D0149645

Praise for *Political Animals*

"Politics in America has this *Alice in Wonderland* quality: what makes sense often doesn't happen, and what happens often doesn't make sense. Drawing on science, history, psychology, mounds of evidence, and political insight, Rick Shenkman's masterful book shows us why. What Malcolm Gladwell's *The Tipping Point* does for society, *Political Animals* does for politics."

—Leonard Steinhorn, professor of communication and affiliate professor of history, American University

"For generations political scientists have argued over whether voters address political issues rationally. Rick Shenkman vigorously asserts that for the most part they make decisions that more closely resemble the instinctual behavior of animals and early prehistoric man. He further argues that our institutions encourage such choices. Clearly written and accessible to ordinary readers, this book is an important contribution to an ongoing debate."

—Alonzo L. Hamby, author of *Man of Destiny: FDR and the Making of the American Century*

"A fascinating, well-told account of how our nature both prepares and ill-prepares us for politics in the modern age."

—George E. Marcus, professor of political science, Williams College

"In *Political Animals*, historian Rick Shenkman makes excellent use of the latest research in behavioral sciences to indicate why we Americans so often fail politically. And in highly readable prose he also provides wise advice on how we can do better."

—Walter G. Moss, professor emeritus of history, Eastern Michigan University, and author of *An Age of Progress?: Clashing Twentieth-Century Global Forces*

"The most predictable thing about politics is that it's often unpredictable. In his fascinating and illuminating new book, Rick Shenkman discovers the problem isn't with our fancy statistical models or forecasts, it's with our brains. When it comes to politics, humans sometimes do things that just don't make sense."

—Taegan Goddard, founder and publisher of *Political Wire*

Political Animals

Political Animals

How *Our* STONE-AGE BRAIN GETS *in the* WAY *of* SMART POLITICS

RICK SHENKMAN

BASIC BOOKS
A Member of the Perseus Books Group
New York

Published by Basic Books
A Member of the Perseus Books Group

Books published by Basic Books are available at special discounts for bulk
purchases in the United States by corporations, institutions, and other
organizations. For more information, please contact the Special Markets
Department at the Perseus Books Group, 2300 Chestnut Street, Suite 200,
Philadelphia, PA 19103, or call (800) 810-4145, ext. 5000, or e-mail special.
markets@perseusbooks.com.

Typeset in 10.5 point Guardi by the Perseus Books Group

Library of Congress Cataloging-in-Publication Data

Shenkman, Richard, author.
    Political animals : how our Stone Age brain gets in the way of smart politics /
Rick Shenkman.
        pages cm   33614056456493
    Includes bibliographical references and index.
    ISBN 978-0-465-03300-3 (hardcover) — ISBN 978-0-465-07382-5 (e-book)
1. Political psychology—United States. 2. Personality and politics—United
States. 3. Political culture--United States. I. Title.

JK1726.S54 2015

320.01'9—dc23
                                                                    2015024591

10 9 8 7 6 5 4 3 2 1

For my remarkable mother, Phyllis Shenkman,
who, in going back to school in her eighties, left a
powerful example in the way she lived her life
for the way I want to live mine.

Contents

Introduction:
The Mismatch

Why we can't trust our instincts

1.

One day in 1891, a wealthy world traveler who enjoyed puncturing public myths offered $500 to anybody who could prove that a shark had ever attacked a human being off the East Coast of the United States. The offer drew headlines. People were sure he'd have to make a payment. They were wrong.

This came as no surprise to the country's leading shark experts. They had long reached the conclusion that the man-eaters that sailors often talked about darkly were highly unlikely to appear in our non-tropical waters. There simply was no proof, the experts categorically stated, that sharks found in the vicinity of America's East Coast seaside communities ever went after human beings, except perhaps by mistake. What then lay behind the grave fear of sharks among people living along the coast? The experts chalked it up to pure superstition. They maintained this for decades.

In 1916, on the eve of the summer vacation season, as they had on occasion in the past, the experts reassured the public that they had nothing to fear from sharks. This wasn't a matter of opinion, they insisted. It was science.

And then the calendar page flipped to Saturday, July 1.

That day, the Vansants of Philadelphia crossed the Delaware River into New Jersey in time to catch the 3:35 P.M. train from Camden to the Jersey Shore. A little after 5 P.M., they arrived in Beach Haven, an elegant resort community some twenty miles north of Atlantic City, and then checked into the Engleside Inn, one of the finest hotels in the area. While his parents relaxed, Charles Vansant, dressed in a black swimsuit that stretched from his knees to his neck, headed to the ocean for a swim. It was shortly before 6 P.M.

Vansant was a college man. He had made varsity in two sports, golf and baseball. Upon hitting the water he fearlessly swam farther out than anybody else. But as a group of onlookers watched him playing with a paddling dog, he suddenly began to shriek for help. Something was dragging him under.

It was a shark. As Vansant fought for his life, his blood turned the seawater bright red. A brave lifeguard quickly swam to help, dragging Vansant toward shore. But the shark hung on. Not until the fish scraped the pebbles on the bottom of the ocean as they neared shore did it finally swim off. By then it was too late. Little more than an hour after he had stepped off the train from Camden, Charles Vansant, athletic and fearless, was dead. He was twenty-five years old.

Five days later Charles Bruder, the bellboy captain at the Essex and Sussex, a top-notch hotel in Spring Lake, forty-five miles north of Beach Haven, went for a swim on his lunch break. In full view of hundreds of tourists, including the well-known socialite Mrs. George Childs, a shark attacked him. Mrs. Childs reported seeing the shark dart at Bruder "just as an airplane attacks a Zeppelin." As he screamed, the shark took off his right leg above the knee and then went after his left foot. Women watching the gruesome scene vomited and fainted. Charles Bruder, in shock, died shortly thereafter on the beach, his body a tangled mess of bones and cartilage. He was twenty-eight years old.

More shark attacks followed. In one attack, a shark ventured up a creek all the way to the small New Jersey community of Matawan, sixteen miles inland, far past where anybody had ever thought a shark might go, and killed a boy out for a swim and a man who tried to save him. Finally, a seasoned angler, fishing from a beat-up boat early one morning, caught a shark and killed it. Though no one was sure this one shark had been responsible for all of the attacks, its death ended the terror that had gripped the seaside communities of New Jersey for two weeks and ruined the local economy. No one else that summer felt the jaw of a shark sink into their flesh.

The lesson of 1916, it seems obvious, is that no matter what the experts say, you should follow your instincts. Sharks are large and dangerous, and you should fear them. When the experts told people not to worry about shark attacks, they were wrong. Four people had died. Listen to the experts? They were as wrong as wrong gets.

But is the seemingly obvious lesson the real lesson? Aren't distinctions necessary? The experts weren't wrong about sharks in general. They were right. Only a few species of sharks out of hundreds pose any danger to humans, and they aren't native to the East Coast. The real lesson of 1916 isn't that we should ignore experts. The real lesson is that context is everything. If you see a shark swimming offshore, get out of the water. If you see one swimming toward a group of boys, try to get off a warning to them. Err on the side of caution. But if sharks haven't been in the news and none have been spotted in years, feel free to take the plunge on your next Atlantic Ocean holiday. Enjoy yourself. That's the real lesson.

That is exactly the conclusion the people of New Jersey drew in 1916. Once the danger passed they didn't let the fear of sharks keep them away from summer fun. The following year they returned to the beaches and resumed swimming in the ocean. Their instincts told them doing this was okay. Their instincts were right. Their instincts were carefully calibrated to the circumstances in which they found themselves. They knew when to be fearful and when not to give in to fear.

Our instincts are not only nuanced, they are also automatic. When a rock is thrown in your direction you don't have to think about what to do, you just do it. Instincts are quick. That's the whole point of an instinct. If you had to think about how to stop a rock from hitting you, it would hit you before you had a chance to protect yourself.

When you stop to think about it, the fact that we can rely on our instincts to avoid getting hit by a flying rock is a stupendous achievement of neural engineering. Instincts, quite simply, are amazing. Think of what your brain has to do before signaling that you should be fearful and take action. First, it has to make a correct assessment of the environment. This assessment can involve one or two or all of your senses. Which senses this time? That's a decision your brain has to make, and that's just one of many it has to make in an instant. After that your brain has to decide on the context. Is that a rock coming at you or just a ball? Is a friend or a foe throwing it? Is it a big rock or a little rock? Then there's the decision of how to react. That's a decision the brain makes using an "if/then" formula. If it's a big rock, then duck. If it's a small rock, then block it. And so on and so forth through a myriad of "if this/then that" possibilities. And all of this has to happen in milliseconds, usually out of conscious awareness.

We rely on our instincts in all kinds of situations. When we hear the squeal of tires as we are crossing a street it is our instincts that tell us to halt dead in our tracks or risk getting run over. When we find ourselves in a dark alley late at night and suddenly detect someone else's presence,

xii   *Introduction: The Mismatch*

it is thanks to our instincts that our body instantly tenses and we become incredibly aware of our surroundings. Fight or flight? That's a decision we make using our instincts.

Animal behavior is almost wholly driven by instinct. We possess higher cognitive abilities that give us the power of reason. But scientists say we possess dozens of instincts—perhaps even thousands depending on your definition—and they involve virtually any human activity you can think of. William James, the father of American psychology, held that instincts guide us from birth. He even included crying and sneezing as instincts. You don't have to be taught to cry or sneeze, after all.

Instincts work so well so often in our personal lives that we inevitably draw the conclusion that we can always trust them. Nature teaches us to trust them. We feel good when we do.

But we shouldn't in all cases. Sophisticated as they are, our instincts don't always work. What happens then? What happens when our brain makes an incorrect assessment of a situation? What if it doesn't get the context right? We don't have to wonder. Look around. That's our problem with politics.

2.

In the pages that follow I am going to tell you the stories of people who behave in ways that seem absurd. We'll meet a mother who becomes a lifelong supporter of John F. Kennedy after making brief eye contact with him at a campaign appearance. We'll get to know a group of supporters of Richard Nixon who remain so loyal to him that four decades later, they have yet to come to terms with Watergate. And I'll introduce you to people who think that Barack Obama was born in Kenya and is a practicing Muslim. As we get to know them and others, I will show you that it's not just kooks and ignoramuses who get politics wrong. We all do. That mother who fell for JFK? She was educated and - intelligent. The same goes for those Nixon supporters. That's even true of many of the people who think Obama is a Muslim. Political professionals, politicians, and presidents—even those who know politics inside and out—frequently make egregious political miscalculations. *They* get politics wrong, too.

As we follow their stories I will be focusing on behavior associated with four specific kinds of failures: 1) Many of us frequently disengage, becoming apathetic. 2) We often don't correctly size up our leaders. 3) We punish politicians who tell us hard truths. 4) We often fail to show empathy in circumstances that clearly cry out for it.

What is striking about all four of these failures, which I will explore in depth in the chapters to come, is how puzzling they are. Let's take up the first, the evidence that tens of millions of Americans—literally tens of millions—are so disengaged that they don't know enough about politics to be able to cast an informed vote. This is an astounding failure. Humans are by nature curious about the world. Infants at nine *minutes* of age are known to take an interest in other people's faces. As we grow into adulthood we evince an extraordinary ability to absorb new information. And with a few strokes on a computer keyboard we can find the answer to any question that occurs to us. And yet millions cannot figure out where Barack Obama was born or what his religion is.

The second failure, our difficulty in getting a good read on politicians, is equally confounding. In general, we have a gift for reading people. The ordinary person can glance at a friend and know in an instant that he or she is having a bad day. We cannot literally read other people's minds. And, because much of what motivates us takes place out of conscious awareness, we often cannot read ourselves. We are "strangers to ourselves," as one social scientist put it. We think one thing is motivating us, and actually it's something else. Furthermore, scientists tell us we aren't particularly good at telling whether someone is lying to us. But they also report that one of the critical differences between us and all other creatures is our ability to read one another's intentions, which develops by the age of four. This ability, say scientists, may be one of the chief reasons why human beings came to dominate the world. So how come we can't read politicians better? Why are we constantly surprised when they turn out to be different from what we expected?

The third failure, our inclination to punish politicians who tell us hard truths, is understandable. We'd all rather avoid unpleasant truths. But we couldn't have got very far as a species giving in to wishful thinking. When a leopard's in your path, you have to deal with it. You can't wish it away. So why then do we consider it a gaffe when a politician blurts out the truth? Don't we want the truth?

The fourth failure, the lack of empathy, is downright puzzling when you consider how often we demonstrate empathy in our own lives. The news media are constantly highlighting examples of people who in a disaster help other people, even when it entails great sacrifice. Science has confirmed that we are inclined by nature to feel empathy for others. Neuroscientists have now shown that when we see a person in physical pain, we can experience their pain; we don't literally feel their pain, but we experience the same emotions they are feeling. So why aren't we more sensitive to the suffering of drug users, prisoners, the impoverished, and other misfortunate people?

What's our problem?

The answer is that in each of these cases an evolved psychological mechanism—or what I have been calling, a bit crudely, an instinct—has gone wrong. Curiosity. Mind reading. Realism. Empathy. These are all in their own way nothing more than instincts. And in politics, I want to prove to you, they often don't work: they malfunction, misfire, and lead us astray. I go even further. I argue in this book that when it comes to politics, the times when we can unquestioningly go with our instincts are almost nil.

What is it with politics that makes our instincts go haywire? Why in our personal lives can we so often trust our instincts, but not in politics? Why do our instincts help us whether we are confronting a jaguar in the jungle or Jack the Ripper in a dark alley, but not when we are trying to get a read on a politician or deciding for whom we should vote?

To go even further, why do so many of our instincts not only fail under modern conditions to do what they're supposed to do, but lead us to make foolish choices? The answer is that modern politics is so different from anything experienced in the Pleistocene—when instincts were baked into human DNA—that we frequently sabotage ourselves, upending our democracy in ways none of us intended. We do this because we were not designed for the modern world. We were designed for the Pleistocene.[*] Most of the time that's not a problem because our ancient instincts can still work to our advantage. Fight or flight is the same whether we are confronting a jaguar or Jack the Ripper. And finding a spouse involves many of the same calculations today as it did eons ago, with women still choosier than men because they have to be: women alone bear the burden of childbirth.

But we did not evolve to prosper in today's political world. We adapted to survive and reproduce as hunter-gatherers. That's how we and our direct ancestors lived for millions of years—that's 99 percent of the time we've been on this planet. We do politics badly today—failing to vote, misreading our leaders, falling for slippery shibboleths, and showing indifference to the

---

[*] My use of the word "design" may be misleading. I use the word in this book for convenience. I do not mean to imply that human beings were designed by a creator. We evolved. No one designed us.

poor—because we are ill-equipped to do politics well as it is now practiced. To do politics well, on instinct, as we are inclined to do, we as a species would have to have changed fundamentally since the Pleistocene. And we haven't. Biologists estimate that fundamental changes in species (such as changing our major instincts) take up to 25,000 years—a thousand generations. How long has it been since the Pleistocene, when humans lived as hunter-gatherers? Just 10,000 years—four hundred generations. That gap is what we are up against. As two of the founders of evolutionary psychology, Leda Cosmides and John Tooby, put it: "The key to understanding how the modern mind works is to realize that its circuits were not designed to solve the day-to-day problems of a modern American—they were designed to solve the day-to-day problems of our hunter-gatherer ancestors. These stone age priorities produced a brain far better at solving some problems than others."

This doesn't mean that because of the way our brain is constructed we are fated to behave as cavemen presumably did, even though we might be inclined to think that, based on the morning's headlines. Though it's sometimes said that we are hardwired to behave in certain ways, psychologist Gary Marcus convincingly argues that it is better to think of ourselves as prewired. That helps account for the wide variety in human behavior. A trait can be innate, but whether it determines how you behave on a particular day in a particular situation depends on a range of factors. Find yourself on a crowded highway behind a slow-moving driver on a day when you are late for an appointment and you will likely feel rage. But if you were schooled as a Buddhist or even just happened to pass a billboard with smiling faces that momentarily put you in a good mood, you might not. Even our level of energy can affect our behavior. When we're tired we behave differently from when we're fully charged after a good night's sleep. The more tired we are the less self-control we possess. Fatigue sabotages our brain's EF—executive function. That's why we snap at people when we're tired.

Culture is an especially important factor in shaping our behavior. It's the reason why we are less violent today than we were thousands of years ago, according to the research of Harvard evolutionary psychologist Steven Pinker. In the modern world violence is usually regarded as unacceptable except in special circumstances. A police officer can discharge his weapon to stop a murderer, but you can't shoot your neighbor should he leave a junked car in his driveway for months on end.

Nonetheless, our prewired traits are our prewired traits. They haven't changed. As Cosmides and Tooby succinctly sum up: "Our modern skulls house a stone age mind."* And that's problematic. In many ways our instincts are obsolete. As we will see, they are particularly ill-suited to the political tasks we face in the modern world. While we are more or less matched to our daily challenges, in politics, we often are not. There's a mismatch. Many traits, helpful as they were in the Pleistocene, are less helpful today. As the biologists say, they are maladaptive.

3.

Maladaptation is the clear lesson of the fascinating story that Christopher Achen, a political scientist at Princeton, unraveled.

It was in 2002 and Achen was visiting Micawber Books, a store in downtown Princeton, when he happened upon two recently published books about the 1916 shark attacks—yes, we are back to the shark attacks—prominently displayed on the front table: *Twelve Days of Terror,* by Richard G. Fernicola, and *Close to Shore,* by Michael Capuzzo (both of which I turned to when writing my account, above, of the 1916 calamity). Achen found himself fascinated by these shark stories. As he stood in the store reflecting on the effect the attacks must have had on the people of New Jersey, he remembered a conversation he'd had with another political scientist, Larry Bartels, a Princeton colleague. "I was talking to Larry about the standard political science view of elections, namely that when times are bad, people vote against the party in office, regardless of whether those officeholders have any responsibility for the problem," he recalled. "Humorously, Larry said, 'If a meteor hit Arizona, they'd vote against the incumbents.' Larry doesn't remember saying it, but it struck me as a crucial remark—a logical consequence of what we all believe, but an implication that hadn't been spelled out."

That's when Achen had a classic eureka moment. "All of a sudden, standing there in the bookstore, I thought, 'There's our meteor.' It seemed obvious to me that if Larry and I were right, then the shark attacks should have reduced the vote for Woodrow Wilson in the fall of 1916," when President Wilson was running for reelection. That was because the attacks had meant economic catastrophe for the beachfront communities that depended

---

* The Stone Age began two and a half million years ago when our ancestors started making stone tools in the Paleolithic period, an archeological time frame that is said to have ended with the invention of metal tools, first made out of bronze, about 10,000 years ago. The Stone Age corresponds roughly with the geological period known as the Pleistocene, when the earth was generally colder than it is now.

on the summer trade for their sustenance. After the second attack cost Charles Bruder his life, the summer tourists panicked. A place identified with fun and frolic suddenly came to be known for sharks and death. Hotels emptied out, and little businesses that catered to the tourists went bankrupt. As Fernicola reports, the attacks cost New Jersey about a million dollars in business ($16 million in today's dollars).

To test his hypothesis, Achen, who had a fellowship at the time, retreated to the bowels of the Princeton library for weeks of tedious and dull research. The first thing he had to do was find out how people in New Jersey voted in 1912 when Wilson first ran for president, and then compare those results with the returns of 1916. This meant digging out relevant county and township returns that no one had ever reviewed. He also had to read up on the shark attacks themselves and become an expert on local politics. "I thought to myself," Achen likes to joke, "if there's nothing here, I am going to have a hard time explaining why I spent a month studying the impact of shark attacks on election outcomes. And the people who gave me the fellowship are going to want their money back."

Chances were high that Achen was on a wild goose chase. Woodrow Wilson had not only served as the governor of New Jersey before becoming president—which meant he had a powerful bond with the state's voters—but he also had a particular connection with the people living along the Jersey Shore because he summered there even after moving into the White House. Also, he had served as the president of Princeton University. Furthermore, when the shark attacks hit the news, he had taken extraordinary steps to show he was engaged. After holding an emergency cabinet meeting, he had ordered the National Guard to patrol the beaches. In the fall, Wilson would run as the president who had kept the nation out of World War One. But in the summer of 1916, faced with the onslaught of shark attacks that had put the public on edge, he had vowed to lead a "war on sharks." So the idea that voters might have turned against Wilson on account of the shark attacks seemed far-fetched. Common sense told you they wouldn't.

What did Achen find? Statewide, Wilson retained roughly the same support he'd had four years earlier, but in the four counties where fear was highest and the economy was impacted the most following the attacks, his support declined by about 3 percent. More dramatic was what Achen found when he further broke down the returns by township. In the two beach communities most affected by the attacks, the decline in support for Wilson was precipitous. In Spring Lake, where Charles Bruder was killed by a shark, Wilson's support dropped 9 percentage points. In Beach Haven, where Charles Vansant was killed shortly after stepping off the train from Camden, Wilson's support dropped 11 percent. No other factor but the shark attacks and the effect they had on the economy accounted for the drop. When Achen checked to see what impact the Great Depression had on Herbert Hoover's vote in New Jersey in 1932, he discovered the results were roughly comparable. Let me restate this for emphasis. The shark attacks in 1916 had the same effect on the voters of Spring Lake and Beach Haven that the Great Depression had on voters statewide in 1932.

That is scary. No rational voter should have let what happened in July affect his choice in November. Leaders should be held responsible only for what they can reasonably be held responsible for. We should vote against politicians only when they fail us, not when things out of their control leave us feeling vulnerable. Wilson did not deserve to lose a single vote because of the shark attacks. He was not responsible for the attacks and couldn't conceivably do anything to stop them. The main thing he could do was show concern, and he did that. That's why he held that crisis cabinet meeting and sent out the National Guard. But for the people in Beach Haven and Spring Lake, that wasn't enough.

And if there was ever a year when sober deliberation was needed in deciding how to vote, it was 1916. Europe was in flames. For two years, millions of soldiers had been engaged in a slaughter the likes of which the world had never before witnessed. And the United States was in danger of being dragged in. Here are some headlines that ran during the campaign:

GERMANY IS PRESSING SUBMARINE WAR: 194 Ships Sunk from
    Aug. 1 to Sept. 11
FRENCH SMASH LINES SOUTH OF SOMME: Big Battle Still
    Rages
AMERICANS LOST IN BRITISH VESSEL SUNK BY U-BOAT
FRANCE DYING, HINDENBURG SAYS: Will Have No Soldiers
    Left if She Continues the War Much Longer.

Even reading these headlines today, as I did using the *New York Times* online website, summons up frightening images. But those war headlines didn't drive the voting in those beachfront communities, according to Achen, one of the country's leading quantitative political scientists. It was those summer shark attacks, which brought fear and economic loss.

Shark attacks.

If you asked those who voted against Wilson why they opposed his reelection, they undoubtedly would have given you an answer that sounds reasonable. Reasons to vote against Wilson were not hard to come by. Militarists like Teddy Roosevelt thought Wilson was a pacifist pussyfooter. Peaceniks in the mold of William Jennings Bryan, who'd resigned as Wilson's secretary of state, believed the president wasn't pacifistic enough. The Irish considered him too close to Britain. Many business leaders considered him too progressive. Suffragettes ridiculed him for his reluctance to back congressional passage of an amendment giving women the right to vote. And on and on. Under the circumstances, it was easy to sound reasonable. Any one of these positions was defensible. Chances are good that if you asked one of those anti-Wilson voters in Spring Lake to explain their vote, they would have come up with something reasonable. We all want to sound reasonable, don't we? We need to sound reasonable to earn one another's respect and to keep our own. But, the fact is, we often lie about our reasons for doing what we do in politics. We don't just lie to others. We lie to ourselves.

Achen's research shows that if we want to get at the truth about people's motives we shouldn't think we can simply ask them. We have to study their behavior as a group. Only then can we detect patterns that can help give us insight into the forces that are really shaping their thinking. In those patterns, we can see truths we cannot see when we confine our study to individuals, even when the individual in question happens to be yourself. We think we know ourselves well. But actually we hide things from ourselves. Even when we are brutally honest, we are not in a position to truly know ourselves since so much of what happens in our brain happens out of conscious awareness. As I have pointed out, the only way to break open the locks is by studying our behavior as members of a group. That's how we can get at the truth. That's what Christopher Achen discovered in the bowels of the Princeton library in 2002.

We think that because people offer reasonable explanations for their political behavior they are being reasonable. We fall into the trap of taking people literally—ourselves and others. But we shouldn't. The electorate in Beach Haven and Spring Lake weren't voting reasonably. They were voting unreasonably. They just didn't know it.

We naturally think politics is about what we see in the newspapers and on television. But the truth is that politics is also about what we cannot see. It's about the hidden patterns social scientists such as Achen have to dig out of musty records, patterns we can't detect any other way. The patterns are critical in helping us understand what's driving our political behavior.

Understanding those patterns is critical if we are to stop making the four mistakes we will be exploring in the rest of *Political Animals*—mistakes to which we are prone and which are undermining our democracy.

4.

When Christopher Achen reported the results of his shark research to colleagues, he was met with instant skepticism. Most political scientists do not want to think that a shark attack can have a significant effect on voting. Like economists, their models are based on what's known as the "rational actor" model. And while political scientists are quick to acknowledge that voters do not always act in their own self-interest, and that they vote against incumbents when times are bad whether the incumbents are responsible or not, the general assumption is that for the most part voters do act rationally. If Achen wanted to prove this wasn't the case, he needed more evidence.

To help him do the needed research he teamed up with Larry Bartels, who had made the crack about the impact that a meteor striking Arizona would have on voting. They decided to focus on the impact of the weather on elections. Their suspicion was that the weather might be a key factor in politics since weather has been so important to humans throughout history. It might be, they thought, like the shark attacks. So they set out to determine if they could establish a correlation between elections and bad weather. Why focus on bad weather and not good weather? Political scientists had long ago established that extraneous forces have political consequences when the effect is negative. Psychologists such as Harvard's Daniel Gilbert have an explanation for this: the human brain is designed to focus on the negative. As we'll see later, this is an evolutionary adaptation that helped save the human race.

Bartels and Achen started by looking at what happened in Florida in the Bush-Gore election of 2000. That was a puzzling election. While Florida is a swing state, it shouldn't have been much in play that year. The state's economy generally was in good condition. The unemployment rate was a low 3.8 percent. In a rational world a battleground state like Florida in 2000 should have tipped decisively toward the Democrats. Just as voters typically vote against an incumbent administration when times are bad, the political science literature suggests that they should be inclined to vote for the incumbent administration when times are good. That means they should have voted in large numbers for Al Gore, the current vice president. But they didn't. How could that be? Was weather possibly a factor?

This is a map produced by the National Oceanic and Atmospheric Administration (NOAA). It shows the counties in Florida in January 2000 affected by drought. Darker colors indicate moderate drought conditions.

Lighter colors show areas unaffected by drought. As you can see, only a few counties were suffering. The maps showing drought conditions in February and March look about the same.

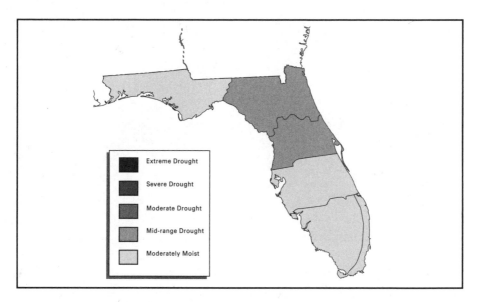

Then, in April, the map changes, as can be seen below. As you can see, drought conditions were spreading.

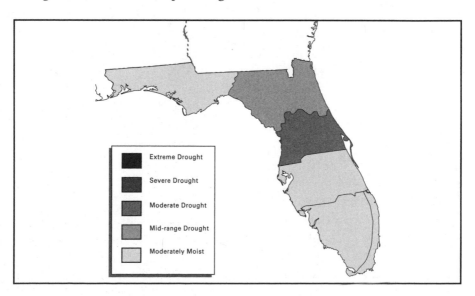

Below is the map for May. See all those darker patches?

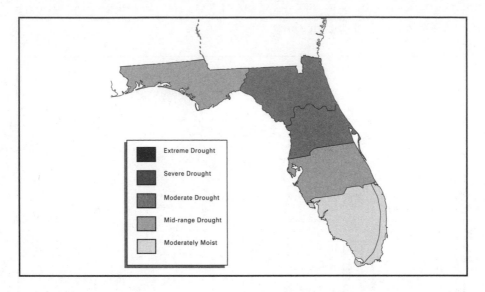

Here's the map for June. As you can see, the area affected by hard drought conditions now covered half of Florida, from the belly of the state, just above the I-4 corridor stretching from Tampa in the west to Daytona Beach in the east, all the way up through the panhandle.

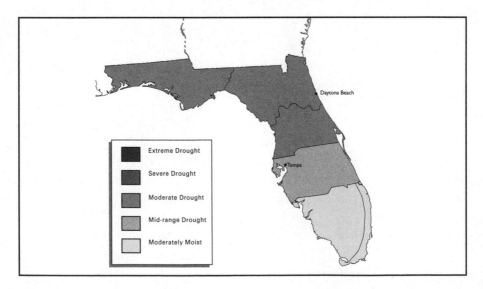

By August, conditions were worsening everywhere. The dark shaded area indicates extreme drought conditions. Those conditions prevailed in half the state.

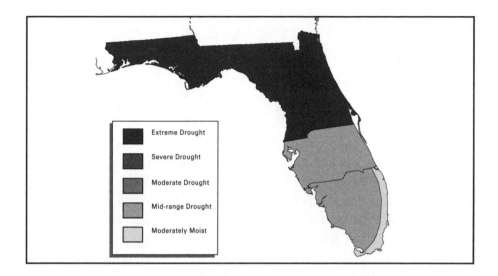

Fortunately for Floridians, the period of extreme drought ended by September, but bad drought conditions remained throughout much of the state, with the belly suffering the worst right through the November election.

The drought should have been a big "so what?" as far as the presidential election was concerned. It wasn't bad enough to adversely affect the overall economy of the state. And anyway a drought shouldn't affect the vote citizens cast in a presidential election because presidents can't be held responsible for the weather any more than they can be held responsible for shark attacks. Though there conceivably are circumstances when public policies might be blamed for the effects of a drought—as was the case with the Dust Bowl in the 1930s—there were no demands in 2000 that the presidential candidates take a stand on any issue related to the drought. Nobody considered the drought a factor in the election. You can read everything that was published in 2000 about the presidential campaign without coming across a single reference to that drought. In presidential elections, the weather almost never seems relevant—except in cases where an early-season snowstorm affects the November turnout (though this might change as global warming becomes an increasing reality).

But when Bartels and Achen analyzed the data, they found through regression analysis that the drought affected many voters' decisions in Florida. People who should have been expected to vote in favor of Al Gore based on historical averages voted instead for George W. Bush. And these voters numbered in the thousands. An election that was decided by 537 votes in Bush's favor actually should have ended in a good solid victory for Gore, irrespective of the design flaws of the butterfly ballots and the other factors that worked to Bush's advantage. Florida never should have led to a Bush win. Gore should have won by thousands of votes and become president.

Could the weather really be that critical?

By now, Bartels and Achen were convinced they were really on to something. So they extended their analysis to the entire country. If the weather affected the vote in Florida, maybe it also affected the vote in other states.

When the two political scientists examined the data that is just what they found. Using a sophisticated model that takes into account three different versions of the government's drought index, they compared past returns with those in 2000 and found that the weather affected the election's outcome not just in Florida, but also in Arizona, Louisiana, Nevada, New Hampshire, Tennessee, and Missouri. The aggregate number of people who let the weather affect their vote could be counted in the millions. Bartels and Achen, who are regarded as luminaries in the political science profession, reported that roughly 2.7 percent of the total electorate, or about 2.8 million people, "voted against Gore in 2000 because their states were too dry or too wet."

Al Gore lost the 2000 election by 5 electoral votes. If he had picked up the states he apparently lost due to the weather, he would have won by 139 electoral votes. Bush would have received 199 votes to Gore's 338, turning Gore's defeat into an impressive electoral college victory, comparable to Bill Clinton's twin wins in 1992 and 1996.

Now that Bartels and Achen had established that the weather affected not just Florida's vote in 2000 but the vote in half a dozen other states as well, they decided to spread their electoral net even further. Using what they had learned about the effect of the weather on voter behavior in 2000, they reviewed all of the presidential election returns for an entire century, going back to 1896, cross-checking the returns against the weather statistics supplied by NOAA. Over and over again they found the same pattern. Voters in states suffering from either floods or droughts registered a strong bias against incumbents. Here's their startling conclusion:

"The strength and consistency of these results across a variety of regression analyses employing different versions of our drought index should leave little doubt that droughts and floods in general have a negative effect on electoral support for the president's party. That negative effect is not coincidental; nor is it simply a matter of voters rationally punishing particular presidents for failing to prepare adequately for or respond adequately to particular disasters. It is a pervasive risk to the reelection chances of every incumbent party, and no more controllable than the rain."

Overall, Bartels and Achen found, adverse weather conditions cost the incumbent party 1.5 percentage points. In close elections, that could spell the difference between a win and a loss. (More than half of presidential elections since 1900 have been won by five points or less.)

Given these results, does it make sense for us still to be discussing politics as if all that matters is what politicians do and say, or what voters tell pollsters—the usual fare of public debate? If hidden forces like shark attacks and droughts can shape our politics, shouldn't we be trying to figure out why? Is it possibly our instincts that are responsible?

5.

In the United States, March is the month when Americans go crazy over college basketball. It's known as March Madness. Using Google you can see just how crazy. Just look up the words "March Madness fans" and up will pop thousands of news stories, diary entries, and videos, all attesting to the fans' love of the games put on by the National Collegiate Athletic Association (NCAA). One of the videos that you'll find is called: "Texas v Wake Forest—Crazy Fan's March Madness. Fun."

What the video shows is a fan in 2009 watching as his beloved Texas Longhorns are playing the Wake Forest Demon Deacons. They're losing, and he's beside himself:

"They're going to break my heart."

"Inside. Go inside. The big guy fouled out, go inside. INSIDE." Screaming now. "INSIDE!"

"Yes, yes, yes! YES! Whooooooooooooo!" He jumps out of his chair and does a little dance.

"Come on, guys. Yeah, baby. Let's go!"

A few minutes later. . . .

"Are you kidding me?"

"They are doing everything to lose this, man."

Another few minutes pass. At one point, the Longhorns had been up by eight points in overtime. But then comes the buzzer. They've lost.

"I told you they were going to break my heart." He starts swearing.

Below, on the discussion board, there's this sympathetic comment: "Love it for what it is, pure emotion. I used to be that guy before the wife told me to stop. So now I go outside and yell."

Now suppose for a moment you're that guy. Basketball means everything to you. And now it's time to go and vote in an election. Would you think for even one minute that the Longhorns' loss might affect how you vote? I'm guessing the answer would have been no before you read about the effect of the shark attacks and droughts on voting. But now you know what the answer is and you're right. In a study published in 2010 in the *Proceedings of the National Academy of Sciences,* Andrew Healy, Neil Malhotra, and Cecilia Hyunjung Mo reported that sports contests color how voters assess incumbents. When the social scientists asked fans of teams that won in the third and fourth rounds of March Madness in 2009 what they thought of President Barack Obama, his ratings went up by a clearly measurable amount: 2.3 percent.

They also tested football fans' reactions. Same results. The fans whose teams won felt more favorably about incumbents than the fans of teams that lost. If their teams scored victories in the two weeks before an election, the fans' support for the incumbents rose by 1.05 percent. This led the social scientists to report: "We find clear evidence that the successes and failures of the local college football team before Election Day significantly influence the electoral prospects of the incumbent party, suggesting that voters reward and punish incumbents for changes in their well-being unrelated to government performance." Their overall conclusion: "These results provide evidence that voting decisions are influenced by irrelevant events that have nothing to do with the competence or effectiveness of the incumbent government."

Hearing this and what we heard earlier from Bartels and Achen, it is sorely tempting to conclude that democracy is hopeless. Like Walter Lippmann a century ago, we seem to have little choice but to write off public opinion as irrational and erratic. But that's too easy. It implies that we are making decisions for no reason at all, that when we are being irrational, we are just being irrational. That's almost certainly not the case.

It is not just Americans who let natural forces like the weather affect their vote. Social scientists report that an earthquake in Chile in 2010 affected elections there the same way droughts and floods have here. Is it likely that people in Chile and New Jersey had a similar reaction to a natural event just by coincidence? What evolutionary psychology teaches is that when people from various countries and cultures evince the same reaction to events, a reaction that doesn't seem justified by those events, we can be pretty sure it has been triggered by an evolved psychological mechanism. A modern cue is setting off an ancient instinct, as the social scientists put it. And that explains a lot, as we will see in the coming chapters.

IN THE FACE OF SCIENTIFIC EVIDENCE, it is no longer possible to pretend that political debates are being waged and won strictly on the merits of applying pure reason. But we like to think they are because we know we are capable of rational thought, and the way we settle political debates is by making arguments that give us every indication we are being rational. The trap we fall into is thinking that rational arguments alone are what move us. We persist in thinking this even though the evidence is abundant that public opinion is often not rational and that multiple forces, some unseen, are shaping our response.

Our problem isn't that voters are stupid, a point I will elaborate on in chapter 2. It is that there's a mismatch between the brain we inherited from the Stone Age, when mankind lived in small communities, and the brain we need to deal with the challenges we face in a democratic society consisting of millions of people. That mismatch explains why our instincts so often mislead us in politics. Our instincts arose to help us survive as members of a small group competing with other small groups, not as members of a mass society competing with other mass societies. Whatever the deep psychological reason for those New Jersey voters going against Woodrow Wilson, it wasn't a suitable reason given the way politics operates in the modern world. Forcing leaders to take the blame when things go bad, no matter what the circumstances, may have been a sound if imperfect general strategy in the Pleistocene. And people who by instinct followed that strategy may well have had an advantage over those who did not, enhancing their fitness—the ability to pass along their genes to the next generation. But it certainly isn't a wise strategy in a modern, multiparty, mass democracy subject to a complicated array of natural and social forces.

What about the nefarious role of emotion in our politics, of which we hear so much? Our problem is not emotion per se, it is emotion wrongly applied as a result of those ancient instincts. If we want to understand politics we have to come to terms with the many ways those instincts play havoc with us—and why. The answer to which we will keep coming back is that our instincts don't work in politics as they should because we get the context wrong.

In the end, our politics are the result of a tug-of-war raging inside the brain between our instincts (and the emotional responses they trigger) and higher-order cognition. Though politics is usually framed in terms of the résumés, ideology, and personality of the candidates, it's not really about them. It's about us and what's going on inside our brain.

Until recently it was not known in what ways we are mismatched with the modern world. But science has advanced to the point where we can now say with confidence how many of our most important instincts probably came about—and how they are affecting our politics. We no longer have to guess. In the last generation, and in some cases in just the last few years, science has begun to reveal the secrets of our decision-making processes. The brain is no longer a sealed black box. Science has begun to pry it open, giving us the opportunity for the first time to understand the sources of our instincts so we can better understand ourselves—which takes much of the mystery of human behavior out of politics. In *Political Animals* we'll explore the scientific breakthroughs that are giving rise to these new insights.

It is important to note that no single branch of science is responsible for our new understanding of the brain. It is only by consulting the work of a now-dizzying array of disciplines in the sciences and social sciences that we can peak inside the box. These include neuroscience, genetics, evolutionary psychology, anthropology, behavioral economics, political science, political psychology, social psychology, and even game theory. Throughout this book I cite studies in all of these fields, and others. As you read the book I hope to share with you the excitement I felt while doing the research. As a journalist and historian I often felt like a tourist traveling in a foreign country as I made my way through the studies cited in the endnotes. But the metaphor is imperfect. While the math that scientists use was foreign to me, the places I was traveling to were as familiar as my hometown. I was visiting the same streets with the same trees and the same houses, but they no longer looked the same. Science helped change my perspective. I hope it changes yours.

With the help of science we will be able to get answers to the four questions *Political Animals* addresses:

1. Why aren't voters more curious and knowledgeable?
2. Why do we find reading politicians so difficult?
3. Why aren't we more realistic?
4. Why does our empathy for people in trouble often seem in such short supply?

You may well be asking yourself, as I did as I was writing this book, what good it does to be able to answer these four questions. What good is it to know about all these instincts? Your first impulse might be to think, not much good at all, because our instincts are our instincts, right? As I say throughout this book, we are going to react the way we react. Our deep biases are going to persist even when we are made aware of them. The great psychologist Daniel Kahneman, whom we'll encounter later, confesses in his memoirs that he continues to succumb to biases he himself helped identify. Social scientists report that subjects in experiments who are made aware of the role of biases do not show any less susceptibility to them. Partisans are generally unable to view candidates from their own party or the opposition objectively. As we'll see, we simply aren't built to be objective. (See chapter 7.)

But it turns out there are many steps we can take to shape the way we respond to events. We may not be able to change our instincts, but we can neutralize many of those that undermine democracy and enhance others that are helpful. There is only one overarching requirement and that is that we acknowledge the role that instincts play in the formation of our beliefs. And that is something easily within the reach of most human beings. We don't have to be able to see the instinctive biases in our own thinking to admit, in theory at any rate, that we are susceptible to them. Then we can take the measures I outline in the Conclusion to try to offset them.

One of those measures grows out of the lesson of the shark story. Context matters. If what's wrong is that many of our instincts don't work because the context is wrong, what we need to do is find a way to change the context whenever possible so that they do work. This is one of the most urgent tasks we face: figuring out how to make our instincts work in favor of democracy instead of against it. As I will explain later, one of the ways we can do this is by tricking ourselves to approach politics with a more open mind by exposing ourselves to diverse sources of information. We can do this thanks to what is one of our bedrock instincts: our social instinct, or our "hivishness" as psychologist Jonathan Haidt puts it. We love groups and define ourselves by our group. By choosing to live in a community (a group) composed of people who are drawn from diverse backgrounds and ideologies, our thinking can become more diverse. You have heard of voting with our feet. This is thinking with our feet. To be sure, this requires us to override another instinct: the drive to live among people like ourselves. But that's hardly a major obstacle, thanks to yet another instinct: our attraction to cities. History suggests a majority of human beings love urban life. Thanks to evolution, we aren't the product of just a handful of instincts all tending in the same direction. This gives us the freedom to chart our own path—if we have the will to do so.

Finally, our instincts may be our instincts, but we are more than the sum of them. As even evolutionary psychologists acknowledge, evolution isn't destiny. Women today don't have to answer to their husbands the way women did in the Pleistocene. Culture matters. That's why, though Maasai women in East Africa may be wholly subjugated by their husbands, Khasi women in northeast India are not. In their matriarchal society, they rule.

We are not the prisoners of our evolutionary past. As I emphasize in the Conclusion, there are concrete measures we can take to help free ourselves. Science is giving us that opportunity—if we can only seize it.

PART I:
CURIOSITY

1

The Michael Jordan Lesson

*Why people who don't vote and don't follow
the news don't think they need to*

1.

This is a book about politics, but a sports story illustrates one of its
themes—that voters don't seem to be very good at their job—better than
any political story I know. The story is about the most famous basketball
player in history. Even if you do not follow sports you know his name:
Michael Jordan. This is because Jordan was such an exceptional athlete, he became a phenomenon. ESPN says he was the greatest athlete
in North America in the twentieth century. The Associated Press lists
him as second best—just behind Babe Ruth. Jordan's most famous feat
was literally flying across the court from the free throw line for a slam
dunk. The soaring maneuver earned him the nickname Air Jordan. In
the early-1990s he led the Chicago Bulls to three NBA championships in
a row—a three-peat. A few years later he led the Bulls to a second three-
peat. He is known the world over for his athletic accomplishments. This
is how Ira Berkow, the longtime sports columnist at the *New York Times*,
opens a profile on Jordan:

> One day I found myself on a boat wending its way up the Bosporus,
> which not only divides a city—Istanbul—but splits two continents as
> well. The guide for this morning tour for two was a young Turk who

3

was doing his job by the numbers. At one point, leaning over the rail—it was the Asian side, not the European side, if memory serves—he asked what I do for a living in America. I told him. He came alive. "Have you ever met Michael Jordan?" he asked. I said that I have, that in my line of work he's rather difficult to avoid. The guide said, "Oh my God!"

In between his three-peats Michael Jordan did something that shocked the world. He retired from basketball and became a baseball player. The news was carried on the front pages of newspapers on every continent.

The very best baseball player in history, judging by batting average, was Ted Williams, who hit .406 in 1941, the highest ever in a single season. The player with the best career batting average was Ty Cobb. His score was .366. At the other extreme are players who hit below .230. They are considered inferior batters.

So how did Michael Jordan, the greatest basketball player in history, do at baseball? On his first try, playing for a team in the minor leagues—the Double-A league, which is below Triple-A—he batted .202 and hit three home runs. On his second try, playing in the Arizona Fall League, which is comprised of Double-A and Triple-A players, he batted .252. That was respectable, but still disappointing. In basketball Jordan had been a star. In baseball, he wasn't. "Bag It, Michael!" a cover for *Sports Illustrated* blared.

After playing baseball for two years Jordan went back to basketball to the cheers of Bulls fans, who had watched their team lose its championship status without him. Once again, Jordan ruled the court. In his second game out he scored 55 points. The next season he averaged 30 points per game, making him the league's top player. With Jordan the Bulls resumed their old winning streak. His first full year back, the Bulls won 72 games and lost just 10. It was the best regular season record of any team in the history of the National Basketball Association.

In high school a student who is a star in one sport is often a star in another. As you flip through the pages of your high school yearbook you will see many of the same faces pop up on multiple sports pages. The star featured on one page with a baseball bat is found on another wearing a helmet and clutching a football. The star of the tennis team doubles as a guard on the basketball team. But college is different. In college, student athletes specialize. It is rare for a college athlete to play in multiple sports. The reason is that in college sports there is often a great deal of money on the line. Schools want athletes playing the sport they are best at. Most are

much better at one sport than another. With the intense competition in college sports, even a gifted all-around athlete can't play all sports equally well.

On Wikipedia there's a fascinating page that lists professional football
players who have won renown in other sports. The list is short. Of the more
than 10,000 people who have played pro football through the years, just 116
made the list. On another Wikipedia page there's a list of people who won
Olympic medals in different sports. More than a hundred thousand athletes have competed in the Olympics. Just 81 have won medals in different
sports. What these lists suggest is that it is rare for star athletes to excel in
different sports. But that's not all. When you begin to examine these lists
carefully a pattern shows up. Here is the tabulated list of the football players
who excelled in other sports:

49 baseball
24 track and field
20 basketball
7 soccer
5 martial arts
4 wrestling
3 lacrosse
3 golf
3 boxing
1 car racing
1 American Ninja Warrior
1 ice hockey

Notice anything? These athletes aren't excelling in two entirely different sports by and large. They are shining in sports that require similar
skills. Football has a lot in common with baseball and basketball. All three
sports require athletes to possess either good eye-hand coordination or fast
legs. The similarity between football and track is less obvious. We think
of football players as bulky and track stars as skinny. But track stars who
can throw a javelin can probably also throw a football, and several of the
football players who did track were expert javelin throwers. The other sports
on the list are outliers. Significantly, some sports don't show up on the list
at all. No football players made their mark in swimming or tennis. This is
striking.

You see the same pattern when you review the winners in the Olympics.
The athletes specialize. They either participate in the summer games or the

winter games. Just four medal winners in the summer games ever won a medal in the winter games. Just four—and that's in the whole history of a competition that draws athletes from around the world. Only one person—Deion Sanders—has ever played in both the World Series and the Super Bowl. Then there's Bo Jackson. What's special about Bo? In the opinion of many sportswriters there haven't been any other athletes like him; a star in both baseball and football, he was courted by teams in both sports after he won college football's Heisman Trophy. The man who made a documentary about him for ESPN says Jackson is even great at surfing and rollerblading.

What this suggests is that human beings, even highly talented human beings, aren't supermen. This is the Michael Jordan Lesson. People are good in some things but not all things. They can excel in one sport but not all sports. When do these star athletes succeed? When their skills match the challenges they face. When do they fail or flail? When they apply those same skills to tasks for which they are not naturally suited. This explains why swimmers like Mark Spitz don't play football and football players like Joe Namath don't compete for swimming medals in the Olympics.

Does it also explain why voters have so much trouble keeping up on the news and making informed decisions?

2.

For as long as mankind has been trying democracy, there have been people who have said it won't work. The reason that is most often provided is public ignorance. Plato's "The Simile of the Cave" is the best known of the early indictments. The story begins with an account of a group of prisoners who have been confined from childhood in a cave. The prisoners are shackled in such a way that the only thing they can see in the dim light thrown off by a fire behind them is the wall they are staring at. They cannot look around or even turn their heads. They can only stare ahead. Behind them there's a stage, the kind marionette players use. Plato asks us to imagine that, on this stage, performances are constantly being held featuring various objects—a figure of a horse, a little statue of a man, and the like—which the manipulators (out of sight like marionette puppeteers) move back and forth across the stage. What the prisoners see are not the objects themselves, then, but the large shadows the objects cast.

Those shadows form the only world the prisoners know until one day one of them is released. As the freed prisoner rises and starts moving about he notices that what the prisoners have been looking at all these years is not the objects themselves, but the images of the objects. As he makes his way out of the cave and into the light and his eyes adjust, he encounters the real world and real objects. "And when he remembered his old habitation, and the wisdom of the den and his fellow-prisoners," Plato asks, "do you not suppose that he would felicitate himself on the change, and pity them?" The answer of course is that he would.

But this is not the end of the story. Plato wants us to consider what would happen if the freed prisoner were to return to the cave to tell his former colleagues what he has found. If you expect his former colleagues on prisoner's row to be grateful to learn what the real world is like, you are in for a disappointment. What actually would happen, Plato predicts, is quite different, and it would be tragic:

> While his sight was still weak, and before his eyes had become steady (and the time which would be needed to acquire this new habit of sight might be very considerable) would he not be ridiculous? Men would say of him that up he went and down he came without his eyes; and that it was better not even to think of ascending; and if any one tried to loose another and lead him up to the light, let them only catch the offender, and they would put him to death.

The grim ending to Plato's story—which suggests that people who see the light will be punished for their insights by people who lack vision—sounds extreme. But he was speaking from experience. Plato's teacher, Socrates, paid for his willingness to speak the truth with his life. In the advanced democracies of the modern West, visionaries are no longer put to death. Instead, they are given book contracts. In their books these modern-day Platos raise a hue and cry over the problem ignorance poses to democracy, turning alarmism about ignorance into a virtual cottage industry. Walk into any bookstore and you will find volumes like Stephen Prothero's *Religious Literacy: What Every American Needs to Know—and Doesn't*, which warns about the dangers of ignorance about religion, and Mark Bauerlein's *The Dumbest Generation: How the Digital Age Stupefies Young Americans and Jeopardizes Our Future*, which charges that young people raised on Google don't read literature, can't understand basic scientific concepts, and have no idea how our government functions.

Bauerlein's book suggests that the young belong to a special category of ignoramuses—and perhaps they do—but critics have been beating the same horse for generations. Mass man is ignorant. See almost any of Walter Lippmann's books, especially his 1922 treatise, *Public Opinion*, in which he raises Plato's ghost to try to scare the country into addressing the problem of gross public ignorance. Books like Lippmann's became especially popular after World War Two. Nazism scared people. It turned liberal democrats into worrywarts, or as one historian calls them, "The Nervous Liberals." Democracy no longer seemed the cure; it was the problem. Nazism showed that even in an advanced nation like Germany millions could succumb to ignorance. Adolf Hitler didn't take power in a coup. He rode a wave of popular discontent into office (even if he never won a majority in a free election).

One of the most popular of the early-postwar critiques was written by Bergen Evans. Evans was exactly the sort of figure you'd expect to find selling America on the idea that ignorance is costly. A Rhodes Scholar, he had gone to Harvard and become an English professor. He became so well known that the quiz show "The $64,000 Question" hired him to oversee the selection of the questions the contestants answered. He even got his own show, "Of Many Things," which mixed fun material on pop culture with serious discussions of events from history. He wrote two books exposing the public's ignorance. The first, *The Natural History of Nonsense*, came out in 1946, just after the war. Its opening salvo is memorable: "We may be through with the past, but the past is not through with us. Ideas of the Stone Age exist side by side with the latest scientific thought. Only a fraction of mankind has emerged from the Dark Ages, and in the most lucid brains, as Logan Pearsall Smith has said, we come upon 'nests of woolly caterpillars.'" Millions, he points out, still believe in witches, informing his readers that "between 1926 and 1936 the *New York Times* carried stories of more than fifty cases of witchcraft," fifteen of which were in the United States. How near we are to darkness, he warns. For "few people think rationally." Skepticism, "the life spirit of science," is rare. The book was so popular he followed it up with another, *The Spoor of Spooks*, a few years later. It too was a hit. The popularity of his books suggests that educated readers shared his alarm.

After the war university professors became consumed with the problem of public ignorance. One is worth singling out, for he devoted himself to the subject for decades. His name was Thomas A. Bailey, and he was a giant in the field of history, elected by his peers to lead the Organization of American Historians. Bailey had the white hair of a stereotypically distinguished historian and a friendly, intelligent face. His name may ring a bell. He was the author of one of the most popular textbooks ever published: *The American Pageant*. Half a century later it remains in print. If you are lucky, it was the textbook you read when you were in high school. Unlike many textbooks, it reads like an actual human being wrote it. Like his book, Bailey was witty. Once, a college student eager to meet the great historian who'd written *The American Pageant* sought out Bailey on a visit to Stanford, where Bailey taught. He found the historian in his large first-floor office literally surrounded by open boxes of photocopied papers, thousands and thousands of them. As Bailey looked up, catching the student's surprised expression as he took in all those boxes, the professor wisecracked, "These days it's Xerox or perish."

Bailey was trained as a diplomatic historian. But he became fascinated with public opinion after it dawned on him that every foreign policy crisis in US history was shaped decisively by public opinion, an observation that formed the basis of the first chapter in another of his textbooks, his hugely popular *A Diplomatic History of the American People*. It wasn't the diplomats who controlled events. It was the masses. As the nineteenth-century British political economist John Stuart Mill observed: "In politics it is almost a triviality to say that public opinion now rules the world."

Bailey did not find this reassuring. He laid out his concerns in *The Man in the Street: The Impact of American Public Opinion on Foreign Policy*, which was published in 1948 (Mill's quote is featured on page 1). The book reads like a ride through a foreign policy house of horrors. Every few pages the "Man in the Street" is on the brink of bringing America to disaster. During the 1898 Spanish-American War, the masses living along the Atlantic seaboard demand that the navy divert key warships from the West Indies, where they are awaiting the arrival of the Spanish fleet, to protect the coast from a nonexistent threat. Bailey observes: "If the Spanish fleet had been stronger, the tale might well have had a less happy ending." That is, we might have lost the war. In World War Two, a loud "get-Hirohito-first" crowd crows so loudly that the army feels intense pressure to change its decision to focus on Hitler first, "and thus prolong or even lose the war."

Ignorance, in Bailey's opinion, was driving these wrongheaded moves. "An appalling ignorance of foreign affairs is one of the most striking and dangerous defects of American public opinion," he acidly observes. As evidence Bailey points to a poll concerning the Atlantic Charter—which defined the Allies' war aims and gave soldiers and voters an understanding of the war's meaning. It's regarded as one of the great documents of the twentieth century. In 1942, eight in ten Americans admitted they had no idea what the Atlantic Charter was. This was just several months after FDR and Winston Churchill signed it.

Two generations later, in the late 1980s, another author, inspired by both Bergen Evans and Thomas Bailey, began plowing the same fields. His special concern was with the myths of history, a subject Bailey also addressed in several books. "Americans, despite everything you hear, know plenty of history," the writer starts off in his debut book on myths. "They know that the Pilgrims landed on Plymouth Rock, that Teddy Roosevelt charged up San Juan Hill, that Columbus discovered the world is round, and that Eli Whitney invented the cotton gin. The punch line, of course, is that Americans know all of these things but that none of these things are true." Like Bergen Evans's books, this book was also a best seller. After the author went on the "Today Show" the publisher had to scramble to meet demand. The books literally came flying off the presses so fast, they didn't have time to dry, eliciting complaints from booksellers that the books were arriving with warped covers. The author made a virtual career out of debunking myths, turning out two more books along the same lines. A few years later, frustrated by the continuing evidence of public ignorance, he put out a polemic. It was called *Just How Stupid Are We: Facing the Truth About the American Voter.* The author of the three debunking books and the polemic was me. (I was also the fresh-faced college student who visited Thomas Bailey with all his photocopies.)

In the early years of the twenty-first century, evidence of public ignorance is omnipresent. These are just some of the findings that have attracted attention:

- A majority of Americans who supported the war in Iraq believed that Saddam Hussein was behind the 9/11 terror attacks. They supported the war chiefly for this reason. In their minds, we went to war in Iraq in retaliation for 9/11.
- Nearly 25 percent of high school students cannot identify Adolf Hitler.
- About 25 percent of Americans have an opinion about Panetta-Burns—a piece of legislation that doesn't exist. A newspaper invented the legislation to see if people guessed the answers to the questions pollsters ask.
- A majority of American voters in 2010 believed that President Obama raised taxes on the middle class during his first two years in office. Obama actually lowered taxes during that time for 95 percent of Americans.
- Nearly 60 percent of Americans cannot identify the chief justice of the Supreme Court.
- A majority of Americans do not know there are three branches of government.
- Nearly 30 percent of Louisiana Republicans in 2013 blamed President Obama for Hurricane Katrina. The hurricane occurred in 2005, when George W. Bush was president.

- Nearly 25 percent of high school graduates cannot pass the army's rudimentary math, reading, and science entrance exam.
- A near majority of Republicans believe that ACORN, the leftwing activist group, stole the election for Obama in 2012. ACORN did not exist after 2010, having been driven out of business by hostile Republicans.
- A majority of Americans do not know which party is in control of Congress.

And that's not the worst of it.

Not long after Barack Obama became a viable candidate for the presidency in 2008 journalists began noticing what seemed like a peculiar phenomenon. A lot of people seemed to believe that Obama was a Muslim. According to the polls, first as many as one in ten believed it, then later, one in five. Many Americans professed not to know what his religion was at all, though Obama had gone to great lengths to identify himself as a Christian. About four in ten Americans in Ohio told pollsters in 2008 that they had no idea what Obama's religion was. Birtherism—the belief that Obama was born in a foreign country—was also popular. A majority of Americans said they did not know in what country Obama was born. Millions believed he was born in Kenya. At anti-Obama rallies voters began demanding to see his birth certificate.

To journalists these poll results seemed the height of ignorance. The facts were well known. Obama had been born in Hawaii. And he wasn't Muslim. He'd attended a Christian church for two decades. His Christian pastor, the Rev. Jeremiah Wright, even became for a time the subject of front-page news stories after a tape of a sermon surfaced in which he seemed to suggest that America deserved to be hit on 9/11. "America's chickens are coming home to roost," he had thundered. How, journalists wondered, could Obama be castigated one moment as a Muslim and the next for his close association with a Christian pastor (who had married the Obamas, no less)? It didn't make much sense. So one day, determined to get to the bottom of the mystery, the *Washington Post* sent a reporter, Eli Saslow, out to the heartland to find the answer.

Saslow ended up in Findlay, Ohio—a city that Congress officially designated Flag City USA in 1974. There he came across Jim P., a quintessential heartlander. He had worked until retirement at Cooper Tire. He was an Air Force veteran. He had two children. And on top of all that he was flying four American flags from poles planted in his front yard. Perfect! You can imagine the glee Saslow felt when he found Jim P. Saslow popped the question:

what did Jim P. think of claims that Obama was a Muslim born in Kenya? The answer was so good that Saslow opened his story with it. The answer was, Jim P. wasn't sure what to think because he kept hearing conflicting stories about Obama. "It's like you're hearing about two different men with nothing in common," Jim P. said. "It makes it impossible to figure out what's true, or what you can believe." A reporter lives for a quote like this.

But it was strange. The mainstream media had, by this point, repeatedly debunked the myth that Obama was a Muslim born in Kenya. Shouldn't the media's exposé of this falsehood have buried it completely? And it wasn't just the Obama nonsense that had been widely debunked. So had the other phony stories, such as the claim that Saddam was behind 9/11. That there should be rampant ignorance when the relevant facts are as easily available as they are today was puzzling. Why then did these stories not only remain in circulation but also attract millions of adherents? Why were people so ignorant about so many things?

That we have to ask this question is troubling. It suggests that human beings are not very good at something we should by all rights be superb at: figuring out the basic facts about our world. As a species, humans excel at discovering the basic facts about the physical world. It is to understand the world that we come equipped with five senses. We are built to understand the environment in which we find ourselves. For instance, vision helps us pick out predators and friends, and our sensitive hearing allows us to detect the direction from which a sound is coming.

Curiosity is built into our brain. We know this by virtue of one of the great discoveries of the twentieth century. It was made by the Nobel Prize–winning neuroscientist and biologist Eric Kandel in the unlikeliest of ways, in lab experiments on Aplysia, an ordinary sea slug researchers love to study because its brain consists of just 20,000 neurons (the human brain, in contrast, has 86 billion neurons). Kandel spent years poking and prodding Aplysia and measuring their response to various stimuli, including electrical impulses. His most significant finding? When they first encounter a stimulus their brain neurons fire like crazy. But the more they experience the same stimulus, the less they respond. By the tenth stimulus their response declines to nearly one-twentieth what it was initially.

This was an amazing discovery because it suggested that the animal brain doesn't consciously decide to ignore habitual stimulation—sea slugs lack consciousness. Rather, the brain does this automatically. In his insightful memoir about his decades-long experiments on Aplysia, Kandel explains why evolution favored this development. It saves energy. The first time you hear a fire bell go off, a chill runs down your neck and you expend a lot of energy trying to assess the implications and deciding what to do. But if after investigating you discover there's no fire, what do you do when five minutes later the bell goes off again, and then goes off again, and then again and again and again? Each time you pay less and less attention. By the tenth time it has gone off it's just background noise. Your reaction saves you from wasting energy. And that enhances your chances of survival. It gives you an opportunity to focus on something else that might come along that actually is a threat. Curiosity may kill the cat, but it doesn't kill us. It saves us.

As it happens, our natural attention to novelty is often helpful in discovering the truth. Why do we read newspapers? Because they tell us what's new. Reading newspapers is how we find out how the world has changed. And that's a well-traveled road to the truth. Focusing on what's novel keeps things real, saving us from overly ideological explanations of world events. Other animals, too, are able to focus on what's new, but none match humankind's cognitive ability to make sense of the world. That's one of our trump cards.

Why, then, do we often evince indifference to facts that are vital to understanding the modern world? We are back where we started, even more puzzled than ever. If as a species we are naturally curious, why are so many millions of people confused about Barack Obama's religion and birthplace? Why, back in 2003 when we invaded Iraq, couldn't voters get the basic facts right about 9/11, the most important event of our time? Shouldn't curious people have wanted to seek out the facts?

These are the kinds of questions that have puzzled social scientists for decades. But there may be a straightforward answer. Remember the Michael Jordan Lesson?

But before we return to Jordan, whose experience can help us solve the problem, we have to determine what exactly our problem is. That's not quite as easy a task as it would appear.

2

We're
Political Animals

So why aren't we better at politics?

1.

This is a list of websites designed to help American voters in recent elections:

congress.org

congressionalreportcards.org

e.thepeople.org

electionland.com

electionu.com

epolitics.com

politics4all.com

popvox.com

quora.com

visiblevote.us

vote411.org

votizen.com

votesmart.org

The list is incomplete. There are actually hundreds of websites like these. What do they have in common? All of them are designed to help voters become more knowledgeable about the issues in the news and the candidates running for office. If you go to congress.org you can find information about the bills before Congress and discover how your representative voted. If you go to votesmart.org (Project Vote Smart) you can find out who represents you in Congress and where they stand on the issues. If you visit Quora you can find the answers to basic questions you might have about an issue you've wondered about. These websites, in short, directly address the problem of

15

ignorance we identified earlier. They help voters become more knowledge-able. In a word, they help voters become smart.

That sounds like a worthy goal. Imagine what it would be like if voters suddenly knew the facts. It would be like living in a democratic Camelot. Or would it? Until 1988 no one knew. Then, that year, James Fishkin, a political scientist who now teaches at Stanford, came up with the idea of a deliberative poll. In a normal poll a voter is asked a bunch of questions about subjects he may or may not know something about. That is the extent of the interaction between the pollster and the voter. The pollster then moves on to the next person. In a deliberative poll a voter is asked a bunch of questions about subjects he probably doesn't know much about and is then educated about those subjects—usually at a weekend conference where he has the opportunity to study materials from all sides and engage in in-depth discussions about what he's read. Experts are brought in to help participants make sense of the material they are given. At the end of the conference, by which time he has become an educated voter on the issues under review, he is surveyed again.

So what happens? Do voters perform differently? Does education make a difference? In 1994, in England, a conference using the deliberative poll approach was televised. Three hundred people, drawn from a represen-tative sample, participated. The pool included clerks and teachers, blue-collar workers and white-collar workers, doctors and lawyers, and an equal number of men and women. The result? Voters who hadn't known much about a myriad of issues suddenly became extremely well informed about them. And all it took was one weekend. People from all demographic groups showed the capacity to grow. After being exposed to relevant information, people changed their opinions. They became more nuanced. They found the simple answers politicians usually offer inadequate. For example, while they remained tough on crime and insisted that prison should be "tougher and more unpleasant," they embraced reforms they had earlier rejected. They now favored rehabilitation and became sensitive to the procedural rights of criminals.

The first televised deliberative poll conference held in the United States took place in the presidential election year of 1996 in Austin, Texas, over the weekend of January 19–21. The conference attracted 460 people. They rep-resented all walks of life and were drawn from diverse geographical popula-tions in both Red and Blue states. A quarter of the participants came from families with an income of less than $20,000 a year. One woman agreed to attend because she would be able to stay in a hotel with hot running water. Jim Lehrer of PBS served as the anchor. Trained moderators led the discussions. As a precaution against bias, the materials given to voters were reviewed ahead of time by two members from opposite parties, Democrat Barbara Jordan and Republican Bill Frenzel. Once again voters picked up an enormous amount of basic information, and once again they changed their opinions, moving from simple-minded answers to the sixty-six questions that were asked, to more nuanced positions. And, no, they didn't always move in a more liberal direction. While opinion shifted in favor of bigger budgets for child care and education, the voters decided that the safety net programs would be better left to the states to manage. This suggested that ingrained ideological biases are no match for facts. Both liberals and conservatives in the group seemed willing to let the facts shape their opinions. When conservatives became informed about the benefits of child care they swung behind programs to help the poor rear their children. So much for the belief that conservatives are so rigidly ideological that facts don't matter.

James Fishkin has run his conferences around the world. Every time he holds one he gets the same results. They are nothing short of extraordinary. Voters aren't dumb. They are ignorant. When you expose them to the relevant information they are able to digest it and make sense of it. This suggests that democracy can work. It means charlatans can be stopped. Fishkin notes that in 1996 Pat Buchanan, when he was running for president, was asked if he would cut Medicare to balance the budget. No, Buchanan answered. He would protect Medicare, which was the politically safe answer. But he added that he would cut foreign aid. This too was a safe answer—foreign aid is wildly unpopular. But it was also a classic nonsense answer. Foreign aid consumes less than 1 percent of the total federal budget. It's a rounding error. But most voters don't know that. So they think it's a serious answer. You see? What voters need are facts. Facts can protect them. Fishkin's optimistic message is that we can make democracy function if we just get the facts into voters' hands. In other words, what we have is not a stupid-voter problem. We have an information problem.

That, at any rate, is what seems to be the lesson of Fishkin's conferences. People are educable. Ignorance can be cured. But was that ever really in doubt? We send children to school, after all, because we believe they can learn. We spend billions on the higher education system because we believe that if you give students the opportunity to learn about complicated subjects, they will. Proving that unknowledgeable voters can be turned into knowledgeable ones doesn't actually prove much that we didn't already know. Ignorant voters lack knowledge, but their problem is not that they have trouble learning. The problem is that on their own they don't try, relying instead on biases of one sort or another to guide their thinking.*

We think we have an ignorance problem. But do we actually have a motivational problem?

The people who attend Fishkin's conferences are plenty motivated, but that's because Fishkin uses incentives. He pays people to attend his conferences. People who went to the Austin conference got a $300 honorarium. He also picks up the cost of their meals and puts them up at a hotel. Attendees from faraway places are flown in. All that begins to suggest why people attend. Being invited to a conference like this is exciting to many people, especially when there's the promise of national media attention. For most attendees this is the first time they will have the chance to meet somebody like Jim Lehrer who can be seen on national television. Fishkin goes to great lengths to encourage people to participate. In his book about the Austin conference he explains that he was able to get a Chicago voter who'd never flown in an airplane to agree to come by flying a friend along to keep her company.

This suggests that if we want smart voters we need to start paying them. If we want people to follow the news closely we should set up a website where people can take a weekly current-events quiz, and if they pass, pay them. Want people to vote? Pay them. Want people to join with their friends every few months to debate public issues? Pay them. Incentives, we know, help motivate salesmen and CEOs. Why not use them to help voters become better voters? As we've seen in Fishkin's project, incentives work.

Is this the solution for which we've been waiting? In a perfectly rational world—one run by economists—it might be. But the world is not run by economists, and it isn't very rational. In the real world Americans generally balk at spending public money on elections. Over the last few years they have even turned against the modest reforms of the Watergate era, which provided for the public financing of presidential elections. After the effort to extend the Watergate reforms at the federal level faltered, reformers moved to the states. Clean-election reforms, which are designed to take private money out of politics by publicly financing campaigns, were tried in ten states at various levels of government. None captured the sustained imagination of the public. Many of the reforms were subsequently rolled back, declared unconstitutional, or defunded.

---

* While Fishkin found that facts could overcome voters' biases, numerous studies that test specifically for bias show that outside the setting of one of his conferences voters generally have trouble rising above it, as I alluded to earlier and will explore in further depth later.

No one, to be sure, has tried paying voters directly to become more knowledgeable about issues and candidates. But that's for a reason. It's not because of moral qualms about paying voters, though a strong argument can be made that we shouldn't pay voters, because paying them cheapens the meaning of citizenship. The reason is practical. Voters would find it insulting to be told that they have to be paid to make them do what they should do of their own volition. Anyone who dared suggest that voters need to be paid because they are citizen delinquents would instantly be branded as elitist and anti-American.

2.

An alternative to paying people is to change the culture. In Scandinavian countries, for example, where civics education is baked into the culture like a thick chocolate filling in a perfectly balanced communal soufflé, voters take a lively interest in politics. When Scandinavians are quizzed about the issues and the structure of their governments they know the answers as well as students who have just completed a high-level civics course. Culture, it turns out, can work as effectively as the incentives James Fishkin employs. The lesson of the Scandinavian experience is that if you teach people civics in school and then continue to emphasize civics in adult education courses—75 percent of Swedes participate as adults in civics-study circles at some point in their lives—they will retain the information they learned in school and will continue to express an interest in politics. You don't have to bribe them.

What seems especially helpful is creating a vast reserve of social capital on which people can draw. People need to feel their voice is heard and that their leaders are responsive. The system has to seem fair. As people review their standing in society they have to feel that under democratic institutions they have prospered—or at least have had a chance to prosper. And people can't bowl alone, to borrow the phrase popularized by sociologist Robert Putnam. They have to join groups. In which countries do people join voluntary organizations the most? The Scandinavian countries, surveys show.

But is it really all that simple? If, for example, social trust is the critical factor, as is often claimed by civics reformers, then we should expect to see the highest voter turnout in local elections. Which elected officials do American voters say they trust the most? Their local officials. Which elections in the United States draw the least number of voters year in and year out? Local elections. In Los Angeles in 2013 the mayoral primary drew just 21 percent of the registered voters, and this was after $16 million was spent by the candidates in a campaign with no incumbent, which should have triggered higher interest, but didn't. In New York City in 2009 so few people showed up to vote in the Democratic primary for mayor—11 percent of registered voters—that the *New York Times* put the story on the front page under the headline "A Primary Turnout So Low It May Be a Modern Record."

Evidently, whatever lies behind the Scandinavian miracle is not easily identified. We know it's in the culture, but we can't be sure what in the culture is exactly responsible or what the right mix of cultural elements is. There are a lot of unknown unknowns. And we cannot know if what works in Scandinavia, a region marked by demographic homogeneity, will work in the United States, a country made up of peoples from across the globe. That is a known unknown. Together, these facts lead to a lot of unknowns.

Americans clearly have not made a commitment to a vibrant civics culture in the Scandinavian mold. But we have tried. The results, unfortunately, have been underwhelming. In 2000 Senator Robert Byrd of West Virginia, convinced that Americans' ignorance of history was putting the Republic at risk, got Congress to pass a program to improve the teaching of history by teaching the teachers of history better methods. Fifty million dollars was spent on the effort over a few years. The teachers thought the program was well worth it. Studies showed that it had no impact on students. Byrd then got the Congress to spend an additional $119 million on the project. The result was the same. Teachers raved. Students showed no improvement.

Supreme Court justices have been especially prominent in the campaign to raise civics standards. In the 1980s, Chief Justice Warren Burger became so committed to the cause of teaching Americans about the Constitution that he resigned from the Court on a seemingly quixotic campaign to ignite popular interest in the upcoming bicentennial of the Constitution. Resign from the Court for this? People were taken aback. But Burger thought it was vital work. Unfortunately, no evidence was ever adduced to demonstrate that his efforts left a lasting impression. Americans remained as ignorant as ever.

When Justice Sandra Day O'Connor left the Court a generation later, she became convinced that ignorance about the Constitution remained rampant. To do something about it she founded a group expressly for the purpose of teaching young students civics. On the group's website, iCivics, students can play games designed to help them learn about the Court, immigration reform, voting, and other topics. The games are compelling. Here's one everybody might find handy: Responsibility Launcher. "Have you ever wanted to knock some civic sense into someone?" the game asks. "In Responsibility Launcher, you can. You'll remind citizens that their civic duties aren't just responsibilities, they help get things done!" Sounds promising. There's even an appealing mischievousness uncommon in civics efforts. Students are told that if they can't knock sense into someone they should try an anvil. A picture of an anvil then appears, as if the advice should be taken literally. But there's no proof this or any of the other games are having much of an impact. On the day I checked the website the anvil game had garnered just 77 Likes on Facebook. By contrast, Apu, one of the more obscure characters on the "The Simpsons" cartoon show—he's the owner of the Springfield convenience store—had 27,943 Likes.

3.

Has failure accompanied our efforts because we haven't tried hard enough? That is the orthodoxy embraced by civics reformers everywhere in the United States. It is what they tell themselves at conferences and what they tell the public: if only we did more, we could finally make some headway. This is why the cry you hear at civics conferences is always the same: spend more money. In a rich country like ours, which has conquered polio and gone to the moon, this sounds right. We think that with money we can solve any problem we face. But that supposes that ours is a money problem. Is it?

Why, after all, should it take either money or culture to get people to perform their civic responsibilities? Shouldn't people want to be involved? Shouldn't they want to be informed? Politics is, after all, supposedly in our blood. As Aristotle famously said, "man is by nature a political animal." We naturally fall into groups. We have millions of years of experience living in groups. So why are we indifferent to how our groups are run? Why do so many people tell pollsters they don't know much about politics? Logic suggests that evolution must have favored people who are good at politics, and in particular, people who are good at sniffing out relevant facts, because people who seek out facts are less likely to be manipulated. In the contest for resources a person who can protect himself from manipulation will in the course of things be favored over people who can't. The more resources one has, evolutionary psychology teaches us, the more likely it is that we will be in a position to pass on our genes to the next generation and the generation after that. Being good at politics, in other words, should be good for our genes. So what's our problem? Our being bad at politics doesn't make sense. Was Aristotle wrong? Are we not by nature political animals?

3

Your 150 Closest Friends

How many people do you know?

1.

Our indifference to politics is so common that it is tempting to leap to the conclusion that Aristotle was wrong—that man is not by nature a political animal. But before you do, consider this. While members of hunter-gatherer groups are obviously susceptible to myth and are largely ignorant about questions involving science that lie outside their knowledge base, there is no evidence that they suffer from political apathy or that individual members remain stubbornly ignorant about facts commonly known to the larger community. These deficiencies are modern phenomena, common everywhere in the modern world, except, as noted, in Scandinavia. What is it, then, about modern society that afflicts us? Could a single, overarching cause be responsible?

There are so many differences between hunter-gatherer societies and our own that it seems almost a fool's errand to try to settle on a single difference that might be accountable for the ubiquity of political apathy in our world. You could make a case for any number of key differences that might be involved. You could suggest that under modern pressures families have grown weak and left individuals adrift. Or, just as convincingly, you could insist that in the modern world people have to juggle so many tasks that they can't attend to them all, so they ignore the ones that cause the most aggravation, like politics. Then there's the argument economists make, which turns the question upside down. Civics reformers make the assumption that apathy and ignorance are an irrational response to politics. But the economists say apathy and ignorance are actually perfectly rational. Their argument is that since no individual's single vote is ever likely to affect the outcome of an election, it makes no sense for an individual to devote scarce resources to the study of politics. Apathy is therefore rational. Why keep up on something you can't affect? Why vote if your vote doesn't count? The costs outweigh the benefits. And so on and so forth. You could ask ten experts and get ten answers—or, more likely, a hundred answers.

To a young political scientist named Michael Bang Petersen, who codirects the Politics and Evolution Lab at Aarhus University in Denmark, the question of voter apathy is actually less complicated than it seems. Petersen breaks into a smile easily, and he has the informal bearing of someone who is highly approachable. His picture on his university website homepage shows him wearing a light-brown plaid shirt, the kind you'd wear on your day off (his white T-shirt underneath is prominently visible). He confirms every physical stereotype there is about Scandinavians. He is tall, blond, and thin. He has authored or coauthored more than fifty social science papers (in both English and Danish).

The subject of most of these papers is the idea—which is just beginning finally to take hold in the social sciences more than a century after it was first proposed by William James—that you can only understand the large psychological forces driving human behavior when you take an evolutionary perspective. This is known today as evolutionary psychology—EP. The central finding of EP is that we aren't blank slates. We are born with a particular psychology. This makes it meaningful to speak of human nature. It is not just a phrase. There really is something called human nature. It was formed in response to the conditions we faced during the Pleistocene, as I alluded to in the Introduction. You want to understand human beings? Don't try to figure out why we are able to survive in the modern world. We didn't mainly evolve under modern conditions. To understand us you have to go back to the Pleistocene. That is when we underwent the major evolutionary changes that made humans human—nature selected for traits that would help us survive back then, not now.

Why do humans cringe when coming across a snake? Because in the Pleistocene snakes posed a danger. People who possessed a healthy fear of elongated animals that slither through the grass were more apt to survive and pass on their snake-fearing genes to their descendants (us). Why do feces and rats disgust humans? Because in the Pleistocene we developed a faculty for disgust to help protect us from microbes that could kill us.

Why are humans afraid of people with diseases? Because in the Pleistocene exposure to people with a disease could be fatal. Why are we not afraid of automobiles, which kill tens of thousands of Americans every year? Because our ancestors did not have automobiles in the Pleistocene, a clever point made by evolutionary psychologist Steven Pinker.

And what is one of the most important facts about the way humans lived in the Pleistocene? They lived in small groups. Of all the various factors that shaped our evolution, this is the one, Petersen says, borrowing from the established literature on evolutionary psychology, on which we need to place the most emphasis. Our genus, Homo, first walked the earth 2.5 million years ago. From that time until the agricultural era began—just 10,000 years ago—Homo lived in groups no larger than the number of people you can squeeze into a college lecture hall: about 150. This was true for people around the world. How do we know that humans seem by nature to be geared to groups of a small size?

All humans at all times in all places seem to find small groups particularly attractive. What is the size of mountain communities in eastern Tennessee? About 150. Mainstream American Protestant church congregations? About 150. Amish parishes? About 150. There seems to be something about the number 150. As evolutionary psychologist Robin Dunbar, one of the great social scientists of our time, discovered when he surveyed studies from across the world, humans seem to naturally favor groups that range in number from 100 to 500, with the median landing at around 150. What do leading business experts say is the optimal size of a department? One hundred fifty. When do employees report feeling high job satisfaction? When they work in an environment with about 150 or fewer colleagues. When do managers report that morale starts to break down? When the number of employees exceeds 150. What is the number of Christmas cards that people in the UK send out to friends and family? It's about 68 cards by one study. How many people are in the households who receive those cards? Between 125 and 150! This suggests that the natural size of an individual's network is about 150.

Midway through the great Mormon trek westward from Illinois to Utah in 1847, Brigham Young had his pioneers sit out the winter in modern-day Nebraska. Twenty-five hundred camped there. In April he organized a vanguard party to break a path through the Rocky Mountains. Because the trip was expected to be dangerous—there was a concern that Indians might stage raids—the planning was exceptionally detailed. So the party brought along enough provisions to last a full year. Livestock included 93 horses, 66 oxen, and 52 mules. The party consisted of 143 men, three women, and two children—just two shy of what's been dubbed the magic number, 150. Mormon historians report that Young found this to be the ideal size of a pioneer group. As he moved 5,000 of his flock to Utah he repeatedly broke them into groups of 150. The Mormon trek was one of the most remarkable and successful migrations in human history.

Robin Dunbar became so fascinated with these findings that he began to wonder if there is biology behind the phenomenon. It would make sense if there were. Evolutionary psychologists have shown that human behavior is shaped not just by the environment but also by our genes. But where to look? Dunbar wasn't sure. Eventually he settled on the size of the animal brain. Scientists had long speculated that the size of an animal's brain corresponds to its intelligence. Animals with big brains, it was believed, are smarter than animals with small brains. That made intuitive sense. But it turned out not to be true. Neanderthals had bigger brains than we do, yet we are smarter.

As Dunbar searched he detected a fascinating pattern. It wasn't the overall size of the brain that mattered. What counted was the size of the neocortex in relation to the rest of the brain. And then he hit upon a groundbreaking discovery. When you divide the volume of the neocortex by the volume of the rest of the brain, giving you a neat mathematical ratio, it turns out that the ratio corresponds exactly to the size of an animal's average network. The bigger the ratio, the bigger the network. The animal with the biggest ratio? Humans. The animal with the biggest social network? Humans.

We now have the biological answer to why humans seem to gravitate to groups of 150. It's because that's roughly the network size our brain can handle. We can't keep track of thousands of people. We can only keep track of around 150. Why is there a limit of just 150 when it would obviously be advantageous to have much larger networks? Imagine if we could handle networks of 2,000 people. You could walk into an average business convention and not have to struggle to pick out a few people here and a few people there to get to know. You could strike up conversations with every person you had time to meet, and grow and maintain a relationship with each person. The only limit on your social network would be the time it takes to initiate a relationship and occasionally tend to it. The effect on the economy would undoubtedly be enormous. But this would only be an advantage in the modern world. During the Pleistocene, when Homo was evolving into Homo sapiens, our ancestors didn't need to know thousands. To survive and flourish all they needed was a network of 150 or so. So evolution selected for people who could keep track of groups of that rough size.

Evolution over millions of years gave us the brain we needed at the time we needed it, not the brain we might need down the road. Nature doesn't throw in extra brainpower we might someday find useful. The reason is that brains use up a lot of energy. The human brain—three pounds of neurons, gray matter, and other stuff—consumes 20 percent of the energy our body produces. If our brain were designed to maintain networks of thousands of people, it is likely our brain would need to be larger and consume even more energy. Today we could supply the brain with that extra energy. But in the past? The answer is yes, but only when times were good. What about when times were bad? Then what? Then the survival of the species might have been threatened, and for what? A capability we didn't need? Evolution doesn't work that way. It doesn't impose costs that a species can pay only when times are good.

It's also possible that our brain would have to be so large to be able to keep track of thousands that it would be too large for our existing body size. To keep us from tipping over, our bodies might have to be larger to accommodate our larger brain. Another problem is that our brain might have to work so hard to keep track of thousands that it would be in danger of literally burning itself out. Brain tissue can only tolerate so many electrical and chemical synapses before it begins to scorch. This puts a natural limit on the size of the human brain. It may be that we would not need to increase brain capacity to accommodate our desire to maintain thousands of relationships. Some people are able with the existing human brain to do so. President James K. Polk was famous in his day for being able to remember the names and faces of people he'd only briefly encountered decades earlier. So we can dream. But thus far the ability of a human to remember thousands of people has not proved to be an evolutionarily advantageous ability.

2.

How important is it that we are able to keep track of 150 individuals? It is apparently so important, say scientists, that it may well be responsible for us having big powerful brains.

For many years scientists believed we developed big brains in order to be able to best predators and find food. But today the thinking is that we evolved big brains to deal with the complexity of our social groups. That is, nature selected for individuals with higher cognitive abilities because intelligence paid off. The bigger your brain power, the more able you are to dominate others and obtain greater resources for yourself and your kin. It's called the Machiavellian Intelligence Hypothesis, and it was proposed in the

1970s by a scientist who studied primates and made a startling discovery. Nicholas Humphrey was visiting a colleague's lab when he began to take pity on the monkeys locked in cages. Here is what he saw:

> They live in social groups of eight or nine animals in relatively large cages. But these cages are almost empty of objects, there is nothing to manipulate, nothing to explore; once a day the concrete floor is hosed down, food pellets are thrown in and that is about it. So I looked—and seeing this barren environment, thought of the stultifying effect it must have on the monkey's intellect.

But then one day Humphrey realized he'd been mistaken.

> . . . I looked again and saw a half-weaned infant pestering its mother, two adolescents engaged in a mock battle, an old male grooming a female whilst another female tried to sidle up to him, and I suddenly saw the scene with new eyes: forget about the absence of objects, these monkeys had each other to manipulate and to explore. There could be no risk of their dying an intellectual death when the social environment provided such obvious opportunity for participating in a running dialectical debate. Compared to the solitary existence of my own monkeys, the setup in [my colleague Robert] Hinde's social groups came close to resembling a simian School of Athens.

As he thought about it, Humphrey realized that getting along with others, whether you are a monkey or a man, requires tremendous skill. At any moment social order can collapse into chaos because everybody is pursuing their own interests. To keep this from happening primates have to have powerful brains.

Getting along is complicated. As Albert Einstein is said to have remarked, when asked why man can figure out the structure of the atom but not a way to stop atomic war, "That is simple, my friend. It is because politics is more difficult than physics." Politics is complicated because people are complicated. There's great truth in the old wisdom passed on to students in high school sociology classes: All men are like some other men. Some men are like some other men. No man is like any other man. While the standard issue human is born with two arms, two legs, and ten fingers, we differ by the groups we join and our individual likes and dislikes. Getting us to get along is an enormous challenge.

A few years after Humphrey's epiphany a young primatologist named Frans de Waal took a job at Arnhem Zoo in the Netherlands. Arnhem was the perfect place for a primatologist. It houses the largest number of captive chimpanzees in the world. De Waal worked there for six years. In a diary, he kept track of the behavior of the chimpanzees. Like Humphrey, he noticed that they are intensely social and that they behave like humans. During a power struggle between two chimpanzees he was observing, Yeroen and Luit, Yeroen began throwing tantrums. The tantrums reminded him, de Waal recalls in one of his books, of a famous scene in *The Final Days*, the Watergate book by Bob Woodward and Carl Bernstein. This is the scene where Nixon collapses on the carpet and, crying out loud, moans, "What have I done? What has happened?" When things went badly for Yeroen, he seemed caught in a similar grip of despair: "Yeroen began to have tantrums after the conflict had been raging for about a month. With an unerring sense of drama he would let himself drop out of a tree like a rotten apple and roll around the ground screaming and kicking. . . . These hysterical outbursts gave an impression of scarcely suppressed despair and abjectness."

De Waal eventually came to the conclusion that chimpanzees not only behave like we do when they are down (or up), they have politics like we do, and play politics in remarkably similar ways in some critical respects. With whom do they form coalitions? It's not with chimpanzees they happen to like. It is with those they need—just as humans do. Careful observations made over a long period of time convinced de Waal that chimpanzee leaders have to demonstrate more than pure strength. They have to curry favor with the crowd—just as humans do. The outcome of a power struggle among chimpanzees, he writes, does not determine the social relationship. The social relationship determines the outcome. Luit triumphed in the contest with Yeroen not because of brute strength—physically, they were roughly matched, though Luit was younger—but because after several weeks of struggle Luit began winning over more allies. Yeroen threw so many tantrums, he alienated his base of support. The more tantrums he threw, the less the other chimpanzees cared for him and the less attention they paid to his tantrums. Luit came to seem the more natural leader. Luit's triumph, however, was temporary. After his defeat, Yeroen struck an alliance with another strong male. Together they were able to dethrone Luit.

On the evolutionary timeline, humans are closest to chimpanzees. In fact, some scientists argue that humans are merely a branch of the chimpanzee line. That is, we are chimps too. But we are different. Our brains are bigger. And what do our bigger brains allow us to do? Form bigger groups.

Nonhuman primates can form groups at the upper limit of only about seventy individuals. Our groups, as we've seen, are typically composed of about 150 individuals. That difference is in part one of the reasons why we are running the world and chimpanzees aren't. Groups are that important. And in the modern world we have proved our capacity to form groups that number in the millions.

Why can't chimpanzees grow their networks like we did? As you might imagine, scientific opinion on this question is divided. Robin Dunbar convincingly argues it's because they cannot talk. Talking is essential for a lot of reasons, obviously. But Dunbar notes that it's especially important in creating group cohesion. In fact, it's probably the reason why language evolved. We need language to bond. We use language to communicate how we feel toward one another and what has happened to us during the day. What's the number one topic of discussion among humans? Humans. We are most fascinated by ourselves and we talk about ourselves constantly. When social scientists began studying the conversations humans have, they discovered that two-thirds of the time the speakers are discussing social topics. Broadly speaking, what we like to do when we talk is gossip. This is true of both men and women. By nature both men and women are born gossips.

What's a striking difference between humans and chimpanzees? We talk. They groom. The next time you visit a zoo take a moment to watch the primates and note the amount of time they spend grooming one another. But animals can only spend so much time grooming, about 20 percent of the day, say scientists. More than that and the animal would have to forgo other important tasks like finding food and eating. Thus, there is a natural limit to the number of other animals with whom a primate can bond. In general, humans can bond with three times as many individuals as other primates. What allows us to do that is language. Language is simply far more efficient than grooming. You can only groom one individual at a time. But you can use language to communicate with several people simultaneously. Studies show that humans are capable of connecting face-to-face through spoken language with as many as four people at the same time. Any more than that and people have to strain to hear. But four is a large number. In an hour, a good conversationalist can roam through a room full of strangers and participate in multiple conversations involving four people, meeting many more people in an hour than a chimp can groom in a whole day. Grooming limits our natural networks. Language expands them. And in our world, of course, we can communicate through language to audiences numbering in the tens of millions, a key advantage over other primates.

But which is better at bonding, language or grooming? Grooming is. When a monkey grooms another monkey its brain activates an opiate that rewards the behavior. Grooming feels good. That feeling of warmth promotes intimacy and empathy of a sort. Although primatologists deny that monkeys feel empathy in the same way we humans do, a monkey who has just groomed another monkey will be sensitive to that monkey's cries for help—and actually follow through and offer help. Grooming creates tight bonds. Language doesn't work the same way.

Merely speaking words to another human being doesn't stimulate the brain to produce opiates. What does? Smiling and laughing. It's not language per se that creates bonds. It's the grin or the chuckle. There is a bagel store in Seattle that I patronized for years because they had the best bagels in town. But eventually I realized I didn't like going there. The reason was that I was never greeted with a smile. It was a family-run business. But whether it was the mother or her son who took my order, I never got even a hint of the warmth that comes with a smile. Going there was depressing and got my day off to a bad start. So I stopped going even though that meant giving up my favorite bagel. I didn't mind (all that much). At the new bagel store I started going to, I got lots of smiles. That was more important, but I sure missed the taste and texture of the bagels from the other store. Fortunately, there's a happy ending to this story. One day, hungry for my good old favorite bagel, I went back to the old bagel shop. The son was at the counter. He didn't smile. But this time I told him off, telling him he was rude. Out of the corner of my eye I saw his mother standing nearby, watching. It looked like she was listening respectfully to what I was saying. Might my outburst make a difference? Curious, I returned the next day. The son was gone. And when the mother saw me she broke into a large smile. I now start each day with my favorite bagel and get a smile along with it.

We rely on smiles and laughter as important social cues. They let us know we count. A lecturer who can get his audience laughing bonds with them. Both speaker and listener get a literal charge in the brain as opiates are released. Primates groom. Humans smile and laugh. That's one way we turn strangers into friends. Look at the pictures of friends and family that people keep on their desks. What expression is on their faces? Quite often, they're smiling. What's my favorite picture of my mother? It's one where she's caught in an obvious moment of incredible joy and laughter. It sits on my office desk, right next to a picture of my father. My father is smiling too. Only after I was doing the research for this book did I realize why I had chosen these photographs over others.

What is the significance of the fact that groups are important and that for humans the natural size of a group is about 150? This is where the Michael Jordan Lesson comes in. In his natural environment—the basketball court—Michael Jordan was a star. His skill set perfectly matched the challenges he faced. But on the baseball diamond he was average. His skill set didn't match the challenges. While basketball and baseball are similar in the demands they make on athletes, they do not make the exact same demands. A person can be great in one sport but not the other. There is a mismatch, in other words. This, it turns out, is the problem voters have. We are mismatched with our environment. We are designed, says the social scientist Michael Bang Petersen, to thrive in a world of small groups. We are ill-suited to deal with the group in which we find ourselves today—the large modern state—a group that consists not of 150 members, but millions. Why are we apathetic? Why are there so many politically ignorant people? We no longer live in groups of the right size for us.

We don't have an information problem, or a motivation problem, or a money problem. We have a human-being problem.*

3.

Imagine, for a moment, a misfit. What comes to mind? I would guess it is someone acting in some visibly inappropriate way: a guy who shows up at a church wedding in dirty shorts and a T-shirt, an oddball who jokes around at a funeral, the loud, noisy person speaking on a cell phone in the quiet car on a train. Suppose I ask you to imagine a political misfit. Now what comes to mind? Perhaps it's the followers of Lyndon LaRouche you see in public squares passing out pamphlets containing wild conspiracy theories, pure nonsense, like the charge that the Queen of England is a drug trafficker or that the World Wildlife Fund is pushing the world to war (two charges LaRouchites actually have made). What all of these misfits have in common is that they are easy to spot. We know them when we see them. But not all misfits are so easily identified.

Think about the voters on the Jersey Shore in 1916. When many of them voted against President Wilson, apparently because of the shark attacks—attacks Wilson could not have stopped if he had ordered the army, the navy, and the marines combined to storm New Jersey's beaches—they were acting

---

* As we will see in later chapters, ignorance is a complicated phenomenon. So while membership in a small group is apt to cure us of certain problems, it cannot cure us of them all. Indeed, certain problems grow worse when our groups are small.

irrationally. Democracy demands that voters exercise wisdom when making political choices. But these voters clearly were not. They weren't up to the job. They let local events dictate their decision in a national election.

To all outward appearances they didn't look like misfits. They didn't act out in public the way we imagine misfits act out. They didn't go around saying crazy things. They didn't dress inappropriately. They didn't leave any outward sign that they were misfits. Nonetheless, they were.

But they weren't misfits in all contexts. In July, when their lives were at risk from an immediate threat, their instincts helped them reach the right conclusion. Their instincts told them they shouldn't wade into shark-infested waters no matter what the experts said—and their instincts were correct. But in November, when they were voting for president, their instincts led them to a wrong conclusion. The voters of Beach Haven and Spring Lake were exposed to the same war news as everybody else in New Jersey. But they were not in the same place as everybody else. Those shark attacks changed them, triggering an ancient instinct that affected how many of them cast their ballot. The change was so well hidden that nobody realized it until Christopher Achen, eighty-six years later, uncovered the truth.

How can we tell when we should follow our instincts and when we should not? How do we know when it's July and when it's November? Earlier, we learned that the real lesson of 1916 was that context is everything. There are times when our instincts tell us to act cautiously and other times when our instincts tell us not to worry. Shark in the water? Get out. No sharks around? Don't worry. But there is yet another set of circumstances to consider, where context is equally important. That's when our instincts don't work at all. In some contexts it's helpful to go on instinct and in other contexts it's not. *Political Animals* is about knowing when it's not—and why that's so often the case in politics.

Acting on our instincts, we forget the context. And context is everything—as we learned in the lesson of the shark story. You cannot just decide as a result of a two-week ordeal that sharks are always out to get humans and that you should therefore never swim in the ocean. You have to temper your fear instincts by taking the context into account.

In a sense, we are all misfits. We don't fit in the modern world. We weren't made for it and don't naturally come equipped with the instincts needed to navigate it well in the political arena. This has consequences.

But what's the Michael Jordan Lesson? It's not only that we excel when we are put in a situation naturally suited to our abilities. It is also that training helps. Jordan became a better baseball player his second season because he worked at it. He became the top basketball star in history because he worked at that too. Humans, whatever their inherent abilities, improve when they set themselves to a task and work hard at it. We aren't dumb animals. We are smart. We may not be able to stop ourselves from thinking the thoughts that come naturally to us in a flash when certain circumstances arise—as I've said, we're going to react the way we react to things that happen to us—but that doesn't mean we have to surrender to our instincts and give up the hope that we can think and behave more rationally and humanely. There's a reason why we no longer take pleasure throwing live cats into open fires, as both kings and peasants once did. Our culture has trained us to think this is abhorrent. That's promising.

PART II:
READING PEOPLE

4

Why We Are Surprised When Our Leaders Disappoint Us

The mistake even smart voters make

1.

Remember James Fishkin's voters, the ones who worked hard to study up on the issues? His work is premised on the belief that you can develop smart voters by teaching them how to be smart. He has proved you can teach them about immigration, and taxes, and gun control. But a funny thing happened on the way to nirvana. They didn't seem able to do something we all think we are pretty good at, and that's to read people well. No matter how much they studied, no matter how many videos they watched, they did not seem able to get at the truth about the political leaders who run for office.

In 2004, Fishkin assembled a panel representative of the country's voters to see whom they'd pick as the Democratic Party's nominee for president. Seven hundred voters participated. Each week for five weeks they studied up on the issues and the candidates. They watched the candidates' campaign commercials and read reams of impartial materials. By the end of the process they had become near-experts. And whom in the end did Fishkin's smart voters pick? John Edwards, the telegenic hair-perfect candidate, whose career went up in smoke just four years later after it was disclosed that while his wife was battling cancer, which ultimately took her life, he had had a mistress, put her on his campaign payroll in flagrant violation of federal law, according to officials, and fathered her child, whom he initially denied flatly was his. Today, he is considered one of the biggest phonies ever to run for president.

To be sure, Edwards fooled even political professionals. Then Senator John Kerry, after all, selected him as his running mate. But what influenced Kerry undoubtedly was Edwards's poll numbers. Those poll numbers blinded him to Edwards's flaws, which became abundantly clear as the campaign progressed and insiders came to rue the choice. The question then isn't why Kerry proved less than perspicacious. As Republican Senator John McCain demonstrated in his selection of Sarah Palin as his running mate in 2008, presidential nominees are often so desperate for victory that they'll run with almost anybody they think will help them win. Ambition blinds them. But what blinded Fishkin's voters?

2.

In Pleistocene times the most common group that humans lived in was the band—which is the smallest social group involving unrelated people that exists. A tribe typically consists of a hundred or so members. A band has maybe twenty-five. That is so small a community it is hard for us to grasp. When we think small we think "small town." Being in a band is like living on a compound with a few families. The small scale on which life played out affected everything. People knew each other like brother and sister and husband and wife. When a couple had sex, their neighbors (and children) probably knew because they could hear the thrashing or perhaps were even in a position to watch. Everyone knew who was good at gathering food and who wasn't. Everyone knew who worked hard and who didn't. Everyone knew who was good at hunting and who wasn't. Everyone knew who was trustworthy and who wasn't. Everyone knew who was generous and who wasn't. Everyone knew who got along well with others and who didn't. Everyone knew who the best parents were. This knowledge, all of it, was critical to the success of the group. It gave the members of the band the information they needed not only to make good social judgments, but good political ones as well. They did not have to guess who could be trusted with power. They knew.

Consider, for example, the interaction that takes place between leaders and followers. Hunter-gatherers interacted with their leaders face-to-face. This meant they could use the evolved mechanisms humans possess to assess how a leader performed. They could make full use of the human powers of vision, hearing, and touch in deciding if a leader showed leadership abilities when needed. Does he wear a brave face in battle? Does he falter when under physical attack? Does he know how to think in a crisis? These are the most important questions followers needed answered, and they are all questions humans are fully capable of answering. We possess the ability to read people. This allows us to detect fear in a flash and, if we are in a position to read their body language, to sense if somebody is preparing to attack or retreat. Though—as we'll see—our judgments are hardly infallible, we can usually tell if someone's in a bad mood or a good one, and whether they mean us well or ill. Moreover, we can tell not only what others are thinking about us, but also what they are thinking we are thinking about them—which psychologists call a Theory of Mind. This ability sets us apart from all other species and is one of the features that makes humans human. Reading people comes so naturally to us that we often don't pause to think how incredible this ability is. But it's absolutely amazing. It's better than any magic trick Houdini ever performed.

Now, contrast the situation hunter-gatherers were in with ours. What do we know about our leaders? Very little actually. We don't come into daily contact with them. We don't get to know them as friends or neighbors. What we do know about them we learn through intermediaries like the media and from fleeting glimpses on television. That is, we know them only at a distance and through heavily filtered lenses that cloud our vision. The hunter-gatherer took in the whole person when evaluating leaders—the good, the bad, and the complicated. We have to get by with a cartoon version: They're strong. They're weak. They're an insider. They're an outsider. And that is often not enough to go on.

Why is that? Our evolved mechanisms, as Michael Bang Petersen points out, are designed to help us evaluate people in our midst. They are less good at helping us evaluate people at a distance. Our natural gifts of reading people are largely neutralized when we are reading politicians. The circumstances in which we get to know them are so artificial, it's impossible most of the time to get a whiff of the real person beneath the fictional character created for public consumption. We think we know our politicians well. But we barely know them at all.

What Fishkin's voters proved in 2004 is that even smart voters are hobbled in making wise leadership choices about people they don't really know. Studying doesn't hurt, of course. The more we know, the more we know. Charles Peters, the founding editor of the *Washington Monthly*, figured out that John Edwards was a lightweight after hearing a story from a reliable source in 2003. Here's what Peters learned: "One evening while he was campaigning for the Senate in North Carolina [in 1998], Edwards was faced with a choice of several events he might attend. An advance man suggested, 'Maybe we ought to go to the reception for Leah Rabin.' Edwards responded, 'Who's she?' 'Yitzhak Rabin's widow,' replied the aide. 'Who was he?' asked Edwards." John Edwards did not know who Yitzhak Rabin was, or that he had been murdered? Rabin, the Israeli leader, had been struck down by an assassin in 1995 after signing the Oslo Accords that recognized the authority of the Palestinians over Gaza and much of the West Bank. The Accords had been front-page news around the world. Bill Clinton had commemorated the agreement in a famous photo op at which Yasser Arafat and Rabin shook hands at Clinton's instigation. The photo of them shaking hands is one of the most remarkable photos ever taken. And John Edwards was unfamiliar with Rabin? And he was running for a seat in the US Senate? And now he wanted to be president?

But how many of us have reliable sources, as Charles Peters did, to whom we can turn for the inside scoop? All most of us have to go on is what we pick up along the way during a campaign. And that doesn't give us the kind of insight we really need to make truly informed decisions, even if we study really, really hard.

3.

In his memoirs former defense secretary Robert Gates recalls that in the weeks leading up to the first inauguration of President Barack Obama, he wondered what it would be like working with Hillary Clinton, who'd been named secretary of state. He had never met her. But he had, he confesses, a strong negative impression. Then they started meeting and getting to know one another. He was flabbergasted. Her media image did not at all match the woman he was getting to know. This led him to conclude, he says, that he should never again assume he knew what someone is really like without working with them.

Robert Gates worked for eight different presidents, yet he was lulled into thinking he knew who Hillary was from her newspaper clippings and media reports. Not even someone of his caliber and experience could rely on his instincts. They misled him.

You want to read someone? You have to actually know them.

There is a compelling example of this in the story of the Kennedys. If you asked an ordinary American in 1961 what he liked about John and Jacqueline Kennedy he probably would have said, among other things, their marriage. They looked like the perfect couple. After the election millions of Americans were so inspired by the Kennedys that they began to model themselves after them. American men stopped wearing hats because Jack went hatless. American women began donning the pillbox hat because Jackie wore a pillbox hat at the inauguration. Film of the parents playing with their adoring children, John and Caroline, warmed voters' hearts, reinforcing the impression that the Kennedy family was exceptional.

It was, of course, one big lie. Jack was a philandering, insensitive lothario. He even cheated on his wife when she was eight months pregnant. In 1956, tired and morose after losing a bid for his party's vice-presidential nomination, he went off to France with a buddy, Florida senator George Smathers. While there, according to Smathers, Kennedy had multiple trysts. Then, one day, word came that Jackie had suffered a miscarriage and her life was in danger. A priest was called to administer last rites. But Jack declined to fly home. Her condition stabilized, and he remained in France for three days until Smathers finally convinced him he was risking a divorce and political suicide. "I told him," Smathers recalled, "I was going to get him back there even if I had to carry him." Joseph Kennedy, Jack's father, reportedly promised Jackie a million dollars to keep the marriage going.

And this was just one of the stories that eventually came out about Kennedy's philandering. John Kennedy didn't commit adultery once or twice. He was a serial adulterer. Not even his election to the presidency stopped him. With the help of aides, who introduced young women they thought he'd like, he had one affair after another. He had to have sex every day, he confessed to a British diplomat, or he'd get a headache. The list of his paramours included the girlfriend of a mobster, the wife of a friend, the White House secretaries dubbed Fiddle and Faddle, and even a nineteen-year-old White House intern, whom he seduced just months before she got married. How did he meet the intern, who was a virgin? One of Kennedy's closest aides arranged for her to take a dip in the White House swimming pool while he was there, swimming in the nude. And these are the affairs that have been confirmed. Kennedy has also been linked to several actresses, including Marilyn Monroe.

At the time of his presidency there was no way Americans could know any of this. In the election of 1960 Richard Nixon, Kennedy's opponent, expressly forbid his staff from circulating stories about Kennedy's private life. And the media failed to report on his philandering, considering it off-limits, though it made him vulnerable to blackmail of the very sort that FBI Director J. Edgar Hoover practiced. (Hoover would inform the administration of the rumors his agents picked up to let the Kennedys know he was on to JFK's lasciviousness, even as Hoover professed a desire to "protect" Kennedy from the kind of blackmail to which Hoover was subjecting him.) But what is puzzling is that Americans were so sure they knew Kennedy well. They hadn't met him, except perhaps fleetingly at a public appearance. They didn't know his friends. And yet they were sure they knew him. They were so sure that when the evidence of his serial philandering began to surface in the 1970s, their reaction was absolute shock. They thought they'd known this man. They hadn't.

4.

When you stop and think about it, the firm belief that we know our politicians well is downright peculiar given the frequency with which we find ourselves surprised by their conduct. You would think that we would learn to be cautious in our judgments. But we don't. In 1972 Richard Nixon won reelection to the presidency in a landslide. Eighteen months later, following the Watergate revelations, a majority of Americans told pollsters that if the election were held over again they would vote this time for Nixon's opponent George McGovern. In effect they were admitting they had misread Nixon.

One of the biggest shocks of all was that Nixon swore. A decisive turning point in the scandal came when White House transcripts of secretly recorded conversations were published. The transcripts were dotted with references to expletives that had been deleted. Nixon had been in the navy during World War Two. It is well known that sailors swear. But the image he had created for himself was of a man who did not swear. Many supporters who thought they'd known him suddenly felt they didn't know him at all. (That voters weren't aware of his swearing is further evidence of how little they actually know about presidents. Swearing, after all, is something a casual acquaintance would pick up about a friend after spending little time with them.)

By the mid-1970s both of the candidates in the 1960 election, Kennedy and Nixon, had been thoroughly demythologized. But then came Jimmy Carter, with his big wide grin, and people all over again succumbed to myth, this time the myth of a competent leader who'd never lie to them. Carter's competence seemed unquestionable. In the navy he'd served in a high position on a nuclear submarine and worked directly for Hyman Rickover, a four-star admiral famous as the Father of the Nuclear Navy. Carter's honesty seemed self-evident. He was a farmer from a small town, after all. Many people thought he had an honest face.

Then came his disastrous presidency, with inflation out of control, the national debt rising, and the economy teetering. Even Democrats by 1980 believed Carter wasn't a very effective political leader. He was considered so weak that he drew a primary challenge from Senator Ted Kennedy. Early on in the race for the nomination Carter's position improved immensely thanks to Iran's decision to take our diplomats hostage. (As we'll see, in a crisis Americans rally around their president.) But then came the botched mission to rescue the hostages, and Americans once again turned against Carter, though too late in the political game to help Kennedy. In the general election, low in the polls, Carter jeopardized his reputation for honesty. As the campaign heated up he let his staff leave the impression that the Republican candidate, Ronald Reagan, was a mad bomber. That backfired badly after Reagan appeared on stage with Carter at the first presidential debate. Whatever you thought of Reagan, there seemed no reason to think he was itching to get us into a war. Between the two of them, Reagan looked the more presidential, Carter coming off as a little desperate. (It was in this debate that Carter invoked his twelve-year-old daughter Amy in support of his nuclear weapons policy.)

The public had thought that in electing Jimmy Carter they were getting a courageous Boy Scout leader like Frank Capra's Jimmy Stewart in *It's a Wonderful Life*. Instead, they got another failed politician willing to squander his reputation in the squalid hunt for votes in the course of an ugly campaign in which the president of the United States sunk to demonizing his opponent. Once again the public felt let down.

Like most elections, 1980 was a referendum on the past. People generally don't vote on the basis of what they expect will happen in the future. The future is abstract. The past, in contrast, is concrete. As emotional human beings we respond most forcefully to the concrete. People didn't vote *for* Reagan so much as vote *against* Carter.

They didn't even share Reagan's conservative political views. Polls consistently showed that 1980 did not mark a sea change in the public's social views or political ideology. Voters did not adopt new opinions about abortion, drugs, or social welfare programs. Fully 40 percent had no ideological orientation at all, confessing they didn't know whether they were liberal or conservative. Nonetheless, millions in both parties showed genuine enthusiasm for Reagan. And the reason for that was that many people found him immensely likable. They found his voice soothing, his reassuring optimism inspiring, and his simple answers appealing. They felt comfortable with him.

Why is this important? Because social science studies show that when we feel comfortable with someone we convince ourselves that we know them. And this is one of the reasons why Americans were willing to trust the presidency with Reagan. The public may have been voting against

Carter, not for Reagan, but a strong majority approved of Reagan the man and that was critical. Voters usually decline to turn out incumbents, even ones with whom they are disillusioned. In the twentieth century, not counting Carter, only three elected presidents were voted out of office: William Howard Taft (in an election in which the Republican vote was split as a result of the third-party candidacy of Teddy Roosevelt), Herbert Hoover (who was associated with the Great Depression), and George H. W. Bush. By nature we are cautious. We go with the devil we know, not the devil we don't know. But voters felt they *did* know Reagan.

This was strange. Ronald Reagan is one of the least knowable presidents we've ever elected. To his friends and family, the people who knew him best, he was all but inscrutable. His own son, Ron Reagan Jr., says he could not penetrate his father's self-protective shield. As we'll see later, neither could Reagan's own personal biographer. Yet Americans thought in 1980 that they knew Reagan well enough to trust him with the presidency, and they still think to this day that they know him.

5.

Why do we think we know our politicians well? One of the most important reasons is simply that we can see them. Seeing them on television gives us the illusion of intimacy, which in turn makes us think we are in a good position to read them, when actually we aren't.

This is part of the mismatch. Hunter-gatherers *were* in a good position to read their leaders. We aren't in a good position to read ours. But our brain plays a trick on us. Evolution teaches us that if we can see someone we can size him or her up. Our brain doesn't stop to consider the difference between seeing someone briefly on TV and seeing them in the flesh over time. Seeing them is all our brain cares about.

One of the powerful lessons evolution teaches us is that we can believe our own eyes. If you are a hunter-gatherer in the woods and a stranger with a spear comes at you, seeing is believing. To survive as a species we had to be able to trust our eyes. It was the same with other species. What accelerated the Cambrian explosion, starting about 540 million years ago, when life-forms on earth increased dramatically from a mere three organisms to thirty-eight? Vision, say scientists. Which sense was most critical to the very development of a world divided into predators and prey? Vision, say the scientists again.

And what activity do we engage in more than any other, including sleep? Consuming media, points out political scientist Maria Elizabeth Grabe.

And what does it usually take to comprehend media? Vision. Of the human being's five senses, vision is dominant. If your ears tell you one thing is happening but your eyes tell you something else is, you are going to believe your eyes. Here's how we know this. If you watch someone saying *ba* over and over again, *ba, ba, ba,* as you watch their lips, you will hear *ba, ba, ba.* But what do you think happens if the person saying *ba* looks like he's saying *fa*? This is what happens—you hear *fa.* The BBC has a video you can find on YouTube that shows this. You can find it by Googling "The McGurk Effect."

Harry McGurk was the psychologist who accidentally discovered the phenomenon in the 1970s. The BBC video, in a close-up shot, shows an individual saying *ba.* Then the video shows the same individual mouthing the sound *fa* while running the audio from the previous clip in which he's saying *ba.* As you watch the video what do you hear? You hear *fa.* To prove this isn't a trick, the BBC then shows you the clips side by side. On the left is the individual mouthing *fa,* and on the right is the same person mouthing *ba.* The audio is *ba, ba, ba,* always *ba.* When you look at the face on the right mouthing *ba* you hear *ba.* But when you look at the same face on the left mouthing *fa* you hear *fa.* As your eyes shift back and forth what you hear changes. Look at the face mouthing *fa,* you hear *fa.* Look at the face mouthing *ba,* you hear *ba.* Back and forth and back again. It's always the same—even though the audio you are actually hearing never changes. It's always *ba.* In your brain vision trumps hearing.

More than half of the brain is taken up with tasks related to vision. The brain processes visual information faster than information provided by any of the other senses. Smell is processed at the rate of 100 bits per second (bps). Taste: 1,000 bps. Hearing: 100,000 bps. Touch: 1,000,000 bps. And visual information? Ten million bps.

We don't have Superman vision. We can't see X-rays. Nor can we see radio waves. Actually, we can only see a narrow segment of the full visual spectrum. We did not develop the capacity to see more because we didn't need to. And there is such a thing as seeing too much. Neanderthals had bigger brains than we do, and it was because their vision was better. (In the low European light where they predominated, greater vision was helpful.) But there was a trade-off. So much of their brain was devoted to visual tasks that they didn't have room left over for all the social capabilities human brains possess. Which would you rather have? A bigger visual brain or a bigger social brain? Evolution's answer was the latter.

But vision is important enough to humans that evolution privileged visual images. Neuroscientists say that the more an object can be visualized, the more likely it is to be recognized and remembered. This faculty is so powerful that they have given it a name, says John Medina, a neuroscientist at the University of Washington. It's called the Pictorial Superiority Effect—PSE, for short. In *Brain Rules*, which summarizes the findings of neuroscientists who have investigated vision, Medina reports that people can "remember more than 2,500 pictures with at least 90 percent accuracy several days post-exposure, even though subjects saw each picture for about 10 seconds. Accuracy rates a year later hovered around 63 percent." Years later many people could still remember an impressive number of the images they'd seen.

Pictures are superior because we remember them more easily than text or spoken language. Our brain remembers them because our brain has been taught by evolution that images are vital to survival.

Lesley Stahl, the *60 Minutes* correspondent, tells a story in her memoirs about a night she was dreading in 1984. That day she had aired on the *CBS Evening News* a very long news story about Ronald Reagan's use of stage-managed events to convey false impressions. "Mr. Reagan," she reported, "tries to counter the memory of an unpopular issue with a carefully chosen backdrop that actually contradicts the president's policy. Look at the handicapped Olympics, or the opening ceremony of an old-age home. No hint that he tried to cut the budgets for the disabled and for federally subsidized housing for the elderly." She expected the White House to be livid and braced herself for an irate call after the broadcast. Instead, she found herself being congratulated. "We loved it," said Richard Darman, an assistant to the president. "You what?" she said, puzzled. "We loved it," he repeated. But "how can you say you loved it—it was tough! Don't you think it was tough?" Darman responded, "We're in the middle of a campaign, and you gave us four and a half minutes of great pictures of Ronald Reagan. And that's all the American people see. . . . They don't listen to you if you're contradicting great pictures. They don't hear what you are saying if the pictures are saying something different." Darman understood what Stahl, even though she is a television reporter and television is all about images, oddly didn't. Images grab us.

6.

Let's try a thought experiment. Think for a moment about John F. Kennedy. What comes to mind, excluding the assassination, which obviously is memorable, and the stories of his adultery, which I just mentioned, and which are therefore easily called up from memory? I will guess that it is an image of some kind: Kennedy on his sailboat, his hair flying in the wind. Or

Kennedy playing touch football on the lawn of the family estate in Hyannis Port. Or Jack and Jackie out for a stroll. Or Kennedy (hatless) delivering his inaugural address: "Ask not what your country can do for you. . . ." Or, my favorite, a tanned Kennedy wearing his Ray-Bans and an Izod Lacoste open-collar shirt.

Why is it important what images come to mind? I think it helps us understand something that is almost incomprehensible. When Americans are asked—today—to name the greatest presidents of the United States, they routinely mention Kennedy among the top three. This is difficult to understand. Any fair estimate of his legacy is that it was modest. The only major legislation he got passed was a tax cut lowering the top rate from 90 percent to 70 percent. His foreign policy record included one out-and-out disaster (the Bay of Pigs invasion of Cuba, which had to be abandoned); one near-disaster (the Cuban Missile Crisis, which he successfully defused but inadvertently triggered, partly as a result of a flawed performance at a summit months earlier with the Soviet leader, who concluded that Kennedy could be bullied); and a disaster-in-waiting (Vietnam, to which Kennedy sent 16,000 "advisers"). The civil rights laws, with which he is closely associated, were actually passed by Lyndon Johnson.

So what can account for Kennedy's enduring popularity more than fifty years after his death? Historians tell us it's owing to many factors, which they cited in the numerous studies and articles that appeared in 2013, on the fiftieth anniversary of his assassination. These include, they said, his charisma, his soaring rhetoric, his support for the civil rights movement (which Democrats like), his advocacy of tax cuts (which Republicans like), his identification with the prosperous 1960s economy, his peace speech at American University in 1963, his commitment to inspiring national projects, including the moon landing and the Peace Corps, and, of course, sadness at his gruesome assassination. A poll commissioned by the political scientist Larry Sabato, the author of one of the anniversary assassination books, found that older Americans who have living memories of Kennedy rank him a little higher than those who don't, which suggests that his presidential record, hazy as it may be, is probably affecting the way these older Americans think about Kennedy. But both young and old Americans hold roughly the same views. Asked to state which American president they'd want living in the White House today, Kennedy was the pick in 2013 of 16 percent of those over 54 and 11 percent of those 54 and under.

But could the historians be making this more complicated than it actually is? Is how we think about Kennedy really influenced by a deep knowledge of his achievements? Recall what came to mind in our thought experiment a moment ago. It wasn't Kennedy's achievements, it was those regnant images. This suggests that Kennedy is remembered by ordinary Americans as a great president because the pictures of him in our head are compelling and positive and mythical. It's not his accomplishments that matter so much—most people, after all, don't know much of anything about his record—but all those images. John F. Kennedy looked convincing as a leader. That's why he became Hollywood's idea of a president. Presidents in the movies don't look like Dwight D. Eisenhower (though historians rank him a better president), they look like John Kennedy. The man and the myth come together in pictures. And the pictures in our head come easily to mind because the pictures are readily available to us. We don't have to struggle to call up flattering images of Kennedy. The human brain allows us to call them to mind quickly because our brain readily digests information in the form of images. Remember, around 50 percent of our brain is devoted to visual tasks. Pictures are readily recalled. This leads us to trust them as a source of good information.

What all this suggests is that Kennedy cannot be considered apart from his images. They are a powerful part of his legacy. Indeed, it is hard to imagine that Kennedy would be lionized by young people today but for these images. Vision is that critical.

7.

Why do we persist in going with our instincts when we are trying to read other people? It's not just our confidence in our own eyes. We believe we can trust other people's eyes, too.

One day during his 1960 election campaign, John Kennedy took to the streets of New York City. He rode in an open car waving to people as he went along. Standing on the sidewalk was a young mother of two who lived in the suburbs, but happened to be in the city that day. As Kennedy drove by he briefly caught her eye, looked straight at her, and smiled. In that moment he won the loyalty of that mother for life. Fifty-two years later, as she lay on her deathbed, she recalled the moment. "He looked right at me," she said delightedly, in a voice that suddenly sounded strong and vibrant. "*Right at me*. Our eyes locked." The woman was my mother. I heard this story a thousand times growing up. It was one of my favorites.

The historian Robert Caro returns time and again in his magisterial multivolume biography of Lyndon Johnson to LBJ's legendary ability to read people. Caro reports that Johnson would try to teach this skill to his young staff members when he was a senator:

Teaching them to peruse men's weaknesses, he said that "the most important thing a man has to tell you is what he's not telling you; the most important thing he has to say is what he's trying not to say"— and therefore it was important not to let a conversation end until you learned what the man wasn't saying, until you "got it out of him." Johnson himself read with a genius that couldn't be taught, with a gift that was so instinctive that one aide, Robert G. (Bobby) Baker, calls it a "sense." "He seemed to sense each man's individual price and the commodity he preferred as coin." And Johnson also had a gift for using what he read. His longtime lawyer and viceroy in Texas, Edward A. Clark, was to say, "I never saw anything like it. He would listen at them . . . and in five minutes he could get a man to think, 'I like you, young fellow. I'm going to help you.'" Watching Lyndon Johnson "play" older men, Thomas G. Corcoran, the New Deal insider and quite a player of older men himself, was to explain that "He was smiling and deferential, but, hell, lots of guys can be smiling and deferential. Lyndon had one of the most incredible capacities for dealing with older men. He could follow someone's mind around, and get where it was going before the other fellow knew where it was going."

And what was the most important thing Johnson told his young staffers about trying to read people? "Read eyes. No matter what a man is saying to you, it's not as important as what you can read in his eyes."

Poets say eyes are the windows to the soul. Psychologists have a more prosaic take. Eyes provide us with the ability to gauge other people's intentions. It is by looking at someone's eyes that you can figure out whether they are bored, or excited, or engaged. We are hardwired to glean important signals about people from their eyes. (Our behavior may be prewired, but our brain functions are hardwired.)

By the time an infant is around a year old it can figure out what someone else is looking at by following their gaze. This is incredibly important in humans. People who cannot do this cannot read other people's intentions. This is the core problem autistic people confront. Lacking this ability, they miss key social cues. How do we know someone is angry with us? They look away. How do we know they are ready to make up? They look at us. How do we decide who's the most powerful, high-status person in a group? We look to see whom people are looking at. Our eyes tend to rest on those who are on top of the social pyramid. A baby looks to its mother; adults look to leaders. When Bill Gates walks into a room all eyes turn to him and stay on him. If you missed his entrance you don't have to worry. By looking at others you'll soon see what they see. And in that instant you'll start looking in his direction too.

Can we read people we see on television? We can read their body language, but it is very hard to read their eyes. To read someone's eyes you need to see their eyes close up. This is simply not possible on television in most situations. The faces of candidates for office are seldom shot with a tight enough focus. When they are—as on *60 Minutes*, which has made the close-up a staple of its program—we can follow their eye gaze. It's one of the reasons why *60 Minutes* interviews are so riveting. Eyes fascinate us. They are vivid. But since most of the time we don't have the opportunity to watch politicians' eyes close up, we cannot glean from their eyes the social information we need to make informed judgments about them.

What do we miss by not seeing an individual's eyes up close? Well, for one thing you can't see their pupils. This is significant because pupil size corresponds to attentiveness. When we are bored our pupils close up. When we are engaged they widen. If you can't see someone's pupils it can be hard to tell if they're really engaged. You don't have to consciously be aware of their pupil size. It registers on your brain unconsciously. A recent study indicates that the size of a pupil corresponds to an individual's decision-making abilities. Subjects in a test were shown a cloud of dots and asked to tell if they were moving in one direction or another. Who did best? It wasn't the people whose pupils were really wide, as you might expect. They were too aroused to make a sound judgment. The sweet spot was in the middle, indicating the subjects were aroused but not too aroused. Pupils send a message that our brain unconsciously picks up. But if you can't see someone's pupils you're missing the message.

Another thing we miss is the subtle but distinct crinkling around the eyes that takes place when we are happy and smile. That crinkling, done just so, which is all but invisible to your conscious brain, is the signal that the smile is genuine. If your brain doesn't see crinkling it knows to be wary. The smile may be fake. But your brain can usually only detect the crinkling when you are face-to-face with someone. On television it's usually hard to see.

What we have here is yet another example of a mismatch. In the modern world, we frequently don't get to use our ability to read politicians' eyes. Even if we do have the opportunity to see their eyes, as my mother did when she got a glimpse of JFK in person, it's usually just for a fleeting moment. And that's just not long enough to draw reliable inferences. To be able to read someone well, to read people the way LBJ read people, you have to spend time with them. And even then you can make mistakes. LBJ made mistakes. As Robert Caro goes to great lengths to explain: LBJ, "this great reader of men, this man who thought he could read any man, . . . read one man wrong." That man was JFK, the same man Americans read wrong. The same man my mother read wrong. LBJ's mistake was his belief, based on his close observation of Kennedy in the Senate, that JFK was little more than a playboy: "weak and pallid—a scrawny man with a bad back, a weak and indecisive politician, a nice man, a gentle man, but not a man's man." That mistaken reading of JFK was partially what gave JFK the edge in the presidential sweepstakes in 1960. It was one of the reasons why JFK found himself at the top of the ticket and LBJ found himself at the bottom. LBJ underestimated Kennedy. He didn't see in Kennedy's eyes what he needed to see. He saw more than most Americans saw. He knew JFK was a philanderer. But he didn't see what else there was to see. He couldn't because he couldn't get past JFK's charm. He couldn't see the grit in the man, the kind of grit needed to ascend to the highest office.

The obvious lesson of Caro's story about LBJ and JFK is that no one should think their judgments about other people are infallible. But this isn't a lesson we are likely to learn. We trust our instincts too much. Worse, we don't stop to consider how important context is, and that under modern conditions we are in no position to judge politicians we know through television because knowing them through television means not really knowing them at all. We are back again with the same problem we have with images. Our brain doesn't send up a red flare to warn us that we are drawing a conclusion about someone for whom we lack critical information—in this case, what their eyes tell us. So we don't realize how handicapped we are. This has serious consequences because we put a lot of stock in our ability to read minds. Years of experience convince us we can. Because we flatter ourselves that we possess superb mind-reading instincts, we don't feel the need to learn a lot about our leaders from independent sources. All we have to do is trust our instincts. Here again, our instincts mislead us. This is as good an example of a mismatch as there is. An evolved mechanism that should help us navigate the complicated maze that is modern politics, doesn't. It's neutralized. But we don't realize it. In our state of blissful ignorance we are lulled into thinking we know more than we do.

What don't we get? We don't realize that the context is vital. Our instincts only work well when we are in the right situation.

8.

The problem is not just that we cannot literally see the eyes of our politicians. It is more complicated than that. Our brains evolved to operate at peak capacity in situations where we are face-to-face with others. When we realize someone is looking at us our heart literally begins to pump a little faster. The neurons in our brain fire faster. Remember, we are designed from birth to pick out faces. This has important consequences, the chief one of which is that face-to-face interactions alert us to pay close attention. If someone isn't looking directly at us we tend to drift off. We lose focus. When we watch our leaders on television, therefore, we are not as engaged as we would be if they were in close proximity to us. The word for this is apathy. Why don't we hear that hunter-gatherers alive today are apathetic about their leaders? Because they communicate with their leaders face-to-face. We don't.

This has an effect on our leaders as well as on us. Because we don't pay them much mind if they show up in a TV commercial or in a TV debate as a talking head talking reasonably about issues, they have to employ evocative language or stunts to attract notice. This warps our politics by giving demagogues an advantage. Demagogues connect with us. Other leaders, operating under a code of restraint, have a harder time. The more noise there is in politics, the more politicians are likely to feel pressure to exploit emotions as demagogues do to break through.

A more subtle effect on our politics of our reliance on TV (and other impersonal forms of communication) in place of face-to-face interactions is that our leaders try to define themselves by a simple mindless message—which they repeat over and over again. Even politicians who cringe at the practice find that they have to adopt it. When it was suggested to Barack Obama that he have a slogan—"yes, we can" was the slogan—he thought at first it was schlocky, a biographer tells us. Nonetheless, he adopted it. It came to define his campaign for president in 2008. Why was it so influential? What shapes our response to a person isn't just their face but a host of cues. While we could see Obama and we liked what we saw—he smiled a lot, after all, and we know how important a smile is—the slogan helped shape our response to his image. How he looked was consistent with what we believed we knew about him and wanted to believe about him.

MERELY SEEING POLITICIANS ON TV convinces us we know them and that we can read them. It's an illusion, but a forgivable one. You can pick up a lot of information about a person you see on TV, even if it's not as much as we think we can. But what about a simple picture? Can you read someone's character from their picture?

5

167
Milliseconds

The amazing speed at which we
draw conclusions about people

1.

Why don't we at least try to make a rational assessment of our presidents?
Why do we seemingly rely on images of little relevance to provide an answer?
It's because evolution teaches us to think quickly. In the life-and-death setting
common in the world of hunter-gatherers, speed was of the essence in sizing
up both people and situations. We couldn't let anything get in the way of our
making up our minds, not even an absence of facts. In circumstances where
we lacked facts—a common occurrence in the real world—we found other
bases upon which to make a decision. The point was to act. Dillydallying
could kill you.

The legacy of this evolutionary inheritance is that today we leap to make
decisions even when we don't need to. Instead of waiting for facts we rush to
judgment. Though in the modern world we are seldom called on to render a
lightning-fast, life-or-death judgment involving a politician, that's what we
do. We can't help ourselves. We are hardwired to think fast rather than to
reflect at length.

Fast thinking (also known as System 1), as the pioneering psychologist
Daniel Kahneman points out, is easy. It doesn't require us to dwell. It really
doesn't require us to think at all, at least as most people define thinking.
That's because it mostly happens in the unconscious, where most of our

brain functioning actually takes place. As psychologist Michael Gazzaniga informs us, "98 percent of what the brain does is outside of conscious awareness." When Michael Jordan dunks a ball he doesn't think through all the steps he needs to take to gain lift, angle his arms, and provide thrust. He performs these tasks automatically. If he suddenly tried to think about what he's doing when dunking a ball he'd probably stumble. Reflection gets in the way of the performance of tasks that are usually left to the unconscious. Why is that? Reflection takes time. It's slow thinking (System 2). Literally slow. Operations in the brain involving the unconscious are five times faster than those involving consciousness.

How do we arrive at a quick decision? We use shortcuts, what social scientists refer to as heuristics. Quick—which of these capital cities in Africa has the most people?

1. Libreville
2. Asmara
3. Cape Town

The answer is Cape Town. How do you know this? Because you have heard of Cape Town (pop. 3.74 million), and you probably haven't heard of Libreville (pop. 797,000) or Asmara (pop. 649,000). Your brain concluded that since you haven't heard of either city, chances are they aren't very big. This is an example of the recognition heuristic. If we recognize something, our brain automatically assumes it must be because it's important. Why do we vote for people whose names we recognize on the ballot even if we know nothing about them? It's because we recognize their names. Our mere recognition of them must mean that they are known for something, and in the absence of a strong negative cue, we naturally believe it must be something positive. In fact, social scientists have discovered that familiarity seems to have the same effect on us as happiness. We get a charge in the reward center of our brain when we experience the familiar. And when do we become less analytical? When we are engaged in System 1 thinking.

Another shortcut is to turn questions we can't answer into questions we can by a method known as substitution, which was identified by Kahneman and his colleague, Amos Tversky. Here's how it works. Say you are asked to make a prediction about the stock market's performance in six months. This is obviously a very hard question to answer. It would baffle even an expert. The world is so complicated that predictions about the stock market are often wrong. There's always some factor it's easy to overlook that can prove to be decisive. So what do you do when you face a hard question for which there's no obvious answer? You answer a question you can answer. You unconsciously make a substitution. In this case, the obvious shortcut answer is to rely on how the market is doing right now and assume things won't change much. Using the substitution heuristic is the approach many voters follow when asked about Kennedy's legacy. They have no idea what his legacy is—that's a hard question even for specialists. So they resort to substitution and answer the easy question they can answer: how they feel about John Kennedy. That's an easy question because of the power of all those images that flood our minds anytime somebody mentions Kennedy's name.

2.

Here's another quick-thought experiment. What do you suppose would happen if I asked you right now to answer the question, *Was John Kennedy a great president?* How would you likely respond?

Because you just read a litany of complaints about him in the last chapter, it's almost certain you'd include a few negative points. My negative assessment of his record would instantly come to mind. As psychologists say, my list would prime you to think negative thoughts about him. But how would you answer that question in a month or in six months? By then you would probably have forgotten what I wrote about his record, for my judgment was rendered in the form of mere text. What would come readily to mind instead would be the powerful images already in your head. And because those are positive images you would probably be inclined to provide a positive assessment of Kennedy's presidency. That would be strange. Remember, I didn't ask for an assessment of Kennedy as a man. I asked for an assessment of him as a president. But what would come to mind would be pictures of him as a man, a person. Why is that? How we think is a function of the way the brain was wired in the millions of years our ancestors spent as hunter-gatherers. We go for the quick-and-ready answer, not the thoughtful answer, and we do that because it feels right. We do it by instinct. And the pictures that come to mind in an instant heavily influence the quick-and-ready answer.

Furthermore, as many social-science experiments have shown, we give priority to the information inside our heads over information picked up from an external source. Our first impulse when encountering information that conflicts with what we already believe is to discount it. If you have it in your head that Kennedy was a great president, a belief that is married to images showing him to advantage, images that reinforce your belief, would you be likely to jettison your belief just because you read something contrary to it? Of course not. That's not how our brain works. When we encounter something new we immediately search for a memory to make sense of it. Information that doesn't jibe with our memories is far less likely to be taken seriously. Why is that? Taking that contrary information to heart places a heavier load on our brain than ignoring it. As Daniel Kahneman reminds us, using a memorable metaphor, our brain is lazy. It is far easier to slip into System 1 thinking than to engage in System 2 thinking. System 2 thinking literally requires more energy: more neurons have to fire, more oxygen has to be consumed, and more chemical synapses have to be made. So when our brain has a choice between System 1 and System 2, what does it do? It engages System 1. That's the default system. We don't make a conscious decision to use System 1. We just do.

So what is your brain likely to do with the litany of negative comments I made about John Kennedy? If my list of his errors is new to you, it's unlikely you'll remember it a few months from now. By then the details will have become hazy. What *will* you remember instead? It will in all likelihood be all those wonderful images you already possess.

Here we begin to understand another dimension of the mismatch. In the time of hunter-gatherers they didn't need to rely on images of their leaders to fill in their idea of them. They had a clear idea because they literally knew them. They spoke with them. They ate with them. They worked next to them. Scientists say that hunter-gatherers almost never met strangers. Today, we don't know our leaders directly at all, but that doesn't seem to faze us. Thanks to the power of images, we can be ignorant about our politicians without feeling ignorant. Lacking the feeling that we are ignorant, we blithely go with the flow. Is it any wonder then that we make so little effort to actually learn the facts and dig for information? In the hoary past of the hunter-gatherers, they did not have to motivate themselves to learn about their leaders. They knew them. We do have to motivate ourselves to learn about ours. But nothing hardwired in us tells us we need to. Unless we consciously make an effort to learn about them, using System 2 thinking, we rely on our default mechanisms. Those System 1 mechanisms—like the substitution heuristic—tell us to go with the images in our head.

We are back to the problem of scale. Our brain is wired to deal with communities composed of small numbers of people. It isn't designed to help us grapple with leaders we know only at a distance.

3.

Earlier, we noted how important it is to see someone's eyes. But it's not only an individual's eyes we are by nature designed to evaluate. It's also their face. Faces fascinate us. When a newborn looks at its mother it automatically looks at her face. If you show a two-month-old baby a picture of a face and a picture of, say, a cow, the baby will zero in on the face. It gets even better. If you show a baby a piece of paper with three dots on it arranged in the form of a face—two dots for the eyes and a single dot for the mouth—the baby will focus on the dots as if they're meaningful. Turn the page upside down so that the dots representing the eyes are at the bottom and the dot for the mouth is at the top, and the baby suddenly loses interest and shifts its gaze. As we saw earlier, one study, conducted in 1975, shows that babies who are nine minutes old follow faces.

Does this mean that humans are hardwired to recognize faces? Until a few years ago many scientists doubted we are. Questions were raised about the methodology of that 1975 study. And it was thought that babies might just focus on faces because experience teaches them to look at faces. That made sense. They respond to faces because faces are familiar. After all, they are constantly looking at faces. They don't respond in the same way to a picture of a cow because they aren't constantly looking at cows. But then fresh studies came in that proved there is something more going on here. Using modern technology like an fMRI to look inside the brain as it's working, scientists discovered that the brain lights up differently when someone is looking at a face as opposed to an object. And it lights up in a particular place, in the fusiform gyrus, just above the ears.

When babies are tested to determine how acute their sensitivity to faces is, it turns out that they can easily distinguish between faces. You can remove all the hair from someone's head so all you can see is a round hairless face and a baby can still tell one person from another. When scientists studied monkeys they found that they too have a special affinity for faces. And if that isn't convincing enough, the scientists found that there's a whole category of people who lack the ability to process faces. They can be married to someone for life and never remember what they look like. Show them a picture of the house they grew up in and they can recognize it instantly. But show them a picture of their spouse of thirty years and they can't. This strongly suggests that there's a special module in the brain that is helpful in recognizing faces and that in some people it's damaged. The condition, which is known as face blindness or prosopagnosia, runs in families. So facial recognition is genetic.

Another experiment provides additional evidence that face recognition is built into us at birth. It's similar to the face test administered to babies. The test, remember, shows that babies lose interest when the dots making up a face are inverted. In this other experiment adults were asked to look at inverted snapshots of faces and objects. The hypothesis being tested was that adults would find it harder to identify inverted faces than inverted objects because our facial recognition module is designed specifically to identify faces right side up. An upside-down face wouldn't register with the facial recognition module, it was surmised. The hypothesis turned out to be true. Show someone an upside-down house and they can remember what it looked like. But show them an upside-down face and they can't. We can more easily identify by memory a dog whose picture we've seen upside down than a human face seen upside down.

Humans are able to not only recognize faces, but also recognize them quickly—sometimes too quickly. When you glance at a cloud and think you see a face, that's your brain's facial recognition module at work. It's why we are quick to spot the man in the moon or Jesus in a coffee cup.

Experience teaches us that we can learn a lot about people from their faces. If they smile at us we can be pretty sure they do not mean us harm. If someone is angry, we know we should be on our guard. Faces reveal the mood people are in. Beaming and scowling are as reliable social cues today as they were in hunter-gatherer days of yore. No mismatch here. And because on TV you can see a politician's face you can make use of your powers of facial recognition, which can come in handy. When Texas governor Rick Perry mentioned in the course of one of the interminable GOP presidential primary debates in 2012 that he planned to eliminate three government agencies but then could remember only two, an expression of sheer panic and embarrassment briefly crossed his face and everybody in the audience immediately picked up on it. When Newt Gingrich appeared on camera in the debates he frequently came across as arrogant and angry. Again, the audience easily detected it. (Whether his arrogance was helpful is doubtful, but his anger? Studies show that anger moves voters. It increases their commitment to a candidate they are already predisposed to like while it simultaneously stops them from thinking. Angry voters go with their gut.) When Barack Obama in a 2008 Democratic primary debate told Hillary Clinton she was "likable enough," a lot of people thought they saw a hint of condescension that they hadn't previously detected.

Faces seem to tell us so much that some people have suggested that we don't have to worry about ignorant voters. For ignorant voters possess the same face-reading ability as smart voters. Why worry if they don't know the ins and outs of the Affordable Care Act or other complex legislation, as long as they can read the faces of politicians. In the end, after all, save for when we are voting on a referendum or initiative, it's not policies we vote on at the ballot box, it's people. And as long as we can read people by reading their faces, we will make reasonable choices. But how well do we read people's faces?

In the popular view, we are really good at it. After all, we have been studying faces since birth. This makes us experts. Like an art critic who can discern the most nuanced strokes in a painting by Matisse or Picasso, we can take in a face and draw sophisticated conclusions. When it comes to faces, we are art critics of the highest order. We can see honesty in a crease and charisma in a crinkle. Ask us if someone looks intelligent, and we feel confident enough in our face-reading abilities to be able to tell.

But how good are we at evaluating politicians' faces?

4.

A few years ago social scientists began trying to find an answer. Daniel Benjamin at Cornell and Jesse Shapiro at the University of Chicago were two of the first to try to quantify our ability. They got together 264 students, most of whom were Harvard undergrads, and showed them ten-second clips of gubernatorial debates that had been shown on C-Span. The clips came from fifty-eight elections. After watching each video the students were asked to answer several questions, the most important of which was simply: "Who do you think actually won this election for governor?"

The results floored political scientists. On the basis of a ten-second clip, 58 percent of the students correctly guessed the winning candidate. This was better than the record of many seasoned pundits, who use all kinds of sophisticated tools to predict election outcomes. What was equally fascinating was that the students did better when the sound was off. Hearing the candidates actually interfered with their fortune-telling powers. Ten seconds, no sound. That's all elections come down to? A ten-second silent-movie clip?

Over the past few decades evidence has mounted that people are capable of making quick assessments. The social scientists call it thin slicing. Author Malcolm Gladwell tells the story of John Gottman, a psychologist at the University of Washington, who studies couples. Gottman puts a married couple in a room and videotapes them for an hour. Then he analyzes what he sees, assigning a number to some twenty different behaviors. Disgust? Check. Anger? Check. Sarcasm? Check. And so on. At the end of the process, relying on just that single, one-hour video, Gottman is able to predict if the couple will remain married. He reports that his accuracy rate, based on the analysis of some 3,000 couples, is 95 percent.

That's very impressive, but it's not nearly as revealing as the study by Benjamin and Shapiro. Gottman needs an hour of video to make his predictions. He needs hours more to analyze the video and score it. The subjects in the experiment run by Benjamin and Shapiro needed just ten seconds of video and zero time for analysis. There are limits to the comparison, to be sure. Different things are being measured. Predicting if two people will continue to get along for years is different from predicting which of two people will win an election. This is a classic apples-and-oranges comparison. Furthermore, Gottman's doing a real analysis based on years of experience—experience that has taught him what to look for. He's gotten so good at identifying the telltale signs of marital conflict that he claims he can identify couples in trouble he just happens to come across in a restaurant. (Most obvious sign couples are headed for divorce court? They treat each other to a heavy dose of sarcasm.) What voters are doing is different. Voters aren't studying politicians with rigor. They aren't using a spreadsheet like Gottman to record each and every sign of emotional reaction they can identify.

But just what exactly *are* they doing? That wasn't yet clear.

Around the time that Benjamin and Shapiro were conducting their experiment, Princeton's Alexander Todorov was running a similar one. But in his experiment he wanted to know if the snap judgments we make about candidates correlate with election outcomes when all we have to go on is a photograph—a head shot.

Suppose I showed you a head shot of a candidate. Looking at his picture alone, could you rank him on these seven traits?

Trust
Likability
Leadership
Honesty
Charisma
Competence
Intelligence

I'm guessing that no matter how confident you are in your face-reading abilities, your answer would be that you couldn't. A single photograph just isn't enough to go on. When we read people we are performing a sophisticated analysis. We are reading their body language. We are reading their eyes. We are watching to see how they react to other people. We are listening to their voice and studying its timber. Do they sound sincere? Do they look trustworthy? Are they intelligent? This, at any rate, is what we think we are doing. But are we?

Todorov asked his subjects—Princeton students in this experiment—to rate the candidates' traits using the list above. The pictures were of candidates who ran in US Senate and House races in 2000, 2002, and 2004.

His subjects fearlessly plunged in. How did they do in rating the candidates' traits? Before I tell you, I want you to think about the impossibility of this task. It is impossible, social scientists agree, to read traits in a still photograph. Impossible. We can read body language in a video, and from that deduce something about an individual's personality. That's what Gottman does. He looks at a video and sizes people up. Thin slicing works. You can, if you are deliberate and analytical, make important and telling observations. If voters took the time to analyze candidates they see on television as carefully as Gottman analyzes the video of the married couples who come to his lab, they would be in a position to make accurate deductions—even if they couldn't see the candidates' eyes and didn't have face-to-face interactions with them. But there is no science behind the belief that you can look at a photograph and from that photograph alone deduce what a person is like. Gottman, expert as he is at detecting the problems couples have, couldn't tell from a photograph how good their marriage is.

So, how did Todorov's subjects do? It turns out they had difficulty measuring the candidates by all seven traits. On the basis of a single photograph they couldn't really make distinctions between a lot of the traits. They didn't know enough. So they lumped categories together. If they thought a candidate showed leadership ability they also thought he was intelligent and competent and gave him the same score on those traits. They also gave a candidate the same score for likeability as for charisma. This suggests that the subjects recognized at some level that their assignment was insane. From a single photo you simply cannot rank someone by all seven traits. But the results indicate that they did believe you could detect from a single photo three broad clusters of information: competence, trustworthiness and likability.

Even this isn't really possible. As I indicated above, social scientists say it's impossible to draw any rational conclusion about someone's personality or character from a single photograph. But if that's the case, then we have a mystery on our hands. Because here's what Todorov found. He discovered that the score a candidate got on the competence cluster correlated nicely with election victory. In election after election, the candidate with the higher competence score won. Overall, Todorov reports, "the candidate who was perceived as more competent won in 71.6% of the Senate races and in 66.8% of the House races."

This is astounding. Todorov, in effect, found that he could accurately predict the outcome of an election on the basis of his students' response to a still picture. This suggests that when voters go to the polls many aren't really doing anything more than his students. *They* are assessing a candidate's competence in the same way. They think they are doing it on the basis, in part, of a candidate's résumé, party identification, and reputation, and in part on what they glean from television and YouTube clips. But many people—perhaps even a majority—are apparently strongly influenced by their gut response to a static and meaningless facial feature. As other studies show, they see a broad jaw and think a person is strong. Or they see a baby-faced individual and think that person's weak. This is true not just in politics, but in all realms of life. Studies of criminal defendants show that those who are baby-faced receive lighter sentences. It's not politicians' behavior we are judging, then. It is the physical contour of their faces. We see significance in the bumps, ridges, and curves of the face the way phrenologists in the nineteenth century saw significance in the bumps, ridges, and curves of peoples' heads. Depending on the circumstances, we go for one kind of face at one time and another kind at other times. During wartime, studies show, we favor square faces (these presumably strike us as stern and tough). During peacetime, we prefer round faces (these seem warm and friendly).

It gets even more alarming. In Benjamin and Shapiro's study, subjects were given ten seconds of video to go on. In Todorov's they got just one second to examine a still photograph. One second. And that's not even the most devastating finding of the social scientists. When they tried to pin down exactly how long it takes humans to reach a judgment about a politician's personality and character based on exposure to a still photo, they found that it doesn't even take one second. In another experiment Todorov discovered it actually takes people just a tenth of a second to draw an inference about someone's traits. When you give subjects more time, they simply use it to grow more confident in the accuracy of their inference. At this speed, humans aren't making a thoughtful judgment. They are simply reacting. The speed with which they are reacting is astonishing. Todorov found that we begin to form an opinion at 33 milliseconds. A millisecond is one thousandth of a second; 33 milliseconds is a third of a tenth of a second. He reported we finish forming an opinion by 167 milliseconds. How fast is that? It's faster than it takes to blink (300 to 400 milliseconds). This mental operation is like Michael Jordan's dunk shot. It is taking place out of consciousness. Support for Todorov's findings came in 2014 when a study by neuroscientists tracking the brain's amygdala activity found that subjects distinguished trustworthy from untrustworthy faces at 33 milliseconds. And we may be processing visual information even faster than that. A recent study reports that we understand a visual image after just 13 milliseconds.

We now have our answer to the question of what many voters are doing when they make their choice of candidates. They are making up their minds in an instant. This explains why those Harvard students who looked at just a ten-second silent-movie clip were able to predict with such uncanny accuracy who won and who lost, and why there was a high correlation between winning candidates and the ones Princeton students believed were competent after a flash review of still photographs. It was because many voters are making the same kinds of calculations.

One final study is worth recalling. In this study, social scientists asked people to rate candidates from a photo. Unbeknownst to the subjects in the experiment, their own image was morphed into that of some of the candidates. The finding, which by now will hardly shock you, was that people favored the candidates who looked like themselves. Disconcertingly, the subjects had no idea why they seemed to favor one candidate over another. Of course, many factors affect how people vote—from party identification and genetic predisposition to the state of the economy and so on—but these studies don't give us much confidence that pure reason is playing much of a role in the decision.

5.

This, when you think about it, is a damning indictment of democracy as it is practiced in the modern world. We are back to the Kennedy problem we encountered earlier. We are making quick work of a task that actually requires time. It's another mismatch.

Still another problem is that we draw irrelevant inferences from an individual's racial and ethnic makeup when we look at their face. We see a face and instantly and automatically surmise where they're from, and both consciously and unconsciously make various inferences. We are on an equal footing with our ancestors in this regard. Seeing someone on television is little different from seeing them in person when assessing their background. But in the Pleistocene it was helpful to know if someone came from different stock. Almost certainly someone who did posed a potential danger. But in the modern world in which we live? In our multiethnic and multiracial society, knowing a candidate's ethnicity or race is not an advantage, but a disadvantage. It inclines us to leap to unwarranted conclusions about our leaders and is the source of great mischief.

Politicians have learned that they can win over many voters simply by playing on a bond based on a common ancestry. They have learned we can be manipulated into voting for them merely by establishing this connection. The mischief comes when a politician and his acolytes decide to exploit this bond by whipping their own kind up into an ethnocentric frenzy and demonizing rivals who lack the connection, which, in turn, can lead to physical attacks on outsiders or, at the very least, social stigma. When Barack Obama ran for president in 2008 he was frequently ridiculed for being a professor who didn't understand white working folk. In the South and elsewhere this was often code for racism. It was deemed an acceptable way of drawing attention to Obama's race without explicitly doing so. In effect, the indictment suggested that Obama wasn't "one of us." People who felt this way began saying that they wanted "their country back." Who had taken it? Though unspoken, it was pretty clear. Tribalism of this sort leads to polarization. It pits group against group. In a pluralistic democratic society it can be devastating. And it can turn a potentially smart voter who succumbs to appeals of this nature into a dumb one.

Now, for a moment, compare how we go about choosing our leaders and how our ancestors did. We look at photographs and video. They actually engaged with their leaders. They didn't look at a headshot and decide on the basis of that whether someone was competent. They decided the competence question the way you should, by watching for signs of competence as someone performs various tasks. People aren't competent or incompetent generally. As our case study of Michael Jordan demonstrated, people are good at some tasks and bad at others. In the Pleistocene our ancestors had the opportunity to find out which tasks people were good at and to match them up to those tasks. In other words, they were in a better position to pick their leaders than we are to pick ours. Despite all of our educational advantages, democracy made more sense for them than for us. Like us, they would have been inclined to make a quick judgment about an individual's capacity. But, unlike us, they had the luxury of experience. They could monitor their leaders' behavior up close and in real time. We, unfortunately, cannot. So we go with the flimsiest of intuitive hunches. Eventually, we usually do find out through the media how our politicians actually perform and who they really are—as we eventually found out what John Edwards was capable of. But years can go by in the meantime. And all the while we can be deceived by our intuitions. And even then, as the Kennedy example demonstrates, we can be fooled by pictures into thinking a person is one way when he is another.

6.

Knowing people is difficult. We don't even know ourselves all that well, say scientists. As I mentioned earlier, we are "strangers to ourselves" because so much of what happens in our brain is inaccessible to consciousness. Put an individual you know in a situation that is unfamiliar, and there's no telling how they will react.

And what takes place when we elect politicians to high office like the presidency? They are promptly put in just such a situation.

What is it that every person who becomes president says? That nobody knows what it is like to be president unless you have been president. Such are the demands of the job that Harry Truman compared it to riding a tiger. Under stress, presidents do all sorts of things they might otherwise not do. But this is not only a feature of the presidency. It is, to a lesser extent, true of all positions that come with power. We can pretend we know the people we elect to these positions and that we are therefore capable of predicting how they will respond to the pressure, but these are illusions. The only way to know how a person will respond to pressure in a leadership post is to observe them in a leadership post while they are under pressure. That is what hunter-gatherers were able to do. They did not have to fall back on the fiction that they knew how someone would perform in a job because they knew the person. But we do—even though we have less reason to believe we know our leaders than they knew theirs.

We are inclined by nature to believe we can predict how people will react based on our understanding of their personality. But social scientists report we are correct only 30 percent of the time. That's because human personalities, stable as they seem, aren't a good predictor of behavior. Even after an individual's personality is formed—this takes place around age twenty-five—our behavior is subject to numerous contrasting forces. We shift and wobble and sway. As the social scientists say, our impulses are in a state of constant tension. A minor trigger can tip us from one form of action to another.

In one well-known experiment, divinity students at Princeton were told to walk across campus to deliver a talk on what it takes to be a Good Samaritan. Some students were told they were late and had to hurry while others were told they were early. As they made their way to the venue one by one, the students encountered a person in need of help. It was a man in obvious distress who was bent over and coughing. Who stopped to help? With the exception of just a few students, those with more time on their hands paused to provide assistance. Those who thought they were late hurried past. The lesson? Even divinity students on their way to deliver a talk about Good Samaritans can let the pressure of an appointment get in the way of their being one.

Situations matter. We think it's the person that counts, but it is often the situation that does—or some intriguing combination of person and situation. That's why presidents from different parties often continue the policies of their predecessors. Institutional pressures lead them to do so. This is one of the findings of presidential scholars who study the presidency as an institution. Much as we are enamored of particular presidents and their styles, their freedom of action is usually circumscribed. This explains why Barack Obama disappointed so many of his supporters. To take just one example, Obama indicated prior to his election that he abhorred George W. Bush's expansion of the national security state, which included spying on millions of Americans. This led many to conclude Obama would dismantle it. But once he became president he more or less retained the system he inherited. This demoralized many supporters—including a CIA contractor by the name of Edward Snowden. Snowden later confessed that he decided to go public with the government's secrets when he concluded Obama was little better than Bush when it came to the issue of spying.

This is not to say that personality doesn't count in the presidency. It does. As the Princeton political scientist Fred Greenstein notes, presidents make a difference. Both Dwight Eisenhower and Lyndon Johnson, Greenstein points out, faced similar crises over Vietnam—Ike in 1954 when the French suffered great losses at the Battle of Dien Bien Phu, and LBJ in 1965 when the South Vietnamese government seemed in danger of collapse. But Ike decided not to commit the United States to action and LBJ did. Presidents matter.

But just who they really are and what they are capable of is far less clear than it usually appears or that we are willing to concede. Ronald Reagan offers a good example. When Reagan was elected president, his supporters were convinced he'd play tough with the Soviet Union. After all, for years he'd denounced détente. In an early speech as president he condemned the USSR as an "evil empire." Consistent with his stated views, he raised defense spending by hundreds of billions of dollars. But then Reagan opened the door to negotiations. This got many hard-right conservatives worrying that Reagan had gone soft. They grew particularly alarmed when he offered to strike a deal with the Soviets to abolish all nuclear weapons. This didn't.

sound like their Reagan at all. His friend, actor Charlton Heston, warned him to "resist the temptations of a Yalta waltz with the Soviet bear." Conservative ideologue Howard Phillips quipped that Reagan had become a "useful idiot for Soviet propaganda." William F. Buckley Jr., founder of the conservative magazine *National Review*, was incredulous and charged that Reagan's overture was "on the order of changing our entire position toward Adolf Hitler." Columnist George Will declared bluntly: "Reagan has accelerated the moral disarmament of the West by elevating wishful thinking to the status of political philosophy."

What had happened? The cause of the change seems obvious. In quick succession, two old-fashioned and ailing Soviet leaders—Yuri Andropov and Konstantin Chernenko—died, leading to the selection of the youthful and broadminded Mikhail Gorbachev, who was clearly a different kind of leader than the Soviet Union had ever had. New Soviet leader, new American policy. Simple. But when experts began sifting through Reagan's papers they discovered something fascinating. Reagan had not changed his position *after* Gorbachev's selection. He had changed it *before*. Gorbachev didn't come to power until 1985. Reagan began changing his approach to the Soviets in 1983. This suggests that his personality had undergone a metamorphosis of some kind. But that wasn't it. The cause actually was a change in his situation.

After a close examination of the evidence, political scientist Beth Fischer identified four critical events, all of which took place in the fall of 1983. The first was the Soviets' downing of a civilian airliner, Korean Air Lines flight 007. The Reagan administration publicly called the Soviet attack barbaric. But behind the scenes officials concluded it had been an honest mistake. That frightened Reagan. The incident, he noted privately, "demonstrated how close the world had come to the precipice and how much we needed nuclear arms control. If . . . the Soviet pilots simply mistook the airliner for a military plane, what kind of imagination did it take to think of a Soviet military man with his finger close to a nuclear button making an even more tragic mistake?"

Just five weeks later, on October 10, 1983, Reagan watched a made-for-TV movie that amplified his growing fears about nuclear war. It was *The Day After*, which depicted in graphic detail what would happen to Lawrence, Kansas, in the event of a nuclear war between the United States and the Soviet Union. The movie, Reagan confessed in his diary, "left me greatly depressed." He added: "We have to do all we can . . . to see that there is never a nuclear war."

Later in October Reagan attended his first briefing as president about the plans the United States would implement in the event of nuclear war.

The secretary of defense explained that in a full-scale nuclear exchange the United States would target 50,000 sites. Millions would die. But Pentagon officials assured the president a nuclear war was winnable. "I thought they were crazy," Reagan admitted.

A few weeks after this briefing the United States and NATO conducted one of the largest war games in the Cold War involving 300,000 people. It was called Able Archer 83 and it spooked the Soviets. At the highest levels some officials became convinced that America was preparing to use the games as cover for a secret attack. (The Soviets' own plans included just such a ruse against the United States.) At the height of the games, the Soviets put a dozen nuclear-armed fighter aircraft on alert and ordered forces in East Germany and Poland to prepare for nuclear war. It was the closest the United States and the Soviet Union had come to nuclear conflict since the 1962 Cuban Missile Crisis.

Conservatives had been sure they understood Reagan. But after what he went through in the fall of 1983 Reagan changed his approach to the Soviets. The threat of nuclear war, which formerly had been an abstraction, suddenly seemed very real. By the end of that year he decided to do whatever he could to prevent an accidental war with the Soviets and to cool their fears of a deliberate one. Privately and publicly he began making overtures assuring them he wanted peace. In the 1970s he had ridiculed arms negotiations. Now he embraced them.

Like those Good Samaritan divinity students, Reagan hadn't really changed. He had always been afraid of nuclear war. It was the reason why he insisted on funding the anti-missile system known as the Strategic Defense Initiative (SDI). He wanted to protect Americans from nuclear incineration just as his character in the 1940 film *Murder in the Air* had tried to protect them from other forms of attack using a futuristic "Inertia Projector"—a death ray. But even close friends and supporters hadn't realized the depth of Reagan's commitment to a kind of utopian peace. When they heard he had seriously considered abolishing all nukes they were left in a state of shock. They'd missed the complex jumble of motives that drove Reagan. So when the situation changed—which prompted him to change course—they thought *he* had changed.

This happens all the time. That's one reason why we keep being surprised by how presidents turn out. They surprise us because they don't stick to the simple script in our head. We think personality is everything and that once you think you know what someone's like they'll always behave in a certain way. But it's just not true.

PART III: TRUTH

6

Lying to Ourselves

The high cost of self-deception and
why we can't stop ourselves

1.

Just two hours east of Seattle, on the other side of the Cascade mountain range, is the small city of Ellensburg, which has a population of about 18,000. Ellensburg is the home of Central Washington University (CWU), but until 1980 it was really only famous for one thing and that was for losing out to Olympia as the site of the Washington state capital. As a kind of consolation prize Ellensburg got a small teachers college that eventually became CWU. As universities go, CWU is not well known. It's barely visible to residents within the state, let alone those outside. But in 1980 there appeared on campus someone who actually was world famous. She wasn't a distinguished professor. She had never graduated from college. But she had a gift. She was adept at American Sign Language (ASL). Her name was Washoe. She was a chimpanzee.

Washoe was the first chimpanzee in the world to learn ASL. By the time she was five years old she knew hundreds of signs—hundreds—and she could reliably use 132 signs herself. If she saw a dog she'd sign DOG. If she wanted a hug she'd sign HUG. If she was hungry she'd sign FEED ME. Remarkably, she could string together individual words she had learned to form a thought. Mornings she would greet the psychology professor who trained her, Roger Fouts, with a series of signs: ROGER HURRY, COME HUG, FEED ME, GIMME CLOTHES, PLEASE, OPEN DOOR.

Fouts was responsible for bringing Washoe to CWU along with two other chimpanzees when he moved from the University of Oklahoma. People thought he was crazy to make the move. His department at OU was ranked thirteenth in the nation. CWU, as he recalls in his memoirs, was an "academic backwater." But in tiny Ellensburg he had one thing he didn't have at OU, and that was the freedom to treat chimpanzees the way he thought they should be treated. The director of the primate institute at OU thought of chimpanzees as brute animals. He made them wear a padlocked collar, the kind slaves in the eighteenth century were forced to wear, not because it was helpful—it wasn't—but because it reminded the chimpanzee it was subject to the will of the trainer. The director also made Fouts use a cattle prod on his chimpanzees. And when he took them out for a walk he was required to keep them on a lead leash. All this appalled Fouts. He was having conversations with the chimpanzees. They were telling him when they were hungry and when they wanted to go outside and when they wanted a hug. And he had to put them on a leash like some wild animal? This was wrong, he was convinced.

When Europeans got their first glimpse of chimpanzees early in the seventeenth century people found them fascinating. But there was a problem. They looked like us. When England's leading anatomist, Edward Tyson, dissected a chimp he discovered that they not only look like us, they are built like us. Their brains are built like our brains. They even possess central nervous systems. But if they were so like us, didn't that make us less special?

For nearly two thousand years, from the time of Aristotle and Plato, Western man had believed that a Great Chain of Being connected all things—God, cherubs, human beings, dogs, lions—right down to sunflowers and sand. Everything was linked, but everything was separate. God was God. Man was man. Animals were animals. And everything existed in a strict linear hierarchy. At the top was God. Below God, angels. Below angels, human beings. Below human beings, domesticated animals. Below domesticated animals, wild animals, and so on. And here was the chimpanzee, and it looked like a version of a human being, suggesting that the line separating man and animals might not be as clear as everybody thought. Tyson reassured people that though chimpanzees are built like us, they weren't really like us after all. They didn't have emotion and they didn't have a mind, he claimed. And for the next few centuries his view prevailed in Europe and America. Down through the years to the early-1960s, the charts published in biology textbooks put chimps in one family and humans in another.

Scientists then began making a series of discoveries that upended the old orthodoxy. What made humans human suddenly seemed in doubt. Where the line fell between humans and other animals seemed unclear. One of the bedrock assumptions of anthropologists had been that toolmaking is one of the distinguishing characteristics of hominins. Then British primatologist Jane Goodall reported observing chimpanzees making tools, and suddenly nobody was sure anymore what divided us. Kenyan archaeologist Louis Leakey wrote: "We must now redefine man, redefine tool, or accept chimpanzees as human!" That sounded extreme, but shortly thereafter two biologists, Vincent Sarich and Allan Wilson, found that there was virtually no difference in the molecules of a blood protein from chimpanzees and humans. And then, little more than a decade later, came the discovery that chimpanzees and humans share 98.4 percent of the same DNA (later upped to 98.7 percent).

By the 1980s a consensus had emerged that chimpanzees and humans are not from different families. We are from the same family. As recently as six million years ago we shared a common matriarch. In evolutionary terms, that isn't very long. Mammals first appeared on earth 350 million years ago, after all. So it is rather astounding that it took until the 1980s for Europeans and Americans to see that chimpanzees and humans are really close. Roger Fouts was floored by it. If you spend any time with chimpanzees, he thought, it is obvious, unless ideology blinds you, that they are very similar to us. African tribes that lived among chimpanzee colonies understood this, he recalls in his memoir. The Ivory Coast's Oubi tribe referred to chimpanzees as "ugly human beings."

What's really striking about chimpanzees? They behave like children, Fouts discovered. When they don't get their way, they throw a tantrum. When they want something from you, they will nag until they get it. When you want them to do something, you can bribe them with candy. Fouts had become a father around the time he started working with chimpanzees. He couldn't help but notice that the chimpanzees behaved like his child. Dog owners might say the same thing about their pets. But dogs cannot communicate their displeasure through sign language.

Not long after Fouts began working with chimpanzees he discovered something else about them. They know the difference between what they should and shouldn't do. They know that if they come upon a cabinet that is always locked, they shouldn't open it. They know they shouldn't poke at a human being or pull a human's hair.

And when they misbehave and get caught, what do they do? They try to cover up their crime. Time and again in his fascinating memoir, *Next of*

Kin: My Conversations with Chimpanzees, Fouts cites example after example of this happening. Covering up, it seems obvious, is not something chimpanzees have to be taught. It's just something they do by instinct. Fouts is nonchalant about this. He saw it so many times it didn't faze him after a while—though it's vital to understand this about chimpanzees, and until recently people did not. It was believed that one of the things that distinguish humans from all other animals, including chimpanzees, was that we alone are capable of deception. Clearly, this was not true, Fouts realized.

But even Fouts was surprised when one day Lucy, a chimpanzee he was training to sign, used sign language to try to cover up what she had done. He had never seen this before. No one in human history ever had. Here was a chimpanzee who was not only covering up misbehavior, but also lying about it—just like a human. It happened, he reports, when Lucy "defecated in the living room when I wasn't looking." Here's the remarkable exchange that then took place, conducted wholly in sign language:

Roger Fouts: WHAT THAT?
Lucy: WHAT THAT?
Roger Fouts: YOU KNOW. WHAT THAT?
Lucy: DIRTY DIRTY.
Roger Fouts: WHOSE DIRTY DIRTY?
Lucy: SUE (a graduate student).
Roger Fouts: IT NOT SUE. WHOSE THAT?
Lucy: ROGER!
Roger Fouts: NO! NOT MINE. WHOSE?
Lucy: LUCY DIRTY DIRTY. SORRY LUCY.

Notice what's going on here? Fouts and Lucy are standing across from one another. They are face-to-face. Lucy is lying to Fouts's face. That is remarkable. It is one thing to lie to someone behind their back. But to their face? That shows how deeply ingrained lying is in chimpanzees. What also is worth noticing is that Lucy made no attempt to tell the truth until she was pressed hard for the truth. Her default position was to lie.

When more chimpanzees started learning sign language they too began using signing to lie. Mary Lee Jensvold, the co-director of the primate institute Roger Fouts established at CWU, says that chimpanzees regularly lie to her face. One thing that happens, she says, is that a chimp will come up to you and poke you. "And it's not very nice to be poked. And you'll say, using sign language, 'Are you going to be good?' and they'll sign back, YES. SORRY. And the next moment, boom, it happens again." When she was a young mother she used to bring her six-month-old to the institute. One day one of the chimpanzees displayed—this means the animal roared and made a scene—and Jensvold's baby grew frightened. "She developed a sort of nervousness around chimpanzees." The chimpanzees knew it and tormented her. This went on for years.

Tatu was the name of everybody's favorite chimpanzee at the institute. She was known, says Fouts, as "the family's precious angel, the good girl." Fouts says in his memoir that "there was no need for padlocks and keys around Tatu. Unlike Washoe, she never ransacked the cupboards or raided the fridge. . . . Her room was neat and tidy with toys lined up in a perfect row. After she played with one toy she would put it back in its place before playing with another." But even Tatu would torment Jensvold's daughter, as Jensvold told me in an interview.

From behind a wall of glass, "Tatu would set her up and get her to come really close, and then, boom, bang on the glass and scare her. One day Tatu did this—my daughter must have been four or five at the time—and she just had her bawling. Tatu gets a kick out of it. It's like the mean, big sister, right? So I took my daughter out of there. The next day Tatu asks about her," using the sign for a baby—folded arms, moving back and forth, as if she's rocking a baby. "And I said, 'Oh, I know, you made her cry yesterday.' And she says, signing, SORRY" and asks Jensvold to bring her back. By this point Jensvold's daughter was onto Tatu and no longer falling for the trick. But on a return visit to the institute, Tatu again "held her hand up to the glass really still—and she had such a sincere look in her eye—and then boom." Jensvold laughs at the memory. But at the time her daughter was terrified.

Chimpanzees are not human beings. The differences between them and us are profound. The differences include our higher intelligence, our ability to speak, our dexterity with languages, and our superior ability to form large groups and maintain them. We possess a fully developed appreciation of moral codes—they don't. We blush—they don't. But to people like Roger Fouts and Mary Lee Jensvold, people with an open mind who have spent extended time around chimpanzees, the similarities are obvious and overwhelming. Visitors to their primate center in Ellensburg are taught that chimpanzees and humans even develop similarly. Gestation period for chimpanzees? Thirty-five weeks. For humans? Forty weeks. Weaning for chimpanzees? Four to five years. For humans? Zero to five years. Loss of baby teeth in chimpanzees? Five to six years. In humans? Five to ten years. Start of puberty in chimpanzees? Eleven to thirteen years. In humans? Ten to sixteen years. Average life span for chimpanzees? Thirty to sixty years. Humans? Thirty to eighty years. Remember Frans de Waal, the primatologist who studied chimpanzees for years at Arnhem Zoo in the Netherlands? What did he conclude? That chimpanzees form coalitions like we do and play politics like we do. In short, we're similar.

But why? There can be only one of two reasons, biologists say. One, we are similar because we share a common ancestor. This is known as a homologous similarity. Two, we are similar because in the past we faced similar environmental pressures, and these pressures in turn prompted similar adaptive changes. This is known as convergence.

Adding up all of the similarities we have identified between chimpanzees and humans, and keeping in mind that chimpanzees and humans are in the same family and that we are each other's closest animal kin, it is hard to avoid the conclusion that many of our similarities are homologous. That is, we are similar in so many ways because we share a common ancestor. Why is that important? Because it means chances are high that the trait for deception is probably ancient, and that the capacity for deception has been part of our primate ancestors and us for millions and millions of years. Unlike speech, which arose in just the last half a million years, deception is probably associated with the ancient part of our brain and arose long before Homo sapiens emerged around 400,000 years ago. If true, that would suggest that deception is among the human traits that are most automatic. The age of a trait correlates positively with automaticity. Traits associated with the parts of the brain that emerged earliest—like our emotions—operate fastest and out of consciousness.

Studies are only now being undertaken to determine where in the brain we process deception. But one recent study confirmed that when we lie, our blood oxygen levels are elevated in multiple parts of the brain—in the bilateral superior frontal gyrus, the bilateral parietal lobule, the bilateral cuneus, the right precuneus, the right lingual gyrus, and the left postcentral gyrus. You do not need to be familiar with these abstruse appellations to understand that something that involves this many brain regions—they involve speech, vision, and touch—is fully integrated with our brain.

Lying, in other words, comes naturally to us. Just like chimpanzees, we don't have to be taught to be deceptive. We are deceptive by instinct. Lying is one of those evolved psychological mechanisms that shape our response to events, often operating out of conscious awareness. And this instinct is powerful.

2.

This is a list of twenty-five presidents:

1. Thomas Jefferson
2. James Monroe
3. William Henry Harrison
4. James K. Polk
5. Franklin Pierce
6. James Buchanan
7. Ulysses S. Grant
8. Rutherford B. Hayes
9. James Garfield
10. Chester Arthur
11. Grover Cleveland
12. Benjamin Harrison
13. Teddy Roosevelt
14. Woodrow Wilson
15. Warren Harding
16. Franklin Roosevelt
17. Dwight D. Eisenhower
18. John F. Kennedy
19. Lyndon Johnson
20. Richard Nixon
21. Ronald Reagan
22. George H. W. Bush
23. Bill Clinton
24. George W. Bush
25. Barack Obama

What do these presidents all have in common? All were guilty of documented deceptions. They either blatantly lied to the American people,
their friends, or family, or misled them in some manner. Wilson, following
a series of strokes, misled the country about the state of his health. FDR,
eager to convince the public before Pearl Harbor of the danger the Nazis
posed, framed them for a supposedly unprovoked attack on an American
destroyer. Eisenhower lied about the U-2 spy plane incident. Kennedy lied
about the missile gap. And on and on. . . . You can read in the endnotes
about the lies the others told.

More than half the presidents have been caught telling out-and-out lies.
If you count the occasions on which presidents have told half-truths to con-
fuse the public about their position on an issue, the list would include every
last one of them except for George Washington, who never lied because he
didn't need to. Even when his enemies (he did have some) accused him of
misconduct—and he might complain that a common pickpocket received
more respect than he did—he held the allegiance of the vast majority of
Americans, whatever their party. Where telling a half-truth often redounds
to the benefit of presidents caught up in political gamesmanship, it would
have damaged Washington where he was strongest because he was considered to be above politics. Telling the truth strengthened him, while it often
weakened others who came after him.

Given what we have just learned about the long evolutionary history of
deception, it is no surprise that our leaders tell lies. We all do. And they
have more reason than the rest of us to lie. Gaining and keeping power is
difficult. It's been getting more difficult with every generation. All George
Washington needed to win the presidency was to gain the support of a few

thousand men. A single generation later, presidential candidates had to curry the favor of hundreds of thousands of men, and shortly thereafter, millions, as the franchise was extended again and again. By the time of the Civil War, presidents had to begin pulling in the support of immigrants, easterners and westerners, rural folk and city folk, and, a generation later, union members and populists. In the twentieth century, they had to win over an entire new voting bloc—women—and they had to learn how to adapt to radio, then television, and finally to social media and the Internet. It's no illusion that politics is more complicated today. It is. Our leaders, in response, feel compelled to lie to us about more things, more often, using every form of media available to them.

But why have so many gotten away with it? Why did most of the presidents get away with their lies?

The answer that leaps to mind is that they got away with their deceptions because the media let them. That sounds convincing when you think about the history of the media in this country. Until the 1972 Watergate Conspiracy, reporters seldom scrutinized politicians the way they do today. Cozy with people in power, journalists frequently failed to call politicians out. Think of FDR's ability to fool the public into thinking that he could walk. Franklin Roosevelt could not walk after he contracted polio in 1921. To use the brutal language of his time, he was a cripple. But the voters never realized it. And they did not know it because the media went along with FDR's request to keep the full extent of his disability a secret. One biographer reports that out of some 40,000 still photographs of Roosevelt only two show him in a wheelchair, and neither of those was published during his lifetime. When FDR moved about the country to give speeches, special ramps had to be built everywhere to accommodate his disability. The public never knew. This was deception on a grand scale in which the media were wholly complicit.

Watergate is supposed to have marked a sea change in the media. But think of what Ronald Reagan got away with. His own son, Ron Reagan Jr., says his father showed signs of dementia three years into his first term. Leslie Stahl reports that when she visited Reagan in the Oval Office in 1986 to bid farewell as a White House correspondent, "Reagan didn't seem to know who I was." He still had two years left to his term. But did Stahl say anything publicly? She didn't. She kept quiet about what happened, not revealing the details until she published her memoirs—after Reagan was safely out of the White House. And this was after the media had come to be dominated by scandal-obsessed journalists eager to become the next Woodward and Bernstein.

The explanation that the media are to blame is, in the end, too simple. There is another reason presidents can get away with lying. It has to do with us. Which brings me to Grover Cleveland.

In 1893, six months after his second election as president, Cleveland one day noticed he had a growth in the roof of his mouth. It was the size of a quarter. He had it checked and was told it was cancerous and had to come out. On the evening of June 30, 1893, he quietly slipped aboard a yacht anchored at Pier A on the East River of New York City. The following day, unbeknownst to the world, Cleveland underwent surgery. It was 1:24 P.M. Cleveland was seated in a large chair located in the ship's saloon. The chair was fixed to the mast to keep the patient steady as the yacht, now un-moored, sliced quickly through the water. Working carefully on the obese president, who weighed more than 250 pounds—his nickname was Uncle Jumbo—doctors removed the cancerous tissue and part of his upper left jaw. Two weeks later, they performed a second operation to remove sur-rounding tissue they had missed. A plate made of vulcanized rubber was designed to fill the gap left by the surgery so that Cleveland's normal speech pattern wouldn't be affected.

Of all this, Grover Cleveland breathed not a word in public, not then, not ever. Only one cabinet member was let in on the secret ahead of the opera-tion, the secretary of war, and only one more was told afterward. Congress was kept in the dark and so was the vice president—though the risk that the portly Cleveland might suffer a stroke was so great that a specialist was brought in to monitor his blood pressure.

To keep his illness hidden Cleveland had to lie. The president's lead doc-tor held a news conference to explain Cleveland's absence from the public stage—to recuperate, the president spent the month of July at his vacation home on Cape Cod—but it didn't go well. The cover story the doctor put out—that Cleveland was simply feeling out of sorts with a bad tooth, a swollen foot and some rheumatism—raised suspicions. One reporter asked directly if the president had cancer. The doctor said no, but wasn't convinc-ing. It turned out he wasn't a very good liar. But the reporters decided to stick to the White House script. For now, the lie held.

In August, Cleveland returned to the White House and resumed his public duties. His recovery was so swift that another of his doctors thought it was no longer necessary to maintain the fictional story that had been spun to explain his absence. In an interview with the *Philadelphia Press*, which was published on the front page, the doctor revealed what had taken place aboard the yacht. He spilled all the secrets. Cleveland had had cancer. He'd been operated on. He was now cancer-free.

The president was aghast. He did not want people to know the truth. It wasn't just the cancer operation he wanted to keep secret. It was that he had lied to keep it secret. The lie itself had to be protected now, just as much as the illness. He had to lie to protect the lie he had told to conceal the truth.

So *that* is what he did. He had his aides ridicule the account and insist that *he* was the victim of lies.

So what do you suppose happened next? The way this story is supposed to play out, the way it would play out in a movie starring Jimmy Stewart, is that senators and representatives would stand up in Congress and demand a full accounting of Cleveland's health history. An investigation would be launched. Witnesses would be put under oath and required to testify in open hearings so that the country could discover the truth. As the truth slowly emerged, protesters would march through the streets demanding the president acknowledge he lied.

But what actually happened? Nothing. Absolutely nothing. The story was forgotten. This was not a situation where the media failed to do their job. The media did their job. They told the truth. They revealed that Grover Cleveland had lied. And the public didn't care.

What's going on here? We didn't believe the truth because we didn't want to. It was unpleasant. And by nature, we are believers. This is something that was first surmised by the Dutch philosopher Baruch Spinoza in the seventeenth century. But not until recently did we have proof. The proof came when scientists began to use fMRI machines to take pictures of the brain while people were being asked to answer questions about their beliefs. What the scientists found, according to Harvard psychologist Daniel Gilbert, is that our brain consumes information in a two-stage process. In the first stage, the brain takes in information and assumes it's true. Only then, in the second stage, does it subject the information to tests to determine if it is true. Often, the brain does not perform this second function. In other words, our brain privileges credulity. At heart, we are not Doubting Thomases. As Gilbert says: "Doubt is less quickly and easily acquired than belief." By nature we are gullible. Or, as another psychologist colorfully put it in a reference to the leading characters on the hit television series *The X-Files,* we are much more like FBI Special Agent Fox Mulder (who takes every claim of alien abduction seriously) than Agent Dana Skully (who always expresses open skepticism).

Our brain in effect is the unwitting coconspirator of manipulative politicians. We are predisposed to believe what they want us to believe regardless of the merits of the belief. We do this because it's easier on our brain. Skepticism takes more brainpower. I mean this literally; for the brain to go to the second stage identified by Daniel Gilbert it has to use more energy. And as Daniel Kahneman tells us, our brain is lazy. If it can get by without using energy it will. Think of the effort that we have to put into skepticism. Like detectives working a homicide we have to build a case piece by piece, and all of the pieces have to fit together. It's much easier to assume the belief we encounter is innocent and not go to the bother of proving it guilty. We don't want to have to go to the trouble of proving a belief guilty unless we have to. This works to the politician's advantage.

As a practical matter, life would be nearly unbearable if we were natural skeptics. A natural skeptic would have to subject everything that happens in the course of a day to intense scrutiny. Imagine waking up in the morning and having to ask yourself—before you even put your feet on the floor—if you can be sure of the floor's existence. That would be tiresome. After assuring yourself the floor exists and that it will carry your weight, you would have to worry as you headed over to the bathroom if water were going to come out of the nozzle or something else, perhaps something poisonous. You can see how deadly tiresome this constant questioning would become. If every minute of every day we had to be on high alert, we'd quickly exhaust ourselves. We simply cannot remain at attention, eyes focused, mind concentrated, for long periods of time. We aren't built that way.

Fortunately, most of the time the world works as we expect it to, leaving us free to focus on anomalies. The floorboards hold our weight without sagging or breaking. The shower shoots out water. We only need to ask questions when there's a mismatch between the world in our heads and the world outside.

Another factor related to our natural credulity affects our response to politicians. It's so self-evident it's easy to overlook. It is the simple drive to believe in our leaders because they are ours. It's for this reason that as we head into the voting booth we often fall into the habit of thinking and hoping that the individual we favor is another George Washington or Abraham Lincoln. It's usually ridiculous to think this. George Washington today couldn't be George Washington. There's no room on the national mantle for more than one patriarch statue and that statue is the eighteenth-century Washington. And anyway, no one else will ever be in the position Washington was. He was above politics. Who could be above politics now and win? And there's little chance we will find many more Lincolns—politicians with the common touch and extraordinary intelligence and communication skills that Lincoln possessed. But at every turn, it seems, one politician or another is compared with Washington or Lincoln. In the run-up to the election of 2008 liberal reporters frequently compared Obama to Lincoln.

The Obama campaign played on these comparisons, expertly exploiting the perception that Obama was a *rara avis*. To reinforce the comparison, on the eve of Obama's inauguration, they even staged a trip on an old-fashioned train that followed the course taken by Lincoln himself on the last leg of his trip from Philadelphia to Washington, DC, for *his* inauguration in 1861. The train ride struck conservative voters who weren't enthralled with Obama as a little weird. But to Obama supporters it made perfect sense.

It's not just our leaders we want to be proud of. It's our country. We want to believe our country is the best in the world. And we don't stop there. We like to believe we are the best people in the world. This is one of the most powerful of all forces driving human behavior, and it shows up in children by age three. It's a form of tribal ethnocentrism and it is in evidence everywhere, in all countries and at all times. The Jews think they are the Chosen People. Americans think they are exceptional. Mormons think they are "God in embryo." Evolutionary psychologists report there isn't a society known to researchers that hasn't believed in its own virtue.

3.

It may seem as if I am leading up to the conclusion that we are by nature suckers. But that would be going too far. We aren't gullible as all that. Nature made sure of it. Rampant gullibility cannot long survive in a population. Cheaters would quickly arise to take advantage of the suckers. Over time, the suckers would be weeded out while cheaters would succeed in accumulating the most resources—resources that would help them attract the most desirable mates and enhance their fitness (their ability to pass along their cheatin' genes). Pretty soon all that would be left would be cheaters. This is one of the key insights of evolutionary psychology.

But just as a society of the utterly gullible wouldn't long survive, neither would a society consisting wholly of cheaters. You cannot have a community made up of people who cheat all the time and get away with it. Community requires cooperation. And you cannot have cooperation if everybody is cheating everybody constantly. That's a recipe for community suicide. It's all against all.

What then is the magic formula that saved us as a species from rampant gullibility and rampant cheating? What saved us from ourselves? What stopped cheating from destroying us? Evolution provided two remedies. Both are essential to the survival of cooperation.

First is the inclination of members of a group to punish violators of social norms. This is something that comes naturally to humans and only humans. Chimps, our nearest relatives, don't punish violators. This, says Jonathan Haidt, is the reason they can't achieve the level of cooperation we can. It's why, he says, quoting a fellow psychologist, Michael Tomasello, you'll never see "two chimpanzees carrying a log together."

Second is that we humans come equipped with powerful cheater-detection abilities. As we learned in chapters 4 and 5, we are endowed with the ability to read people. Reading people helped save us. When you can accurately read someone's intentions you can stop them from cheating you. (What also helps is that word spreads when someone cheats. People who cheat a lot get a reputation for cheating.)

The world is not actually made up of just cheaters and non-cheaters. In reality, we're all cheaters to a certain extent. From the individual's perspective, cheating, up to a point, works. We are taught to believe that deception is a bad thing. But it's actually essential in everyday life. You cannot get through a day without resorting to deception. What is deception at its essence? It's manipulation. What is required to navigate the social world? Manipulation.

Benjamin Franklin said after the American Revolution that we are all politicians now. It was a memorable observation, but fundamentally misleading. All humans are *by nature* politicians. Life requires us to be politicians. We are constantly looking for allies and assessing our place in groups. We are always trying to improve our standing. And how do we do that? By manipulating others. How do men win over the women they want? By showing off. Men are peacocks. In every society on earth, men try to impress women that they are worthy of marriage by proving they are exceptional in some way. That's why men show up for a date in a nice car. They do it to help get what they want. It screams, *I am worthy of you.* That's a form of manipulation. What do women do in return? They demand proof that the men who want them will stick around after childbirth. How do they arrange that? By asking for proof of the man's long-term investment in their relationship. That's what diamond rings are all about. In most societies through history, men literally had to pay a price—it's known as a bride price—for the right to marry. That was women manipulating men.

Nature rewards manipulation. Why does the male bowerbird spend months building a beautiful nest? It is not because he needs the nest to live in. He needs it to attract a mate. When the female bowerbird comes calling she inspects the bower to see if it's well built. A well-built bower is a signal that the male is strong and knowledgeable. His genes presumably will produce offspring with a better chance of survival. If the nest passes muster she'll consider moving to the next stage in their courtship.

Why do we have a big powerful brain? According to the Machiavellian Intelligence Hypothesis proposed by Nicholas Humphrey, you will remember, it's because the demands of social groups are enormous. To learn to get along and to succeed we have to be able to make intelligent assumptions about other people: what they want, how we can win them over, whether we are doing well or badly. What comes in handy in dealing with other human beings? An ability to practice deception on them.

Deception in the human being is in evidence from an early age. Scientists keep pushing back the date in the life cycle when we display a capacity for deception. The latest research demonstrates that babies at *nine months* are already manipulating their parents. By that early age they possess the ability to tell their mother they do not care about something when they actually do care about it. And what else have scientists found? According to the evolutionary biologist Robert Trivers, "the brighter children are . . . the more often they lie." Furthermore, "the smarter the species, the more deception occurs." As Trivers nicely puts it, "dishonesty has often been the file against which intellectual tools for truth have been sharpened."

What Roger Fouts noticed in chimpanzees, that they are capable of deception, is even more pronounced in human beings because we are smarter. Because we are far more adept in communicating, we can manipulate others better. The sign language chimpanzees use is limited. Their vocabulary is limited. The ideas they can express are limited. And there is no evidence that chimpanzees ever developed sign language on their own, though once they have it, they can pass it on—Fouts made the amazing discovery that a chimpanzee who signs can teach another chimpanzee how to sign. In contrast, human language is unlimited. Every year the dictionary makers find hundreds of new words that have begun to circulate. And we, of course, can use language to express complicated ideas. When we lie, we can lie in really sophisticated ways beyond the capacity of other primates. Literally, more of our brain's networks are involved in lying than theirs. So though we and chimpanzees are both capable of deception, we are better at it. It's more a part of our nature than it is of theirs.

What we have here, ironically, is a classic virtuous circle. For what happens when someone smart behaves deviously in a smart way? They get ahead in life. This favors their offspring over others'. What happens to the people with superior cheater-detection brains? They too get ahead in life. This favors their offspring. Replicated over and over, millions of times, the competition between cheaters and people who are good at detecting cheaters—often the very same people—leads to an ever-smarter population. Deception, in other words, was not, as might be expected, a drag on our development as a successful species. It was a spur to our development. What appears at first glance to be a negative was actually a positive.

What keeps us on the straight and narrow path most of the time? A powerful urge to obey rules and to see to it that others do as well. The name for this psychological mechanism is deontic reasoning. (The adjective comes from the Greek *deont*, which means "being right.") That's reasoning that involves rights and obligations. See the traffic light turn green and you start walking? That's your deontic brain at work. You know it's okay to walk because your brain tells you to be alert to rules. Children demonstrate this ability by age three. By then they are able to determine that in life there are obligations, permissions, and prohibitions.

One of the distinguishing features of deontic reasoning is that it is accompanied by a policeman's sensitivity to lawbreaking. When we see someone violate a deontic norm our instinct is to punish the violator. This powerful instinct is what helps a community establish norms and maintain them. The detection of cheaters is so important that evolution favored people who possess the ability to remember the faces of cheaters. In one experiment subjects were shown pictures of cheaters and non-cheaters. A week later they returned to identify who was who. They had trouble recalling the faces of those who were trustworthy, but the cheaters? They remembered their faces easily. Another experiment showed that we remember the names of cheaters more easily than those of non-cheaters.

4.

Given our cheater-detection abilities, you would think we would be able to read our presidents better, even given the handicaps we labor under in the modern world—as alluded to in Part II. But something stops us. In the next few pages try to guess what that "something" is as we review what presidents have in common. It's something so obvious we usually overlook it.

Here is a list of seven of presidents and the ages at which they first made their mark in life:

Abraham Lincoln	Age 23	Runs for a seat in the state legislature
James Garfield	Age 26	Appointed president of a college
Teddy Roosevelt	Age 23	Elected to a seat in the state legislature
Warren Harding	Age 19	Appointed a newspaper publisher
Franklin Roosevelt	Age 28	Elected to a seat in the state senate
Lyndon Johnson	Age 29	Elected to the US Congress
Bill Clinton	Age 32	Elected governor

What is obvious from this list? These presidents all demonstrated ex-traordinary ambition very early in life. It is no surprise to most people that Bill Clinton shows up on the list. We know he's an ambitious person because his political enemies have long made an issue of his and his wife's ambitiousness. But Lincoln? He ran for a seat in the state legislature at age 23? Lincoln, by his own admission, had little more than one full year's schooling. He had no money. No connections. No nothing. Just months before he announced he was running he was still working on his father's broken-down farm for meager wages. Yet he had the nerve to run for a state office. I think you'll agree that is downright astounding.

And Harding? Warren G. Harding was ambitious enough to become a newspaper publisher at age 19. That's astounding, too. Who thinks of Harding as ambitious? If you read a Harding biography you'll discover that his wife Florence is always described as the ambitious one in the family. But Harding obviously was ambitious as well.

It's not just the presidents on the above list who demonstrated ambition at an early age. Nearly all of them did—even George Washington, despite his reputation as a saint. Washington was so eager for advancement as a young man that he tried to get himself a commission as the Adjutant Gen-eral of Virginia even though, as one biographer points out, at the time "he had never worn a uniform, never drilled a corporal's guard of soldiers, [and] never seen a fortification except one he had visited in Barbados." He failed in the effort, but succeeded a short time later in winning a commission as a colonel. In this position he ignominiously became involved in a skirmish in the Ohio Valley that led to the surrender of a fort, cost the lives of thirty of his soldiers, and prompted the start of the French and Indian War. He was all of twenty-two.

When professional historians examine the career paths of presidents the verdict is nearly unanimous that all of them demonstrated extraordinary ambitiousness at an early age. By age twenty-five, Thomas Jefferson, James Madison, and James Monroe had all won seats in Virginia's colonial legis-lature. By age twenty-seven, John Quincy Adams had achieved the status of an international diplomat, Jackson had been elected a congressman, and William Henry Harrison ("Tippecanoe") won an appointment as a territo-rial governor. And on and on it goes, down through the presidents elected before the Civil War, after the Civil War, and in the twentieth century. Even George W. Bush, who is widely thought not to have demonstrated much ambition until he quit drinking in his forties, ran for a seat in congress at age thirty-one.

When you read a lot of biographies of presidents you begin to discover similarly revealing patterns. One of the most astonishing I remember coming across when I was writing my book *Presidential Ambition* is the one that shows up in their marriages. I had never paid much attention to the people presidents married when one day I began reading up on James Buchanan. Buchanan's is a pure poor-boy-makes-good story. Born in a log cabin, he managed to get himself into college, where he earned the best grades of any student, and then apprenticed as a lawyer in Lancaster, Pennsylvania. At age twenty-one he was admitted to the bar. His career seemed set and he made friends easily. But there seemed something a little too calculating about Buchanan. One of his two best friends was Amos Ellmaker—who just happened to be the only Yale graduate his age in Lancaster. Buchanan's other best friend was Molton Rogers—who just happened to be the son of the governor of Pennsylvania. Those friendships did not seem to be matters of coincidence.

The same year he was admitted to the bar Buchanan announced his engagement to Ann Coleman. This looked like another good move. But from the moment of the announcement people expressed suspicions. Did he really love Ann? Or was he after her because of who her father was? Ann's father was Robert Coleman, an ironmaster, one of the richest men in the United States, who owned several mansions. Ann dismissed the rumor-mongering. But after their engagement was announced Buchanan suddenly grew distant, declining opportunities to get together. This suggested to many people that there was a reason to doubt his motives. He did not want to spend time with her, it appeared. He just wanted to marry her. When Ann complained, Buchanan explained that he was busy with a big case that required him to make frequent trips to Philadelphia. Mollified, she agreed to continue the engagement. But then she found out that he had spent an afternoon at a friend's house at which a beautiful young woman was present. This was too much for her. In a rage, she broke off the engagement and sank into a depression. Alarmed, her father sent her to Philadelphia to be with her sister. There she suffered wild mood swings, one minute engaging in polite repartee, and the next turning hysterical. Six days after she arrived at her sister's, Ann was found dead. Her doctor said she was the first person he knew who ever died from hysteria. More likely, she committed suicide.

Had Buchanan gone after her for her money? That is impossible to know. But after reading about the tragic story of his abortive marriage I remembered something Robert Caro noted in the course of his biography of LBJ. As a young man out looking for a wife, Johnson had gone after the daughters of three of the richest men living in his corner of Texas. I then began to closely examine the love stories of other presidents. And time and again the same pattern was detectable. Preparing to marry, they made every effort to marry into power and money. Washington courted and married the richest woman in Virginia. Lincoln went after the daughter of one of the few aristocratic families in Springfield. Garfield married the daughter of the president of the college where he was teaching. William McKinley married the daughter of a prominent newspaper publisher. Taft married the daughter of the richest banker in town. FDR married Teddy Roosevelt's niece while TR was in the White House. JFK married an aristocrat's daughter. This pattern was not the exception. It was the rule.

It may not strike you as surprising that presidents are social climbers. It's a common enough practice, and social scientists have a name for it: hypergamy ("marriage into an equal or higher caste or social group," according to Merriam-Webster). But the pattern of presidents marrying up *is* actually unusual, and it's unusual for one reason. All of these presidents were male. Hypergamy is almost always associated with females. The reason for this is that women, as I mentioned earlier, have to be choosier than men in the selection of their mates since they alone bear the burden of childbirth. They have to be sure their mates will stick around to help with child rearing. Men, unburdened by such considerations, are in a position to go after women whom they simply find desirable. So why were these men being so choosy? They had to be as choosy as women to get what they wanted—which was power and status.

When you consider the presidents' marriage histories in combination with their early march up the political ladder, a picture emerges of nearly unbounded ambition. One sign of this is that once they started running for office, they could not stop themselves. Most presidents spent their whole lives running for something—congressman, senator, governor, whatever—until finally they captured the top prize. And even then they did not stop running. Virtually all of them ran for reelection, running even when they hated being president. They ran whether they experienced great success as president or utter failure. It didn't seem to matter to them. Some presidents kept running and running and running. Martin Van Buren ran for reelection in 1840 and lost, ran again in 1844 and failed, and then ran again in 1848 and failed again. Millard Fillmore, one of the worst presidents in history, who failed even to win his own party's nomination after succeeding to the presidency upon the death of Zachary Taylor, ran again four years later as the candidate of the loathsome Know-Nothing Party. James Buchanan ran for president four times, in every election from 1844 to 1856. Cleveland ran three times. TR, succeeding to the office upon the death of McKinley, served out McKinley's nearly full term, then ran for a second, and then, after a four-year gap, ran yet again, this time against the man he had hand-picked as his replacement and in violation of a promise he had made earlier not to ever run again, a promise he later said was the greatest mistake of his political life. Wilson ran twice, and in his second term, after suffering a massive debilitating stroke, floated the possibility of his running for a third. From his deathbed he plotted a return to power, going so far as to draft the inaugural address he planned to deliver after winning reelection. FDR ran once for vice president and four times for president. Eisenhower ran for a second term a year after suffering a heart attack. LBJ, after serving out JFK's term, ran and won a term on his own, and then famously bowed out in 1968, announcing he would not be a candidate for reelection. But when political scientists examined his papers they discovered that he had schemed be-hind the scenes to be named the Democratic Party nominee at the Chicago convention. A surprise appearance was supposed to trigger such a fervent response that it would lead to a Johnson stampede. Only the anti-Vietnam War riots in Chicago prevented his coming, dooming his plans.

As Lincoln, with more self-awareness than most, confessed, "No man knows, when that presidential grub gets gnawing at him, just how deep it will get until he has tried it."

And not even all that begins to suggest the lengths they were willing to go to in order to gain power and keep it. In many cases they demonstrated an egomaniacal tunnel vision, running even when their loved ones raised serious objections. Nine ran for president over the opposition of their wives. One, Franklin Pierce, knowing of his wife Jane's feelings on the subject, concealed from her his maneuvering for the office, pretending that when it came his way it was by chance. Shortly before his inauguration, they were traveling on a train when it suddenly derailed, killing their young son Ben-nie. Both Pierces went into mourning. But then virtually on the eve of the inauguration Jane finally learned the truth that the office had not come to him, he had gone after it. That shattered her and virtually destroyed their marriage. She refused to attend his swearing in and delayed moving into the White House. Blaming their son's death on her husband, she concluded that God had taken away their child to punish Franklin for his lies. A pathetic figure, she held séances in the White House to try to get in touch with her dead child. And Pierce? Despite a lackluster record and the personal tragedy of the death of his son and the near collapse of his marriage, at the end of his term he signaled he wanted to run again.

The ambition of people like Pierce is predictable. Evolution rewards am-bitiousness. Members of the same species—conspecifics—are in a constant state of rivalry for resources. Which ones win? Often it's the ones with the most drive. Put two crayfish in a tank and they'll battle it out for dominance until one finally gives up (or is killed). Presidents are like the crayfish winners. They yearn for dominance, which in the case of humans is fueled by testosterone. The more testosterone in their system the more feverishly they want to win. And each time they win they enjoy an increase in testosterone. Many environmental factors can affect an individual's drive, from the desire for social status to an adult child's wish to live up to their parents' expectations. But the one biological factor that affects ambition above all is testosterone. More testosterone = more ambition.

It's not just society that rewards ambitiousness. So does the brain. When crayfish win they get a serotonin charge in the reward center of the brain. When humans amped up on testosterone win they get a dopamine charge. Dopamine gets the attention of the conscious brain. It screams: *Hey, do whatever you just did again and I'll reward you by making you feel good*. So presidents run again and again.

But why do presidents keep pressing for victory even after losing? That's a mystery at first glance. Losing a hard-fought contest in life usually diminishes testosterone. That's evolution's way of helping the defeated steer clear of battles likely to end in their death. So why do presidents keep pushing on even after they lose? A clue can be found in the behavior of the crayfish. When a loser crayfish that has never achieved dominance loses, it stops competing, ultimately accepting its position of inferiority. But when a winner crayfish suddenly experiences defeat, what does it do? It repeatedly returns to the battle and keeps trying to recover its former position of superiority. Presidents who cannot stop running even after running is fruitless are like those winner crayfish. They can't help themselves.

An additional factor, identified by psychologist Daniel Kahneman, may be in play. As he discovered, humans hate to lose. In fact, we feel losses more intensely than gains. Presidents who have tasted power and then lose it may feel so traumatized by loss that they are willing to risk even humiliation to regain what they had. Then again, this may not be a peculiarly human phenomenon. It may be true of all primates. What did Yeroen do after he was defeated by Luit? After sulking, he regrouped, struck an alliance with another chimpanzee, and went on to reclaim his crown.

Evidence accumulated by evolutionary psychologists shows that ambitiousness is rewarded even in sexual selection—as the behavior of women on the verge of marriage demonstrates. When a young woman in a traditional society is sizing up a suitor, what does she look for? Quite often, it's ambition. Young suitors usually lack resources because at that stage in their lives they have not yet had a chance to accumulate a lot of resources, as the evolutionary psychologist David Buss observes. Many are flat broke. But that's okay. They can still be considered a good catch as long as they possess the drive to succeed. Ambitiousness assures the young woman that a suitor is likely in the future to be able to accumulate resources to take care of their children, and that's what matters. At least that is how things worked until recently. Today, women have far more opportunities than they ever did in the past. Now it may be the woman who is responsible for providing for the kids, and the man who stays home with the children. No matter. One of them at least needs to be ambitious in the outside world.

But this isn't the ambitiousness presidents need to demonstrate. To make it to the top rung of American politics you need to be ruthlessly ambitious. You need to be willing to sell out your friends, compromise your principles, exploit your family, conceal malfeasance, slam your adversaries, scrounge for contributions, wink at racism, prevaricate, and worse. You may even need to play politics with national security when lives are actually on the line. What does the former secretary of defense Robert Gates say in his memoir, *Duty*, about Hillary Clinton and Barack Obama? Both confessed in private in his presence that they opposed President George W. Bush's surge of troops into Iraq for political reasons. This is the reality of American politics.

Testosterone helps explain the pattern of ruthlessness. Testosterone suppresses the levels in the brain of oxytocin, the so-called love hormone associated with compassion. It's no wonder then that we associate ambitiousness with ruthlessness. Testosterone makes people more ruthless. The more one wins, the higher one's levels of testosterone are likely to go. Win a touchdown in the middle of a regular season National Football League game and you feel pretty good. Win the winning touchdown in the Super Bowl and you will feel godlike. The more one wins, the more ruthless one is likely to become. This applies to both men and women, though men naturally have more testosterone than women (which may explain the oft-noted finding in trust games that women are more generous than men; they have less testosterone to interfere with their natural oxytocin levels).

Reviewing the pattern of presidential ruthlessness it is hard not to conclude that we voters are fools for believing that presidents are paragons of moral virtue. The strong temptation, after reviewing the evidence of the way politics is actually played at the highest levels, is to conclude that presidents put one over on us. That all the while they are telling us that they decided to run because of their great love of country, the truth is that their love of country probably had less to do with their decision than their burning hunger for power and status.

The inescapable conclusion appears to be that they are guilty of nothing less than rank hypocrisy. But that does not seem to be the case. You can look through the memoirs and papers of presidents and their friends and family for evidence that they consciously flimflammed us, but it does not exist. Presidents do not believe themselves to be frauds or intellectually dishonest. Just the opposite. They believe in their own rectitude. When they compromise their principles or sacrifice their friends, they do it only because they feel they have to. That's politics. In any case, what they do, they do for their party, or their country, or some larger cause—not for themselves. Ambitious? No, not at all, they insist. Ambition isn't what they're about.

Here is Bill Clinton in 1992, when he was running for the Democratic nomination for president: "The reason I'm still in public life is because I've kept my commitments. That's why I'm still here, and that's why I'm still standing here. And I'm sick and tired of all these people who don't know me, know nothing about my life, know nothing about the battles that I've fought, know nothing about the life I've lived, making snotty-nose remarks about how I haven't done anything in my life and it's all driven by ambition. That's bull, and I'm tired of it."

Bill Clinton was as ambitious as any man who ever ran for president. But he's angry anyone should even think he's ambitious. Ambitious? Me?

This is standard behavior in human beings. When we ourselves take a morally dubious action we usually think it's in response to the situation in which we find ourselves. We don't consider it a reflection on our character. We therefore give ourselves a pass. That's what presidents do.

In 1964 George H. W. Bush surprised the political world in Texas by announcing that he would run for a seat in the US Senate. Bush, who'd grown up in Connecticut, had to prove he was a real Texas conservative. Consequently, he sidled up to right-wing members of the John Birch Society and criticized his opponent, Democrat Ralph Yarborough, for voting in favor of the Civil Rights Act. Bush nonetheless lost the election. Afterward, he confessed to his Episcopal minister, "You know, John, I took some of the far right positions to get elected. I hope I never do it again. I regret it." But Bush didn't think he was a bad person. He simply did what he felt at the time he had to do to win.

5.

What stops us from reading our presidents accurately, jamming our cheater-detection radar? It's our presidents' sincerity. This is the answer to the question I raised earlier about our inability to read presidents well. We get snookered because they are able to convey the appearance of sincerity.

To understand why this happens let's examine what takes place when someone consciously lies to your face. They give themselves away, right? They grow anxious. According to scientists who have studied lying, liars give themselves away in at least five different ways:

1. They speak more slowly because they have to edit themselves in real time.
2. They often twitch uncontrollably.
3. The pitch of their voice rises.
4. They avoid the use of "I" and "me" words.
5. They use fewer qualifiers, preferring instead to speak in short, punchy sentences. Truth Teller: When I went to the store it was raining and I took Twelfth Street. Liar: When I went to the store I took Twelfth Street.

This seems to mean that if someone lies we are likely to catch them because of our wonderful cheater-detection antenna. We can sense when someone's feeling anxious about lying. We may not consciously notice that a liar is twitching or that their voice is rising. But we feel it.

Often though, liars fool us. Social scientists say that, absent training, our ability to detect lies is actually quite low—little better than chance (especially when we don't know the person doing the lying). Why are we fooled? The answer is that people who want to lie possess the ability to make themselves believe—when they need to—that they are not really lying.

Think about the implications. If you believe what you are saying, you won't be anxious and you won't give yourself away. This isn't just something politicians do. It's what we all do. We lie to ourselves. We do one thing and say another and believe what we are saying at the time we are saying it. We do this because we cannot hide our lies from others unless we believe them ourselves. Who makes the best salesman? The salesman who believes what he's peddling. What made Lyndon Johnson such an effective liar? His biographer Robert Caro says it was LBJ's conviction when he was telling his lies that he was telling the truth:

Lyndon Johnson could make himself believe in an argument even if that argument did not accord with the facts, even if it was clearly in conflict with reality. He "would quickly come to believe what he was saying even if it was clearly not true," his aide Joseph Califano would write. "It was not an act," [White House press secretary] George Reedy would say. "He had a fantastic capacity to persuade himself that the 'truth' which was convenient for the present was the truth and anything that conflicted with it was the prevarication of enemies. He literally willed what was in his mind to become reality." He would refuse to hear any facts which conflicted with that "reality," to listen to anyone who disagreed with him. His oldest Texas associates, men like [Edward] Clark, called the process the "revving up" or the "working up," explaining, "he could start talking about something and convince himself it was right" and true—even if it wasn't.

Or take Ronald Reagan. Reagan was famous for self-deception. He hid himself so well, he drove his biographer Edmund Morris wild. Morris found Reagan impenetrable, to the point that he finally gave up trying to write a standard biography. You couldn't get at the truth of the man that way, he concluded. So he novelized his biography, inserting himself into the book as a fictional character. Most critics panned the work. But you can understand Morris's frustration. He worked on the book for years. He spent hours and hours with Reagan privately. He had more access to Reagan than any independent biographer in history has ever had to any other president. And still he could not figure him out.

Reagan, to be sure, seemed more inclined to self-deception than most. He claimed, for instance, to have witnessed the liberation of the German concentration camps in April 1945, though in fact he never left Southern California during the war. He apparently mixed up seeing movie footage of the camps with his actually seeing the camps in person. That is some self-deception and suggests that the reason Morris found it hard to come to terms with Reagan was because Reagan himself did. But is Reagan's self-deception actually any less palpable than the self-deception of most presidents?

To take another example, consider Bill Clinton's lies about Monica Lewinsky. Here is what the Starr Report says happened on their first significant encounter: "According to Ms. Lewinsky, she and the President kissed. She unbuttoned her jacket; either she unhooked her bra or he lifted her bra up; and he touched her breasts with his hands and mouth. Ms. Lewinsky testified: 'I believe he took a phone call . . . and so we moved from the hallway into the back office. . . . [H]e put his hand down my pants and stimulated me manually in the genital area.' While the President continued talking on the phone (Ms. Lewinsky understood that the caller was a Member of

Congress or a Senator), she performed oral sex on him. He finished his call, and, a moment later, told Ms. Lewinsky to stop. In her recollection: 'I told him that I wanted . . . to complete that. And he said . . . that he needed to wait until he trusted me more. And then I think he made a joke . . . that he hadn't had that in a long time.'"

Was this sex? Yes. But Bill Clinton seems to have convinced himself it wasn't because he and Lewinsky never had intercourse. This was no ruse he offered just to wiggle out of the tight corner in which he found himself once the affair came to light. He actually seems to have believed it. That's the only thing that makes sense. Otherwise, why wouldn't he have gone ahead and had intercourse? His wife wouldn't care that he had gone up to a certain line and not crossed it. Once he had oral sex he crossed it. That's all she would care about. So why did he establish a line and not cross it if it was a meaningless line as far as his wife would be concerned? The explanation is that it was not meaningless to him. He needed to believe there was a line he hadn't crossed so that he could convince others, including his wife, that he had remained faithful to her if he was asked if he had been faithful. For him to lie convincingly he had to tell himself a lie. It was an act of self-deception and it worked. Clinton successfully insisted that he had not had sex, and both his wife and his cabinet believed him—until the infamous semen-stained blue dress surfaced, providing physical evidence of his affair.

Deception can work if we are able to convince ourselves of our own sincerity. Sincerity is the Gibraltar Rock on which we anchor our lies. Sincerity is vital because it's our defense against detection. How do others evaluate our truthfulness? By determining if we seem sincere. Cheater-detector mechanisms are designed to detect cheating by detecting insincerity. In the absence of insincerity, cheater-detector alarms fail to go off.

Evolution, remember, favors both the cheater and the person who can detect cheating. Both have at their command powerful tools. The cheater's is the ability to believe his own lies.

Our natural inclination in conversation is not to tell a lie. It is to tell the truth. That is why when we first tell a lie—a real lie, not a white lie (our brain knows the difference)—scientists can actually measure our anxiety rising. But when we need to lie—and we all need to lie on occasion—we can. Lying gets easier the more we do it. And after we have lied about something many times, we ourselves grow so used to the lie that we come to believe it. If we were designed to tell the truth we would never grow used to lying. The fact that we do lie is further confirmation of the belief that lying is an evolutionary adaptation. That is, people with the ability to lie had an advantage over people who did not lie and over people who could not lie convincingly.

It used to be thought that the main purpose of self-deception was to fool ourselves. You find yourself in a tight corner where everything looks hopeless, so you lie to yourself to keep up your spirits, what one social scientist calls the "hidden power of self-deception." But in recent years scientists such as Robert Trivers have concluded that this is not the primary purpose of self-deception. Actually, we fool ourselves so we can fool other people. As Trivers notes, nature would not design an organism to deceive itself except in rare, perhaps life-threatening, circumstances. In the main, organisms need to understand their environment. Their chances of survival are improved when they are able to make correct assessments of risks and rewards. Planes crash when pilots deceive themselves about the risks of bad weather. But if it helps to deceive others about our motives—and obviously it often does—then self-deception in those situations can be highly desirable.

But there's a cost. To deceive others, politicians have to deceive themselves. In the Pleistocene that might not have been a particularly dangerous inclination in a leader, or at least not so dangerous as to be prohibitive. A leader in a small community who's monitored daily by the members of that community is unlikely to plunge it into catastrophe. There are too many other eyes watching. But in the modern world? In our complicated world, it's dangerous when a president can't see reality for what it is—and that's a particularly likely circumstance given the bubble in which presidents live. And who pays the price when they misconstrue reality? In the Pleistocene a leader who erred was likely to pay with his own life. But in our world it's not the decision-makers who usually have to bear the costs when things go wrong. Other people do. The leaders generally go on to live out their lives in comfort and security.

Only one significant cost is borne by a leader when he lies and things go wrong. His reputation for honesty and competence suffers. That is not insignificant. Lie once too often and you get a reputation as a liar. This is especially damaging when leaders get a reputation among other leaders as a liar. Politicians accept the fact that from time to time they have to lie to voters. But lie to each other? That's frowned upon. When a leader lies to another leader, deal-making becomes impossible and the wheels of government grind to a disastrous halt.

But presidents usually find they can easily escape a reputation for lying to voters. Grover Cleveland lied. No one cared because he didn't lie very often. His reputation for truth-telling carried him through.

Our challenge as voters is to remember that we are by nature believers, and that it's rather easier than we think to be taken in. Relying on our gut to tell us when politicians are lying isn't sufficient. We don't really know who they are or what they're up to most of the time. Just as the residents of those New Jersey beach towns, trusting their instincts, went wrong, unfairly holding Woodrow Wilson accountable for the devastation wrought by the shark attacks, we shouldn't trust our instincts when we evaluate politicians by their demeanor—as we do all the time from their appearances on television. It makes us vulnerable to connivers and deceivers. That's one reason why televised debates are a problem. What do we do when watching a TV debate? We judge politicians by how they conduct themselves. That makes sense to us because that's how we judge people in our intimate circle. But that's not how we should judge politicians. Though television gives us the illusion of intimacy, we aren't really in intimate contact with the figures we are watching. We are back once again to the fact that our brain was designed for social life in a small community. It was not designed to help us live in a society consisting of millions of people. We therefore get the context wrong.

While we are sorely tempted to trust our eyes and ears, we can't. They cannot supply us with the depth of information needed to make a full and fair assessment of a candidate's character and personality—two key factors we should be taking into account when we head to the polls. That's one of the vital lessons science is teaching us.

7

Do We Really Want the Truth?

*Why we often seem less interested
in the truth than we profess*

1.

Think about the way we remember Watergate. The story begins with the break-in at the headquarters of the Democratic National Committee at the Watergate complex overlooking the Potomac River. Ace *Washington Post* reporters Bob Woodward and Carl Bernstein investigate, and explosive headlines follow. The Senate Watergate Committee—headed by the avuncular Sam Ervin, the soft-spoken, white-haired senator from North Carolina who speaks in a folksy Southern drawl—grills officials. John Dean, the White House counsel, testifies about the cover-up. Then a low-level bureaucrat reveals that Nixon had installed a taping system to record everything that was said in his presence. Nixon initially refuses to release the tapes, citing executive privilege. The special prosecutor demands the tapes, and the Supreme Court orders Nixon to turn them over. The decision of the Court is unanimous. Sixteen days later, after the "smoking gun" tape is released—this is the tape showing that Nixon ordered the CIA to block the FBI investigation of Watergate on national security grounds—Nixon resigns. Two thousand and twenty-six days after he assumed office Richard Milhous Nixon walks up the steps of a waiting helicopter on the White House lawn, turns and delivers his signature V-for-victory salute, and flies off into history. At noon Gerald Ford becomes president, declaring "our long national nightmare is over."

On the day Nixon left office, August 9, 1974, 80 percent of the American people believed that it was time for him to go. That is an extraordinary number. Americans don't even agree by that margin what the national sport is (34 percent say it's football, 16 percent baseball). So to have 80 percent of us agree on anything, let alone something as controversial as Watergate, was truly remarkable.

You hear a statistic like that and you think that public opinion must be rational. Voters followed the evidence where it led and made the appropriate judgment, even though it was painful. This seems to be one of the plainest lessons of Watergate. You can trust public opinion. And because of that you can trust American democracy.

But how did voters react to Watergate as events unfolded?

The break-in took place on June 17, 1972. At the end of June, after the media reported that the burglars included James McCord, the security director of the Committee for the Reelection of the President, and E. Howard Hunt, a former CIA spy who had worked at the White House as recently as March, Nixon stood at 56 percent in the polls. In July John Mitchell, his former attorney general, resigned as the manager of the campaign just before the *New York Times* reported that the burglars had paid for bugging equipment with donations to the campaign laundered through Mexico. Nixon's poll rating remained at 56 percent. In August the *Washington Post* reported that a "$25,000 cashier's check, apparently earmarked for President Nixon's reelection campaign, was deposited in April in a bank account of one of the five men arrested in the break-in at Democratic National Headquarters here June 17." The General Accounting Office reported that the Nixon campaign had apparently violated the Federal Election Campaign Act. Nixon's approval rating? Fifty-nine percent, the start of a slow *increase* in his numbers. In September a federal grand jury indicted Hunt and the five Watergate burglars including G. Gordon Liddy, a member of the covert investigations unit known as the White House Plumbers, who led the break-in. Just before the end of the month the *Post* dropped a bombshell: "John N. Mitchell, while serving as U.S. Attorney General, personally controlled a secret Republican fund that was used to gather information about the Democrats, according to sources involved in the Watergate investigation." September polls showed Nixon holding on to the growing edge he had in August.

The headlines grew more ominous. In October the *Post* had another bombshell story: "FBI Finds Nixon Aides Sabotaged Democrats." The paper reported that the acts of sabotage included: "Following members of Democratic candidates' families and assembling dossiers on their personal lives; forging letters and distributing them under the candidates' letterheads;

leaking false and manufactured items to the press; throwing campaign schedules into disarray; seizing confidential campaign files; and investigating the lives of dozens of Democratic campaign workers." Nixon's approval rating? It went up. It was now 62 percent.

By Election Day, you couldn't escape news about the scandal. Though the coverage hadn't yet become an avalanche as it would later, the story was being reported in all media: newspapers, radio, television. While the *Washington Post* clearly held the lead in Watergate scoops, other papers, including the *New York Times* and the *Los Angeles Times*, scored blockbuster scoops of their own. It was the L.A. *Times* that nabbed an interview with the former FBI official who served as the burglars' lookout man: "Bugging Witness Tells Inside Story on Incident at Watergate." Many papers ran scathing editorials like the *New York Times*'s "Time to Come Clean." Even the *Chicago Tribune*, an avowedly pro-Republican paper, published front-page stories about Watergate thirteen times during the campaign.

Television, the chief source of news for most Americans, devoted hours to the scandal. Twenty percent of NBC's campaign coverage featured stories about Watergate, with the other two networks not far behind. CBS in the final two weeks before the election ran two specials on Watergate, the first taking up half of the evening news broadcast. A Harris Poll asked, "Have you heard, or not, about the men who were caught trying to install wiretaps in the Democratic National Headquarters in Washington?" Seventy-six percent answered they had. That was more than could name their own member of Congress or even knew there are three branches of government. Voters generally don't pay much attention to politics. But they were paying attention to Watergate. And still Nixon's polls didn't suffer.

Nixon was able to make a strong case for reelection. His opening to China and détente with the Soviet Union were historic, and the economy was doing well. He also had a not-so-secret weapon: his opponent, US Senator George McGovern, the balding and boring former history professor who was easily demonized (falsely) as an extreme left-winger who favored amnesty, abortion, and acid. His election campaign fizzled within weeks of his nomination after reports surfaced that his running mate, Senator Thomas Eagleton, had undergone electroshock therapy. McGovern said he was behind Eagleton 1,000 percent. Five days later he dumped him.

On Election Day, Tuesday, November 7, Nixon won 61 percent of the popular vote in one of the all-time great landslides in presidential history. He carried forty-nine of the fifty states, the most impressive tally since James Monroe's smashing victory in the election of 1820, 152 years earlier. (Monroe won every state.) No president since the dawn of mass democracy had ever beat his opponent by a greater margin, except for FDR. What of Watergate? Historian Keith Olson, after an exhaustive study, concluded that the scandal "played no perceptible role in the casting of votes in the 1972 election."

After the election, with McGovern now out of the picture, the voters could focus solely on Nixon. But his poll numbers didn't change substantially then either, not even after the trial of the Watergate defendants began in January 1973, which kept the story constantly in the news. In February Watergate again made headlines when Nixon nominated L. Patrick Gray to replace J. Edgar Hoover, who had died, as head of the FBI. Gray confirmed that the bureau had dug up evidence that the Committee for the Reelection of the President had played dirty tricks on the Democrats. He also said that John Dean had lied to investigators, which confirmed suspicions that the White House had been engaged in a cover-up. Nixon's poll numbers didn't budge. In March one of the Watergate burglars confessed to the judge in the case that he had committed perjury to protect the White House. In leaked testimony he reported that John Mitchell had known about the Watergate burglary in advance. Nixon's poll numbers dropped ten points, but he still retained a higher favorability rating than many presidents. Not until April 30, when Dean was fired and White House aides H. R. Haldeman and John Ehrlichman resigned, did Nixon's numbers drop substantially, finally falling in May below 50 percent. Here's the scorecard:

59% December
67% January
67% February
57% March
54% April
48% May

This is the disturbing story of a country asleep. The Watergate break-in happened on June 17, 1972. But Nixon's poll numbers didn't begin to collapse until May 1973, *eleven months later.* Why?

That's an obvious question, but we haven't seen fit to ask it. One reason is that it undermines the morality tale that came to define Watergate, a story with mythical overtones as old as civilization: a bad leader is run out of town by good men appalled at his crimes. This is a powerful narrative. It allows us to skip over the fact that the public elected Nixon twice so we can focus on the ending, when we rid ourselves of our bad king. This narrative gives Watergate a happy ending.

But something else is at work as well that explains why we don't pause to wonder at the public's long delay in coming to terms with Watergate. The delay makes no sense to us. Once you come to view the political subterfuge of Watergate as immoral, as everybody does who thinks Watergate ended well (it ended well because the crooks got what they had coming), you cannot imagine that voters didn't see things the same way from the beginning. It's inconceivable to us that a voter could have a ho-hum reaction to a headline about the attorney general's slush fund and spying operation.

People are supposed to be capable of reading a story about political corruption and taking away the right lessons. Facts are supposed to matter. Responsible journalism is supposed to be able to find a sizable audience. Voters are supposed to pay attention and want the truth. The system is based on all of these assumptions. If the assumptions are wrong, the system is flawed. And we are self-deluded.

So are we?

2.

In 1940, social scientists at Columbia University undertook the first scientific analysis of voting in American history. What they wanted to find out was why people vote the way they do. It was a simple question, but no one had a scientific answer. While polling had by then become commonplace, polls didn't provide the kind of information needed to answer the question. In a traditional poll you ask a random group of voters what they think at a particular moment. What you get is what pollsters refer to as a snapshot of the electorate, but it's superficial. Using this method you can't find out how events affect voters' thinking because the next time you do a poll you select a different group of voters. If you want to find out why people vote the way they do you need to keep going back to the same group of people over and over again so you can track the changes that take place in their thinking. But that had never been done.

The social scientists decided to try. To begin they had to pick a representative community. They selected Erie County in Ohio. Although the social scientists carefully noted that "there is no such thing as a 'typical American county,'" Erie came close. For forty years it had "deviated very little from the national voting trends." Another virtue of Erie was that it was small. It has just one principal city: Sandusky. This was important because the plan was to use interviewers to ask a large sample of voters for their views. Erie was "small enough to permit close supervision of the interviewers." After contacting three thousand voters—one in every four households—the social scientists winnowed the list down to 2,400. They subdivided this group into four groups of 600 voters each. Three of the groups were interviewed just once. These were the control groups. The fourth was returned to repeatedly throughout the 1940 presidential election cycle. By interviewing the members of this fourth group over and over it could be determined why they voted the way they did.

And what did the social scientists find? The result was wholly unexpected. Based on everything they had studied before, they had believed that voters were influenced to a great extent by the media. That made sense. Campaigns largely focus on the media. Getting good coverage is one of the chief aims of a campaign. The assumption was that what a politician says in a campaign matters. What he does matters. All of that is assumed because people, listening to the media, presumably hear what is said and what has been done. The candidates make news and the voters follow the news. That was what everybody believed.

It wasn't true. For all the hullabaloo of a campaign, it didn't really attract sustained attention. It turned out that only political junkies actually followed the twists and turns of the campaign. This was true, even though voting participation in Erie County was high: 81 percent of the eligible voters voted. By modern standards that percentage is almost unheard of. And yet even these conscientious voters didn't track the campaigns closely. The startling conclusion of the researchers was that even at the height of the campaign, the final two weeks of October, "about half the population ignored stories on the front page of their newspapers or political speeches by the candidates themselves, and about 75% of the people ignored magazine stories about the election. In short, the flood of political material at that time, far from drowning any of these people, did not even get their feet wet."

And this was in 1940, before television, before Facebook, before video games—before, that is, all of the modern distractions people today like to blame for the public apathy of both the young and the old. And it was in an election year when war was in the news and Franklin Roosevelt was on the ballot. Roosevelt was one of the most polarizing figures in American political history. Many Republicans hated him—"That man!" they'd bellow—and he returned their hatred. In 1936 he had famously said of the enemies of the New Deal: "Never before in all our history have these forces been so united against one candidate as they stand today. They are unanimous in their hate for me—and I welcome their hatred." But not even FDR could make politics for the people of Erie County exciting enough for a majority to follow the campaign closely over a long period.

So did the media have an impact on anybody? The social scientists assumed that if they did it would be on the people who knew the least about politics and were the most undecided. In theory, they would listen to the news, pick up information they hadn't considered, and then make an informed decision. If the media had a big impact on this group you could conclude that the media indeed play a powerful role in elections. But the confounding finding of the researchers was that "the group the campaign manager is presumably most eager to reach—the as-yet undecided—is the very group which is less likely to read or listen to his propaganda." These were the people who couldn't name the chief justice of the Supreme Court or the three branches of government. We think that the media in a democracy are vital instruments of education. But the people who could benefit the most pay the least attention.

So who paid the most attention? Who, in other words, formed the main audience for the election? This was perhaps the study's central finding. It was partisans—the people who had already made up their minds. The key audience wasn't the people who had an open mind. It was the people who had closed minds. They didn't follow the news to get educated. They followed the news because they found it interesting. The media had virtually no impact on their views. When they heard what they wanted to hear, they cheered. When they heard what they didn't want to hear, they ignored it. For the most part, Democrats ignored what the Republicans said and the Republicans ignored what the Democrats said. The partisans' willingness even to engage the other side in argument was limited.

While members of each group were willing to debate economic issues—about which each side felt it had the better of the argument—they declined to argue about the issues for which they felt the other side could make a reasonable case. The best argument of the Republicans, for example, was that FDR was breaking the two-term tradition by making a third run for the office. They hammered that argument repeatedly. But the Democrats didn't bother answering it. The best argument Democrats had for electing FDR was his experience. This time it was the Republicans who sat out the argument. When the interviewer asked them to provide a response to the claim that FDR was experienced, they switched to the anti–third term argument—their "good" argument.

How does someone become a partisan? What makes a Democrat a Democrat and a Republican a Republican? This is a complicated question only somewhat related to the issues addressed in this book. But it's worthwhile pointing out that all of the main theories that purport to explain partisanship rest on the shared assumption that our stated views rarely account for the rich variety of factors that influence us. Our social circles, social scientists tell us, are often decisive in shaping our views. It's not the media, in the main, that influence how we vote. It's the people closest to us. If your parents voted Democrat, you probably do too. But this doesn't begin to suggest the complex forces at work.

Recently, researchers have discovered that our politics are to a certain extent influenced by our genes. There is no liberal or conservative gene. But some of our behavior is correlated with different genes. The best predictor that someone votes conservatively? It's how often they go to church. The more they go to church, the more conservative they probably are. And what do we know about churchgoing habits? To an extent they are inherited. That is, religious fervor is in part genetic. So, therefore, is political ideology. Social scientists now believe that up to 50 percent of our ideology may be traceable to our genes. One study found that even our body odor is telling. Researchers discovered that we are attracted to the odor of people who share our views. Some studies suggest that what ultimately distinguishes liberals from conservatives is the degree to which they welcome change. Liberals in general react positively to novelty, while conservatives react negatively, seeing in novel situations the possibility of threats. Our attitude toward novelty is largely genetic. All this is seriously at odds with the assumption that we arrive at our political beliefs on the basis of conscious reasoning.

And, as we saw earlier, wholly extraneous factors like shark attacks and basketball games can affect voting behavior. We are always worried about demagoguery, but demagoguery is usually pretty obvious. Subtle framing effects like sports events are not obvious, and yet they can be decisive too. And recent studies show that our attitudes are so plastic that social scientists have found they can change how we think with fart spray. Scent the air with a zap of fart spray—yes, there's a company that makes it, social scientist David Pizarro informed me—and people's thoughts become more negative. Hang a hand sanitizer on the wall, and people in the vicinity suddenly become more moralistic.

This doesn't make campaigns irrelevant. They activate voters, stimulating them to take an interest in elections. Twenty-eight percent of the voters in the Erie County study who in May had said that they had no interest in the election decided by the end that they had enough interest to vote. So campaigns do matter; and the media matter. But few voters switch sides: in 1940 in Erie County just 8 percent did.

The lesson of the 1940 Columbia study is that by nature we aren't impartial umpires. We are fans. We want to see our side win. We cheer when our opinions are celebrated and we boo when contrary opinions score. As the Harvard psychologist Steven Pinker has observed, we don't want the truth to prevail, we want *our* version of the truth to prevail. Because we are programmed to try to win, we muster every argument we can think of to help us achieve victory. In the end, it is not the truth we care so much about as winning.

That explains, says French cognitive scientist Daniel Sperber, why the evidence that we are biased in favor of our own opinions—which is known as Confirmation Bias—should not surprise us. Nor should it's opposite, Disconfirmation Bias: the inclination to discount facts that undermine our opinions. So what wins arguments? It's not being in the right—though that can help. It is pigheadedness, research shows. Stick with your opinion in an argument through all challenges, and you have a good chance of bringing people around to your point of view. Grinding down the opposition works.

Experiments at Yale University by social scientist Dan Kahan demonstrate that we generally don't evaluate issues on the merits or privilege the truth. Instead, we rely on our intuition. And how does our intuition work? It's often self-serving. His research shows, for example, that when a corporate CEO is told that the earth is warming the CEO isn't likely to focus on the facts but on the implications. As soon as he hears the words "global warming," he thinks, *this is a problem bound to require government intervention.* And once he thinks that, his thoughts turn negative. Government intervention is a red flag. The result of this mental hopscotch is that before he can even begin to evaluate the merits of the argument he's reached a conclusion. In an instant he's become a climate change denier. It's not because he is against science. It is because his brain has made a connection between the problem and the likely solution, a connection he finds alarming to his side in political debates. When a businessperson scoffs at climate change it's not climate change he's likely thinking about. It's government regulation. This is what makes debates about climate change frustrating. Environmentalists and businesspeople are often talking past each other. The environmentalists are holding a conversation about science, while the businesspeople are discussing government regulation.

It is not just businesspersons who let their self-interest affect their political opinions. We all do. Social scientists Jason Weeden and Robert Kurzban recently published a book that claims *nearly all* of our political opinions reflect our self-interest. Immigrants generally favor looser immigration standards. African Americans generally favor affirmative-action programs. Jews and atheists almost uniformly oppose prayer in public schools. This is no accident, they argue. Immigrants, documented or undocumented, stand to benefit when the country embraces immigrants. Blacks generally stand to benefit from affirmative-action programs. Jews and atheists benefit when government refrains from sanctioning religious activity. Why are liberals pro-choice? Weeden and Kurzban daringly assert it is because liberals have multiple sex partners prior to marriage and therefore embrace the practice of both birth control and contraception, including abortion. So-called freewheelers vote Democrat to protect their right to the freewheeling lifestyle they prefer. Ring-bearers—people who marry young and have lots of children—vote to restrict abortion and other methods of contraception to impose costs on a lifestyle they find threatening. Why should they care if someone else is having sex with multiple partners? In part, because it reduces the supply of virgins.

3.

Partisanship is just one of many biases that shape our politics along with Confirmation Bias and Disconfirmation Bias. What are we to make of them all?

A clue lies in what evolutionary psychologists have dubbed Error Management Theory (EMT). This is what might be called the Fire Alarm Bias. When a fire alarm goes off at work, what do we do? We immediately prepare to exit the building. Faced with a potential danger, we assume the alarm is real and act on the assumption. Of course, quite often fire alarms turn out to be false. But we still react as if they are real when the alarm is first sounded. This is because that's the safe response—the same reason we want smoke alarms to be on hair-trigger alert. If it turns out that the alarm is false, we simply return to our desks and get on with our work. Responding to a false alarm won't get you killed. But if you fail to react? That just might. A missed alarm can end in death. So who was evolution likely to favor? People who take a better-be-safe-than-sorry approach. This is why we share a fear of missed alarms. We'd rather overreact than underreact. This bias shapes our response to events in all sorts of ways. It's one reason that, for example, we seem inherently biased against strangers. Who is likelier to take advantage of us? A stranger or someone we know? A stranger, right? So when we come across people who seem unfamiliar by virtue of the language they speak or the clothes they wear or the color of their skin, our instinctive reaction is wariness. That's the better-be-safe-than-sorry approach.

Or, to take another example, consider McCarthyism. When Joe McCarthy warned Americans that communists by the hundreds had infiltrated the national government at the highest levels, voters instinctively responded with fear. Their reasoning reflected the play-it-safe bias. McCarthy might be wrong, but if he is, so what? A few hundred falsely accused people might be hurt, but life would go on as normal for most. But if he is correct and we ignore his warnings? Our very survival as a nation might be at risk. Danger lies in the missed alarm, not the false alarm. In the case of McCarthy, this was flawed reasoning. As people eventually figured out, McCarthyism came with its own heavy cost. Accusing innocent people of a crime undermines the confidence people have in the fairness of their society; that confidence is the glue that holds society together. But what did voters act on initially after McCarthy began leveling his charges? Their fears. Nobody wants to miss an alarm. Our instinctive error management strategy sees to it that we do not.

What these two examples suggest is that evolution favors biases that help keep us safe and assure our survival. Seen in this light, biases aren't errors that put us at a disadvantage. They contribute to our survival and are therefore an advantage. Or, as scientists put it, "biases represent adaptive solutions to the decision-making problems of our evolutionary past." What they don't do is favor the truth above all else.

Here are some of the most common cognitive biases identified by social scientists.

Availability Bias
Perseverance Bias
Source Confusion
Projection Bias
Self-Serving Bias
Superiority Bias
Planning Fallacy
Optimism Bias

Do any of them privilege the truth? The answer is no. Not one. They privilege survival.

Let's take each of these biases one by one, starting with the Availability Bias. This refers to our tendency to respond to a question with the first answer that pops into mind. Quick. Who was our greatest president? According to a Gallup Poll in 2011, Americans are most likely to say it was Reagan. Upon a little reflection, that's obviously not the right answer. No historian would argue that Reagan ranks with Washington or Lincoln. But Reagan is the name people mention more than others when asked because his presidency is frequently discussed in glowing terms. His name is easy to call up. And what do we assume, say social scientists? We assume that information that comes quickly to mind is bound to be correct. So when the pollster asks who's the greatest president, people answer without thinking, "Reagan," and they do so with confidence. (This bias is apparently what lies behind the myth that you should go with the first answer that comes to mind when you are taking a multiple-choice test. Research actually shows the first answer is usually *not* the correct one. But that's not a lesson students have learned. Instead, they go with their instinct—their first choice.)

Why do we go with the first answer that comes to mind? Because in the Pleistocene, as we found earlier in our discussion of mind reading, speed was of the essence. It was usually more important to get a quick answer than an answer based on reflection. A quick answer that was good enough was usually better than a thoughtful answer that took time. Truth was not unimportant to our hunter-gatherer ancestors. But good-enough answers were usually all they needed. And the Availability Bias met their needs.

The Availability Bias does not meet *our* needs, not in politics at any rate. In politics we very rarely need the quick answer. We need the thoughtful answer. As a voter you seldom have to come up, on the spot, with a decision about the candidate you support or the policy you favor. You have time to think about it. Even if a pollster asks you for your opinion and you haven't got one, you don't have to invent one. You can just say you don't know. But by instinct what do we do? We come up with an instant answer and convince ourselves it's the right answer. And we do it, say social scientists, whether we know a lot or a little. In one experiment, subjects with nothing to go on but a photograph and a name were asked to predict how an individual would behave under various conditions. Would they call home once every three months? Would they comb their hair just before having their picture snapped? And what was invariably the subject's response? They not only were willing to make a prediction, they were overwhelmingly certain that their prediction was accurate. They were just a little less confident in the accuracy of their predictions than subjects who were given the chance to actually interview the individual and learn a lot about them. This suggests two things. First, we are by nature opinionated. Second, once we have an opinion we're likely to think it's correct whether it's based on encyclopedic knowledge or just a hunch. That's frightening.

It gets more frightening, thanks to what's known as the Perseverance Bias. This refers to our inclination to stick with an opinion once we have enunciated it. Studies show that once we have formed an opinion we don't easily give it up—not even after contradictory evidence surfaces that undermines our position. Once again evolution easily accounts for the bias.

It simply did not behoove hunter-gatherers to reconsider their beliefs because those beliefs were likely to have been born of hard experience. They formed their opinions by and large on the basis of things that happened to them, their family, or their closest friends. Hard experience was likely to produce opinions that were good enough to assure their survival because those opinions were based on what they *knew*. And it was an advantage not to keep revisiting those beliefs. That saved time and energy. But us? Our opinions in politics are usually not based on hard experience; they are based on something we read in a newspaper or saw on TV that happened to somebody else. For most of us, the knowledge we come to by personal experience is likely to be of little help in forming opinions about the political questions that come before us as voters.

Worse, our political opinions are often based on little more than a headline. We hear about something that's happened and immediately form an opinion about it even though we lack the basic facts. Worse than that is that we are unlikely, say social scientists, to remember where we pick up information. This is known as Source Confusion. While you are watching a television ad that slams a politician you are aware at that moment that the source is biased. But after a week or two? You are likely to remember what was said but not where you heard it. And there's no surefire way to protect ourselves from this sort of thing except to not watch the ad in the first place. Want to keep your head clear of nonsense? Don't expose yourself to it. Treat bad information like a disease and avoid contact with it.

Projection Bias is responsible for most of our worst foreign policy disasters, including the Iraq War. Going into the war policymakers believed that we would be greeted as liberators. We figured that's how we'd respond if somebody helped us overthrow a brutal dictator. We'd be grateful. But that is not how most Iraqis responded. They used our intervention to settle scores. Why did we err so disastrously? We didn't know how they think. Instead of finding out, we projected on them the way we think. The CIA refers to this as the "everybody thinks like us mind-set." In other words, when we look at others we see ourselves as if we are staring into a mirror. A warning against the bias is prominently addressed in *Psychology of Intelligence Analysis* published by an arm of the CIA (see chapter 4, page 33). The warning is threaded throughout the book. Finishing it, you think, *This is great! The CIA gets it!* It's particularly reassuring to read in the foreword, which was written by several high-ranking CIA officials, including the agency's former deputy director, that the CIA regards the author of the study, Richards J. Heuer, a CIA official for some three decades, as one of its leading lights. You think: *The CIA is paying attention. As a country we won't make the Projection*

Bias error again. But is this really the good news it appears to be? *Psychology of Intelligence Analysis* was published in 1999—four years before the Iraq War.

They didn't get it, after all. That's the grim conclusion we are sorely tempted to reach. But it may not be quite accurate or fair. You can understand a bias without being able to do much about it. That's the thing about biases. They operate in the background, lurking just outside conscious awareness. As I noted earlier in the book, Daniel Kahneman admits he still finds himself succumbing to biases, and he is the one who first identified many of them.

Why would evolution favor Projection Bias? What seems to be the likeliest explanation is that it was an error without consequence in the Pleistocene. While knowing your enemy is always useful, mirroring—thinking your enemy thinks like you do—is only dangerous when your enemy thinks differently. And in the Pleistocene, how often were our hunter-gatherer ancestors likely to encounter other hunter-gatherers who thought differently than they did? Probably not very often. Most everybody they were likely to encounter lived the same way they did and faced similar hardships. Especially before language was introduced, culture counted for less. So most of the time mirroring probably worked.

Perhaps the most common of all biases is the Self-Serving Bias. When something good happens, we take the credit. But when something bad happens? That's somebody else's fault. This is easily explained. Evolution rigged the system to favor people who favor themselves. The last thing anyone wants to be reminded of is the truth, which is that we often make mistakes and, on the flip side, that other people often get things right. Who wants to hear that?

A related bias is the Superiority Bias. Nearly everybody thinks they are above average. One survey, done in the 1970s, captured the ludicrousness of this bias. It found that 85 percent of Americans think they get along with others better than ordinary people. As one social scientist put it, this is mathematically impossible. Eighty-five percent of people cannot believe they are in the top fiftieth percentile. But when you survey public opinion this is invariably the result you get. Take almost any skill. Leadership. Driving. Whatever. When researchers ask people where they believe they rank, the percentages are nearly always laughably skewed. By overwhelming proportions, most of us think we are more capable as a leader than the average person, a better driver than the average person, a better everything than the average person. When university professors were asked to rank themselves against other professors, more than 80 percent said they are in the top half. As with the Self-Serving Bias, evolution seems to have favored people who think highly of themselves.

The Planning Fallacy afflicts everybody from homeowners building a house to the officials who design grand public projects. It's no more complicated than this: in the planning stages people tend to underestimate the time and cost of a project. We do this so often that Hollywood has taken notice, producing movies like *Mr. Blandings Builds His Dream House*, the 1948 comedy starring Cary Grant that begins with hope and ends in near disaster as costs mount far beyond what the couple building the home anticipate. As for public projects, it is the rare one that doesn't go haywire. Remember the Big Dig, Boston's vast network of highways and tunnels? It was estimated to cost $2.8 billion when planning began in 1982 and was supposed to be done by 1998. The actual cost in inflation-adjusted dollars was $8 billion—nearly three times the initial estimate. It was not finished until 2007, nine years late. Why do we nearly always underestimate costs when we make plans? Why would evolution favor people with this bias? It's no mystery. We need to take risks in life. Underestimating costs helps us cope with those risks by minimizing them. If we were sticklers for the truth, we might never try building our dream house or a major, complicated highway project. If I had made a realistic estimate of the effort it would take to write this book, I never would have started it.

What do the Self-Serving Bias, the Superiority Bias, and the Planning Fallacy all have in common? They are based on a kind of insane optimism. When bad things happen it's always other people's fault? That's the gist of the Self-Serving Bias. And that's crazy. Compared with most others, we are superior? That's mathematically impossible. When we plan a project it will come in on time and at cost? In what world?

These biases suggest that we are designed for optimism. It turns out we are. The neuroscientist Tali Sharot reports that 80 percent of us are by nature optimists. This is true not only of Americans, but of people from around the world. Chinese, Germans, Brazilians—all of us. When she puts subjects into an fMRI machine, she discovered, two parts of the brain light up when questions about the future are posed. When people feel optimistic the left inferior frontal gyrus shows activity. When they feel down on the future the right inferior frontal gyrus is active. Good news registers in the left hemisphere, in other words. Bad news registers in the right hemisphere. But which shows more activity time and again? Which lights up more and with greater intensity? The left hemisphere. We respond much more powerfully to good news than we do to bad news. And the more hope we have, the higher our levels of testosterone. And we know what happens when that's the situation. We show more drive. The more drive we possess the likelier it is that we'll succeed in a chosen task.

This explains a lot. For the Optimism Bias doesn't affect just ordinary people. It affects political leaders too—who, after all, need vast reserves of testosterone to succeed. This helps clear up the mystery of Joseph Stalin's head-in-the-sand reaction to warnings that Hitler, in violation of their 1939 pact, planned on attacking the Soviet Union, a story Sharot retells in her fine book about her research into optimism. It was actually obvious Hitler was going to pull something like this. In *Mein Kampf* he had written openly about invading the Soviet Union. Fifteen years later, in the months leading up to the invasion, Soviet spies repeatedly warned Stalin that they had uncovered evidence that Hitler planned an attack. Leopold Trepper, Stalin's own spy, masquerading as a businessman in Europe, found out that Hitler had signed an order for the invasion. In Trepper's dispatch reporting this news to Stalin, he gave the exact number of divisions Hitler was withdrawing from France and Belgium to divert to what would become the eastern front. "I sent the proposed plan of attack, and indicated the original date, May 15, then the revised date, and the final date," Trepper later recalled. His communications indicated the attack would take place on June 22, 1941. Another Soviet spy told Stalin that Hitler was amassing a giant army on the Russian border. Franklin Roosevelt slipped a warning to Stalin through our ambassador. And when did the attack take place? June 22, 1941, just as Trepper had predicted. But Stalin disbelieved what he was told even though he had long believed that Hitler eventually planned on attacking the Soviet Union.

This was truly insane. It cost Stalin and the Russian people dearly. Unprepared for war with Hitler, Stalin had to scramble to stave off defeat. In the ensuing battle-to-the-death, the USSR lost tens of millions of Russians. But Stalin's optimism that Hitler would not attack was no more curious than the optimism that blinds us all. We all want to believe things will turn out well. Consider the chance you will get cancer. Do you think it's small? Most Americans by a wide margin, more than 60 percent, believe neither they nor a close family member will "be diagnosed with a serious illness like cancer." In reality, 50 percent of all men will get cancer. Or consider the chance you'll divorce. Very few newlyweds believe their marriage will end in divorce, though the divorce rate is north of 40 percent. Sharot reports that even divorce attorneys underestimate the chance they will divorce. And they know the facts.

This is less surprising than it seems. We are prewired to believe that bad things happen to other people, not ourselves. Even after subjects in a study were told how high the risk of cancer is, they believed their personal risk of getting the disease was low. Virtually nobody, Sharot informs us, changed their mind after learning the facts—more evidence that facts don't matter as much as we think they do. And with one exception, it doesn't seem to matter what kind of person you are—conscientious or not conscientious, agreeable or not agreeable—it doesn't seem to make a difference. When students in a study were asked if their health is at risk from drunk driving, smoking, or sex, their personality type did not affect their response, except for neurotics. Neurotics showed more pessimism. The study confirmed the consensus view that we think others are susceptible to ill health from risky behavior, but not ourselves.

Other studies have found that if a doctor tells a patient they have an 80-percent chance of surviving an operation, most patients will agree to go under the knife. But if the doctor frames the issue the other way around and tells the patient they have a 20 percent chance of dying? In those circumstances most people say no to the operation. Of course, both reflect the exact same odds. But we respond much better to problems framed in an optimistic manner. An 80 percent chance of survival sounds a lot more promising than a 20 percent chance of dying.

In his memoirs, former vice president Walter Mondale defends his decision to tell Americans in his acceptance address as the presidential candidate of the Democratic Party in 1984 that he planned on raising their taxes. "Let's tell the truth," he stated with passion from the Moscone Center in San Francisco. "Mr. Reagan will raise taxes and so will I. He won't tell you. I just did." He insists that it was not only the right decision, but also that it made sense politically because voters respect a politician who tells them the truth. It was one of the worst political decisions of all time. Voters, as we have seen, do not want the truth. We want hope. If the truth robs us of hope, we don't want to hear it. What's the percentage of Americans who are optimistic by nature? Eighty percent. That's the largest constituency there is. The Catholic vote, the women's vote, the black vote—all pale in comparison with the optimist vote. Mondale still can't see that? That's a good example of Perseverance Bias.

Given a choice between a hard truth and a softheaded optimism, which are we likely to select? Optimism. That is not hard to explain. In the Pleistocene, life was often so hard and conditions so harsh that the only way to carry on was to deny reality. Survival often depended simply on the hunter-gatherers' ability to hang on. To make it to the spring, you had to survive the winter using any means you could think of, and if you couldn't think of a way, well, you just lived on hope. Who survived under the circumstances hunter-gatherers faced? Optimists. Nature favored them. Hope was, therefore, a sound strategy. But in the modern world, a world in which millions interact in complicated ways within the confines of well-established institutions, hope isn't a correct strategy. It's not a strategy at all. It's the abandonment of strategy. Often, it's a recipe for disaster, as the Obama administration discovered when it debuted the website of the Affordable Care Act in the fall of 2013 without adequate advance testing. In the modern world it's not optimists we need, it's realists.

A lifetime of research has convinced the psychologist Daniel Kahneman that human beings are poor reasoners. Our biases, he says, get in the way of clear thinking. But this is not quite the whole story. As Gerd Gigerenzer, another gifted social scientist and Kahneman's chief critic, has found, many biases serve a still-useful purpose, such as the Recognition Bias we explored earlier in the book. It's thanks to that bias that you knew that Cape Town was bigger than Libreville or Asmara. You've heard of Cape Town, so you assumed it's bigger. As evolutionary psychologists argue, our biases are not "design flaws," they are "design features." They helped hominids (that's us and our great ape ancestors) survive for millions of years. While our world is far different from what it was in the Pleistocene, it's not entirely different. We often face similar challenges. If a stranger appears at the entrance to your cave or your McMansion you'll be wary.

Where does this leave us? Can you or can you not trust your instincts in politics? What I have been trying to convince you, of course, is that much of the time you cannot. There are just too many tasks required of us in our capacity as citizens where instincts mislead us. Consider the Recognition Bias as it comes into play in politics. What do voters using the Recognition Bias do when filling out their ballot? They vote for the candidate whose name they recognize. Does that make sense? It could be that the candidate was able to plaster his name all over town and television because he raised a lot of money. But does that mean you should vote for him? Shouldn't you wonder where he got all the money he spent on advertising? It might well be from special interests who don't have *your* interests at heart.

Given the realities of American politics we might be better off if, by instinct, we had an un-Recognition Bias. That would tend to balance the system against candidates who sell out their principles in exchange for donations from powerful groups. It might be that you recognize a candidate's name because he's the incumbent. But is that a good reason to give him your support? It might be a good reason if you think things are going well and you consider your vote a stamp of approval for the status quo. But using this approach could well lead you to support an individual who does not merit it. Blanket support for incumbents is bound to lead to bad choices. Worse yet, familiarity, social scientists report, leads to a positive feeling, the same kind of feeling we experience when we are happy. And what happens when we are happy? We become less analytical. Name recognition leads us to lower our guard and become more susceptible to manipulation.

Confirmation Bias, like the others we've just reviewed, stops us from digging for the truth. Biases put a premium on easy answers when hard answers are more likely to be the correct answers. Further, the 1940 study of Erie County voters shows that voters need more than information. And that's important to know, for it undermines the naïve assumption of civics enthusiasts. Give voters the facts, we are told, and they will reach the right conclusions. But actually, we know, they often don't. Americans had all the facts they needed in the fall of 1972 to conclude that Nixon was abusing his power, but that wasn't enough to change their opinion of Nixon. For eleven months they resolutely stuck by him. Once they had made up their mind about him—and by the time the Watergate break-in took place, most had—they refused to let facts contrary to their opinion color their views. What counted weren't the facts, just their opinion—a classic illustration of Perseverance Bias.

4.

This is less strange than it might appear. If you think that poor people are lazy and you come across a study that shows they are not lazy, that they just lack opportunities, are you likely to give up your underlying assumption that poor people are lazy? Probably not. Much more likely is that you are going to find ways to dismiss the study or ignore it. One reason for that is that our opinions reflect our general understanding of the way the world works. And who wants to question that? Who wants to change the assumptions underlying our understanding of the world? No one. Rethinking assumptions is hard. And we know from Daniel Kahneman that our brain takes the easy path whenever possible, because, as he instructs us, our brain is lazy. We'd much rather *not* think. Thinking takes cognitive energy. So if we come across a finding that is at odds with our understanding of the world, we'd much rather dismiss it out of hand than deal with the implications. *What? This study claims poor people's problem is that they lack opportunities?*

Once we learn something about the way the world works, we don't want to keep relearning the same lesson over and over. Our brain is literally designed not to revisit an issue once we have figured it out. In monkey studies a few years ago scientists rewarded a group of animals with a juice drink 60 percent of the time when they looked in a certain direction. So what did the monkeys do? Once they had been trained, they stopped looking in the other direction. They stuck with what experience taught them. Look this way, not that way. When the scientists measured the monkeys' brain activity, they made an unforeseen discovery. Once the monkeys had learned it was beneficial to look one way and not the other, their brain activity virtually ceased when faced with a decision about which way to look. As far as their brain was concerned, no decision needed to be made. Experience proved you should do this, not that. This is a major factor in our reluctance to change our opinions. Why waste time on it? We are cognitively inclined not to. This isn't a decision we make consciously. Our brain makes it for us unconsciously. Once we make a decision we are inclined to stick to it and will find ways to justify our decision. According to several studies, when voters are asked after they vote what they think of the candidate they just voted for, they usually are a lot more sure he is all they hope he is than they were just minutes earlier before they cast their ballot.

Once voters had decided that Nixon deserved reelection, they didn't want to entertain the possibility that he didn't. They did not want to revisit an issue they had decided was settled. Deciding who should be president is the voter's most significant political decision every four years. *And we got that wrong?* That's not a conclusion most people are likely to welcome. Abandoning Nixon by the fall of 1972 would have been akin to abandoning a basic outlook on life. If Nixon was the wrong choice, that opened the possibility that a lot of other choices were wrong as well. Maybe Nixon's Vietnamization policy was wrong. Maybe the openings to China and Russia were wrong. Maybe it was wrong to side with the police against protesters. Who'd want to reopen all of those questions?

Watergate on paper was all about Nixon's abuse of power. But in reality it was about a lot more. Proof of that is what happened after people eventually abandoned him. Many dropped the political positions with which he was associated. Many voters who abandoned Nixon moved left on issues like abortion and busing that had nothing to do with Watergate. To take just one example: more than half of male pro-life Democrats who supported Nixon in 1972 switched to a pro-choice position on abortion after they decided to withdraw their support for Nixon as a result of Watergate. Did that make sense? Of course not. Watergate had nothing to do with abortion.

Why did these voters switch? A psychological mechanism inclines us toward consistency, especially when our beliefs and behavior are in conflict. While we often hold contradictory views, obvious contradictions make us feel uncomfortable. By nature we aren't Walt Whitmans. "Do I contradict myself? Very well, then I contradict myself, I am large, I contain multitudes," Whitman says in his poem "Song of Myself." But that's not how the brain operates. The human brain does not like cognitive dissonance—as social psychologist Leon Festinger dubbed the phenomenon in the 1950s. Rather than live with contradiction, we figure out a way to reduce it. How far are we willing to go to do this? Pretty far.

In his landmark study of cognitive dissonance, *When Prophecy Fails,* Festinger tells the remarkable story of a Chicago housewife turned mystic who became convinced that the world was coming to an end. A great flood, she predicted, would envelop the globe, ending humanity. She learned this, she claimed, via a message from another planet. All but she and her followers would be lost, she said. They would be saved after being flown in a flying saucer to another planet, Clarion. In anticipation of the end of the world her followers sold their belongings: houses, furniture—they sold it all. Then the date of apocalypse arrived. It was December 21, 1954. She and her followers dutifully gathered to await their deliverance from the hell that earth was about to become. They expected it to happen as the clock struck midnight. But nothing happened. Perhaps God wasn't on Central Standard Time. So they waited. Minutes passed, then hours. Still nothing. But this did not shake their belief in the prophecy. Once they realized that no flying saucer was whisking them away and that no great flood was coming, they concluded that they had saved the world from destruction. Their example of faith had so moved God that he had decided to spare humanity. They saved us all.

It is easy for us, from our vantage point, to think of these folks as ridiculous believers in magical thinking. But what they fell victim to was a form of thinking to which we are all highly susceptible. We all want to believe what we believe is true. That's the Perseverance Bias in action. Once we settle on a view of the world, we are inclined to persist in it. If forced to confront inconvenient facts—as the Chicago cultists were forced when life on earth didn't come to an end—we are capable of going to great lengths to explain them away. That's because we absolutely hate cognitive dissonance.

Nixon himself benefited from this mechanism twice. In 1971 he went to China, shocking the world and his supporters, who had grown used to thinking of Nixon as a tough-minded anticommunist. So what did they do when he made his stunning announcement about China? By overwhelming numbers, his supporters stuck by Nixon and changed their opinion about China. They reduced cognitive dissonance by flip-flopping on a grand scale. This is what voters usually do when their leaders evolve. It's the reason leaders are able to lead. On most issues, voters' allegiance to their leaders is stronger than their commitment to a stand on a particular issue. In cases like this our instincts actually work to our advantage as members of a mass political democracy.

It's fortunate that they do. Imagine what would happen if we lacked this basic desire for cognitive consistency. Every time leaders decided to push their country in a new direction to take into account new realities, followers would decline to follow their lead. They'd insist on sticking to their original views. What a nightmare. Under such circumstances leaders could seldom lead. Politics would stagnate. Democracy would collapse. We'd never escape the death grip of the past. We'd be like the Bourbon kings that Talleyrand ridiculed: we'd learn nothing and forget nothing.

But cognitive dissonance isn't a tonic for wooden-headedness. Look at what happened in 1972. When Watergate broke, Nixon's voters again faced a contradiction. This time it was the difference between their belief that Nixon was basically ethical and the facts reported in the news media, which suggested he might not be. To resolve the contradiction what did they do? They ignored Watergate. Ignoring Watergate ended the dissonance. In this case the psychological mechanism of cognitive dissonance did not work to the advantage of democracy. It undermined democracy. It was a disadvantage. Democracy only works when leaders are held to account. Here the voters were willing to give Nixon a free pass.

5.

There's a further psychological desire that helps explain why voters were reluctant to cast Nixon overboard. It has to do with our attitude toward change. As a general rule, we don't like it. That's because it upends the expectation that the world is predictable. And what does our mental health depend on? The world working pretty much the way we think it works. We want the world to confirm our assumptions.

As we learned earlier, we cannot remain on high alert all the time. We'd go crazy if we had to. And fortunately, most of the time, we don't have to. Remember what we found in our discussion of credulity. Credulousness works because the world is predictable for the most part. When we turn on a light switch, the lights go on. When we push an elevator button, an elevator generally arrives. Or, to take an example our hunter-gatherer ancestors would have found familiar, the sound of rustling in the bushes nearby probably indicates an animal is hiding there. We don't need to question everything. Most of the time things work the way we expect them to. But it's more than that. The fact is, we *need* the world to work this way. We need predictability so we can focus our attention on everything that happens that is out of the ordinary.

What was more likely to appeal to Nixon's voters after Watergate? The belief that he should be abandoned, or supported? Wasn't the obvious choice to stand by Nixon? If change is frightening, that was the default position. Between Nixon and McGovern, it wasn't Nixon who was more identified with change. It was McGovern. Even as the Prairie Populist issued his fervent appeal, "Come Home, America," the voters were deciding that they already were home—with Nixon. He was the status quo. McGovern, fairly or not, was associated with the turmoil of the sixties. Nixon posed as the defender of the country against the sixties. Our default preference for the status quo, all other things being equal, is the reason we generally favor incumbents. It's not just name recognition that gives them an edge. We are more comfortable with them. A newcomer could be dangerous.

Predictability puts us at ease. An expectation of predictability was built into our psychology during the Pleistocene—that key period when the contours of our psychology at the deepest level were developing. For *millions* of years, life hewed to familiar patterns day in and day out. Everything ran in cycles, as the social scientist George Marcus emphasizes in his work. The sun rose in the morning and it set at night, and this happened every single day. Spring followed winter, and this happened every single year. The calendar. The weather. The seasons. Birth and death. Everything was cyclical. A sameness characterized life. Things were predictable.

This isn't true of the modern world. The sun may still rise and fall, but our lives are marked by unrelenting change. Change is so rapid these days, it's remarkable we don't suffer a kind of collective nervous breakdown. The reason we don't may be because we have now had a few hundred years to begin getting used to the idea of rapid change. While our brain hasn't evolved to accommodate the speed at which we experience life in the modern world—at least there's no sign of it yet—our culture has. But we have found it hard to adapt. Consider what happened to American society after the Revolution. We went on an alcoholic binge. According to research by historian William Rorabaugh, in the three decades after the Constitution was ratified Americans began drinking twice as much as the Irish. He reports that in the whole Western world only Swedes drank more.

It's no wonder. What did the Revolution do to Americans? It upended their daily lives. Who held sway in society before the Revolution? Older people, according to the historian David Hackett Fischer. That makes sense. In a world marked by cycles of history, who is better equipped to help a community navigate safely past the rocky shoals? People who have lived through lots of these same cycles before: older folks. After the Revolution, who suddenly began to command the attention of people? The young. The wisdom of the elderly no longer seemed self-evident or applicable. If history doesn't run in cycles, their experience counts for less. Even clothing styles shifted. Before the Revolution, Hackett found, fashion favored the clothes worn by the old. And after the Revolution? Now people wanted to look young. Before, being older was better. Now, being younger was.

But our basic instincts have not undergone a metamorphosis. We still find change unsettling. It leaves us feeling that things are out of control. When change produces a negative outcome, what do we often do? We turn to conspiracy theories to help relieve the anxiety and confusion we feel. That's why *The Protocols of the Elders of Zion*, the anti-Semitic tract that blames the Jews for the world's troubles, suddenly became popular in the wake of World War One and the Russian Revolution, two decades after its publication. It provided a neat and simple explanation of the events that had upended world order. We are drawn to conspiracy thinking by instinct. No one has to teach us to think conspiratorially. We just do. This is because we resist the notion that bad things just happen, for that undermines the predictability we crave. What is it ordinary people by the millions said after Kennedy was assassinated in Dallas in 1963? There is no way a loser like Lee Harvey Oswald, acting on his own, simply could decide one day to buy a gun through a mail order ad and shoot the president of the United States— and succeed. Big events need big causes. Some nefarious conspiracy must have been afoot—involving the Mafia, or Fidel Castro, or Lyndon Johnson, or somebody big and important, somebody bigger than Lee Harvey Oswald.

Think back on all the big events of the last generation that made us feel bad: 9/11, the Iraq War, Hurricane Katrina. Each time, people by the millions were drawn to conspiracy theories. Deciding to go down that path is usually irrational, but once we do, everything makes sense. The reason is that we settle on conspiracies that build on an existing base of knowledge and worldviews. They don't just come out of nowhere. Thus, people accustomed to finding answers in religion see the hand of God in catastrophe. What is it the right-wing Christian leader Jerry Falwell said after terrorists brought down the World Trade Center towers on 9/11? "The abortionists have got to bear some burden for this because God will not be mocked. And when we destroy 40 million little innocent babies, we make God mad." Falwell believed God had plotted against us. God. It doesn't get much clearer than that. You piss off God and he smites you.

It is not bad news per se that drives us crazy enough to embrace wild theories. It is bad news that undermines the order of our universe. We abhor disorder and uncertainty. Think about our reaction to George W. Bush in the months following 9/11. What did he offer? Certainty. And Americans by the millions rallied behind him. In those terrible, grief-stricken, frightening months, Bush sustained the highest ratings of any president in our history:

September 2001	90%
October	89%
November	87%
December	86%
January 2002	84%
February	82%
March	80%

Later, Bush may have proved to be deeply flawed as a leader. But in those months he gave people what they wanted and needed. The man and the moment met.

Biology reinforces our belief in order. Consider how our vision system works. We think of vision as objective. It's actually subjective. We don't actually see what we think we see. Our brain doesn't shoot documentaries, cinema verité–style. It's Hitchcock. It shoots movies. It assembles its movie from thousands of parcels of visual information. These parcels, says the neuroscientist John Medina, are "ridiculously specific." A vertical line at 40 degrees is picked up by one parcel, while another picks up a vertical line at 43 degrees. What we think we are seeing—a seamless movie—is actually a rough director's cut, sliced, and diced in such a way as to give us in the end the illusion of a sensible representation of the world we see. But it's not the real world. If the brain showed us the world it's photographing, we would see a herky-jerky little movie as abstract as a Picasso painting. We'd see the frames of the movie rather than the flow. And everywhere we went we'd see two little black dots. Where the optic nerve connects to the retina in the back of the eye, there's a blind spot, one in each eye. But we don't notice them. The director, our brain, doesn't want his movie spoiled by dots, so he fills them in. When the movie debuts, we see a world we can navigate easily.

Our brain doesn't let us see the director's cut because it wouldn't serve any purpose. And it would be upsetting. Our brain doesn't want us upset. It wants us to feel in control. As much as it can, it discounts that which might lead us to believe we are not in control. It deliberately blinds us.

This is extraordinary when you think about it. Evolution has given us a lot of highly effective tools to arrive at a representation of the world that is truthful. We see the world in 3D at a speed of twenty-four frames per second. We can distinguish among 120 different levels of loudness, from the faint sound of a snail moving quietly along a garden path to an ear-shattering rock-and-roll concert. We can detect up to ten thousand different odor molecules. Our cognitive powers are sufficiently developed that we have figured out how to split the atom and send a man to the moon. But if the truth is messy, we run from it? We prefer a wrong-headed conspiracy theory to the truth? That appears to be the case. We are like the character played so memorably by Mary Tyler Moore in the film *Ordinary People*. We want our spoons lined up perfectly. We hate mess.

When we go to the grocery store and walk down the cereal aisle, we face literally hundreds of choices. Why do we often reach for a name brand cereal, even though a generic costs less and probably tastes the same? Because, say social scientists, we like no more than three choices. More than that and we grow anxious. That's why so many of us go for Frosted Flakes or Cheerios. Picking those cereals is a way of reducing our anxiety. It takes the mess out of shopping.

Our preference for order is so pronounced that we often turn to name brands we're accustomed to even when blind taste tests show we prefer an alternative. In blind taste tests Pepsi is usually favored or at least draws even with Coke. But Coke far outsells Pepsi, and when people in experiments are told they are drinking Coke, three out of four say they prefer it.

Economists like to think we are rational creatures and that we act in our self-interest. They even have a name for us that reflects our allegedly rational, utility-maximizing nature: homo economicus. But our capacity for rationality is exaggerated. That's particularly true when it comes to politics. The world is messy. But because of our strong desire for order, we see order.

It should by now be clear that the public's eleven-month-delayed reaction to Watergate was no anomaly. It was predictable. The voters' instinct wasn't to get at the truth. Actually, they wanted to ignore the truth as long as possible. When the truth makes us uncomfortable, as Watergate clearly did, that's what we do. That's especially true if the truth makes the world seem unpredictable. The more incomprehensible the truth is, the more we run from it.

Remember what many Americans' reaction to 9/11 was when they saw hundreds of thousands of frenzied people in the Middle East celebrating the attack? They could not get over it. It was almost as shocking as the attack itself. *You mean to say that people actually hate us?* Americans could not believe that. Rather than face that fact they decided our problem was that people did not understand us. That was a palatable truth. But it wasn't really the truth, was it? Many of the demonstrators had a real beef with the United States. They hated us, and they did so because we are big and powerful and sometimes careless with the lives of those who live in other countries. While it's true many didn't understand our motives or our values, understanding us wasn't going to cool them down. They were hopping mad. But we couldn't bear to think people didn't like us. So we misconstrued their rage and concluded, in another classic illustration of bias, this time of Confirmation Bias, that they had no reason to be mad at us.

6.

Not long after the Watergate burglary, the Republicans held their national convention in Miami to nominate Nixon for reelection. After he gave his acceptance speech, delegates and supporters in the hall were allowed to meet the president, who stood on stage as people, one by one, passed by to shake his hand. In the long line that immediately formed was a young man, all of seventeen years of age, from New Jersey. He had come to Miami without a ticket to the convention, but he had managed to wangle one that afternoon. "Mr. President, I'm a Democrat," the young man said when he got his turn. "But I am supporting you." Nixon looked a little flummoxed. Even though he was courting Democrats, he apparently wasn't expecting to be shaking hands with one at this point in the proceedings of the Republican convention.

That fall the young man went off to Vassar College, a bastion of liberalism. There he encountered students who despised Nixon. As the Watergate crisis unfolded they repeatedly piled argument upon argument based on well-established facts showing that Nixon was lying and covering up. Can you guess what happened? By this point it should not come as a surprise that the young man continued backing Nixon. In defiance of the school consensus, he stuck with Nixon through 1972 and 1973. Active in local New Jersey politics, he joined a pro-Nixon group, the local chapter of the Committee to Save the Presidency. He quickly was elected its vice president. Through the Watergate hearings, the Saturday Night Massacre (in which Nixon abused his power to have special prosecutor Archibald Cox fired), and all the rest, he stood by Nixon. Not until June 1974—little more than two months before Nixon resigned—did he finally become convinced that Nixon had been lying.

For years afterward that young man wondered why he had been so slow to face the truth. It haunted him. I should know. The seventeen-year-old student was me. The media had done their job. I had kept up on the news and watched the Watergate hearings attentively. And still I stuck with Nixon?

We shouldn't be surprised to learn that people don't like to face facts when those facts contravene their opinions. It's right there in the most hallowed papers produced by the Founding Fathers, the *Federalist Papers*. In "Federalist No. 10," the most celebrated of all the essays, James Madison observes: "As long as the connection subsists between his reason and his self-love, [man's] opinions and his passions will have a reciprocal influence on each other; and the former will be objects to which the latter will attach themselves." In other words, we love our own opinions because we love ourselves. And if those opinions conflict with the facts? We'll choose our own opinions.

But Madison did not quite grasp the mechanism in play here. As Harvard's Daniel Gilbert points out, we think we are right and others are wrong not because we love our own opinions but because we want to be right. Studies show that people who think they are right all the time do better in life. They suffer from less stress and enjoy better health. This is a critical factor in what he calls our psychological immune system.

Furthermore, we don't hold all of our opinions with equal fervor. We make distinctions. We hold some opinions more dearly than others. Psychologist Elliot Aronson demonstrated this in a famous study. Aronson recruited students—all women—to join a purportedly hot discussion group that promised to delve into the mysteries of sex. But before they could join they had to undergo an initiation rite. For some the rite was fairly innocuous. They had to read aloud a list of words with a sexual connotation, such as prostitute, virgin, and petting. The others went through a much more difficult rite. They had to say aloud in a public setting a dozen obscene words, including fuck, cock, and screw. This was in the 1950s. You can imagine how mortifying this was. Following their initiation, all of the women were allowed to join the discussion, which was already in progress. But when they did, they discovered this wasn't the fun and somewhat daring group they had been led to expect. The subject wasn't human sexuality, it was lower-order animal sexuality. And the other participants (confederates of the researcher) were dull. They spoke in a halting fashion and muttered. You could barely follow the conversation. What had promised to be an interesting experience turned out to be a deadly boring one. Afterward, the students were asked if they liked the group. Which ones would you guess said they did? It wasn't the women who had gone through the easy initiation. It was the ones who had been required to read swear words out loud, an experience that had left them embarrassed.

You would think the ones who went through the more troublesome initiation rite would be more upset and therefore more likely to denounce the group. They had a legitimate grievance. They had been conned into joining a group that wasn't what it was cracked up to be. Instead, they defended it. The explanation is really quite simple. Unlike the other young women who had gone through the easy initiation rite, they had gone through something of an ordeal. They couldn't just write off the experience with an *Oh well*. Saying swear words aloud in a public setting had been traumatic. At the end of the experiment they faced a classic moment of cognitive dissonance. On the one hand, they believed themselves to be smart. On the other, they knew that joining the group had been dumb. This left them in a tough spot. They could either admit to themselves that they weren't as smart as they thought they were, or they could maintain that the group actually lived up to its billing. How would you respond?

What Elliot Aronson's study proved was that cognitive dissonance isn't an equal opportunity phenomenon. Contrary to James Madison, we are not likely to defend all of our own opinions in the face of the facts. We are only likely to insist on our opinions when they involve our own feelings of self-worth. When a decision we make is a referendum on our status as a good and smart person, we are much more inclined to justify it. (The analysis is known as Justification Theory.) Under which circumstance is that likely to happen? When our holding an opinion comes at a cost, as mine did when I defended Nixon at liberal Vassar. As psychologist Carol Tavris puts it, the "more effort we put into something that turns out to be useless or harmful or just plain boring," the more we have to reduce the dissonance we feel—our conviction that we're smart and the reality that we "just put a whole lot of time, money, and effort into something that isn't worth it." The way we do that is by doubling down, defending our original decision to the hilt. That's what I did at Vassar. After a time the fight I was waging for Nixon wasn't about Nixon at all; it was about me.

It's no mystery, then, why voters postponed the day of reckoning as long as they could after the Watergate burglary. They couldn't abandon Nixon without indicting themselves. The election had ostensibly been a referendum on Nixon. But once people decided to support him it was a referendum on them too. For them, Watergate wasn't really about Nixon at all. It was about them. The more they defended Nixon, the more of a stake they had in his survival.

Politics is always about the voters. It's about how they feel. That is so obvious I hesitate to say it. But it's easy to forget. When a politician is about to go on camera, what does he do? He straightens his tie and combs his hair. The assumption he makes—and that we often make—is that an on-camera appearance is about the candidate. Actually, it's not. It's not about how he performs or looks or talks. It's not about how articulate he is. It's about how the people on the other end of the camera feel in his presence. Does he make them feel dumb or smart? Does he leave them feeling optimistic or pessimistic? Whether every hair on his head is in place or whether he chooses his syntax right does not really matter.

Campaigns should never be about the candidate. They should be about the voters. Barack Obama is said to believe that it was his story that got him elected. This is an error in sloppy thinking—because while stories are important to a leader's success, as we'll see, Obama was putting the focus wrongly on himself rather than the voters. While his story was compelling, it worked because it made white voters feel good about themselves. As the Hoover Institution fellow Shelby Steele astutely deduced, Obama made white people feel good about voting for a black man. Voting for Obama was more than a form of redemption for centuries of racism. It gave whites credit for the great racial progress that had been made since the days when Commissioner of Public Safety Bull Connor turned dogs loose on black children in Birmingham, Alabama. That's one of many reasons why Obama won.

Politics in the end is *always* about the voters. For eleven months, that worked in Richard Nixon's favor. Then, as the voters' assumptions about his innocence were washed away in what became a tidal wave of headlines about corruption and scandal, they abandoned him in droves. Finally, the truth mattered. What was the tipping point? A story about a college professor and his rowing crew helps provide the answer.

7.

When the political scientist George Marcus was in his forties doing what other political scientists at that age do—research and writing—he decided suddenly one day to do something a little odd. He and a colleague at Williams College decided to establish a rowing team. This wasn't what professors like Marcus, who was in the process of building a legendary national reputation, usually do. It frankly seemed a little crazy. As it turned out, it probably contributed more to his successful political science career than anything else he ever did.

When he started coaching rowers, Marcus admits, he wasn't very good. As a student at Columbia University decades earlier he had gone out rowing and loved it. Nearly every day he headed out to the Harlem River on the north end of Manhattan to row like crazy for hours and hours. Over time he became a good rower, though he was too small to try out for the Olympics. But it turned out that knowing how to row doesn't make you a good rowing coach. To be a good coach you have to get to know people and learn how to lead them. As he got into the job he discovered that it was really challenging. The job "wasn't just communicating information about the sport or the skills or the methods we were using," he recently recalled, "but teaching young athletes new to the sport and developing them so they could be ferocious when necessary and graceful and fluid when necessary. And all that required insight into the human psyche."

Six days a week, three hours a day, from 4 P.M. until 7 P.M., Marcus went out with his students on the water to train them. First, it was just men, then, later, women. He spent another hour doing scheduling, strategizing, and consoling. This went on for ten or eleven months, year in and year out, for thirteen years. It was, he admits, a great time suck.

Other political scientists thought they didn't have time for extracurricular activities. Marcus found he had to make time for them. What he was learning about human beings out on the water was as valuable, it turned out, as what he was learning in the library and the laboratory. He says it saved him from the fate of so many of his fellow social scientists, who regard themselves as knowledgeable about people because they study human beings in aggregate. Actually, he says, if you want to understand what drives people you have to get to know them. This sounds basic—of course you have to get to know them. So what was Marcus driving at? I wasn't sure.

Then he told me a story. It was about two rowers he had trained for the Olympics, Sue and Ann. Sue was a freshman, Ann a senior. Both were exceptional. But he pushed Ann, the older student, harder, so much harder that one day she came to his office and announced she was ready to quit. Marcus was taken aback. "What's all this about?" he asked. "You're a great athlete." "But you're always on my case, never on Sue's case," she said. The explanation was simple, Marcus explained. Sue is a young pup. She's got years ahead of her to make the Olympic team. But "I have to get everything out of you *now* because if you're going to have any hope of making the team you're going to make it by your fingernails," and it would have to be this year. The Olympics only come every four years. This was Ann's one shot.

I still wasn't sure what this had to do with political science. Marcus explained that it had everything to do with it. He and his colleagues had been doing political science wrong. From the time political science was established as a profession in the nineteenth century, it had become customary to ignore the role of emotion in politics. Instead, political scientists focused on things they could count and measure: voter turnout, public opinion, and the like. But what Marcus was learning about people by coaching his rowers was that emotion was key. If he was going to turn these students into Olympic-class athletes, "you have to explain what you're doing and why. They have to accept what you're doing. And if they don't, they're either going to do it grudgingly or not wholeheartedly or they're just going to quit and say, 'I don't know what you want me to do, but this isn't what I want to do.'"

Marcus says it began to strike him as weird that political scientists could ignore emotion. How on earth could they? As a student at Columbia he had been exposed to the school's famous Great Books program, which included classics such as *The Iliad*. The books all dealt with emotion. Scientific research on monkeys was showing that emotion is critical to their development. In one famous experiment in the 1950s, psychologist Harry Harlow gave monkey babies a choice between a fake monkey mother made out of wire mesh and one made out of terry cloth. Although the baby monkeys got food when they were with the wire-mesh figure, they naturally gravitated to the soft, cuddly, terry-cloth mother. And "we're a lot like monkeys," Marcus said.

So Marcus began studying emotion. This was in the mid-1980s. But he found he couldn't get funding for his projects. Worse, he couldn't get his papers published. "No one wanted to publish anything on emotion." You can see it still stings. Here he was, a college professor who'd graduated from Columbia and Northwestern who had gone on to become a postdoctoral fellow at Yale—and he couldn't get his papers on emotion published? Finally, one journal editor, out of the blue, decided in the late-1980s to accept one of the papers. Marcus, a bit shocked, asked why. "It's interesting," was the reply.

And that was the beginning. Slowly, Marcus found more allies who, in response to scientific findings we'll explore in a moment, were coming to the same conclusion that he was about the importance of emotion. Now, two decades later, emotion is firmly acknowledged as a key concern of political scientists. In part, it was because of the rowers, and in particular, because of Ann and Sue.

Ann didn't quit, by the way. And she made the US Olympic team. Unfortunately, at the last moment, she contracted a bad case of exercise-induced asthma and had to withdraw. Sue, who had years ahead of her to improve her skills, went on to become the captain of the Williams College rowing team. In 1980, she made the Olympic team too.

While Sue worked on her rowing, Marcus, along with a few colleagues, came up with a theory of emotion that helps explain why those American voters who took eleven months to abandon Nixon finally did so.

8.

One of the commonest criticisms of voters is that they are too emotional. As civics reformers like to say, what we need are rational voters. Indeed, it is hard to argue with that. After all, it's an idea with a long pedigree. The

Ancient Greeks wanted us to be rational. Descartes wanted us to be rational. If we were rational we would not have waited eleven long months before finally grasping the gravity of the charges being leveled at Richard Nixon. We would have gotten Watergate early on. Right?

It is common sense to think that emotion should be divorced from reason and can be. But that is not what science is finding. Common sense is wrong. The way the brain works, neuroscientists tell us, is that emotion and reason work together. You cannot separate them. The problem with those voters who waited eleven long months before finally deciding that Nixon had abused his office and violated their trust was not that they had been too emotional, but not emotional enough. They had left their reaction to Nixon on autopilot. Woodward and Bernstein had been breaking stories that should have made voters' hair stand on end. Instead, they barely took notice.

What was missing? Anxiety—one of our key emotions. Voters weren't anxious enough. Science has established that we digest information about the world in two ways, using System 1 or System 2. Because, as we learned earlier, most of what happens in the world is predictable, our brain mostly has to deal with challenges that are familiar. For this, System 1 is perfectly adequate. The way System 1 works is simple. It matches everything it encounters to a familiar pattern. In effect, our brain faces the same challenge as the contestants on the 1960s television game show *Concentration*, who had to guess what they were seeing by matching the fragments on the screen with the images already in their head. As with those contestants, our brain has to figure out if what it's seeing is a dog, a cat, a tree, or something else, using as a reference point its databank of memories. Success comes when it makes a match. The match doesn't have to be perfect. We don't need to match up a phantom "parti poodle" that we happen upon with a memory of one in our brain to know it's a poodle. Even if we have never before seen a poodle of that type (it's rare) we can still figure out it's a poodle. The brain performs this task so seamlessly, we aren't even aware of what it's doing. It just does it.

The brain uses the same system when performing motor functions. When you drink a cup of coffee you don't have to think about it. You don't have to consciously think about every step in the process as your fingers reach for the cup, grasp the handle, and bring it to your lips. Your unconscious brain, using a process known as the habit execution system, handles all of these actions seamlessly by matching what you want to do with a pattern of behavior you previously executed. It does this by using System 1, the system that Michael Jordan uses when he dunks a basketball. He does not consciously order his hands to reach for the ball while telling his legs to speed up as he makes his way down the court. He just automatically does these things. This is what athletes do. They practice like crazy so that when the ball is thrown to them they know what to do with it automatically. This is why practice makes perfect. The more we practice, the less we have to think consciously about what we're doing. We can just let our unconscious brain (System 1) take over. And because our unconscious brain works at a phenomenally faster speed than our conscious brain, we can perform at a level that seems superhuman. This is the miracle of System 1 thinking.

But the world isn't always predictable. That's why our brain is designed to pick out what's novel. A surveillance system in our brain is constantly searching the environment for anything that seems strikingly different from what it has encountered before. It's your surveillance system that goes into action when you see something you can't believe and your eyes widen to take in more of the scene, or you smell something that's a bit disturbing and your nostrils flare to give you a better sniff. Threats get particular attention. And when the surveillance system cannot find a match in its memory for what it has come across, it sends up a flare from the amygdala to our conscious brain to take notice, using System 2 to make sense of it. The emotion you feel when this happens is anxiety.

The reason those pro-Nixon voters took so long to come around to the obvious truth that Nixon was engaged in a cover-up of astonishing proportions was because for eleven months they did not feel anxious enough to revisit the assumptions they had made when deciding initially to vote for him. Flares went up. They were ignored. Not until the Watergate story snowballed with the resignations of Haldeman and Ehrlichman in the spring of 1973 did the avalanche of bad news finally trigger an amygdala reaction of sufficient force that it got voters to do what we humans hate to do: make the decision to change our minds. When exactly does this happen? George Marcus has discovered that it happens when the burden of hanging on to a belief becomes greater than the cost of changing it. That's one of the key findings of what's come to be known as the Theory of Affective Intelligence, the theory Marcus and his colleagues developed when they began studying emotion. Anxiety is particularly important because it's like acid. It eats through the rusting metal of our preconceptions.

What broke our rigid commitment to Nixon in the spring of 1973? What saved our democracy? The emotion of anxiety.

8

Everything
Happens for a Reason

It's not just kids who prefer fairy tales

1.

If I am correct that we crave predictability in politics, crave it above almost everything else, even the truth, this should be something everybody knows, shouldn't it? Any force as powerful as this must be in operation constantly. And yet we don't seem to realize it. How can that be?

The answer is simple. We do realize it. But we call it by another name: stories. Politicians are constantly telling us stories. What do stories do? They put us at ease. In a world where everything is constantly changing, they make things comprehensible. Think for a moment about Ronald Reagan. What was he renowned for? His stories. Jimmy Carter's record of high inflation and military ineptitude in the failed attempt to rescue the American hostages held in Iran had convinced millions that our day had passed. Once a great power, we were now in decline. Then Reagan took over and slowly people began to feel differently. They got their confidence back. What was the secret to Reagan's success? Was it just that he got inflation under control and built up the military? Probably not. A contributing factor was undoubtedly Reagan's success in weaving together a powerful story that made Americans feel good about themselves. He was a great cheerleader. And what made him one was his ability as a storyteller.

Reagan's presidency was just minutes old when he told us his first story as president of the United States. As he was nearing the end of his inaugural address on January 20, 1981, he regaled Americans with the story of one Martin Treptow, who was buried, Reagan indicated, at Arlington National Cemetery, a short distance beyond the great "monuments to heroism" on the Washington Mall, just across the way from where the crowd was gathered. Treptow was a small-town Iowa barber who in 1917 volunteered to fight in France in the 42nd Infantry's famous Rainbow Division. "There, on the western front, he was killed trying to carry a message between battalions under heavy artillery fire," Reagan related. What drew Reagan's attention to Treptow was a diary found on the dead soldier's body. "On the flyleaf under the heading, 'My Pledge,' he had written these words: 'America must win this war. Therefore I will work, I will save, I will sacrifice, I will endure, I will fight cheerfully and do my utmost, as if the issue of the whole struggle depended on me alone.'"

What was the point of the Treptow story? It was to reassure Americans that they had what it takes to confront the great challenges of the hour. "The crisis we are facing today," Reagan told them, "does not require of us the kind of sacrifice that Martin Treptow and so many thousands of others were called upon to make. It does require, however, our best effort and our willingness to believe in ourselves and to believe in our capacity to perform great deeds, to believe that together with God's help we can and will resolve the problems that now confront us."

Many people wondered who Martin Treptow was. Hardly anyone had ever heard of him. It turned out not even Reagan knew all that much about him. For one thing, he did not know where Treptow was actually buried. When researchers started digging they found out that Reagan had erred in indicating Treptow was buried under a marker at Arlington. As the *New York Times* reported the next day, he actually was laid to rest in Bloomer, Wisconsin. Thus did Reagan in his very first address to the nation get the facts wrong in one of his stories, something that was to happen constantly during his presidency. White House officials, thrown on the defensive, admitted that Reagan had made a mistake. But Reagan gave no hint of worrying, this or any other time, when he got the facts in a story wrong. Once he had a story in his head, aides often found they could not stop him from retelling the story, wrong facts and all, over and over again. Michael Deaver, the president's media maestro, said it was because Reagan could never believe that anyone could lie to him. Whatever the cause, aides lived in fear of his picking up a story that wasn't true. Reagan, they came to realize, had a particularly strong Perseverance Bias. Once he believed something, it was very hard to get him to stop believing it. But you know what? Americans did not care any more than Reagan did when he got the facts wrong in one of his stories. So the *New York Times* found he'd misconstrued the facts again? So what? All that mattered was the story, as Reagan speechwriter Peggy Noonan noted in her memoirs. It is not the truth we revere. It is stories.

Why do we like stories so much? Because they offer up something we pine for: plausible cause and effect. In a story 1+1=2. Things add up. Life becomes understandable. Often, stories pit good against evil, a formulation that is particularly appealing. What, after all, is more comprehensible than the forces of lightness and darkness battling it out? Children by the age of five grasp the concept, say developmental psychologists.

Years ago, the distinguished Harvard social scientist Howard Gardner wanted to discover what highly successful leaders have in common. After reviewing the lives of eleven luminaries, from Margaret Thatcher to Martin Luther King Jr., Gardner concluded that their success depended to a great deal on their ability to communicate a compelling story, "narratives that help individuals think about and feel who they are, where they come from, and where they are headed." These stories, he found, "constitute the single most powerful weapon in the leader's literary arsenal." And what did these stories in turn often share? A five-year-old's binary view of the world as a place of lightness and darkness. Why was that critical? Because, Gardner reported, "Adults never lose their sensitivity to these basic narratives."

It was no coincidence, Gardner suggested, that Reagan's Strategic Defense Initiative (SDI), a missile defense system, instantly came to be known as Star Wars. While his critics hoped to discredit SDI by associating it with a movie featuring a simple good-versus-evil formula, the imagery brilliantly worked in SDI's favor. Reagan, like Luke Skywalker, was fighting the good fight.

The reason stories are particularly attractive to leaders is that they are easily understood. Politics is about finding issues susceptible to public debate, issues that don't require a college education, which most voters lack. By using stories, especially children's stories that feature good guys and bad guys, politicians can reach 100 percent of the audience. How does a voter feel in the presence of a politician who bases his appeal on stories? Smart. For everybody understands stories. And as we learned earlier, what's important in politics is not what politicians look like or sound like, but how they make voters feel.

Stories are important in another way that's worth noting. Like myths (more on this later) they help us adapt and change. The historian Yuval Noah Harari asks us to imagine a woman born in Germany in 1900 who lives to 100. In the course of her single lifetime, she would have lived through the Hohenzollern Empire, the Weimar Republic, the Nazi Third Reich, the division of Germany into East and West Germany, and the unification of Germany. Despite living through "five very different sociopolitical systems," her DNA would have "remained exactly the same." What changed each time was not her or anybody's DNA, but the story citizens living under those systems believed about themselves. Change the story, and our behavior changes. Germans living under Hitler behaved differently than they do today.

One of our chief advantages over animals has to do with our storytelling (and story-believing) ability. Animals by and large do not change their behavior, and they certainly cannot do so quickly. They need thousands of years to evolve. We don't—and it's because of stories. We don't need to evolve to change. We can just tell ourselves a new story.

Politicians avail themselves of our susceptibility to stories by changing their own stories to suit our desires. If one election year what we seem to want is an outsider, they'll emphasize milestones in their life story that suggest they're outsiders. If four years later it seems more opportune for them to present themselves as experienced insiders, they'll simply rebrand themselves by changing their story.

Who wins elections? Well, that's another one of those complicated questions. But one of the factors that is often critical is the ability of a politician to tell a convincing story. The reason for this is that stories unify us. A politician with a compelling story can unite people behind him or her.

Why does this work? What is it about humans and stories?

2.

Imagine, for a moment, four common geometric shapes: two triangles (a small one and a large one), a small circle, and a giant rectangle with a flap on one end that opens like a door. Not very exciting, is it? Brain scans show that when we look at still images like these, our brain slips into a state of inactivity. But what happens when you add movement, crashing the triangles into each other as they buzz around madly, in and out of the giant rectangle? In a landmark study in the 1940s psychologists Fritz Heider and Marianne Simmel decided to find out. They showed a two-and-a-half-minute movie featuring the triangles, the circle, and the rectangle to several groups of students. (You can watch the movie yourself on YouTube. Google "Triangle Experiment 1944.") Most interesting is what happened with the first group of thirty-four undergraduates who were asked to describe what they saw because, unlike the subsequent groups, they weren't coached. In the professors' paper you can read the students' responses. One student is matter of fact: "A large solid triangle is shown entering a rectangle. It enters and comes out of this rectangle, and each time the corner and one-half of one of the sides of the rectangle form an opening. . . ." And so on, in her dreary way. Zzzzz. But she is the only one who uses neutral language to describe what she sees.

How do most of the others interpret what they are seeing? They explain the movements of the triangles and circle as if they are people. Typical of the responses is one in which a student perceives the movement of the triangles and the circle as two men fighting over a woman. "A man has planned to meet a girl and the girl comes along with another man. The first man tells the second to go; the second tells the first, and he shakes his head. Then the two men have a fight, and the girl starts to go into the room to get out of the way and hesitates and finally goes in." The student goes on and on in this vein, describing each action sequence in similar terms. The two men chase each other around. One becomes so "blinded by rage and frustration" after the woman decides to leave that he smashes the walls of the house (the rectangle) until they collapse.

What does this sound like? It has all the ingredients of a story, right? The student's natural reaction to a film featuring the movement of geometric shapes was to turn it into a daytime soap opera—all this from a little movie featuring triangles and a circle. Is this not a little odd? It is.

It is important to acknowledge that the triangle experiment, suggestive as it was, did not prove anything. And it certainly did not prove that we are wired to invent and consume stories, but proof was coming. . . .

IN 1962, A PATIENT KNOWN AS W. J. underwent an operation that had rarely been performed on a human being. W. J. had been a soldier during World War Two. On an unsuccessful bombing run over the Netherlands in 1944 his parachute failed to open properly, plunging him to the ground. He broke his leg and lost consciousness. Discovered by the enemy, he was sent to a prison camp, where he was beaten over the head with the butt of a rifle. Over the course of the following months he lost a hundred pounds and nearly starved to death. After the war he returned to civilian life and took a job as a clerk. He regained his weight, but he never became his old self. Then, around six years after the war, he began suffering from long blackouts. Once he got in his car and drove fifty miles, but when he arrived he did not know how he had gotten there. During blackouts, he'd scream, "Bail out, Jerry!" He also began having seizures.

As the years went by his symptoms grew worse and worse. By the late-1950s, he was going into convulsions two or three times a day. The seizures were so terrible he often fell and injured himself. He couldn't hold a job. Life was miserable. When he could take it no longer he decided to subject himself to experimental surgery that doctors hoped would limit the seizures. The plan was to split his brain into two parts, dividing the left hemisphere from the right hemisphere, by literally cutting the thick thatch of neural fibers known as the corpus callosum that connect them.

This was a radical approach. Although it had been tried on a few dozen people in the 1940s and 1950s after an epileptic patient, who had developed a tumor in his corpus callosum, got relief from his seizures—leading doctors to suspect that major epileptic attacks could be held off if the overstimulated neurons firing in one hemisphere could be stopped from triggering overstimulation in the other one by severing the two halves of the brain—the operation was still considered experimental and dangerous. One doctor had reported that his patients suffered no ill effects. But another stopped performing the procedure. Colleagues said he came to regret what he had done to his patients. The operation was just too invasive. You can understand his apprehension. The procedure involves cutting 200 million nerve fibers. Furthermore, scientists performing experiments on monkeys reported that the animals had trouble afterward with coordination. Nobody therefore really knew what would happen when W. J. underwent what came to be called split-brain surgery, a name that suggests just how extreme the surgery is. He and the nine other similarly desperate people in California who agreed to the operation were more than normal patients. They were guinea pigs—desperate guinea pigs.

W. J.'s surgery took place on February 4, 1962, at White Memorial Hospital in Los Angeles. His was the first one and it was a great success. His seizures stopped cold. For the first time in years he was no longer falling down. To anyone coming upon him, he seemed normal. He could speak. He could walk. He had focus. But like the monkeys that had undergone split-brain surgery he had trouble with coordination. He couldn't get his left and right hands to work together. He literally had to sit on his left hand to stop it from interfering with the movement of his right hand. This was because each hand (like each eye) is controlled by only one hemisphere, and with his corpus callosum severed, the left and right hemispheres were no longer communicating. In effect, he was afflicted with what might be called bureaucratism: his left hand did not know what his right hand was doing.

Testing revealed another curious anomaly. When the scientists showed him a spoon visible only to his right eye, he said he was able to see the spoon, which suggested that the hemisphere that controls his right eye was working properly. But when they showed the spoon to his left eye (controlled by his other hemisphere), he said he didn't see it. He said he saw nothing even as he was staring straight at the spoon. Did this mean the hemisphere that controlled his left eye was broken? Could he really not see the spoon?

To find out, the scientists conducted another test. They gave him a Morse code key and told him to strike it using his left hand (which, like his left eye, was controlled by the same hemisphere) when they flashed a light in his left eye. Then they flashed the light. If he hit the key it meant the hemisphere was working. They flashed the light and he hit the key. It *was* working. But then they asked him to tell them what he saw. He said he saw nothing. *Nothing?* We know he had seen the flash of light because when he saw it he tapped the Morse code key, but when you asked him he said he hadn't. Here is what was going on. He saw the light, but he couldn't *say* he saw it because he saw it with his right hemisphere and the speech center is in the left one. What this taught the scientists was that though the hemispheres were working properly, they couldn't communicate. In effect, the patient had two brains.

This became relevant a few years later when the scientists ran more tests, this time with split-brain patients on the East Coast, and another anomaly surfaced. This one was downright bizarre. Using a special device that limited what split-brain patient P. S. could see with each eye, they flashed an image of a chicken claw to his left hemisphere and a snow scene to his right. Then they presented him with a bunch of cards with pictures on them that they allowed him to see with both eyes, just as he normally would. They asked him to pick the single picture that seemed to match the images of a claw and a shovel, which he had just seen. It was like a child's quiz where you are asked to say which objects go together. Each of his hands went for different cards. His left hemisphere had seen a chicken claw and now the hand controlled by the same hemisphere went for a picture of a chicken. That made sense. Chicken and chicken claw go together. His right hemisphere had seen a snow scene and now the hand controlled by the right hemisphere went for a picture of a shovel. That also made sense. Snow and shovel go together. So far, so good. Each hemisphere, working separately (just as W. J.'s had), worked properly.

But then the scientists asked P. S. *why* he chose the chicken and the shovel. This is where things got interesting. This is how neuropsychologist Michael Gazzaniga, who designed the experiment, describes what happened when they asked P. S. why he made the choice he'd made: "His left-hemisphere speech center replied, 'Oh, that's simple. The chicken claw goes with the chicken,' easily explaining what it knew. It had seen the chicken claw." But looking down at the shovel in his other hand, "without missing a beat, he said, 'And you need a shovel to clean out the chicken shed.'"

What? That wasn't why he had picked the shovel. He had selected the shovel because the shovel went with the snow scene, which he had seen with his right hemisphere. But his speech center did not know what had been happening in the right hemisphere. It's in the left hemisphere. So what was his left hemisphere doing when it paired up the shovel and the chicken and P. S. announced, "you need a shovel to clean out the chicken shed"? The left hemisphere, not knowing what the right hemisphere knew, was putting the facts available as it knew them into a context that would explain them. Here is Gazzaniga again: "[The left hemisphere] interpreted the response in a context consistent with what it knew, and all it knew was: chicken claw. It knew nothing about the snow scene, but it had to explain the shovel. . . . Well, chickens do make a mess, and you have to clean it up. Ah, that's it! Makes sense. What was interesting was that the left hemisphere did not say, 'I don't know,' which truly was the correct answer. It made up a post-hoc answer that fit the situation."

In a subsequent experiment with another split-brain subject, Gazzaniga flashed a picture of a naked woman on a computer screen. The subject, a woman, chuckled. When she was asked why, she said, "I don't know . . . nothing . . . oh—that funny machine." That was odd. The picture had been flashed to the patient's right hemisphere. Her left hemisphere had no idea why she had just laughed. But it quickly came up with an answer that sounded reasonable.

What had the brain in these split-brain patients done? Using what Gazzaniga calls our Interpreter, it had confabulated. That is, it had made up a story. It assembled the information it had access to and built a little story around it.

In some people, confabulating is the result of a clinical condition known as Wernicke's encephalopathy, which is associated with brain damage caused by a deficiency of vitamin B1, which is often the result of severe alcoholism. In others the condition is caused by damage to the ventro-medial prefrontal cortex. Whatever the specific cause, in extreme cases patients afflicted with the disorder make claims that are demonstrably untrue. In one recent paper, scientists reported that a retired psychiatrist who was in therapy "after rupture of aneurysm of the anterior communicating artery, was convinced that she was actually working as a psychiatrist at our clinic and repeatedly left therapy sessions in the conviction that she had to see patients. A young lawyer, suffering from limbic encephalitis, desperately searched for her files, convinced that she was expected at court." What went wrong in these patients was that the mechanism in the brain that filters fantasy from reality malfunctioned. The two got mixed up. But you don't have to have suffered brain damage to be susceptible to confabulation. Gazzaniga's split-brain experiments show that confabulation isn't a design flaw. It's another feature. We make up stories to make the world make sense. And we do this because we are hardwired to do it.

Thanks to the Interpreter we are born storytellers. It's no wonder those students viewing the short film featuring geometric shapes turned it into a soap opera. This is what our brain does. While we possess the ability to get at the truth of things, our brain is not biased in favor of the truth. It is biased in favor of stories that make the world comprehensible. In fact, we are so eager to find patterns, says Gazzaniga, that experiments show we will predict that something will happen based on a detected pattern when there's no pattern at all. And because pattern detecting is most highly developed in humans, we'll make this mistake but animals won't.

This really does sound like a design flaw. But it isn't. We see patterns constantly because seeing patterns by and large proved helpful as we evolved. As the science writer Michael Shermer observes: "We are the descendants of those who were most successful at finding patterns. This process is called *association learning* and is fundamental to all animal behavior, from *C. elegans* to *H. sapiens*." The ability to discern difficult-to-find patterns is not only what distinguishes humans from other animals, but also highly creative humans from less creative humans. Seeing patterns is what helps make creative people particularly creative. Where an ordinary person sees just noise, a genius is able to pick out a signal in the noise that's telling.

What distinguishes the brain of the ordinary person from that of the genius? Well, that's yet another of those complicated questions. But one of the distinguishing characteristics is an abundance of dopamine transmitters. The more dopamine in our brain the more likely we are to see patterns. Too little dopamine and you fail to see patterns you should. Too much dopamine and you see patterns that don't exist. Do you know people like that? I do. It's the dopamine in their brain that's likely responsible.

What happens when we see a pattern that doesn't exist? That is, what happens when we get a false positive, what statisticians call a Type 1 error? In the modern world the consequences can be disastrous. You go to the doctor to be tested for AIDS fearing the worst. A few days later you get a call telling you the test was positive and you freak out. But then it turns out, whoops, the test was wrong. You're not infected. Terrible, right? But when hunter-gatherers got a false positive it usually didn't matter. It simply meant there wasn't a snake behind a rock or a lion hiding in a clump of trees. No snake or lion? No matter. You just went on your way. The error was of such little consequence, says Shermer, that we "did not evolve a baloney-detection network in the brain to distinguish between true and false patterns. We have no error-detection governor to modulate the pattern-recognition engine."

This begins to explain why we have such a strong positive reaction to politicians who tell stories. Our brain doesn't immediately distinguish between a true story or a false one. It just hears a story and immediately thinks, *Hey, a story! I love stories.* That gives story-telling politicians a huge advantage over politicians who don't tell stories—and over us. We're so hungry for stories our instinct is to sit in rapt attention when we hear one.

We actually have a chemical reaction in our brain to stories. Recent experiments show that when we see something that triggers a story in our brain, our brain activity goes up. The more action there is in a story, the more chemical reactions there are. All stories, however, are not alike. Our brain distinguishes between positive stories—the kind politicians tell about themselves—and negative stories. Stories that trigger an empathetic reaction lead to the release of oxytocin, the love hormone we encountered earlier. Stories that make us fret and worry lead to the release of cortisol, the stress hormone. Stories, in other words, change the brain. When we take in ordinary information like the instructions on a tube of toothpaste, our brain does not produce either oxytocin or cortisol. It's bored by it. Our brain, in effect, processes stories differently than it processes information. It is not neutral about stories. It privileges stories.

The more complicated the world seems, the more desperate we become for stories to help us make sense of things. And the world increasingly seems more complicated. Even the things we credit with improving our lives, such as Google or other search engines, often contribute to the feeling that life has become unbearably confusing. Google doesn't just do things for us, it does things to us. On the one hand, it's given us instant access to all of the world's knowledge. You can sit at your desk at home and come into contact with a thousand cultures with very different values. On the other, it's exposed us to knowledge from which we were mainly shielded in the past. At any moment we are just one or two clicks away from content that not long ago would have been declared pornographic or seditious. What that does to us is unclear, but by giving us the choice to explore worlds previously closed to us, Google is forcing us to make more decisions. Any one of these decisions can affect our self-identity, whether it's a decision to visit a site about ancient Greek pederasty or the Ku Klux Klan. In the process of satisfying our curiosity we are making a statement not only about our obsessions and our interests, but ourselves. This can be a little unnerving.

The more complicated things become, the more we gravitate to stories that help ground us—just as we opt for name brands in the grocery store when faced with more choices than we feel comfortable making. This is one reason we have become more partisan. As moral clarity recedes and the old verities begin to crumble, we take refuge in our partisan identities, which put at our disposal handy, ready-made stories to help explain what makes the world tick. When the economy began to totter in 2008, Democrats didn't have to wonder who was to blame. The party, recycling a story from the last depression, had an immediate answer: it was greedy bankers. Republicans had their own quick response: Congress, interfering with the free marketplace, had pressured the government-subsidized mortgage lenders, Freddie Mac and Fannie Mae, to loosen standards so poor people could buy houses they couldn't really afford. This was a twofer. It played on Republicans' conviction that government is bad while reinforcing the impression that poor people receive benefits they don't deserve.

A few years ago the historian Rick Perlstein edited a collection of the writings of Richard Nixon. In an editor's note, he observes that "the opening passages of Nixon's memoir put several Nixonian traits on full display." But one trait was "most neglected," he notes. This was the trait that accounted for Nixon's "consistent ability to connect with ordinary voters despite his oft-remarked personal awkwardness." Which trait was that? His ability to tell stories. "Nixon was an outstanding storyteller." This is a useful talent in a president. Among the hats they wear—commander-in-chief, moral leader-in-chief, teacher-in-chief—few are more important than storyteller-in-chief.

Heading into the election of 1972, Nixon had a story that made sense to the American people. He had restored America. He had helped ease Cold War tensions by going to China and the Soviet Union, put America on the road to peace in Vietnam, and cracked down on war protesters and urban rioters. Watergate wasn't part of that story and they ignored it. They explained away any facts that didn't fit the narrative in their heads. That was easier than coming up with a new narrative. Unlike P. S. they were not yet forced to confront the evidence of Watergate as he had been forced to confront the picture of the shovel he was literally holding in his hand.

It turns out there was yet another reason for voters not to take Watergate seriously. It has to do with the power of myths.

3.

In the spring of 1964, leading up to the decision to make the Vietnam War *our* war, the Joint Chiefs of Staff arranged for a war game to test the strategy the United States was contemplating using. The name of the war game was SIGMA I-64. Fifty-six policymakers, drawn from the top echelons of the CIA, the White House, and the Defense Department, participated. They were divided into four teams. The Blue Team represented the United States and South Vietnam. The Red Team represented North Vietnam, the Viet Cong (VC), and the Pathet Lao. The Yellow Team represented Communist China. A Control Team represented everybody else in the world: European allies, the Soviet Union, the United Nations, and the American people—a real multicultural grab bag if ever there was one. Exceptional attention was paid to the execution of the game, down to the decision to require the Blue Team to use Blue paper, the Red Team to use Pink paper, and the Yellow Team to use yellow paper. Twenty military officials, including a rear admiral and several colonels, were assigned to assist the teams.

The goal of the game was to determine how the different teams would react if the United States began aggressively trying to undermine the Viet Cong through a policy of gradual escalation. Gradual escalation was considered the prudent course. It would be less likely than other strategies to lead to an all-out war, which could draw the Chinese directly into the fight. But would gradual escalation work? Would the North Vietnamese reduce their support of the VC? Would the VC melt away? In war you can never accurately predict how the enemy will respond, but war games are used to try to figure out that response as best as humanly possible. It's the way war planners get inside the heads of their opponents. War games are designed, in effect, to blunt Projection Bias, the mistake people make when they project their own perspective on others, as we saw earlier. To protect yourself from the bias, you put yourself in your enemy's shoes.

SIGMA I-64, which was sponsored by the War Games Agency, began on April 6, 1964, at 1300 hours. It was held in the Pentagon in room 1D965A. It lasted three days, ending on April 9 at 1800 hours. So what happened? The game began with the Blue Team (United States) increasing pressure on North Vietnam through covert cross-border attacks by on-the-ground commandos. In response, the Red Team (North Vietnam, VC) stepped up its attacks, shooting down American planes, firing on US personnel and their dependents. This in turn led the Blue Team to amp up its attacks against North Vietnam. Air Force pilots were ordered to bomb the North. Navy teams were told to mine the North's ports and harbors.

Back and forth it went, an attack by one side inspiring a counterattack by the other, leading to a gradual escalation of violence, as the United States held to a tit-for-tat strategy. The longer the war went on the worse the American position became. Not only did the North Vietnamese not back down, they actually increased their support of the VC, who in turn ramped up their attacks. In consequence world opinion began swinging sharply against the United States, perceiving it to be the aggressor. At home public opinion was split. Fearing he was losing control of the situation, the president then went to Congress to ask for a joint resolution authorizing him to use the armed forces of the United States to repel aggressive action by the communist nations in Southeast Asia.

Does this sound familiar? It is eerily similar to what was to actually happen, as one historian notes. Sigma I-64 was like the coming attraction of a terrible horror movie. Coming to a theater near you: the Vietnam War, in all its misery. In its final report, the War Games Agency even warned that public opinion at home and abroad would decisively move against the United States "if the cover for US participation is thin—so thin as to resemble cynical aggression." What happened three months later? President Lyndon Johnson went to Congress to get a joint resolution allowing him to take military action against the communist powers in Southeast Asia after a US destroyer operating in the Tonkin Gulf said it had been fired upon in two separate attacks by the North Vietnamese. This was exactly the thin cover for war that SIGMA I-64 had warned against. As soon became clear, there had not even been a second attack. The radar that picked up signs of ships and gunfire had malfunctioned in bad weather. Johnson later confided to aides: "For all I know, our navy was shooting at whales out there."

Although in the war game's final report officials had held out the hope that the policy of gradual escalation could be made to succeed, the evidence provided in the body of the document offered convincing proof that this was unlikely. Barring some unforeseen lucky breaks, gradual escalation would not work. North Vietnam would continue to provide support to the VC. The VC would continue to operate. World opinion would swing against us. At home Americans would grow disconsolate. In short, we would lose the Vietnam War.

SIGMA I-64 was meticulously designed. Its execution was flawless. Enormous resources were expended on it, including 900 man-hours involving many of the government's most senior officials. At its end, the War Games Agency produced an impressive report carefully documenting the steps each team had taken as the game unfolded, providing an astonishingly accurate forecast of what likely would happen if the policy of gradual escalation were implemented. The report was distributed to each of the fifty-six participants. A cover letter commending their work was attached to the report. The chairman of the Joint Chiefs of Staff, Maxwell D. Taylor, signed it.

And then it was ignored. President Johnson was not told about the results. Policymakers decided in the coming months to adopt gradual escalation as official US policy in Vietnam.

In September 1964, the War Games Agency, at the behest of Walt Rostow, one of President Johnson's key war advisors, decided to rerun the game.
Rostow believed the first game had turned out badly for the United States
because the Blue Team (United States) had made several wrong assumptions. The new game, which included fresh instructions for the Blue Team,
was called SIGMA II-64. Once again, top officials from the government
were asked to set aside their regular schedule to allow full participation. The
list included: McGeorge Bundy, the national security advisor; his brother
William Bundy, deputy secretary of state; John McCone, the director of the
CIA; John McNaughton, assistant secretary of defense; and Cyrus Vance,
deputy secretary of defense. The game began on September 8. This time it
went on for nine days instead of three, signaling a more intense commitment by the government to the game.

Once again the Blue Team, representing the United States, employed
the strategy of gradual escalation—the policy the United States was in the
process of adopting. Once again the policy failed to deter Hanoi from supporting the VC. And once again the VC, in response to the Blue Team's
campaign, increased its attacks. In the final report it was established that
bombing North Vietnam largely did not work because North Vietnam was
an agricultural society. Bombing rice fields did not produce results. There
simply were not enough good targets to justify the hopes war planners invested in bombing. The Joint Chiefs had come up with a list of ninety-four
targets. These included communication lines, military installations, factories, and the like. But even if you bombed every last one of those targets
you could not stop the North from supplying the VC with arms or soldiers.

The US government had run a second war game testing the assumptions that the policy of gradual escalation was based on. For a second time,
the evidence suggested the United States, following that policy, would be
unable to stop Hanoi from supporting the Viet Cong. In effect, the policy
would lead to our losing the Vietnam War. But, once again, the outcome of
the game was ignored.

This is beginning to sound dreary—and it gets worse. In 1965, the
Pentagon went through the whole exercise again. And once again officials
reached the same conclusion they had earlier. Using gradual escalation, we'd
lose the war. This made three times that we lost the Vietnam War. *Three
times.* Not that we admitted this as such. Not once in any of the war games
was the truth stated this baldly. But the implication was there. Gradual

escalation did not work. You could bomb Hanoi over and over again and not succeed in stopping its support for the VC. And yet, while we were discovering this at these war games, we went ahead and adopted this same, deeply flawed, policy.

It sounds ludicrous, but that's precisely what happened. There is no ambiguity about this because Robert McNamara, the secretary of defense, admits to it in his memoirs. He includes a quote from the final report of the SIGMA II-65 game that expressly acknowledged that bombing Hanoi would not work. Here is what the report said, as quoted by McNamara in his book: "There was considerable feeling . . . that [the] punishment being imposed could and would be absorbed by the Hanoi leadership . . . based on the fact that the country is basically a subsistence economy centering on the self-sustaining village. . . . Industrial activities constitute such a limited portion of the total economy that even [its] disruption seemed an acceptable price" to pay. Does this seem in any way ambiguous? Go ahead and bomb, but it won't succeed?

The war games of 1964 and 1965 were designed to give policymakers insight into the mind of the enemy. The games did that and did it superbly. This wasn't a situation in which policymakers were caught off guard. Going into the war, they knew—*they knew!*—that bombing North Vietnam would not stop the VC from operating in South Vietnam. And still they went ahead and bombed.

In his memoirs, McNamara says flatly that the SIGMA II-65 "report's conclusions disturbed me greatly." But then he confirms what the record demonstrates. He writes that the report "seemed to have little impact on others in the Pentagon and elsewhere in the government." McNamara suggests this was because in August 1965 the news from Vietnam was encouraging. In our first major engagement with the forces of the VC we decisively defeated them. But this does not explain why, when things started to go wrong, which they did shortly afterward, the Pentagon continued to ignore the lesson of its own war games.

And it doesn't explain the similarly docile response to the SIGMA war games in 1964, the year before, when events on the ground seemed as if they were careening out of control. Then, too, policymakers ignored the games. In his unpublished memoirs, William Bundy, the deputy secretary of state, admits to bafflement that the games were treated with such insouciance. "At a distance of several years, the account of this may seem astounding," he concedes. "I wish I could recall or accurately state its impact at the time. On me it simply was not great, and I find others felt the same way."

What then accounts for the indifference? Clearly, policymakers showed signs of plain old biased thinking. Their own war games provided evidence that their favored policy would not work, so they ignored the evidence, even though they themselves generated it. This is as clear a case of Disconfirmation Bias as one is likely to find. They also were guilty of Projection Bias. They insisted on believing that North Vietnam would eventually change its behavior in response to a massive bombing campaign because that is what they imagined we would do under the same circumstances. As Lt. Gen. Andrew Goodpaster, in a harsh protest to McNamara in 1964, warned: "Sir, you are trying to program the enemy and that is one thing we must never try to do. We can't do his thinking for him." But even conceding the impact of both Disconfirmation Bias and Projection Bias, something else undoubtedly affected policymakers. And that was their belief that in the end the United States, with all its superior technology and power, simply could not fail. Failure was unimaginable. No matter what their own reports indicated, they could not accept the fact that the United States could lose a war in Vietnam once it became committed to military victory.

This reflects more than a cognitive bias or two. It is wholesale blindness. What could account for this? A myth. In this case, the myth was that an all-powerful superpower that had won World War Two and had never lost a war in its history simply could not lose the war in Vietnam. Losing was inconceivable. Looked at from this perspective, Vietnam was a disaster because of a myth.

This may sound like an exaggeration. But when you consider the important role myths play, is it really an exaggeration to think that a myth could so shape our understanding of an event as to make us blind to what should have been self-evident? What a myth is, after all, is nothing more than a glorified pattern to which we attach special meanings. And we know how the brain loves patterns. Being smart is no protection against a myth. All you need to be susceptible is to be human. Indeed, the smarter you are the more likely it is that you possess the genes that produce the extra dopamine in the brain that enhances pattern-finding abilities. (That's because, as I noted earlier, dopamine is associated with creativity.) This may mean—I am clearly speculating here—that smart people are particularly vulnerable to mythmaking. They perhaps see patterns the rest of us don't—and leap to conclusions they shouldn't. If true, that would help explain why so many really smart people in high positions in the government were blind to the folly of Vietnam. No matter the facts, they saw patterns in high body counts and large bombing runs and other "hard" data that struck them as highly significant—signs that we were winning the war, and in the process fulfilling our American destiny, when the truth was we often were barely maintaining the status quo. In short, a surfeit of dopamine may be a contributing reason for the best and the brightest leading us into the worst foreign policy disaster in our history. Whether that's true or not is unknowable, but we can be sure of one thing: the myth of American omnipotence had dangerous consequences whether bright people were particularly vulnerable to it or not.

4.

Think of all the ways our lives and culture are defined by myths. The Virgin Birth? A myth. The British Stiff Upper Lip? Myth. William Tell? Myth. Everywhere around us, in all directions, in all aspects of life, there are myths. When the president of the United States invokes freedom, he's laying claim to a myth. When we speak of George Washington, what do we have in mind? Not the man, but the monument. Pilgrims landing at Plymouth Rock? Betsy Ross making the first American flag? The Liberty Bell tolling to signal independence? They're all myths. Every society on earth has these so-called Foundation Myths (that have to do with origins) and many others. The universality of myths suggests they are one of our most significant evolved psychological mechanisms. This goes far toward explaining one of the most troubling facts historians have uncovered about myths: they don't die. They just go into hibernation, ready to spring back to life when circumstances become favorable. Take Joseph Stalin. He was officially repudiated by the Soviet Union shortly after his death in 1953. His horrors were fully exposed. But on the sixtieth anniversary of his death, who did Russians tell pollsters was the greatest Russian leader in history? Joseph Stalin. It's not the man Russians were celebrating. It was the myth of the Great Leader. In myths, fact and fable get all mixed up. The facts are incidental. What counts is the meaning the myths have for the people who believe them.

Americans, like others, are susceptible to myths. The reason for this is that myths serve the same purpose for us as they do for others. As the psychologist Jonathan Haidt points out, myths bind groups together. They bind the hive. Myths bring us closer. As a heterogeneous society we have more of a need for myths than homogenous societies. Unlike most people around the world, our history is short—so short, we have not had time to meld into a single people with a common culture. We come from everywhere. Unlike, say, the Germans or the French, we have not lived in the same place for thousands of years. Nor do we share a common tribal identity. *E pluribus unum?* Out of many one? That is what we like to believe, but it's not really true. What unites us is not a common identity but a loose set

of beliefs. This is why myths are so appealing to Americans. They help an-
swer the burning question, to quote the eighteenth-century French émigré
writer J. Hector St. John de Crèvecoeur: "What then, is this new man, the
American?" Two centuries on we still aren't sure, but a clue is in our myths.
Our myths make us, us. We therefore cling to them and can't give them up.
It's who we are. Myths are so important to us that writers and intellectuals
after the Revolution set themselves on a conscious path of mythmaking.
This was to create an authentic American identity. They did not want children growing up on the stories of Robin Hood and Sherwood Forest. They
wanted children to learn American stories. The story of Paul Revere did
not become part of American culture by accident. Longfellow wrote a poem
about him. Plymouth Rock became iconic because Daniel Webster gave a
famous speech about it. Why do we have myths, after all? They tell us who
we are and what values we cherish.

That is why we see such fierce battles over figures like Christopher Columbus and holidays like Christmas. They have become part of American
mythology. We define ourselves by these myths. Plymouth Rock, Betsy
Ross, the Liberty Bell—these are part of the bedrock foundations of American culture. We take them seriously. So when critics challenge Columbus's
virtue and Christmas's universality, many Americans naturally recoil. It's
not the myths that they are defending. It's themselves. Myths R Us.

Is it surprising, then, that when policymakers confronted evidence of a
loss in Vietnam, they went beyond discounting the evidence in front of
them to ignoring it so completely that in retrospect they could not remember what their reaction to the war games was? What did William Bundy say?
"I wish I could recall or accurately state its impact at the time. On me it simply was not great, and I find others felt the same way." William Bundy, by all
accounts, was brilliant. A historian by training, he followed his government
service with a post at Princeton. But he confessed he could not remember
his reaction to war games in which he participated for days on end. He, like
his colleagues, was beholden to the myth of American omnipotence. It's
no puzzle why officials ignored the import of their own war games. Given
the pervasiveness of the myth they were operating under, the real surprise
would have been if they had chosen to act on the evidence before them.

After Watergate a lot of Washington journalists who had been slow to
come to grips with the scandal, happily leaving the field to Woodward and
Bernstein to plow, asked themselves why they had been so slow. The answer
many settled on was that they had suffered from a lack of imagination. They
could not imagine a president doing what Nixon was accused of doing.
"To me, a hard-bitten cynical reporter, it boggled the mind to think that a

president could be involved in a crime like that," reflected Jack Nelson, the Washington Bureau Chief of the *Los Angeles Times*. "Most of the reporters felt that way." Why is that? A myth got in the way of them doing their job. The myth of the American presidency. Nixon's actions seemed wholly inconsistent with that myth.

It wasn't just DC journalists who were under the spell of the myth of the presidency. So were most voters. They found it beguiling. This is yet another reason it took them eleven months to come to grips with the evidence that Nixon had lied and covered up. They couldn't jettison Nixon without jettisoning the myth of the presidency. Instinct stopped them.

9

It's Like It
Was Still 1974

*Why people make arguments so transparently
feeble they leave others dumbstruck*

1.

Timothy Naftali hadn't been head of the Nixon Presidential Library for
long when one day it dawned on him that something was wrong. Naftali
is a historian, and in 2007 he was appointed by the National Archives
and Records Administration to be the first director of the library after
the Nixon Foundation turned over control of the institution to the federal
government. He is prematurely balding, doesn't appear to get much sun
though he's spent years in California, and speaks in full sentences. If you
have a mental image of a historian, he probably fits it. Like most historians he sees parallels with the past everywhere he looks. When he hears a
president give a speech he thinks of half a dozen speeches other presidents
have given on the same subject. When Congress passes major legislation
he instantly finds himself comparing it with the legislation of previous
Congresses. And after just a short time at the Nixon Library he began to
understand something about the people who ran the Nixon Foundation.
They didn't just see parallels with the past as he did. They were stuck in
the past. The calendar read 2007, but for them it was still 1974, the year
Nixon resigned from office.

This was strange, but it began to seem undeniable. The evidence for it
just kept popping up. All you had to do was look at the exhibit on Watergate.

153

The Watergate exhibit, which had been built for the library's debut in 1990, opened with the true statement that Nixon had no advance knowledge of the plan to bug the Democratic National Committee headquarters. But almost everything that followed was untrue, unsupported, or misleading. It was "terrible," says Naftali. "It couldn't be in a federal institution. It was biased. It was a continuation of the cover-up, a product of spin." Why had the break-in been ordered? Because John Mitchell, the former attorney general who served as the campaign chairman, wasn't minding the store on account of his "colorful wife"—which conveniently overlooked the fact that breaking and entering had by then been endorsed several times by Nixon himself to get dirt on liberals and leftwing radicals. Whether Nixon knew in advance of the effort to dig up dirt on the Pentagon Papers leaker Daniel Ellsberg—the White House Plumbers broke into his psychiatrist's office—is unproven, though the head of the operation said Nixon did. But the exhibit didn't mention the Ellsberg break-in at all. Why did Nixon order the CIA to stop the FBI investigation? That was the fault of John Dean, the White House counsel. Dean had suggested it to White House Chief of Staff Bob Haldeman, who had passed along the suggestion to Nixon, and "Nixon agreed"—which made it sound like Dean and Haldeman were responsible, not Nixon.

There was no hint that this was the start of the cover-up and that it was a federal crime—obstruction of justice—one of the central offenses for which the president would face impeachment. It was really nothing at all because two weeks later, when Pat Gray, the acting director of the FBI, came to visit to complain about the CIA's interference, Nixon told him to conduct a full investigation. You see? Nixon's heart was pure. He really didn't want anything covered up. When Dean told him there was a "cancer on the presidency," Nixon responded by waiving all claims of executive privilege so that investigators could get to the bottom of things—which sounds good except that Nixon continued to sabotage efforts to release the key evidence in the case, the White House tapes, and went all the way to the Supreme Court to block their release. When the Court finally ordered him to turn over the tapes, Nixon "immediately" agreed, the exhibit says. In fact, he seriously considered defying the Court.

Why did Watergate cost Nixon the presidency? The Watergate Exhibit suggested it was because of his enemies, deeply flawed people whom the media declared heroes. Senator Sam Ervin, the chairman of the Watergate committee, whom the media turned into a "constitutional hero," was an old racist, the exhibit implied. Just nine years earlier he had voted against the civil rights laws. What of Carl Bernstein and Bob Woodward? They'd committed grave ethical violations, "offering bribes, illegally gaining access to phone numbers, talking to members of the grand jury." And Archibald Cox, the special prosecutor Nixon fired? A Kennedy family cabal of Nixon haters installed him in office. And so on.

The omissions in the exhibit were glaring. Not a word about the enemies list. Not a word about the plan to order IRS audits of those enemies. Not a word about Nixon's anti-Semitic slurs or his singling out Jews in the Bureau of Labor Statistics for special investigation. And what of the Huston Plan, which Nixon approved and then canceled? The Huston Plan condoned the use of illegal wiretaps, burglaries, and other crimes in the name of national security. "Now you remember Huston's plan? Implement it," the president says on the tapes. "I want it implemented on a thievery basis." But about the Huston Plan there was not one single word.

Most astonishing of all was the exhibit's conclusion: as of the start of the summer of 1974 "no evidence" had been presented proving that Nixon had engaged in a cover-up. Only in August did the evidence finally surface. This was the brief six minutes on a single tape—the "so-called smoking gun" tape—when Nixon mentions using the CIA to stop the FBI. That was bad, to be sure. But if the tape had come out a year earlier Nixon easily could have survived. It precipitated his resignation only because of everything else that had happened.

Before the federal government took over the library, the foundation members had agreed to replace the exhibit with something more balanced, but they never did. That was puzzling. If they wanted to make sure the new exhibit came out the way they wanted, all they had to do was produce it themselves. Instead, they left the old exhibit standing. "The United States government insisted that the Nixonians change the Watergate exhibit, that the Nixonians change it before the National Archives took it over," Naftali says. "The National Archives did not want to do it. Now when I come on the scene the Reverend John Taylor of the Nixon Foundation said to me 'we can't do it. We are not able to revise our own exhibit. I can't get consensus.' So I don't know what better evidence I have about the Nixon loyalists' inability to move past 1974 than the fact that they couldn't even figure out a way to revise the Watergate exhibit. Now think about it."

Naftali is incredulous as he recalls what happened. Watergate had taken place nearly four decades earlier. But here was a group of people who didn't seem able to come to terms with it even now. They were so committed to Richard Nixon that they insisted on seeing Watergate only as he saw it. Time had barely altered their views.

2.

It is no secret that we humans often have trouble seeing things as they are. But the popular belief is that in politics, at any rate, it's owing to partisan bias. Democrats give high marks to Democratic presidents because, well, they are Democrats. Republicans are disposed to favor the candidacy of Republicans because they're Republicans. That's what the Columbia study found back in the 1940s, and it's what neuroscientists have reported finding recently when they put subjects into an fMRI machine and asked questions that should have made partisans squirm. In one experiment, conducted during the 2004 general election by psychologist Drew Westen, partisans were shown plain evidence that John Kerry and George W. Bush had made blatantly hypocritical statements. The reaction of the subjects? They over-looked the evidence that incriminated their own candidate. Worse, their brain rewarded them for doing so: ignoring the evidence made them feel good. Here is Westen's explanation of what goes on in our brain when we turn a blind eye toward information we find objectionable: "When con-fronted with potentially troubling political information, a network of neu-rons becomes active that produces distress. . . . The brain registers the conflict between data and desire and begins to search for ways to turn off the spigot of unpleasant emotion." Notice what we don't do. We don't ex-pend cognitive energy to digest the information. Instead, we immediately try to reconcile it with our partisan preferences.

But saying that we are biased hardly begins to account for the behavior of partisans. They don't just overlook evidence, they manufacture it. And when they really get going they can make arguments that leave your head spinning. It is one thing to make a biased argument in favor of your group, quite another to make an argument that is so transparently feeble it leaves others dumbstruck, as the Nixonians' defense of Watergate left Naftali. These types of arguments don't even advance a group's cause—they hurt it. Yet it's a pattern we see all the time. When we join a group, it's often for a rational reason or at least a reason that can be made to seem plausible. Then, by and by, as members work themselves up over some issue, they become more and more extreme.

Consider, for example, the trajectory of the Tea Party. At the beginning it channeled the angst of people like Keli Carender, who were upset with the Obama administration's $787 billion stimulus bill. This is what Carender, the organizer of what's recognized as the very first Tea Party protest, held on February 16, 2009, told the *New York Times*:

It didn't make any sense to me to be spending all this money when we don't have it.

It seems more logical to me that we create an atmosphere where private industry can start to grow again and create jobs.

Some days I'm very Randian [a reference to Ayn Rand, the libertarian writer and philosopher]. I feel like there shouldn't be any of those programs [like Medicare and Medicaid], that it should all be charitable organizations. Sometimes I think, well, maybe it really should be just state, and there should be no federal part in it at all. I bounce around in my solutions to the problem.

Keli Carender's background was utterly conventional, with no hint of extremism. She studied math at Western Washington University. Later, she got a teaching degree at Oxford. Old and ignorant, as the Tea Party stereotype goes? Hardly. She was 30 and wore a ring through her nose. She lived in liberal Seattle.

Three days after she staged her protest, which drew 120 people, came CNBC editor Rick Santelli's on-air denunciation of the Obama administration's plan to save homeowners stuck with mortgages now valued more than their houses. Here is how Wikipedia describes it:

Santelli drew attention for his remarks made on February 19, 2009, about the Homeowners Affordability and Stability Plan, which was announced on February 18. While broadcasting from the floor of the Chicago Mercantile Exchange, Santelli accused the government of 'promoting bad behavior', and raised the possibility of a "Chicago Tea Party". He suggested that individuals who knowingly obtained high-risk mortgages (and faced impending foreclosure as a consequence) were "losers".

If you've seen Santelli's remarks you know they were delivered with passion. Most accounts refer to them as a rant. But his remarks weren't off-the-wall. Indeed, they made so much sense to millions of Americans that they decided to join the Tea Party movement, a movement so powerful that in 2010 it helped the Republicans take back the House of Representatives.

Spring forward a brief three years to 2013. What once had been a movement of aggrieved taxpayers with a fuzzy grasp of economics (most, for example, thought that Obama had raised their taxes when in fact he had lowered taxes for 95 percent of Americans) had become a radical movement of people so convinced of their virtue and their wisdom that they were will-ing to shut down the federal government if they didn't get their way. Defund Obamacare, they screamed, or we'll close down the US government. They went even further. If they didn't get their way, they said, they would block the effort to raise the debt ceiling, which was coming to a vote a few weeks later. They insisted that the economy of the United States would not be damaged by such a move. Virtually every economist in the world disagreed.

Social scientists have found that group membership is often a license for irresponsible behavior and strange ideas. An individual, on his own, will refrain from taking an extreme position on an issue. But put him in with a group of like-minded people, a group with few dissenters, and pretty soon he and the other members will drift inexorably toward more and more extreme positions. If they drive the dissenters out, they'll go even more extreme. Social scientists have even found that the members of a group will flout social norms if one of their own leads the way. In one experiment a group of students at Carnegie Mellon University were given a math test. One of them—who in fact was a confederate of the professor conducting the experiment—flagrantly cheated on the test. What then happened? Others immediately followed his lead and cheated as well. In a follow-up exper-iment the same confederate wore a shirt identifying him as a student at the University of Pittsburgh, Carnegie Mellon's archrival. What happened then? Almost nobody followed his lead and cheated. The shirt marked him as an outsider. Members of a group don't follow outsiders.

What is it about groups?

3.

This is a list of the members of the board of directors of the Nixon Foun-dation posted on its website (accessed September 12, 2013).

Ronald H. Walker, Chairman	Gavin S. Herbert Sr.
John H. Barr, Treasurer	Lawrence M. Higby
Everett Alvarez Jr.	Tod R. Hullin
George L. Argyrols	Kenneth L. Khachigian
Robert J. Brown	Frederic V. Malek
James H. Cavanaugh	Edward Nixon
Tricia Nixon Cox	Maureen Drown Nunn
Julie Nixon Eisenhower	J. Peter Simon
Barbara Hackman Franklin	Pete Wilson
John W. Hamilton	

What is obvious from the list? It's that these are serious people. Lawrence Higby, one of Haldeman's assistants, is a businessman. Kenneth L. Khachigian, one of Reagan's chief speechwriters, is an attorney. Fred Malek is the former president of Marriott Hotels and Northwest Airlines. Pete Wilson was the governor of California.

When we encounter highly esteemed people like this we make an assumption that they take a rational approach to life. But when it comes to Watergate, these people as a group couldn't (though some may have departed from the group's orthodoxy privately). What can we learn from this? One thing is clear. It's not just ignorant people who can become beholden to views that are patently at odds with reality, an assumption we often make. Anybody can. We mislead ourselves when we attribute fantastical views to ignorance, as liberal pundits writing about the Tea Party often do. Ignorance may have nothing to do with it.

What then is the cause? What is it with groups? To find out let's examine a bit more what happened to Naftali as he began to make decisions as the director of the Nixon Library. As he tells the story, every time he tried to open the place up to fresh viewpoints he faced a furious backlash. When he invited the liberal journalist Elizabeth Drew to speak at a library event, the foundation suddenly cut funding to the library's exhibits. Two years later, when he invited John Dean to speak, a storm erupted. "There was a campaign. They wrote letters to every living former president and denounced me personally for undermining the whole [presidential library] system and said you wouldn't have this at your library. Why should we let the National Archives do it here. I never saw the letter but I know it mentioned me personally because the director of the Clinton library wondered who the hell Tim Naftali is. Who is this guy and why is he a threat."

Despite the pressure, Naftali felt he couldn't give in. He was "going to bring John Dean come hell or high water," he says. It was going to happen. "It was a resignation issue for me. Because if Washington had said no, then it's finished. It's over. We're never going to have credibility." John Dean appeared as scheduled. But there were consequences. The acting director of the foundation, who had broken with her colleagues to support Dean's visit, was axed. Then the foundation cut off funding to the library. The Nixon library now became the only library in the federal system not to receive funding from the foundation of the president whose papers it oversees. Shortly after that a hold was mysteriously placed in the Senate on President Barack Obama's nomination of the Archivist of the United States, who oversees all presidential libraries. The new head of the Nixon Foundation subsequently revealed he was behind it: "It was to send a signal to the Archives if Tim's not gonna straighten up and fly right," he admitted to the *Los Angeles Times.*

This was all-out war. And it didn't make much sense. Timothy Naftali wasn't the enemy. In fact, one of the reasons why he had been selected as the library's director by the federal government was because the Nixon Foundation found him acceptable. Unlike many historians who had grown up with Watergate, he was so young he lacked Watergate scars. "I am gay. I am from Canada. I was 12 years old when Richard Nixon resigned," he told the *New York Times* when he was chosen. "I have no skin in the game." And he did everything he could, he says, to get along. He made overtures to Julie Nixon Eisenhower, the president's daughter. He proposed joint exhibits with the Nixonians. He held events featuring old Nixon hands. But repeatedly he found himself at cross-purposes with the members of the foundation.

A distinguishing physical characteristic of Naftali is that the wrinkles on his forehead grow more intense the more agitated he becomes. As he recounted what happened during the five years he spent as the director of the Nixon library his eyebrows began to twitch and his forehead wrinkled like a newborn baby's face. The subject clearly brought to mind a tumultuous period in his life. Though he had explained to the Nixonians that he had to take a balanced approach to establish the credibility of the library, he met resistance every time he tried.

The worst was yet to come. In the summer of 2010, Naftali finished the plan for the replacement Watergate exhibit. It was stunning. Here in one place were all the multifaceted dimensions of Watergate. Not just the break-in at the Watergate complex in 1972, as in the old exhibit, but the events in 1970 and 1971 that led up to the break-in, events that Nixon was determined to keep secret: the Huston Plan, the creation of the Plumbers, the black-bag Ellsberg psychiatrist job, and all the rest. It was everything the old exhibit wasn't. It was broad in scope and it made a powerful impression. It made Watergate, which can be complicated for people who didn't live through it, simple to understand. And it did what the old exhibit failed to do, which was to make the country's ultimate decision to get rid of Nixon comprehensible. The old exhibit had made Nixon's resignation almost seem like an unanticipated and inexplicable event owing wholly to the hatred of his enemies and the media. The new exhibit proved that his enemies hadn't done in Nixon. Nixon had done in Nixon.

Many sections in the exhibit featured new material that filled out the familiar Watergate story. Haldeman, for example, had always insisted that he wasn't present at the meeting where G. Gordon Liddy, the ringleader of the Watergate burglars, was hired. But he was. And Naftali had the proof:

an early draft of the meticulous notes one of Haldeman's aides had taken at the meeting. Haldeman had ordered aides immediately after the break-in to shred evidence implicating him and others in the White House, but the draft had survived. There was also a story that no history book had. One of the tapes nobody had previously heard revealed that Nixon had considered pairing amnesty for the Watergate burglars with amnesty for a group of antiwar protesters arrested in Gainesville, Florida. But there was a problem with the plan: not enough protesters had been arrested to make the pairing appear equitable. So Haldeman suggested arresting more antiwar protesters on trumped-up charges. All this and more was in the new exhibit, probably the most honest exhibit ever planned for a presidential library, where evidence damaging to presidents is usually soft-peddled. And it was all documented.

As a courtesy, Naftali sent the text over to the Nixon Foundation. This prompted another storm. Once again the Nixonians reacted with fury, firing off complaints to the headquarters of the National Archives in Washington. What annoyed them? Naftali's Watergate exhibit told what actually had happened. This naturally reflected unfavorably on Nixon. Their view was that exhibits at presidential libraries should "reflect favorably" on presidents. How could the Watergate exhibit reflect favorably on Nixon when Watergate involved the crimes he'd committed as president—crimes that led to his resignation? By putting them in context, they insisted. That sounds good, but what this meant in practice, the Nixonians made clear, was going back to the defense of Watergate Richard Nixon promulgated during his long struggle to remain in office. The lynchpin of that argument was, as a book of the era had it, *It Didn't Start with Watergate*. Richard Nixon may have committed this or that crime, but he wasn't the first to do so. FDR, JFK, and LBJ made secret recordings of conversations in the Oval Office. JFK's FBI used illegal wiretaps to get dirt on Martin Luther King Jr. Many presidents went to great lengths to stop leaks. Nearly all of them countenanced dirty tricks. Nixon wasn't an exception. He had been a normal president, not the freak show he'd been made out to be.

Reading the Nixonians' objections to the exhibit—which are laid out in an indictment that runs *158 pages long*—can take your breath away. The hush money Nixon and Haldeman agreed to pay to buy the burglars' silence? The Nixonians contended that there was no proof whatsoever that the money went for anything other than the support of the burglars' families during a difficult time. The secret wiretaps on journalists? Until the Supreme Court ruled in a Watergate case that such wiretaps were illegal, there was no reason to believe such taps were illegal. In fact, they weren't illegal until the Court said they were. The Huston Plan? It had no business being included in a Watergate exhibit as it had nothing to do with Watergate. Dirty tricks and espionage? These had no place either in an exhibit about Watergate. Here's how the Nixonians put it: "We object to this entire section as an inappropriate expansion of the Watergate exhibit, which can only be done at the expense of the core Watergate scandal story."

What about the cover-up for which John Mitchell, Bob Haldeman, and John Ehrlichman went to prison? The Nixonians disputed the case made against them: "While Mitchell, Haldeman and Ehrlichman were convicted of all counts in the Watergate cover-up trial, this does not mean that the National Archives can discount all their protestations of innocence. Put simply, the jury did not make specific findings of fact." What about the constitutional crisis: Congress and the president at loggerheads, the president's appeal to the Supreme Court to stop a lower court's order for subpoenaed records? The Nixonians' response was that "there was no 'constitutional crisis' in the proper sense of the word—there was no defiance of a Court Order or Act of Congress." They even disputed the claim in the exhibit that Nixon was sure to face conviction in the Senate if he hadn't resigned: "[The exhibit] neglects to mention that an impeachment trial would most likely have taken well over a year—and that if Nixon had mounted a serious defense, he might have been able to show that many of the charges, however serious, did not reach a sufficient level of legal proof to result in a conviction. While impeachment in the short term was very real, conviction in the long term was not nearly as certain." They didn't even like the exhibit's focus on abuses of power even though the law providing for the federal takeover of the library expressly established that it should be devoted to research into Nixon's abuses of power. Research was one thing, exhibits something else entirely:

> It is important to note [that the law providing for the transfer of Nixon's papers to the Nixon library] deals specifically with the National Archives' archival responsibility to safeguard, preserve, and promulgate these Nixon abuses of power papers and tapes by making them easily accessible to citizens and scholars. [The National Archives] has been meeting that requirement for many years; indeed, the process is ongoing, and it will be greatly facilitated by the opening of the new building at Yorba Linda that will finally house all the Nixon presidential materials together in one place. The extrapolation of [the law's] "abuses of power" archival criterion to govern the Nixon Library's

Watergate Exhibit seems to be an overly broad reading by Dr. Naftali of the intent of the statute.

Here we begin to understand why the Nixonians never mounted an exhibit of their own to replace the old Watergate exhibit. They didn't replace it with something more balanced because they didn't have a balanced view of Watergate. It was now 2010 and they still couldn't get past 1974. While they were prepared to make a few concessions they hadn't made earlier— for example, they now freely admitted that a cover-up had taken place and actually used the word cover-up, something they hadn't done in the old exhibit—their point of view hadn't really changed. Not only did they believe Nixon might have escaped impeachment and conviction, some even believed he should have. All seemed to believe that Nixon got a raw deal.

That solves one mystery. Now we understand why, when the Nixonians were given the chance, they didn't replace the old exhibit. But that leaves us with another, and a far deeper one: why couldn't the Nixonians move on? Why were they still resisting a truth that now seems obvious to just about everybody outside the tight circle of loyal Nixon apologists? Was it something in the water? This is the joke we make when we come across people who seem to hold a warped view of reality. But there may be something to the idea. When people drink from the same fountain of information they are bound to take a common view of things. That is what seems to happen to people who join a group. They listen to information that reinforces their views.

But something else is at work too. When we join a group we often value our membership above the truth. As the psychologist Jonathan Haidt makes clear in his landmark study of human behavior, *The Righteous Mind: Why Good People Are Divided by Politics and Religion*, when we are faced with a choice between the truth and our standing in a group, we usually go with the group. Our survival in the Pleistocene didn't depend on our understanding the truth. It depended on the safety of the group. That, Haidt says, is why we didn't evolve an inner scientist or inner judge to help us make assessments of the truth. We evolved an inner lawyer. And like any lawyer we can argue any side of an issue. The truth may be what we say we cherish—and indeed we often make great sacrifices for it. But what assures our survival isn't our commitment to the truth, it's our capacity for social cohesion. Our morality is social.

Another factor that may have contributed to the Nixonians' insularity is their conservative ideology. According to Haidt's research, conservatives generally display a higher commitment to groups than liberals. Group loyalty is one of six key values that define conservatives. While all humans are hivish, conservatives respond more to appeals to group loyalty than liberals, who are inclined toward what Haidt calls universalism. This suggests there may have been something to the joke attributed to humorist Will Rogers: "I am not a member of any organized party—I am a Democrat."

But evolutionary psychology suggests there may be another reason as well that the Nixonians marched in lockstep, and it's something that affects all of us, conservative, liberal, whatever.

Let's return for a moment to that list of the members of the Nixon Foundation's board of directors:

Ronald H. Walker, Chairman   Gavin S. Herbert Sr.
John H. Barr, Treasurer   Lawrence M. Higby
Everett Alvarez Jr.   Tod R. Hullin
George L. Argyrols   Kenneth L. Khachigian
Robert J. Brown   Frederic V. Malek
James H. Cavanaugh   Edward Nixon
Tricia Nixon Cox   Maureen Drown Nunn
Julie Nixon Eisenhower   J. Peter Simon
Barbara Hackman Franklin   Pete Wilson
John W. Hamilton

What else is worth noticing besides the fact that these are accomplished people? Look for what's missing. With the exception of Julie and Tricia, Nixon's daughters, and Edward, his sole surviving brother, these people aren't related. What's missing, then, is a genetic connection among the majority of the board's members. This is not a family roster. It's a social unit, a group, of like-minded people—people who think the world of Richard Nixon. That, it turns out, is highly significant because of a quality all groups share. But before we can understand what that is, we have to come to terms with what families share. Only by understanding families can we truly understand groups.

4.

A good place to start is with the story of the Donner Party, the sad tale of the ravaged pioneers who, on a bad tip, used an untried shortcut to California in the dead of winter in 1846 and paid for it with their lives. What's the standard lesson of the Donner Party? As historians tell the story, it's this: in extreme circumstances human beings are capable of anything, even cannibalism. But recently, social scientists discovered a new lesson. The social scientists found a new lesson because they asked a new question.

Historians writing about the tragedy always wanted to know what happened, and how members of the party responded, in order to account for the calamity that beset them, thirty-six of whom died out of a total of eighty-one. So the historians wrote stories about the journey and the fascinating people who made it: George Donner, the garrulous, gregarious Southerner who was so well-liked that everybody thought of him as Uncle George, and who in extremis had to dig up his brother Jacob so George's starving children could eat him, as George looked on, tears streaming down his cheeks. Or Lansford Warren Hastings, the ambitious twenty-something who lured the Donner Party with a fanciful tale about a quick route west and then promptly abandoned them. Or James Reed, the opinionated Irishman who was forced into exile after he killed a teamster in a fight, robbing the group of one its few natural leaders. The historians' focus, in other words, was on the individual. The historians' stories throbbed with the pulse of a broken heart over the losses individuals suffered.

The social scientists, writing from the perspective of evolutionary psychology, took a heartless, cold steel, mathematical approach. They weren't interested in the stories of individuals. They were interested in groups. So they accumulated a broad array of statistics and subjected them to a withering number of tests. Did women as a group fare better or worse than men? Did old people fare better or worse than young people? And so on. What they found is shocking. The people who fared worst on the trail? It wasn't old women or children, the people we usually consider the most vulnerable in a physically demanding environment. It was strong, single young men, the very people you'd expect would be able to ride out the winter's harsh conditions the best. They suffered the highest mortality rate of any demographic group. These were people, lacking families, who had no need to look out for anyone but themselves. They were free to behave as selfishly as they wanted. They didn't have to make sacrifices for anyone. And yet the facts are the facts. No matter how many times the social scientists reexamined the data, it came out the same way. The numbers are sobering. Of the fifteen single young men who went on that ill-fated journey, just three survived. Three. Who fared best? The members of families.

The real lesson of the Donner Party tragedy? It's not the grim one that human beings are capable of anything, including cannibalism—the lesson that the broken-hearted historians found. It's that human beings trapped in an unimaginably harsh environment are capable of survival as long as they can fall back on their family for support—that's the lesson of the cold-hearted approach the social scientists took. Why is family so important? Because in a pinch you can almost always be certain your family will be there for you. Family comes first. Family members look after one another. The larger your family, the more people you have looking after you, the better off you are. And indeed larger families during the Donner Party trek west suffered lower mortality rates than smaller ones.

This is one of the most fascinating findings of evolutionary psychologists. Here's another. When they examined the records of the *Mayflower* they found the same pattern. The *Mayflower* pioneers also faced terrible conditions. Just over half of them died during the first winter spent in the New World. And which people suffered least? The members of families.

For eons—literally millions of years—families have proven to be the most dependable of all social units. Families survive. And this is true whether the marriage the family unit is built around is monogamous or polygamous or polyandrous. (In a polyandrous marriage the female has several husbands, who may be brothers.) Nature is morally indifferent to the form a family's organization takes. What matters is the family's ability to survive in the circumstances in which it finds itself. In some circumstances a polyandrous family survives better than a polygamous family. In the modern world monogamous families prevail.

What gives families the edge? That's simple. They behave altruistically toward one another. They help each other out even when it comes at a cost. A parent sacrifices so a child can survive. A brother sacrifices for the sake of his sister. It's a phenomenon we see on display every day.

But until a discovery in 1964 no one knew why. The discovery was made by a craggy-faced British evolutionary biologist who favored long hair like a hippie and in his prime looked a lot like David Gregory, the TV anchorman. His name was William D. Hamilton, Bill for short. And he was one of the twentieth century's greatest biologists. This is what Hamilton figured out:

$$r B > C$$

Translated, this formula establishes that altruism is embedded in our genes. While under normal circumstances individuals compete for scarce resources in the ruthless competition for survival, Hamilton proved mathematically that an individual will help another to whom he is genetically related (that's the r) as long as the cost (C) to himself is lower than the benefit (B) to the other person. (If it's not, he'll just save himself at the other person's expense.) This was a scientific breakthrough. What Hamilton deduced is that when people are altruistic to their kin they are actually serving their own selfish needs, in line with the Theory of Evolution, which is based on the idea that individuals compete for scarce resources. This is because as far as biology is concerned we are our genes. So when we help our kin we are helping ourselves since we share some of the same genes. The more copies of our genes that make it into the next generation and the generation after that, the better. Biologists call this fitness, as I mentioned earlier in the book. Genes are everything. As the biologist Richard Dawkins explains, human beings are the vehicles that genes use to assure their survival into future generations. As he puts it: "We are survival machines—robot vehicles blindly programmed to preserve the selfish molecules known as genes."

Why do mothers look after their families? Because of their genes. They are genetically programmed to do so. Nature makes sure mothers protect their kin even if they are uninclined for whatever reason not to. Say a mother during pregnancy decides that she wants to deprive the fetus of food and resources. She cannot do so without risking injury to herself. And because nature doesn't like to leave things to chance, it is not the mother's genes that determine how a fetus in the womb grows. This task is controlled entirely by the Igf2 gene—a gene that is inherited from her father. Evolution selected for mothers who leave a fetus's growth in the womb up to the father's gene to make sure that mothers place the well-being of the fetus ahead of her own. Mothers literally have no genetic say in the matter.

Once a baby is born the mother will recognize her infant and know it's hers and not someone else's by smell. She doesn't even have to be conscious of this. It's automatic. It's not just mothers who are programmed to protect their offspring. Fathers, brothers, sisters, cousins, aunts, uncles—all are genetically programmed to aid their kin. Family loyalty isn't magic, it turns out. It's a part of us—same as our arms, our legs, and our heart. It's hardwired. That is, it's built into our system.

Intuition tells us that this expression of loyalty is a human quality. But it isn't. Nature favors altruism in animals of all kinds, even animals that give no hint of consciousness, such as birds. Studies confirm that birds are most likely to help another bird feed its young if they are related. We happen to possess consciousness. So we naturally think we are making a conscious decision to help our kin. But actually we are executing our genes' commands. And the genes of mammals—all mammals—are prewired for attachment. This doesn't mean we have no say in the matter. Our brain allows us to override our impulses. Behavior is prewired, not hardwired. But absent a decision to go against our kin, we are inclined by nature to offer help. Nature selected for individuals who favor their kin. Altruistic family members survive better than people who go it alone. That's the lesson of the Donner Party.

We don't favor kin willy-nilly. Hamilton's Rule, as it is known, is that we favor people on a sliding scale, and we do so according to a precise formula.

Our relationships with one another come down to math. The key is the r in the formula, which refers to what biologists call the coefficient of relatedness. This is a measure of the degree to which two individuals are genetically similar. A brother and a sister born of the same parents share 50 percent of their genes. So their degree of relatedness is 0.5. A mother and a child also share 50 percent of their genes as do a father and a child. In these cases, therefore, the degree of relatedness is 0.5 too. The more genetically related people are, the higher the number. The less related, the lower the number. Half brothers share just 25 percent of their genes, so in their case r = 0.25. What this means is that a mother is inclined to sacrifice more for her biological child than half brothers are for each other.

Once Hamilton's Rule became known, researchers began putting it to the test. They began examining real-world situations to see when people behave altruistically and when they don't. If Hamilton's Rule is accurate we should be able to see a difference in how human beings behave toward one another based on their degree of relatedness. And sure enough we do. One of the relationships that has been studied the most is between parents and their stepchildren. Hamilton's Rule suggests that parents will behave more altruistically toward their own biological children than toward their stepchildren. They do. A study of Canadian children, for example, showed stepchildren are sixty times more likely to die from physical abuse than children living with their biological parents.

Everywhere researchers looked they found confirmation of Hamilton's Rule. Sometimes the results were unsurprising, as with the studies of stepchildren, which reflected the ancient folklore wisdom about wicked stepmothers. But often they were eye-opening. Everybody who's ever watched a cop show on television knows that the people who detectives investigating a murder look closely at first are the victim's relatives. The detective shows up after a crime and immediately begins to ask questions that suggest the relatives are under suspicion. If the atmosphere becomes a little frosty the cop quickly reassures them he is just following protocol. He is required to ask these awkward questions, he says sheepishly. But the viewer knows better. A family member is probably guilty. Detroit crime statistics seem to back up the television drama's standard formula. When researchers examined the city's crime records they indeed found that 25 percent of the victims of murder were killed by a member of their own family. But then the experts dug deeper. It wasn't blood relatives who were killing each other by and large. It was spouses—people who don't share the same genes. Just 6 percent of the murder victims were blood relatives—people who did share the same genes. The cop shows are misleading. It's not your blood relatives you have to fear. It's your spouse.

A sign of the importance of Hamilton's Rule was that scientists in virtually every field of study began to test it. Anthropologists wanted to know if kinship classifications are universal. If Hamilton's Rule is right, then every society should have ways of categorizing relationships that reflect the degree to which people are related. Every society should have names for siblings, aunts, uncles, grandparents, and so on. Every society does (though some cultures employ more detailed hierarchies than others). Psychologists wanted to find out how infants react to people who aren't members of the family. If Hamilton's Rule is correct, the studies should indicate that babies show distress when approached by strangers. They do. And if Hamilton's Rule is correct, babies have to have a sure-fire way of distinguishing strangers from family. They do. One way is by smell. Babies recognize their mother's scent just as mothers recognize their baby's scent. Another is by facial features. As we've seen, humans come with sophisticated facial recognition software that allows them to discern who is close genetically. This software is remarkable. Babies just nine minutes old, as I have reported, can recognize a face from other objects. These findings added further confirmation to the belief in Hamilton's Rule.

Evolutionary psychologists made the most significant findings of all.

As I have mentioned many times in this book, evolutionary psychologists believe that who we *are* basically has to do with who we *were* during the Pleistocene, when we survived as hunter-gatherers. If the evolutionary psychologists are right, we should see signs of familial altruism in every human society. No exceptions. If it's truly a part of us we should see evidence of familial altruism in humans everywhere, under all conditions, whether in the modern United States among Iowa farmers and New York City bond traders, or deep in the Amazon jungle among people who still live as hunter-gatherers. We do. But it's complicated. Families don't always get along. Under difficult circumstances conflicts break out. Sometimes resources are in short supply, contributing to familial discontent. Sometimes jealousy and rage trump altruism—as they do in the biblical story of Cain and Abel. Cain kills Abel, after all. He doesn't show him much mercy. The story may be a work of fiction, but it reeks of verisimilitude. The newspapers are filled with stories about rotten people like Cain.

And sometimes raw ambitiousness triumphs. English history is filled with stories of relatives vying for the throne who resorted to murder to literally kill their way to the top. Isn't that evidence that Hamilton's Rule is defective? Little altruism was in evidence when Richard III murdered his nephews, or Queen Elizabeth I ordered the execution of Mary, her cousin, the Queen of Scots. But Hamilton's Rule doesn't say that family members always get along. It says that members will perform acts of altruism toward other members as long as the cost is less than the benefit. In a situation where the English throne is at stake, it's hard to argue that the benefit of letting your cousin become king is higher than your cost of not becoming king. Nonetheless, even British royal history gives strong hints of a familial altruism effect. Since 1066, royal aspirants to the throne committed murder in pursuit of the crown eleven times. But not once did children kill their fathers, or brother kill brother. Murder always involved uncles, nephews, and cousins, people who bore a much lower genetic relationship to one another.

Where r is low the chance for conflict is higher. Where it's high the chance for conflict is lower. This is the iron law of Hamilton's Rule. And it has profound implications for us. It helps account for the mysterious behavior of the stuck-in-the-past Nixonians. But before we return to the Nixonians, let's consider another example of families reacting under pressure. It can help us to understand the key difference between families and groups.

5.

One Monday in April 2013, a fine clear day, two brothers, aged nineteen and twenty-six, got up in the morning, dressed, pulled on hooded jackets, adjusted their backpacks, and put on their caps, one white, one black. The nineteen-year-old wore his backward. Two ordinary-looking young men, they then walked out into the open air and made their way downtown. It was the day of the Boston Marathon. In their backpacks were two deadly pressure-cooker bombs. The bombs contained nails, ball bearings, and black powder. At 2:42 P.M., the older brother planted his bomb next to Jeff Bauman, a young man waiting for his girlfriend to cross the finish line of the marathon. The brother stared straight into Bauman's eyes and then calmly walked off. The younger brother planted his bomb a short distance away. On video, he too looks composed. A moment later the bombs exploded, twelve seconds apart. The next day the younger brother went to the gym and worked out. He tweeted: "I'm a stress-free kind of guy."

Three people died as a result of the Boston bombing attack, including Sean Collier, a twenty-six-year-old campus police officer who worked for MIT. Two hundred sixty-four people were injured, most notably Jeff Bauman, whose legs were blown off. He is the figure you see being wheeled away from the scene just seconds after the bombing. He looks dazed. His face is covered with large black-powder splotches. It is the Boston bombing picture we carry around in our heads.

The ordeal of the Boston bombing ended with the older brother's death and the younger brother's capture. It lasted 102 hours. During much of that time the citizens of Boston lived in sheer terror. The city was closed down.

What was it all about?

Two story lines quickly emerged. The first one was that this was an act of terrorism. The surviving brother reportedly told police that he and his older sibling were self-directed jihadists taking revenge for the wars in Afghanistan and Iraq. They had learned how to make their pressure-cooker bombs from *Inspire*, the improbably named online magazine published by al Qaeda in the Arabian Peninsula.

The second story line was that this was an example of sibling loyalty gone awry. Everybody seemed to quickly conclude that the younger brother—he was just nineteen, remember—had been a good kid who'd been misled by his older brother. Everybody blamed the older brother, a ne'er-do-well, who started out right and then took a wrong turn after his boxing career stalled.

But the second story line has things upside down. The Boston bombing story isn't evidence of sibling loyalty gone awry; it's evidence of sibling loyalty. That's what motivated the younger brother. Focusing on the bad influence his older brother had on the younger brother misses the point. The story of the Boston bombers is the story of two brothers working together. The younger brother didn't seem to have anything personally to gain from the attack. His career hadn't stalled. He was enrolled in college and enjoying social success. Strange as it might seem to think of his support for his brother as an act of altruism, it was. It's a textbook example, in other words, of Hamilton's Rule in action (save for the fact that engaging in terrorism is hardly likely to result in greater fitness). As such, it's a powerful testament to the power of family. It is impossible to imagine that the younger brother would have planted a bomb at the Boston Marathon absent that familial connection. It was what drove him. It was responsible for his hideous decision to explode a device designed to kill lots of innocent people. That is some powerful motive.

And it isn't just the brothers who provide a demonstration of Hamilton's Rule in action. So do the brothers' parents. What was their reaction when they heard the news? The instant the father was told his boys were suspects he adamantly denied it. When confronted with indisputable evidence of their involvement after his older son died in an explosive exchange of gunfire, he couldn't bring himself to admit the facts. But he had to say something. So he claimed his sons were victims of some crazy police conspiracy.

He declared incoherently: "The police are to blame. Being cowards, they shot the boy dead. There are cops like this." The brothers' mother was equally adamant her boys were angels. "I am 100 percent sure that this is a setup," she told *Russia Today*. "It's impossible for them to do such things." She insisted that her sons weren't jihadists. Why was she certain? They'd never mentioned to her that they were. "My sons would never keep a secret," she said. Both father and mother couldn't accept what everybody outside the family could. Their children had committed a heinous crime.

One family member signaled disapproval of the brothers' behavior. An uncle. He famously blasted them in a television interview. He called them barbarians and said the older brother was "a loser." The uncle's judgment was caustic: "They do not deserve to be on this earth. . . . What can I say? They murdered." But he was their uncle, not their parents. He shared far fewer genes with them. The parents' coefficient of relatedness was 0.5. His was 0.25. Later, after the shock of the attack had worn off, he expressed his love for the brothers despite what they did. That was his 0.25 coefficient showing.

On a Facebook page set up to honor the memory of the victims, the parents' defense of their indefensible children drew derision. These are some of the (unedited) comments that people made:

- "I'm sorry but if my children murdered innocent people out of violence. I wouldn't have anymore children. What the hell is there to defend after you murdered people, innocent children and moms and dads, grandma's and grandpa's. There is no forgiveness there, these to MEN need to rot in hell."
- "I have two children and if either of them did something this extreme I would throw them under the bus and make sure they paid for what they did!"
- "I can defend my child when he/she tells a fib but when a child murders and maims hundreds of men, women and children I no longer have a child I raised."

What the Facebook posters overlooked is that when it is your family involved in opprobrious behavior you don't think rationally. Facts don't matter. What matters is rallying around in a circle of common defense. This is what families do when a member is under attack. Given our evolutionary history this reaction is virtually inevitable. Evolution doesn't teach us right and wrong. Being in the right doesn't help perpetuate our genes. What evolution teaches us is survival. And how do we survive? By sticking with our families through thick and thin. That's how we perpetuate our genes. That's the meaning of what happened to the Donner Party.

Let's go back now to the Nixon Foundation. What was so significant about its membership? Only three people were related. It wasn't a family. But the members' reaction to the new Watergate exhibit seemed to be very much like a family's. When they learned what was in the new Watergate exhibit they immediately circled the wagons, loaded their weapons, and commenced firing. No argument seemed too outrageous to make if it could possibly be deployed in the defense of Richard Nixon's actions during Watergate. No concession was made that didn't absolutely have to be made. They didn't even concede that Nixon had condoned the payment of hush money to the Watergate burglars. This is seemingly how a family responds. It's how the family of the Boston bombers responded when they confronted the evidence of their sons' guilt. They shooed it away. Another similarity is striking. The Nixonians, like the Boston bombers' family, indulged in wild talk about a grand conspiracy. The Nixonians' wasn't a conspiracy of the police. Theirs was a conspiracy of the media and Nixon's enemies. Nixon didn't bring Nixon down. His enemies did. But it was the same old conspiracy nonsense disguised as an argument.

What are we to make of this? The answer that leaps to mind is that groups under siege can behave in ways strikingly similar to families under siege. They behave like families even though they're missing the genetic co-efficient of relatedness. This is not unexpected. Families and groups are parallel in many respects. Both exist to help their members through collective action. Both help us stave off mental illnesses (such as depression). Both can inspire intense loyalty. Both are often revered. Members of a group will even say of their fellow members: they're family. But it's an illusion. They aren't. They lack that coefficient of relatedness. And that makes a big difference. A family under attack sticks together the way the Boston bombers' family did. But what happens when groups come under attack? They often splinter.

Consider what happened to "All the President's Men," the people Richard Nixon installed in power, people who professed intense loyalty to him. When the Watergate cover-up began to unravel many members of the group went their separate ways. John Dean betrayed the group, spilling its secrets in open testimony that nearly single-handedly sank Nixon's presidency. Jeb Stuart Magruder, the deputy campaign manager, pleaded guilty to conspiracy and then wrote a book saying he'd lost his moral compass. Hugh W. Sloan Jr., the campaign treasurer, became a secret source for Bob Woodward and Carl Bernstein and resigned when he discovered what the Plumbers had done. Alfred Baldwin, the former FBI agent who served as the Watergate burglars' lookout man, gave up his secrets in an interview with the *Los Angeles Times* while the 1972 campaign was still in motion. E. Howard Hunt, one of the leading Watergate burglars, threatened to talk unless he received hush money. James W. McCord, the campaign's security director and a Watergate burglar, wrote a letter to Judge John Sirica that blew the Watergate conspiracy wide open.

They were the "President's Men" but they didn't stand by him the way the Boston bombers' immediate family stood by them. Under pressure, the President's Men broke away to look after their own interests. Family bonds are forever. Social bonds aren't. They are ephemeral. They are fragile. That missing coefficient of relatedness has consequences. One of those consequences is that groups, unlike families, often impose strict limits on its members' freedom. Because a group can't count on the loyalty of its members the way a family can, the group tries to guarantee loyalty through artificial means. One of the most obvious ways it does this is by imposing strict rules of membership. Only people who clear a number of barriers can join. This helps weed out or exclude people who have only a weak commitment to the group's cause. It's the reason, apart from religious dogma, that Jewish men wear yarmulkes, Catholic priests don't marry, and Mormon men wear special undergarments.

In some cases a person seeking to join a group has to literally make a payment. Want to join the Augusta National Golf Club, the group that hosts the annual Masters Tournament? That will cost you thousands and thousands of dollars. On top of that there are annual dues, which costs thousands more. Until 1990 you couldn't be black and join. Until 2012 you couldn't be a woman and join. Those restrictions undoubtedly reflected rank prejudice, but they also served a purpose favorable to the group's survival. They made the people who did get in feel special. Not everybody could join Augusta. Just some people. Exclusion is a requirement of a group. There always have to be some people who can't join. Otherwise, what's the point? Even trivial groups limit their memberships. Want to join the Ice Cream Lovers Club on Facebook? The very first thing you see is this humorous statement: "This group is for Ice Cream lovers only! :) No haters :)"

What else do groups do to maintain cohesiveness? They may commit their members to a certain point of view on a set of core issues. The Republican Party's idées fixes? Government is the problem, abortion is evil, Ronald Reagan was a god. And the Democrats'? Government is the solution, abortion should be rare but legal, Franklin Roosevelt was a god. In practice, political parties generally are lax about membership standards. They want to win elections, after all. So they allow people who depart from the party script to remain members. That diversity saves them from extremism. But not even their desire for victory can overcome the deep-seated feeling of many that there's a line members should never cross. That's why every election you'll hear some Republicans and some Democrats say that they'd prefer to go down to defeat than support so and so who claims to share their values but really doesn't.

As I was writing this chapter, a fight was raging in the Republican Party between true believers and pragmatists. The true believers wanted to run the pragmatists out of the party. The derisive name for the pragmatists? RINOs: Republicans in Name Only. Leaders of the party in Washington were part of the pragmatist wing. These pragmatists included all the big names of the party machine going back years: Karl Rove, Michael Steele, Ed Gillespie. To them the fight was about the future of the GOP. Either the party embraced moderate Republicans who hold different views on hot issues like immigration, or the party would cease being a national party capable of winning elections in the Northeast and the West. Only the South could be considered GOP territory. At a party conference Chris Christie, the Republican governor of New Jersey, one of the pragmatists, took the true believers on directly. "We are not a debating society," he said. "We are a political operation that needs to win."

What this fight showed is that the GOP, like all political organizations, is subject to enormous stress at the seams because its members are united by little more than ideology and a common history, with a dose of social identity thrown in. And that's not nearly enough to keep them united when things go wrong. That's why parties always look so weak after electoral defeat. They look weak because they *are* weak. They are weak because the ties that bind the members are weak. This weakness is concealed during flush times because in victory people are inclined to remain silent about their disagreements. Winning, in other words, disguises the true nature of political parties. But in defeat the truth comes out. Families in a crisis are strong because families are strong. Non-familial groups in a crisis are weak because they are fundamentally weak.

Families, like other groups, are capable of bad behavior and irrational reasoning. And no one needs to be reminded that families often pass on old resentments from generation to generation. So it's not like families are above the sort of behavior we see in other groups. You might think, therefore, that it may be just as well that groups aren't strong. Do we really want strong groups? Wouldn't a strong group be capable of doing more damage when its members become wedded to crazy views? The answer is unquestionably yes. But as a thought exercise it's worth considering the damage they do as a result of weakness to give us a better understanding of the nature of groups. For what do weak groups do? Being weak, they feel the necessity of resorting to the constant repetition and reinforcement of loaded emotional appeals.

Look at how political parties do it. They tell their members they are the true Americans. They claim their values are more true-blue American than the opposition's. Their national conventions are decked out in patriotic colors. When their presidential nominee is finally selected, red, white, and blue balloons literally drop from the ceiling. No effort to rally members seems too extreme if it works. In the nineteenth century, party activists even strapped live eagles to poles at the head of parades to exploit people's patriotism. As often as possible they attempt to define their mission in almost religious terms, giving members the feeling of belonging to a sacred organization. (This is particularly appealing to conservatives, says Jonathan Haidt.) Parties claim that unless they are put in power the country's decline is assured and the death of the nation looms. The lower their political fortunes the more extreme their rhetoric gets. The resort to chauvinism is a function of weakness. It's the price we pay for the weakness of these groups. If you hate political parties that throw red meat at their base and resort to cheap patriotic claptrap, now at least you know why they do it. They do it out of desperation. At their core, parties, like all non-familial groups, are weak. (I hasten to add that weak doesn't mean crippled. As anyone familiar with the history of the twentieth century knows, groups are capable of extraordinary good and evil.)

There's another cost associated with the inherent weakness of groups. Groups write off people. Families are strong enough that they can tolerate wayward members. Groups can't. What was the reaction of Nixon's inner circle to John Dean after he testified before the Senate Watergate committee? They demonized him. They couldn't tolerate his apostasy. Apostates are a mortal threat to a group's existence. So the Nixonians did everything they could to discredit Dean. Four decades later they were still at it. When Nixon Library Director Timothy Naftali decided that it was essential for the Library's credibility to extend a speaking invitation to Dean, the members of the Nixon Foundation board became apoplectic. They fired the foundation's acting director, who had the temerity to back Naftali. And then they proceeded to try to get Naftali fired. William Safire, the *New York Times* columnist who had served as a Nixon speechwriter and remained ever loyal to Nixon, was so upset with the invitation to Dean that he vowed never to visit the library again.

The difference in the responses of the Boston bombers' family and the Nixonians could not be starker. The Boston bombers' parents refused to write off their sons even though they had committed murder. The Nixonians eagerly wrote off Dean and then tried to destroy him—not for the crime for which he was guilty, participation in the cover-up, but for a "crime" that wasn't a crime: failing to continue the cover-up by confessing to it.

We can now answer, finally, the question we posed at the beginning of this chapter, why the Nixonians refuse to move on—why it's always 1974 with them. The answer is that moving on threatens the very existence of the group. A family continues to exist no matter what happens as long as its members remain alive. Even when a parent tries, as parents on very rare occasions do, to disavow a child who's behaved badly ("he's dead to me" is the refrain we hear in the movies), the child's family identity remains inviolate. Not even going to court to get official records changed can alter the fact that biological parents and children share something no court can dissolve: their genetic ties.

Groups are different. The members of non-familial groups don't share genes. What they primarily have in common are their beliefs. If they suddenly give up their beliefs, they have little to hold them together. What, after all, could it mean to be a Nixonian if you didn't believe in Nixon? That was the problem the Nixonians faced. The only way they could continue to believe in Nixon was to believe in the defense he offered when he was president. There were hard limits to the flexibility they were willing to show. The facts? The facts were too difficult to absorb. You couldn't submit the facts into evidence in the court of history and remain an enthusiastic backer of Nixon. The facts were too damning. So instead the Nixonians denied the facts. They had little choice if they were to remain Nixonians, which they wanted to do for a variety of reasons: a shared history, social status, and their identity.

We are reminded as Americans from time to time to be wary of the influence of powerful families on our politics. This is with good reason. The danger from them is self-evident. A powerful family can dominate a state's politics as the Chandlers did in California, the McCormicks did in Illinois, and the Kennedys did in Massachusetts. While these families often do a lot of good, they also often do a lot of harm. Large, powerful families are in a position to put their own interests above others, as the Kennedys did after Chappaquiddick, snuffing out the chance for an independent investigation of the incident that left a young woman dead in a car as the driver, Senator

Ted Kennedy, swam off. Large powerful families can stifle change, leaving politics sclerotic. People connected to one another by family ties usually feel bound to favor their own families over principle when the two come into conflict, suffocating needed reforms.

These are the reasons we sometimes fear powerful families. We don't usually share the same fears about the members of non-familial groups. We figure they don't feel the same kind of pressure to compromise their principles. You can't leave your family, but you can always leave a group. Membership in a group is always temporary. But leaving isn't always easy. We treasure our social connections. And when membership becomes a part of our identity and our connections pay off in enhanced social status, leaving can be difficult. That is another of the lessons of the Nixonians. We remain in groups even when we should leave. This is the downside of these groups.

Groups like these aren't powerful enough to be able to protect us in all circumstances the way families can. But we are so desperate for the protection they do offer—a lesson evolution teaches; in groups there's safety, as we've seen—that we will compromise our integrity to remain a member if they'll have us. A family doesn't require us to surrender our integrity even as we are inclined to do whatever we can to assure the survival of the family. We can have our individual beliefs and our family membership too. But it's not that way with non-familial groups. They require conformity. The underlying assumption on which every such group is based is: conform or leave. The Nixonians who fought the effort to make over the Watergate exhibit, whether they acknowledged this to themselves or not, placed group membership ahead of the truth. The effect was to stymie change until finally the federal government forced change upon them.

IN THE WINTER OF 2002, the *Boston Globe* published a scoop that rocked the political world of Massachusetts. Secret federal grand jury testimony leaked to the paper indicated that the president of the University of Massachusetts, Billy Bulger, who had served earlier as the president of the state senate for nearly two decades, had tried to protect his younger brother from prosecution. His brother was Whitey Bulger, the notorious leader of the Winter Hill Gang, who was implicated in nineteen murders. For years, Whitey Bulger had been on the FBI's most-wanted list. He was into everything: drugs, extortion, racketeering, and money laundering. Stories of his ruthlessness were legion. This is what one of his thugs said working for Bulger was like: "My job description was simple: From 1985 to 1990, I worked for Whitey as a street soldier, an enforcer, a leg-breaker, a drug-runner. I was the hired muscle who distributed drugs for my boss and broke the limbs of those who disrespected him. I was often sent on missions that made me feel I was pushing up against the icy shoulder of death." An associate said of Bulger: "He could teach the Devil tricks."

The newspaper reported that his brother, the former senate president—who had served in that post longer than anybody else in Massachusetts history—had testified in secret that he had never tried to encourage his brother to give himself up. "I don't think it would be in his interest to do so," he testified. "I do have an honest loyalty to my brother and . . . I don't feel an obligation to help everyone catch him." On one occasion he had deliberately helped his brother evade capture. Suspecting that federal authorities had wiretapped his home phone, he had, at a time when he was president of the senate, made sure to take a call from Whitey at a friend's house. "It's my hope," he told the grand jury, "that I'm never helpful to anyone against him." The *Globe*'s story made national news, drawing the attention of columnists from across the country.

One columnist, writing in the *New York Times*, predicted that Billy Bulger would have to step down as president of the University of Massachusetts (a prediction that was to come true). But he also expressed sympathy for the beleaguered politician. He acknowledged that Bulger, pulled in one direction by his loyalty to his brother, and in another direction by his loyalty to his state, faced an agonizing choice. The name of the columnist was William Safire. He could understand perfectly well the depth of attachment a brother has for a brother, even a brother who's committed murder. This was the same William Safire who couldn't bring himself to sympathize with John Dean and who considered Dean so far outside the bounds of respectable society that his mere presence at an event at the Nixon Library was grounds for never visiting the library again. Why is that? Dean wasn't family. Dean had been a member of the same non-familial group, the President's Men. But that wasn't the same. We put family in a different category.

It is a good thing over all that groups do not command the same intense unwavering loyalty as families. A democracy could not long survive if they did. Democracies require flexibility and change to prosper. The Nixonians offer a classic example of the stultification that results when people put group loyalty above all else.

But that is what we do all the time. Why at the end of Nixon's presidency did 23 percent of the American people still stick by him? We can't be sure. But truth probably mattered less to them than their identity as steadfast Nixon loyalists. That was their group. Forced to choose between the truth and our group, as Leon Festinger proved, we will usually choose the group. That's why the followers of the Chicago mystic who believed the world was coming to an end stuck with her even when the world did not end. We privilege our group identity.

That's one of the reasons why we see the phenomenon of groupthink. We let ourselves be influenced by the group. In one classic experiment by the social scientist Solomon Asch, subjects in a group were shown strips of paper of different lengths. But when several members, Asch's confederates, declared that the strips were the same length, three-fourths of the others at various times went along in defiance of what they were seeing with their own eyes. Such is the power of group conformity. Our brain rewards conformity. When we conform to others' views, we experience a pleasurable dopamine rush.

The problem is that in a democracy truth matters. If truth is vital to the survival of democracy, if it's important for us to see things as they are and not as we wish them to be, then we have to find a way to set aside our loyalty to our group when the facts go against us. We have to work hard at resisting the impulse to just go with the flow of the group. We have to be our own Hollywood hero. Like Henry Fonda in *12 Angry Men*, we have to resist the gravitational pull of groups that draw us into their orbit and keep us there. My group right or wrong? In the Pleistocene, when humans lived in tiny communities made up mostly of members of either their own family or people they'd known their entire lives, blind loyalty, one of our deepest instincts, was often a virtue. In a modern democracy, it's poison.

As we have repeatedly seen, we are unlikely to be able to control our feelings. We are always going to feel what we feel. But we can control which groups we join. That's a decision we can make consciously, with due deliberation, using higher-order cognition—System 2 thinking, as defined by psychologist Daniel Kahneman. The reason that's so important is because whom we hang out with and the group with which we identify will help determine what kind of feelings we experience. Once you join a group, those feelings are going to be shaped by the group. So before we make a decision to join a group, we need to be absolutely sure the group we are joining reflects our values. That's easier with groups that have a track record. It's harder with new groups. It's the new groups we have to be most wary of. They can evolve into almost anything and take us along on the ride.

PART IV:
EMPATHY

10

When It Happens to You

The limits to empathy

1.

On June 25, 1950, a vast North Korean army, 89,000 strong, assembled along the 38th parallel, and invaded South Korea without warning. In a matter of days the force came close to overrunning the South Korean troops putting up a brave defense. Defeat seemed imminent. But then the US Air Force literally flew to the rescue. Just four days after the invasion American planes took control of the skies, giving ground forces a chance to regroup and fight on. One website boasts that by the end of the first month ground forces had "more air support than General Omar Bradley's Twelfth United States Army Group in Europe had during World War II." South Korea was saved.

The lesson the generals took from this was that air power works and that they should use it. And use it they did. This is evident from the statistics the Pentagon keeps, which are mind-boggling. The first month of the Korean War the air force flew two hundred sorties a day. (The North Koreans were flying just sixteen.) Soon the number increased to hundreds and hundreds of sorties daily. While you are imagining what this must have been like on a typical day—the pilots running for their planes, the engines revving up, the crews huddled in their aluminum tubes as they wait on the runway for take off, hundreds and hundreds of times a day—go one step further and imagine this happening day after day for three long years. That will give you some idea of the magnitude of the US air campaign over Korea. If you average out the sorties flown during the entire war, the number comes to more than nine hundred a day—an astounding number. Multiplied by the 1,128 days of the war, that comes to more than a *million* sorties—1,040,708 to be precise.

The statistical record also includes the amount of ordnance dropped by our airplanes. It is also mind-boggling. When the war broke out our planes were dropping around six hundred tons of bombs a day. That amount steadily increased until by the end of the summer it was eight hundred tons. And that was just the beginning. By war's end, on some days, we were dropping thousands of tons of bombs. All that added up to a staggering total over the course of the conflict to 32,000 tons of napalm and 386,000 tons of bombs. If you add in rockets and machine gun ammunition, notes historian Marilyn B. Young in a stunning essay on the history of bombing, the total comes to 698,000 tons. To make that number meaningful, I searched the Internet for a comparison. That is nearly equal to the weight of two Empire State Buildings.

In the years following the war a legend grew up about the immense achievements of the air force. The view of the generals was summed up in the title of a book that appeared in 1957: *Airpower: The Decisive Force in Korea,* to which Young draws attention. What left the generals in awe was the ability of the air force to occupy territory like an army. With air power alone the United States "could capture and control any desired segment of [enemy] territory for as long as the military situation warranted." One campaign seemed particularly significant. In January 1953, the air force made a show of bombing an eight-square-mile target a hundred miles inside enemy territory. Planes bombed the area for twenty-four hours a day for five days. The bombing erased all signs of life and left nothing but "gnarled steel and wretched earth." It was, air force officials boasted, a clear demonstration "of a new concept in war—air envelopment."

There is another way of looking at this record and that is from the perspective of the people on the ground, the people who lived in the path of destruction. For them the air force achievement was a horror. Due *in part* to the effectiveness of the air force, the war cost the lives of 600,000 civilians in North Korea and more than a million in South Korea—greater than the number killed in the American Civil War. After the war, the head of the UN's reconstruction agency called Korea "the most devastated land and its people the most destitute in the history of modern warfare."

2.

In her essay on bombing, Marilyn Young cites an article written by Freda Kirchwey, a prominent liberal journalist in the 1950s, who was appalled at the extent of the destruction in Korea and puzzled that Americans seemed indifferent to it. Maybe, Kirchwey surmised, it was because we had become "hardened by the methods of mass-slaughter practiced first by the Germans and Japanese and then, in self-defense, adopted and developed to the pitch of perfection illustrated at Hiroshima and Nagasaki by the Western allies, and, particularly, the Americans. We became accustomed to 'area' bombing, 'saturation' bombing, all the hideous forms of strategic air war aimed at wiping out not only military and industrial installations but whole populations."

Kirchwey, writing in the *Nation* during the Korean War, acknowledged that the Soviet Union, China, and North Korea were contributing to the horror as well. But nothing "excuses the terrible shambles created up and down the Korean peninsula by the American-led forces, by American planes raining down napalm and fire bombs, and by heavy land and naval artillery." Not even a righteous cause can justify such operations. For "after a while plain horror displaces a sense of righteousness even among the defenders of righteousness, and thus the cause itself becomes hateful. This has happened in Korea. Soon, as we learn the facts, it will overtake us here in America."

Freda Kirchwey could not have been more wrong. The facts came out. Americans did not care. Americans never showed any sign of revulsion at the way the war was being fought. Their main gripe was that it was taking so long to end. It just seemed to go on and on. In 1953, two years *after* Kirchwey's article, polls found that two-thirds of Americans favored a *greater* application of force, not less force. A majority probably would have backed the use of nuclear weapons. Going into the war the Pentagon had concluded that Americans would be appalled if we did *not* use nuclear weapons if it were determined that by using them we could shorten the war. As it turned out, neither Harry Truman nor Dwight Eisenhower chose to authorize the use of nuclear weapons. But that was not because they feared the public's wrath. It was because our allies opposed their use, as did high officials in the Pentagon, who worried that the Soviets might bomb Japan in retaliation. US officials were also concerned that the weapons might not actually stop the war, which would weaken considerably their deterrent power.

There was never much of a chance that Americans during the war, when war fever was high, would suddenly develop the sensitivity Kirchwey expected. But after the war? It did not happen then either. Indeed, it is Republican Party dogma that Dwight Eisenhower ended the war by threatening to use the most dangerous of all weapons, nukes. What does this tell you? Republicans are bragging that Ike threatened to let loose unholy hell on Korea. Doesn't that suggest that rather than worrying about the death of

civilians in war, Republicans are indifferent to it or at least not terribly concerned about it? And it's not just Republicans who seem to take a callous
attitude to the lives of civilians in wars overseas. When Barack Obama became president he immediately expanded the use of drones equipped with
Hellfire missiles. This predictably led to an increase in civilian deaths. But
did Democrats loudly complain? The answer is they did not.

Bombing always entails the risk of civilian casualties. But not even the
pilots of the planes dropping bombs all over Korea worried too much about
the trail of death they were leaving in their wake. Nor did the pilots who a
generation later flew missions in Vietnam. "One thing about napalm," one
pilot in Vietnam recalled, "is that when you've hit a village and have seen it
go up in flames, you know you've accomplished something. Nothing makes
a pilot feel worse than to work over an area and not see that he's accomplished anything."

Nothing could be worse? This makes us sound like Nazis.

One of the legacies of the Korean War is our faith in air power. Since
Korea the Pentagon has turned to the air force in every war we've fought.
Dropping bombs has won such widespread acceptance that the moment a
crisis erupts in some foreign country where military action might be required, the stock suggestion is that we bomb the place. That is what we
heard when, in 2011, the people of Libya turned against Muammar Gaddafi and the people of Syria began to revolt against Bashar al-Assad, and in
2014 when ISIS, the Islamic State of Iraq and Syria, began making a run at
Baghdad. Start bombing. Even liberals backed bombing Gaddafi. As Marilyn Young points out, air power sounds attractive. She astutely notes that
we refer to soldiers as grunts, but pilots as aces. When our gaze takes in an
airplane we feel a rush of excitement. Airplanes are a symbol of our age's
technological prowess. War may be dirty, but air power? It gleams.

3.

But does it work? That is not a question we are used to hearing. Of course it
works! You drop a bomb and see immediate results. How could it not work?
But there are doubters, and there is a strong reason to believe they are right
that air power isn't the panacea it is often made out to be. Remember the
campaign in Korea that the air force was so proud of, the one that reduced
eight square miles of enemy territory to rubble? The one that demonstrated
"a new concept in war—air envelopment"? As Marilyn Young observes,
the same report that used this campaign to show what you can do with
air power also included this fact: in the end air power succeeded in clear-

ing out the area for only eleven days. That's five days of bombing and the six days that followed. And after that? The communists who had fled the scene moved back in and began restoring the infrastructure that had been destroyed. The very first day they came back, a central road was restored. Then came the rail links. Five days of round-the-clock bombing and all we had to show for it was eleven days of inactivity before the "hordes" of "Red laborers and soldiers," as the report put it, were able to start putting things back in order.

In the summer of 1964, Lyndon Johnson shared with his close friend Richard Russell, the senator from Georgia, his plan to use air power in Vietnam. Johnson said he had to do something. Vietnam was collapsing. And he didn't want to send in more American ground troops. Fortunately, he didn't need to. The air force could bomb North Vietnam and stop the slide toward defeat. Russell was incredulous. He was one of the doubters. "Bomb the North," he said, "and kill old men, women, and children?" No, LBJ said, the air force wouldn't bomb people, it would bomb highways and buildings. Russell would have none of it. "We tried it in Korea," he said. "We even got a lot of old B-29s to increase the bomb load and sent 'em over there and just dropped millions and millions of bombs, day and night." He was exaggerating. It wasn't millions. But his point was well taken. "They would knock the road at night and in the morning the damn people would be back travelling over it. . . . We never could actually interdict all their lines of communication, although we had absolute control of the seas and the air, and we never did stop them. And you ain't gonna stop these people either."

What did LBJ do? He decided to use both ground troops *and* air power. In March 1965 Defense Secretary Robert McNamara launched Operation Rolling Thunder, which was designed to bomb North Vietnam into submission. Fifty-five thousand sorties were flown the first year. At its height, our planes were dropping 1,600 tons of bombs a week.

In 1966, a think tank hired by the Pentagon, drawing on the talents of some of the country's most eminent thinkers, subjected the claims made on behalf of Rolling Thunder to extended critical analysis. What they wanted to know was whether the air campaign could stop North Vietnam from supporting the Viet Cong. The answer was a categorical no. The group found that since "the beginning of Rolling Thunder air strikes on NVN [North Vietnam], the flow of men and materiel from NVN to SVN has greatly increased, and present evidence provides no basis for concluding that the damage inflicted on North Vietnam by the bombing program has had any significant effect on the flow."

So naturally the Pentagon called off Rolling Thunder, right? Wrong. It was continued. It remained in operation until October 31, 1968, when Johnson ordered a halt in the bombing in the last week before the presidential election.

Conservative critics of Johnson's leadership of the war frequently complain that he never unleashed the US military. It is true that he hesitated to allow the bombing of certain areas, where large civilian populations were centered, in North Vietnam. He also declined to mass bomb Laos and Cambodia, which the communists used to deliver weapons and soldiers to South Vietnam. But he can hardly be charged with taking a lily-livered approach, as is often implied. During the course of Rolling Thunder the United States flew more than 300,000 sorties and dropped nearly 650,000 tons of bombs. It was, says historian Mark Clodfelter, the "longest sustained strategic air bombardment in history."

Over the course of the entire war we dropped 8 million tons of bombs on Indochina—four times what we dropped in World War Two in both the European and Pacific theaters. We dropped more bombs on little Vietnam, Laos, and Cambodia than we dropped on the enemy in Europe and Asia in World War Two. And we went ahead with bombing even though there was a strong reason to believe it wouldn't work. What does this remind you of? It's the SIGMA war games syndrome all over again. Bombing doesn't do much good, but let's bomb anyway. Failure doesn't seem to matter.

4.

As you read Marilyn Young's essay on bombing it becomes obvious that she shares Freda Kirchwey's shock at the loss of life air power inflicts on innocent populations. It is also apparent Young is appalled that Americans did not rise up in revulsion as Kirchwey predicted they would. Reading the accounts Young provides of civilian casualties it is easy to be appalled. But should we expect human beings to be appalled?

We believe human beings are naturally empathic. We take pride in our capacity for empathy. It's what keeps us human. But our capacity for empathy is limited. Most of the time empathy only works under four restricted circumstances:

1. When a story tugs at our heart.
2. When we are face-to-face with someone in pain or jeopardy.
3. When somebody is going through something we ourselves have experienced.

4. When we identify with a person in pain, either because we
   know them or their group, or we are members of the same
   group.

When people are reduced to numbers—as the civilian victims of bomb-
ings inevitably are—we don't feel their pain. We don't automatically put
ourselves in their shoes, which is by definition what you do when you are
feeling empathic. We have the bomber pilot's problem. We don't feel anything for the victims. We need to see people face-to-face for our emotional
system to become fully engaged. In experiments in the lab social scientists
have found that people are far more generous when playing the Dictator
Game, in which an individual splits a pot of money with another player,
when they can see the other player than when they cannot.

Freda Kirchwey was certain that Americans would react humanely once
they heard the facts. She believed in the rational model of politics. She had
faith that facts matter. But as I hope I have persuaded you by now, facts on
their own usually don't matter all that much. Most of the time people don't
think through public policy questions. They respond with their gut. And
responding in that way isn't likely to elicit an empathetic reaction to the
civilian victims of air power.

We think we can count on our own empathy to provide us with the
necessary warmth and humanity to address issues we face as citizens in
a democracy. But we can't. Our inability to do so skews public debates. It
gives the advantage to the side wanting to take action to achieve a goal that
inconveniences, harms, or kills people we don't know. Once we settle on a
goal, believe it's just, and become convinced that we can get results, there's
nothing that inclines us to pause and consider the effect our efforts are
having on the victims, who remain largely invisible to us.

This pattern can be seen in lots of public policy debates. When Republicans in 2013 moved to drastically cut food stamps, they focused on the
cost of the program. For them, it was a dollars and cents issue. The federal
government is going broke, they said. Therefore, we need to make cuts
somewhere, and this seems like a good place to start. Cut food stamps and
help America! Some murmured that cutting the program would even be
good for the recipients. It would strengthen their backbone. But the recipients were never more than an abstraction. They weren't real human beings.
They were a foil, used to build support for the cuts by appealing to voters'
resentment at people who are supposedly lazy cheats. On conservative talk
radio shows the hosts lambasted the recipients for using food stamps to buy
everything from organically raised meat to wild salmon. One Texas state

senator featured in a clip on *The Daily Show* said flatly that food stamps should only be permitted for the purchase of essentials like ordinary meat and flour. In a debate like this where the humanity of the people who will be most affected by our actions is not acknowledged, can a fair debate be said to have taken place? That doesn't seem likely. How can you debate a public policy and not take the measure of its impact on the human beings who are most affected? You can't. But that is how our debates go for the most part.

Not even factual evidence that our efforts are failing stops us. We fought the drug war for decades. Failure was obvious. But did we stop? No. Prisons filled up during the drug war. The United States' incarcerated population doubled over a few short years to two million—the highest of any country in the entire world. And still people continued taking drugs. Pleas to change the law and show empathy for drug offenders went nowhere. Almost certainly, voters would have felt differently about the drug war if they themselves or someone they knew had ever been sent to prison for drug use. That would have made the policy personal. But how often do we have personal contact with the people policies directly affect? Not very often at all.

And when we do? We see things differently.

3.

In 2011, Senator Rob Portman, a Republican from Ohio, and his wife Jane had a conversation with their son Will. It was like none they'd ever had before. Will, a freshman at Yale, told them he was gay. "He said he'd known for some time," the senator recalled later, "and that his sexual orientation wasn't something he chose; it was simply a part of who he is. Jane and I were proud of him for his honesty and courage. We were surprised to learn he is gay but knew he was still the same person he'd always been. The only difference was that now we had a more complete picture of the son we love."

Senator Portman until then had always been a firm opponent of gay marriage. In 2011, the same year his son came out to him, hundreds of students had protested the senator's selection as a commencement speaker at the University of Michigan over his insistence that marriage "is a sacred bond between one man and one woman," as his spokesman put it. But two years later, after mulling over his son's disclosure, Senator Portman announced that he had changed his mind. He now favored gay marriage. What happened? Suddenly, gay politics was personal.

The same metamorphosis took place when Dick Cheney learned that his daughter Mary is a lesbian. When the Bush administration came out in favor of a federal statute establishing marriage as a contract between a man and a woman, Cheney went on television to say he personally believed this is an issue that should be left up to the states. This is what happens when politics is no longer about some abstract person you read about in the news. As feminists in the 1960s put it, the personal is political.

This is the reason too for our having a greater empathic response to people who look like us and talk like us and dress like us. We naturally favor our own group. When something bad happens to a member of our group we react far more sensitively than when something bad happens to somebody outside our group. It's more personal then. When something happens that affects our group we respond viscerally. It's how our brain is prewired.

Evolution favored the development of empathy. It is one of the critical defining attributes of our species and the basis for group cooperation. The more empathetic we are, the more trusting we are. And trust is essential to our success as a species. The more trusting we are the more prosperous we are. One economist has showed that the key defining quality of successful societies is the inherent willingness of members to trust one another. The more trust there is, the more people trade with one another, and the more they trade with one another, the more trusting they become, creating (once again) a classic virtuous circle.

And as scientists have now shown, trust is built into our brain. That's what oxytocin is doing in there. Oxytocin is what gives us the feeling of well-being when we establish a connection with one another. Without it, we'd be at each other's throats. We'd be all testosterone all the time. And people charged up on testosterone usually find cooperation a challenge, which is one reason why males, who naturally come with more testosterone than females, are much quicker to grab a gun in a fight. It's why younger males are more prone to violence than older males. They have more testosterone. What happens when a male marries and has children? His testosterone levels decline dramatically. This helps make him a better father and husband.

One of the fundamental differences between humans and chimpanzees has to do with empathy. A toddler can follow an adult's gaze, which is a critical skill in understanding what another person is thinking, a vital component of empathy. A chimpanzee at any age can't. This is not because human babies are simply brighter than chimpanzees. A study comparing two-year-olds and adult chimpanzees demonstrated that both are roughly equal in executing key physical tasks. When in one test a chimpanzee needed to use a tool to get at food that was out of reach, he was able to do so as easily as a baby. Both groups received the same score, 68 percent, on this part of the test. But when it came to social skills? The babies easily outperformed the chimps. The babies could follow someone's gaze to find hidden food. The chimps could not. The babies got a score of 74, the chimps, 36.

You can visit a hunter-gatherer community today and see empathy on display under all sorts of circumstances. Like curiosity, reading people, and realism, our capacity for empathy comes naturally. But in the modern world, in public debates involving issues affecting millions of people, our empathic impulse is short-circuited. It often doesn't work. Even when we see a story on TV about someone who's going to be adversely affected by a change in public policy, it's unlikely—unless that story is truly extraordinary—that we will know what it's actually like to stand in that person's shoes.

Think about the difference between seeing someone in trouble in person and seeing that same person in trouble in a video story. If you saw someone on the street getting badly roughed up your instinct would be to help them if you could. Furthermore, you'd feel the blows. As the victim writhed in agony you would feel their agony. If you didn't, you'd think there was something wrong with you and probably conclude you need to see a shrink. You'd realize you aren't a fully functioning human being. Now take the same situation, only this time the scene is on television. It would be different, wouldn't it? First, there'd be no need to call for help. But second, and much more importantly, you would not likely feel the same emotions you felt if you were watching in person. Watching the news is different from living the news.

While I've been writing this book, the war in Syria has been a nightly presence on television. Some scenes have been absolutely horrific. But seeing them on TV isn't the same as seeing them in person. There's a profound difference in the way we process live events happening before our eyes and events we see on the tube. We can eat dinner without pausing while watching a bomb drop on a city. We can't do that in person. The fact is, we don't expect a television news story to produce the same reaction in us as a real event to which we are personally a witness. That's why in the history of the world no one has ever likely scheduled an appointment with a psychiatrist because he failed to feel pain when watching a news story on TV about some bad situation. See something horrible in person and not react? You've got a problem. See it on TV and not react? Pass the salt and pepper.

Psychologists tell us that no matter how hard we try, we cannot actually imagine what it's like to be someone else. Studies show that even when we try really hard we have difficulty. Let's say you are pro-choice, but you want to understand what it's like to be pro-life. So you begin to think up all the arguments you've ever heard from pro-life supporters. What's likely to come of your efforts? Almost certainly, you will assume that pro-life supporters take a much more extreme view than they actually do. When we try to imagine what others feel, we almost always go for the extreme. After all, that's what sticks in our minds when we hear about things. When pro-choice and pro-life advocates are fighting, the battle lines are always drawn starkly. So if you were to try to imagine what a pro-life supporter thinks, you'd naturally remember the arguments that left the deepest impression—those at the extreme. Paradoxically, social scientists have discovered that the harder we try to imagine what others are thinking, the more warped our perspective becomes. We wouldn't show more understanding of pro-lifers if we spent more time thinking what it must be like to be pro-life. We'd show less.

4.

Empathy is hard. It's hard even with people we know and love. Married couples who have been together fifteen years and are asked by researchers to say how their partners feel about a variety of issues, issues as simple as the debt load their family is carrying, have trouble coming up with accurate answers. They do better than chance, but not by much. People are complicated. It's hard to know how they feel, even when it's people we spend time with and think we know really well.

And we think we can empathize with people we don't know and have never met? Short of watching a movie that brings their story to life or experiencing what they feel by putting ourselves in their situation, it's virtually impossible to feel empathy for them. Want to feel what it's like to be homeless, asks the behavioral scientist Nicholas Epley? Spend a month living on the streets. Then you'll know. In other words, if you want to stand in someone's shoes and know what they feel, then stand in their shoes. But how many of us are going to do something like that? Alternatively, he suggests, you can simply ask them how they feel. That works. When the Pentagon was considering allowing gays to serve openly in the military, high officials were concerned that a majority of soldiers, particularly those from the South, where a disproportionate number of soldiers are from, would rebel. Then, Epley relates, Secretary of Defense Robert Gates decided to try a novel approach and actually ask the soldiers how they'd feel about the proposed change. Over 70 percent said it wouldn't bother them.

Another possibility has surfaced to help increase our feeling of empathy. It's to give us a shot of oxytocin. That's the love hormone remember, the same hormone that makes lovers feel close at the moment of highest arousal and that helps mothers bond with their children. Some companies have actually started selling oxytocin for this purpose, producing an atomizer that allows you to spray the stuff on yourself. This doesn't actually work. You need a shot for the treatment to be effective. And in any case, the effect doesn't last very long. But there's one other problem. Studies now show that it mainly increases empathy for members of our own social group, people we are already predisposed to understand. It can actually increase our hostility to strangers.

We are back, then, to more prosaic solutions. Want to know what people think and feel? Ask them. But that's not practical in most situations. Even on the local level it's not very practical. If your local city council is considering passing an ordinance prohibiting the homeless from sleeping in parks, would talking to a homeless person you encounter on the street likely give you a real understanding of the situation the homeless in your city face and the impact the proposed ordinance would have on them? You'd have to talk to a lot of homeless people to get a real sense of the impact. And how many of us are going to do something like that? That's the difficulty we face on the local level. Imagine the complications when an issue is national in scope. Then it's actually impossible for us to feel empathic for the people likely to be impacted by some law, because we can't possibly talk to enough people.

This suggests that the nature of our problem is a familiar one. It's the problem of scale. The smaller a community is, the more we can rely on our own empathy to feel what we ought to feel when bad things happen to people. When a community is tiny, as our hunter-gatherer communities were, our automatic empathic impulses work beautifully. When bad things happen in hunter-gatherer communities, they happen to people who are known to the entire community. This doesn't mean that hunter-gatherers respond to people in pain as a Mother Teresa might. Their response is shaped by the values of their culture, which, for example, might condone infanticide or senicide. But in general, they are likely to feel the pain of the members of their own community.

What about us? With large communities like the ones most of us live in today empathy frequently doesn't kick in. See someone hurt and you'll feel their pain. See five hundred people hurt and you'll feel their pain, too—but it won't be five hundred times the pain. Hear on television that a typhoon has killed a hundred thousand people? You will feel badly, but you won't feel a hundred thousand times worse than you did when you learned that one person had been killed by a typhoon. Empathy doesn't scale. When asked to make a donation to help a single victim of a natural disaster identified by name people are far more generous—as much as 50 percent more generous—than when they are asked to help a large group of anonymous victims.

Even if the Americans who lived through the Korean War had made an effort to come to terms with the facts, which most people did not, could they really know what the Koreans were going through? Can you imagine what it would be like to be bombed? I know I can't imagine it. I've never had so much as a rock come sailing through my window, let alone had a bomb drop on my street. Only people who have been bombed can be counted on to react instinctively the way Freda Kirchwey wanted Americans to react. Kirchwey herself, using her powers of imagination and relying on endless hours of research, probably had a pretty good idea. But the rest of us? We don't have time under normal circumstances to delve and probe and feel our way into somebody else's world. So what do we do? We work off our gut. And that's often inadequate.

There's an additional problem. We think we are a lot more empathic than we actually are. Think of those married couples I mentioned earlier who were asked to guess how their partners feel. They scored just a little better than chance. But nearly all of them were convinced that they had done really well. They believed they were so in sync with their spouses that they understood them as well as they understood themselves. Nicholas Epley, who performed the experiment, says that in his entire career as a scientist he has never seen results as stark as those this study of married couples produced. Their confidence in their own empathy was off the charts. It was also wildly misplaced.

11

— The — Accountant's Error

The danger of relying on our gut

1.

In 1976, the journalist Anthony Lewis penned a column in the *New York Times* that stuck with me ever after. It was seething with anger—which was rare for Lewis. But he couldn't contain himself. What was he so exercised about? Gerald Ford, of all people. Ford had a reputation as a nice man. "If he saw a school kid who needed clothing," his former press secretary said, "he'd give him the shirt off his back, literally." But Ford's policies were not nice. Lewis went through a list. Ford had vetoed the school lunch program. He'd vetoed legislation to regulate strip mining. He'd used "strident language about crime." Lewis even held against Ford something he had said before he became president: "I heard him in a small group express disbelief at the idea that anyone in this country did not have enough to eat." How, Lewis asked, "can such a nice man be so insensitive, politically, to human concerns? How can he so consistently have identified himself, over a long career in politics, with [such] narrow and illiberal causes? How can such a person be President of the United States?"

The answer Lewis came up with was that Ford had lived his life in a co-coon, safe and insulated from the hard world of millions of his fellow Americans. Ford didn't know what their lives were like because he didn't stand in their shoes. Lewis was saying, in effect, what the social scientist Nicholas Epley says: if you want to feel for some other person's condition, you have to talk to them and experience what they experience. Ford had not.

But was this all there was to Ford's insensitivity? It is impossible to know what Ford was thinking. But a clue that more was going on here than can be explained by his mere isolation is that all of the people he seemed to discount had something in common. What do coal miners and hungry schoolchildren and criminals have in common? They are people of low status. That, say social scientists, is highly significant. People of low status generally do not draw an empathic response. When we go into a room our eyes automatically search for people of high status. Even our cheater-detection abilities are geared to people's status. Low-status people get less scrutiny than high-status people. Like it or not, that's how we are built. When we come upon persons of low status we have trouble even seeing them as fully human. We don't get angry with such people. Anger is reserved for people whose behavior we want to change. We don't want to change the behavior of people we consider beneath ourselves. We simply don't want to have anything to do with them. Rather than anger, we feel disgust. What do we do when we are disgusted by something? We avoid it. That's what we do when we steer far clear of a homeless person lying on the sidewalk. We are not angry with them. We simply do not want to engage with them as one human being to another.

We literally pay them no mind, treating them as if they are mindless, says Epley. We reserve mind reading for people who count. Reading the minds of people who don't count is a waste of time. That, at any rate, is what our brain thinks. When subjects are put into an fMRI machine and told to look at pictures of the homeless and other low-status people their brain registers far lower activity in the medial prefrontal cortex (MPFC) than when they look at pictures of high-status people. They literally are paying low-status people less mind. The lower the status, the less activity there is in the MPFC.

It gets worse. The higher status you yourself are, the less likely you are to feel empathy for people who have a lower status. It's not just a stereotype that rich people seem less concerned with the fate of the poor. Studies show the rich actually *are* less concerned. It's one of the consequences of their wealth. Here's where things get really bizarre. You don't actually have to be wealthy to share the wealthy person's state of indifference. You just have to feel wealthy. When subjects playing Monopoly with *fake money* are tested for their capacity for empathy, the amount of fake money they accumulate during the game affects their empathy score. The more fake money they have, the less empathic they are toward strangers. Called away from the game on a pretext that something was happening in another room, most showed less sympathy for a woman they came across who'd spilled dozens of pencils on the floor than players who hadn't accumulated wealth in the game. And this is Monopoly we're talking about.

Then there's this. It turns out that people demonstrate less empathy when they grow more muscles. The stronger people get, the less empathic they get, too. This sounds downright strange except when you consider the effect body strength had on the fortunes of people prior to the creation of the modern state. In a hunter-gatherer community body strength was a major asset. The stronger you were the more likely you could gain and keep resources others wanted. You could literally fight them off. Evolution therefore selected for brute strength. Every man wanted to be dominant. The stronger he was the more likely he could exert his will, though as we have seen in our discussion of alpha-male chimpanzees, in the end it was not brute strength that determined who'd lead, it was an individual's social skills. Why in the end did Yeroen defeat Luit? Because of Yeroen's superior social skills. He was able to take control by forming a coalition with another chimpanzee. So physical strength wasn't everything. But it wasn't nothing. Physically strong alpha males were favored.

It gets even worse than this. Imagine a train hurtling down a track at a high speed. Ahead is a group of five people tied to the track. If you could save those five people by diverting the train onto another track where a bystander is waiting, killing him, would you? This experiment has been done over and over, and every time a majority answer yes. But when social scientists added a wrinkle, denoting the status of the bystander, they got a surprising result. More people became convinced that it was morally acceptable to divert the train if the bystander was of low status. When researchers added that the five people to be saved were of high status, the majority grew even larger.

Recent experiments conducted by Paul Zak, an economist-turned-neuroscientist, show that changes in our status are reflected in the physical functioning of our brain. The higher up you are on the status ladder, the more testosterone is likely to be active in your system. Like presidents who keep running and running for office, the more testosterone you have, the less likely you are to feel empathy for people lower on the status totem pole. Zak is convinced that this is why males so frequently score lower on tests of empathy than women. They have more testosterone in their system. Men are doubly at a disadvantage compared with women. Not only do they generally have higher levels of testosterone, they have lower levels of oxytocin. If you have a choice of bosses, you might want to take their gender into account, he advises. If your boss is female, she'll probably have an easier time understanding you.

This begins to explain how humans, born with the capacity for empathy, could put black people in chains, send Indians on forced marches, and gas Jews. You can only empathize with people whose humanity you recognize. If you drop them into a subhuman category, your MPFC doesn't activate.

So the rich and powerful and strong are out of touch? That's not a sign they're broken. That's a sign they're human. It's human beings operating the way we evolved to operate. A person who behaved this way was more likely to pass on his or her genes than someone who didn't. This doesn't excuse that person's behavior. To think that is to commit what social scientists have dubbed the naturalistic fallacy: the belief that because a behavior is replicated in nature that means it's moral.

Freda Kirchwey was sure Americans would respond empathically to victims of bomb attacks because she knew, she said, that Americans are a warmhearted people. But humans are only warmhearted toward people they regard as human. When we cannot feel another person's humanity, we cannot empathize with them. When we regard them with scorn, as many have regarded blacks, Indians, Jews, the homeless, immigrants, and, in this case, people of color living in foreign lands we were bombing, we feel free to treat them abhorrently.

Anthony Lewis could not understand how Gerald Ford could fail to see the humanity of the people affected by his public policy choices. It made Lewis a little crazy. "How can such a person be President of the United States?" But Ford apparently did not recognize the humanity of many of the least fortunate among us. His contact with them was limited. When he and his advisers were discussing the school lunch program he apparently wasn't thinking much about the kids the program would benefit. He was dealing not with people but with numbers on a spreadsheet. Ford was a wiz with budgets. He was the last president of the United States to pore over the federal budget page by page and line by line. Political scientists regard this with awe. A president who can read a budget! But there's a downside. Ford suffered from the accountant's problem. Call it Accountant's Syndrome. He apparently frequently saw people affected by his policies as numbers. When we do that we cease seeing them as people.

Another factor may have affected Ford's thinking: the fact that he was used to thinking about policy choices as a numbers problem not a people problem. Recent research indicates that when we are performing mental functions involving math we cannot simultaneously exercise the part of our brain that triggers compassion. When our brain is preoccupied with an analytical problem, we cannot successfully intuit what other people are feeling. We can either be analytical or compassionate. We can't be both at the same time because these functions operate like a light switch. They are either on or off. This suggests there may be something to the stereotype about engineers, who, by reputation, often seem to have great difficulty relating to people.

Ford apologists might argue that Ford took the positions he did in 1976 that so infuriated Lewis to blunt the attacks from the right he faced from Ronald Reagan, who was challenging him for the Republican nomination. That may be. But we are still left with the fact that Ford was willing to sacrifice the poor on the altar of his political ambitions. That suggests he regarded them as abstractions.

In the world of hunter-gatherers empathy was easily expressed and felt. Everybody knew everybody. In our world we often need to be empathic toward people we don't know at all. When a policymaker is deciding on the budget for a social–safety net program he can't possibly know personally the people who will benefit from it. When he is making his decision he is not looking at their faces, he is looking at a spreadsheet. Voters are even one step farther removed. They don't have those spreadsheets in front of them. Policymakers have numbers to go by that suggest the magnitude of the hurt that needs to be taken into consideration. Voters don't even have that.

2.

Midway through the primaries in 1976, when Reagan was challenging Ford for the Republican nomination for president, Ford made a trip to San Antonio, Texas. The trip was a disaster. While meeting with a group of Mexican-Americans, Ford was invited to eat a tamale. Ford grabbed the tamale and bit into it. He chewed. He swallowed. The people around him were aghast. As everybody knows who has ever eaten one, tamales come with a cornhusk. Before you take a bite you have to peal back the husk. Ford didn't know that. The next day the *New York Times* ran a photograph of the mishap. The caption read: "Campaigning in Texas: President Ford starting to eat a tamale during a visit to the Alamo yesterday. The snack was interrupted after the first bite so that his hosts could remove the corn shucks which serve as a wrapper and are not supposed to be consumed." Ford managed to eke out a victory over Reagan in the race for the GOP nomination, but he lost in the general election to Jimmy Carter. After the election, he was asked what he had learned campaigning for president in 1976. He answered, dryly: "Always shuck your tamales."

Looking back on the San Antonio event, it is easy to fault Ford for cynicism. His goal in eating the tamale was to establish a bond with

Mexican-Americans he did not actually have. It was an act of ersatz empathy. It's what politicians do. To get the vote of Asians, they go to Chinatown and eat fried rice. To win over Jews, they head over to Moishe's Bake Shop in the East Village in New York City and take a bite out of a babka. To lock up the Irish vote, they duck into a Boston pub and down a Guinness. The temptation is to write off these forays into ethnic communities as acts of naked manipulation, as reporters mostly do. But studies indicate there may actually be more going on here, whether the politicians themselves realize it or not. The physical act of eating a tamale while voters are eating one is likely to trigger a well-known phenomenon of empathy. When two people perform the same action they feel united: both instantly get a jolt of the heartwarming hormone, oxytocin. It's one of the ways we break down barriers between ourselves and others. Watch someone else eat a tamale. Ho hum. But eat a tamale with them? A kind of intimacy is established because we like to imitate others and like them to imitate us. This is why non-drinkers are sidelined when they go out with friends who do drink. We need to perform the same task as our friends to bond with them. Gerald Ford wasn't just appearing to be empathic as he ate his tamale along with his hosts. He was becoming more empathic with every bite.

Why does this work? It's the result of a peculiarity of evolution. We are able to feel what another person is feeling by replicating their actions. You want to know what your friend is feeling when he sees vomit on a rug? You don't have to see the vomit yourself. Just look at your friend and scrunch up your face just as he's doing. You'll feel it. This was unclear to scientists until they began studying people who suffer from Möbius syndrome. This is a congenital condition that prevents its victims from moving their facial muscles. Happy. Sad. Annoyed. They always look the same. They cannot even blink. Their eyes are always open. What scientists discovered is that people with this condition are unable as a rule to intuit the feelings of others. They can see a friend smiling but not feel it the way normal people can because they cannot force their own facial muscles into the form of a smile. You don't have to be a victim of Möbius to understand the effect a frozen face has on one's ability to show empathy. Here's an exercise you can try at home. First, ask a friend standing nearby to frown. Then make a frown yourself. See how this feels? Now, place a pencil horizontally in your mouth. Then ask your friend to make another frown. Now you do it. What you'll find is you can't frown. The pencil stops you. It freezes your facial muscles. What it also does, as Möbius victims know, is stop you from feeling what your friend is feeling and what you felt a moment ago when you frowned without the pencil.

What's going on inside the brain that explains this? That was a complete mystery until the 1990s when scientists working with macaque monkeys in a lab in Parma, Italy, began to notice something. The scientists were trying to figure out how a monkey's brain reacts when the animal performs a particular function. So they hooked up wires to different brain regions to see which light up when the monkey performs different tasks. Then one day something peculiar happened. The event was so momentous that a fascinating story began to be told about it. The story is untrue. But it might as well be true, for it captures the essence of the scientists' discovery. So here's the story the way it's usually told.

A graduate student happened to come into the lab one day with an ice cream cone. When the student went for a lick, all of a sudden the monitor a monkey was hooked up to began to make the sound it makes when the monkey performs an action. Brrrrrip. Brrrrrip. Brrrrrip. That was odd. The monkey wasn't licking the cone. It was merely *watching* someone lick the cone. But the monkey was showing brain activity as if it were licking the ice cream cone itself. This—or whatever happened the day of the discovery—was dumbfounding. Why would the monkey's brain indicate movement when it wasn't moving? The answer was that the same neurons in the brain—which the scientists dubbed mirror neurons—activate whether the animal is performing an action or merely watching someone who is.

You can understand why the discovery drew worldwide interest. Here seemed a clue to the phenomenon of empathy. For it isn't just macaque monkeys that have mirror neurons. So do humans. Mirror neurons make up more than 15 percent of the average human's total brain neurons. And here was a mechanism that seemed to explain exactly how a human being feels what another human is feeling. We feel it by performing in our brain the action they are performing without actually performing it. This is apparently why, when you are watching a football game and see someone tackled hard, you grimace and actually move your body as if *you* were being tackled. Though some scientists adamantly reject the belief that mirror neurons provide the mechanism by which we feel what others are feeling, many scientists accept it. Research continues.

GERALD FORD WAS AFFLICTED with Accountant's Syndrome. But there's a solution. It is to meet people and do what they do. You want to see someone else's humanity? Invite them to eat tamales with you. Proximity counts. You can't phone this in. You have to share the same physical space to get the effect. What Ford needed to do before he vetoed bills affecting schoolchildren and coal miners was spend time with them so he could experience their world as they experience it. It may be that even after he did he might still believe that the measures designed to protect them were flawed in some way and deserved to be vetoed. But at least he would have had a fair basis upon which to make a decision. When we decide the fates of others, that's the least we should do. If it's impractical for a president to visit with them because of his busy schedule, he should make it his business to have people around him who have. That would help balance the scales.

Seeing people as people won't stop cruelty or stereotyping. But it makes it harder. When soldiers in war are forced to engage in hand-to-hand combat, they often find they can't kill the enemy. A soldier (or bomber pilot) can kill at a distance with few moral qualms. But kill someone up close? That's hard. One of the worst commands ever given in a war was the order given in the Revolutionary War to American soldiers in the Battle of Bunker Hill to not fire until you can see the whites of their eyes. That's exactly when soldiers are least likely to want to fire.

Historians examining combat records in World War Two found that some 80 percent of soldiers found themselves incapable of firing a gun at the enemy in close quarters. At a distance of a couple of feet, the enemy aren't the enemy anymore. They're human beings. That became clear to George Orwell when he went to fight fascism in the Spanish Civil War. One day he came upon an enemy soldier who had jumped up out of a trench. "He was half-dressed and was holding up his trousers with both hands as he ran." But Orwell couldn't bring himself to fire a shot though the man was in full view. "I did not shoot partly because of that detail about the trousers," he recalled. "I had come here to shoot at 'Fascists,' but a man who is holding up his trousers isn't a 'Fascist,' he is visibly a fellow-creature, similar to yourself, and you don't feel like shooting at him."

3.

From 1968 to 1980—the years leading up to his election as president of the United States, when he was openly running for the presidency—Ronald Reagan always found that he could connect with audiences when he began discussing welfare. He returned to the subject constantly. It was one of the chief themes of his run against Ford in 1976.

Someone from Mars might conjecture that Reagan talked about welfare so much because he was concerned about the poor. But that wasn't it. We don't talk about welfare in this country because of our empathy for the misfortunate. We talk about welfare because we think there's a problem with it.

On its face Reagan's preoccupation with welfare—and his audience's responsiveness—seems odd. Welfare—defined here as direct cash payments to the poor—simply doesn't cost taxpayers much money. It's never amounted to more than a tiny percentage of the federal budget—less than 3 percent. In 1970, Aid to Families with Dependent Children (AFDC)—the means-tested welfare program at that time—cost federal taxpayers annually about $5 billion. The Pentagon budget just for research and development that year was more than $7 billion. The overall Pentagon budget at the time was $83 billion. And Reagan was preoccupied with welfare?

Reagan, however, wasn't just inventing a problem that didn't exist. In California the welfare rolls were exploding. In 1963, there had been 375,000 Californians on welfare (AFDC). By 1967 the number had risen to 769,000. By 1969 it was up to 1,150,687. And in 1970 it reached 1,566,000. As Reagan complained when he became governor of California, the rolls were increasing by 40,000 a month. That wasn't sustainable. And this wasn't just happening in California. The same thing was occurring in states from one end of the country to the other. Nationwide, between 1967 and 1973, the welfare rolls in many states tripled or quadrupled. This was very strange. During that period—84 months in all—the economy mostly was doing extremely well. Only in 13 out of the 84 months was the country in recession. Yet the rolls were increasing everywhere all the time, going up both when unemployment sank to near record lows—less than 3 percent—and when unemployment rose. This confounded liberals. The surge in the rolls upended their naïve assumption about welfare—that it went up only when unemployment did. They were wrong.

So why then were the rolls going up? Reagan's answer was that a lot of people who did not deserve welfare were applying for it and getting it.

The poster child of welfare abuse was a Chicago African-American woman known to the public as Linda Taylor. Reagan made her famous. Here's how he'd describe her: "She used 80 names, 30 addresses, 15 telephone numbers to collect food stamps, Social Security, veterans' benefits for four nonexistent deceased veteran husbands, as well as welfare. Her tax-free cash income alone has been running $150,000 a year." A journalist has noted that when Reagan would mention her annual haul the crowd would gasp. Then Reagan would add telling details, one of which was that she owned three cars, including a new Cadillac. You can imagine the crowd's response to that. Linda Taylor was the quintessential welfare queen.

Liberals complained that Reagan, once again, had gotten his facts wrong. Actually, it was they who were wrong. A 2013 investigation published by Slate found that, if anything, Reagan *underplayed* her crimes, which apparently included kidnapping and possibly murder. And it wasn't Reagan who first called her a welfare queen, a moniker liberals despised for obvious reasons. It was the *Chicago Tribune*, which ran a series of exposés tracking her criminal career, which culminated in her arrest, trial, and imprisonment.

Linda Taylor was like a villain in a Hollywood movie who is all evil. As such, she was a figure of fascination. But what is interesting is how irrelevant her case was. There was no proof, then or now, that con artists like her on a grand budget-busting scale were abusing the welfare system. All the evidence suggests that the overwhelming number of people who were on welfare were people who needed it: mothers, children, and the elderly. An audit of Pennsylvania's rolls, which had exploded along with California's, found that just 4 percent of recipients did not meet the state's requirements.

So why then had the welfare rolls skyrocketed? It's no mystery. But it was complicated, owing to several critical factors. One was that poor people from the South were migrating north and congregating in cities, changing those cities' urban demographic profiles. In New York City, impoverished blacks and Puerto Ricans moved into the neighborhoods that middle-class whites were leaving behind as they made their way to the suburbs. More poor people, more welfare cases. By the 1970s 10 percent of the city was on welfare. Another factor was the welfare-rights movement. In city after city poor people, inspired by the example set by civil rights activists like Martin Luther King Jr., began making demands for improved living standards. In Washington, DC, welfare-rights protesters occupied the Department of Health, Education, and Welfare. In New York City they began demanding thousands of hearings when people were denied benefits. Their protests resulted in higher benefits and expanded rolls. Still another factor, an exhaustive study concludes, was that the urban riots of the 1960s prompted scared mayors to reduce the social pressures building up in their cities by encouraging the poor to go on welfare—in effect, buying them off.

To summarize: the welfare rolls did not go up because people were cheating. They went up because there were a lot of people in need of welfare services. Even the people being bought off by the politicians legitimately needed services. We simply have a lot of people in this country, then and now, who cannot make it. This flies in the face of the myth of American prosperity. It's something we don't like to acknowledge. But it's a fact. What happened between 1967 and 1973 is that suddenly this fact became visible. Suddenly, it had a face.

The reaction of liberals to the skyrocketing rolls was to finger the econ-omy as the culprit. As we have seen, they were wrong. Reagan's reaction was to blame cheaters. As we have also seen, he was wrong too. But the public thought he was dead right. Why was that?

The stock answer is racism. This seems so self-evident to liberals that the case hardly needs making. What else could account for the harshness of the attacks on welfare? When William Buckley, the publisher of the conservative *National Review*, ran for mayor of New York City in 1965 and denounced welfare recipients as lazy—"No workee, no dolee," he said— wasn't his candidacy designed explicitly to appeal to racists? John Lindsey, the liberal Republican, swept to victory in the Big Apple, but in white ethnic communities Buckley, running as a third-party candidate, won up to 30 percent of the vote. His running mate was a leader of Parents and Taxpayers, an anti-integration group. Alabama governor George Wallace's campaigns for the presidency featured fevered denunciations of welfare. He claimed that welfare recipients were buying Porterhouse steaks with food stamps. Of course racism was behind the belief that welfare recipients are lazy.

But is the stock answer the correct answer? Did whites associate welfare with laziness because they are racist? When the social scientist Michael Bang Petersen, whom we met in chapter 3, surveyed opinions about welfare in Denmark, a society that is overwhelmingly white and homogenous, he made the astonishing discovery that Danes also quickly jump to the conclu-sion that people on welfare are lazy. Once Danes are prompted to think that someone in need is indeed lazy, they cannot remember anything else about them. *Hey, you're a cheater?* That's all we need to know. Indeed, the suspicion that people on welfare are lazy is a worldwide phenomenon. It is not just in the United States that people think that the poor have only themselves to blame for their impoverishment—that's a near universal belief, according to the World Values Survey.

What appears to liberals to have been a sign of dyed-in-the-wool racism may actually have been a sign of something even deeper, an ingrained hu-man suspicion that people who are the beneficiaries of community mu-nificence are lazy. Not even ideological beliefs, strongly held as they may be, undermine this psychology. Danes strongly believe in the abstract in the welfare state. Their society is built on the assumption that everybody deserves government assistance regardless of their work ethic. But when Danes are confronted with stories about people in need, Petersen's work shows they respond just as Americans do. (It should go without saying that this doesn't mean that racism isn't behind a lot of the hostility in the United

States to welfare. The misperception that a majority of welfare recipients are black clearly shapes many whites' attitudes.)

What Petersen's research suggests is that human beings are designed to be suspicious of the needy. This should not surprise us. While evolutionary pressures favored empathy—at any time anyone in the Pleistocene could find themselves down on their luck—you always had to be wary of the people who claimed they needed your help. They might be faking it. They might really not need it. They might just be lazy. Empathy could not evolve in the absence of this suspicion. How could it be otherwise? If all it took to survive was to ask neighbors for help, evolution would ruthlessly have favored parasites until they outnumbered the people willing to help them. The flip side to empathy therefore had to be inbred suspicion. Whenever a human being offered a helping hand they had to be sure the recipient deserved help. Before offering help you had to ascertain that the person receiving it deserved it.

There is nothing wrong with suspicion. But what makes sense in a small Pleistocene community does not make sense in the modern world. In the Pleistocene you'd want to help people because you might one day find yourself in need of help. Life was full of risks. Empathy for neighbors mitigated risks. If you went out hunting for food and did not succeed, you could turn to neighbors for meat with the implicit understanding that they could come to you in the future for meat if they went out hunting and failed to catch anything. This was classic tit-for-tat psychology, and it underlay many of our most altruistic impulses (and still does). But tit-for-tat cannot be the basis for welfare in the modern world. We don't enroll people in welfare on the assumption that someday they might help us out if we are down on our luck. You cannot run a large-scale system involving millions of people that way. It wouldn't work.

More significantly, the moral categories by which people in the Pleistocene judged other people don't apply in the modern world. In the Pleistocene, distinguishing between lazy people and unlucky people made sense. But does it make sense in a world like ours? Are people who find themselves on welfare there because they are morally flawed? Some might be. But isn't it likelier that most people on welfare end up there because of their circumstances? Children, for one, do not wind up on welfare because they are morally flawed, and children make up a substantial part of the population of welfare beneficiaries. But even their mothers and fathers are probably on welfare because of their situation. Maybe racism held them back or their lack of an education did.

Our brain is designed to evaluate welfare recipients on moral grounds, but the morality of the individual is irrelevant during a recession. If the economy is shedding jobs by the hundreds of thousands a month, as it was in 2009 after the financial crisis, it is likely you won't be able to find a job no matter how hard you look. In those circumstances it is not the individuals who are responsible for the situation in which they find themselves, it is the circumstances that are responsible. To think otherwise is to make the Fundamental Attribution Error. This is the error we make when we judge others by a different standard than we naturally judge ourselves by. When we take an action, we usually think it's in response to the situation in which we find ourselves. But when others act? It's because of who they are. When something bad happens to us, we think we're unlucky. This was, you may recall, how presidents get themselves off the hook for all kinds of nefarious behavior. It was, they tell themselves, the situation that forced them to behave badly. When something bad happens to someone else? It's because of some personal flaw. So when we see someone standing on a welfare line who looks physically fit and the thought occurs to us, "they must be lazy," we don't automatically think they're unlucky. We think they are scammers.

And who succeeds in the modern world? It's people who are competent. Specifically, this means people who possess sufficient skills to solve complicated problems. Their morality may bear little on their success. Plenty of egregiously antisocial and immoral people succeed in the modern world. Think of the titans who run many of Wall Street's empires. Are all of these people at bottom highly moral individuals? That's unlikely. From what we know of the financial crisis, plenty were not. The newspapers were filled with stories of businesspeople taking advantage of their fellow citizens, earning millions, and in some cases billions, selling investors worthless securities for houses that had been sold to people too poor to be able to make their monthly payments. When the mortgage market went belly up, some of these same Wall Street wizards turned around and bought up these same properties at distressed prices, earning them millions and billions more. These titans aren't likely to find themselves on welfare. But the people who do? It may well be that they end up on welfare because they lack the critical skills—perhaps even something as basic as literacy—needed to make it in the modern world. When that's the situation, denying them welfare seems cruel. Judging people who are in need today on the basis of moral categories that suited hunter-gatherer communities half a million years ago makes no sense.

4.

During Reagan's two terms as president he failed to reform welfare. At the end of his presidency, historians report, welfare spending was higher than it was at the start. In 1996, President Bill Clinton, working with a Republican Congress, ended AFDC, replacing it with a new program—Temporary Assistance to Needy Families (TANF)—that imposed a strict five-year lifetime limit on benefits, and added work requirements. It was the greatest change in the program since welfare had become a concern of the federal government in the Great Depression when AFDC was first established. The change in the law had immediate and dramatic effects. The rolls became substantially thinner. Overall spending on welfare declined. In the end Reagan prevailed. The United States adopted his approach to welfare. And it worked. Or did it?

Conservatives are convinced that Reagan was right because the welfare rolls dropped. But what no one could say was what happened to the people who left the system. Did they get jobs? Did they suddenly become, as conservatives like to say, productive members of society? No one knew. Then, in 2013, National Public Radio reported the results of a startling investigation that was as demoralizing as it was shocking. The story drew attention to a little-known fact. While the welfare rolls were going down, the number of people on Social Security disability was going up. The website version of the NPR report features two bar graphs. The first tracks the number of families on welfare. It looks like a ski slope, with the slope getting lower and lower on the right the closer you get to the present, reflecting the smaller welfare rolls we see today. The second bar graph tracks the number of low-income people on Social Security disability. This graph looks just like the other one, but in reverse. In place of the downward slope is an upward slope. At every point along the way, where one slope declines, the other increases. The slopes, in reverse, are not just similar. They look identical.

What had happened to all those people on welfare? It appears plausible that after they left the welfare rolls, a lot of them simply moved onto the disability rolls. In Hale County, Alabama, "one in four working-age adults is now on disability," NPR reported. We did not solve the welfare problem, it would appear. We simply moved a lot of people from one program, where they were visible, to another program, where they are less visible. In some respects nothing really changed except the name of the bureaucracy handing out their checks. In 2014, the government reported that for the first time ever the amount of federal aid going to families with disabled children exceeded the amount going to those on welfare.

But in one respect something important really did change, and it is terribly unfortunate. We have made it impossible to tailor government benefits to meet people's true needs. It makes no sense for people who cannot find a job to go on disability if they are not really disabled. They should be on welfare if they cannot take care of themselves and need a helping hand. We have taken a system that, for all its faults, made a certain amount of sense, and replaced it with one that does not make much sense at all. According to NPR, the criteria by which people are designated disabled are arbitrary. One individual might be labeled disabled because he has high blood pressure, while another person with high blood pressure is not. Some people who undoubtedly need assistance are no longer getting it, while others are getting a form of assistance they don't need.

And the reason? We cannot see the people on welfare as people. We see them as potential cheaters. And as Michael Bang Petersen observes, that swamps all of our other responses, including the strong impulse we possess for empathy.

The United States spent decades debating welfare policy. Finally, the policy was fundamentally changed, ending welfare as we know it, as the politicians put it. And in the end? We possibly wound up with a worse system. This suggests that the whole welfare hullabaloo was something of a charade—and a colossal waste of time. Linda Taylor, the symbol of welfare abuse, had never been representative. She had been *sui generis*. But we had responded to her welfare queen story so viscerally that we could not think straight about welfare. That has left us with a warped public policy.

FREDA KIRCHWEY THOUGHT that Americans living in a state of peace at home could feel what Koreans at war were going through thousands of miles away. Anthony Lewis thought Gerald Ford should be able to share the pain of the people most affected by his policies. Both Kirchwey and Lewis thought it should be natural to feel empathic. But when people go with their gut, they often don't. And isn't it with our gut that we react to the news most of the time? We don't attend to the news the way a PhD student listens to a professor's lecture. We don't take notes. We don't think hard. We just react. And that doesn't get us very far.

Conclusion:
A Way Forward

*Solutions are at our
fingertips if only we grasp them*

1.

One day, a twelve-year-old boy, home alone in Wheaton, Illinois, daringly decided to go through his parents' mail even though he wasn't supposed to. As the boy slowly shuffled through the envelopes one by one, opening some as he went, he came across one obviously meant to be secret. He opened it anyway and began reading. The letter informed him that his parents were getting a divorce. The name of the boy was Bob Woodward.

Life was never the same again for Woodward, but because of who he grew up to become, it is not his parents' divorce that has drawn the attention of biographers. It is the fact that he was opening his parents' mail. The story seems revealing. It is consistent with our assumptions about journalists and about Woodward. His is the seamless story of a boy intrigued by secrets who became a man intrigued by secrets, ever alert to the gap between outward appearances and ugly reality.

But is what Woodward did as a boy any different really from what we have all done? Not really. We are all curious and probing. To be sure, Woodward has an extraordinary nose for news, as the cliché has it. He has probably broken more significant stories in his career than any other journalist of his generation. But does his brain fundamentally work differently than those of the rest of us? The answer is that it does not. Brain research proves that we all possess an extraordinary sensitivity to novelty, as I reported in the chapter 1 discussion of Eric Kandel's experiments with sea slugs. We all have a nose for news. It's how we're built as human beings. Like Kandel's sea slugs, we hanker after new stimuli. In this sense, we're all born journalists. As soon as we get used to something, we ignore it so we can focus on what's novel. Our brain is always scanning the world for breaking-news headlines. As the Yale psychology professor Paul Bloom tells his students, we hate to be bored: "You show a baby something over and over again. A baby will learn this isn't interesting." And it will start looking at other things.

But this raises a question. If we're all basically alike in our appetite for news, why aren't we all budding Bob Woodwards? Why did he get Watergate so much earlier than the rest of us?

The answer is that Woodward came to the story with a couple of important advantages. One gave him a leg up over many other reporters. This was the advantage of youth and ignorance. Both he and Carl Bernstein came to the politics beat with fresh eyes since neither had covered the White House before. This circumstance left them ignorant in a desirable way. As James McCartney, a Washington-based Knight Ridder journalist, has explained: "The real secret to Watergate was that it wasn't done by reporters who called [Henry] Kissinger, 'Henry.'"

The advantage Woodward had over his readers was the fact that he got to meet the Watergate politicians, bureaucrats, and party hacks he was writing about face-to-face. He was not just reading what they said. He was hearing them say it to his face. This, as we've learned, is a quite different experience. It is one thing to read a story in a newspaper that quotes a hack, and quite another to actually talk to a hack. When we talk to people we are on high alert, as we saw earlier. We pay attention. And if a person lies to our face? We take it personally. We get mad. And when someone we are talking to lies to us, we are more likely to catch them lying than if we just read their words on a printed page. True, practiced liars can get away with lying relatively easily. But many of the people Woodward was talking to weren't practiced liars. They were just ordinary Americans who got caught up in the scandal. They didn't even have to lie in a brazen and obvious way for Woodward to know something was wrong. They might just twitch. They might not say anything at all when he showed up on their doorstep. But a look might cross their face that told him what he needed to know.

Being able to meet people face-to-face helped Woodward know whom he could trust and whom he couldn't. It was because he actually met Hugh Sloan, the treasurer of the Committee for the Reelection of the President, that he felt he could trust him. As Woodward recalls in *All the President's*

Men, he "was impressed by [Sloan's] care and his unwillingness to mention the names of persons he had no reason to think had done anything wrong."

Woodward wasn't just reading about Watergate as his audience was. He was living the story. That's the advantage journalists have over voters. That is one of the main reasons reporters are almost always out ahead of voters in their appreciation of the significance of events.

Journalists may have a natural interest in politics that puts them in a better position to understand the world than ordinary voters. But their chief advantage is not their aptitude for politics. It is their circumstances. In many ways they are able to perform their tasks in an environment tailored to the cognitive mechanisms we humans developed during the Pleistocene. They get to read people face-to-face. They get to spend enough time with their sources to be able to get to know them. You know the saying, *Washington is a small town.* Being in a small town helps reporters immensely. It's not Pleistocene small. But it's small enough to give reporters the opportunity to meet the subjects of their stories. While that's not always an advantage—it creates the danger, as we've seen, that reporters will get too close to their sources, as those who called Henry Kissinger "Henry" did—but it is *generally* an advantage. Read about politics and you risk boredom and distraction. Write about politics after interviewing politicians? Chances are you're not bored or distracted. Why was Woodward so convinced that Nixon's people were lying? *They were lying to his face.*

Journalists come by facts the way we were designed to come by facts. Through experience. They aren't, like Michael Jordan, playing baseball when they should be playing basketball. They are playing the game humans are naturally good at playing. But voters? They learn just about everything they know about politics secondhand. That's a problem because we weren't designed to take novel facts to heart when we learn them in a newspaper. And facts we read in a newspaper don't register the same way as facts we learn when we experience something firsthand.

Those pro-Nixon voters took eleven months to change their minds, and as a college student I took more than two years? You may have thought earlier that that was strange, but I'm confident you no longer do.

To be sure, our brain is designed to detect novelty. But our instinctive curiosity can be short-circuited by our biases:

- our inclination to stick with what we know like those juice-drinking monkeys who learned to look in just one direction for a reward
- our ingrained partisan bias

- our inclination to discount facts that cause cognitive dissonance
- our tendency as individuals to identify with a group, as Nixonian apologists still do
- our storytelling proclivities
- our susceptibility to myths

Add on top of that the fact that we were picking up information about Watergate secondhand, and it's entirely understandable that Americans took eleven long months to come to terms with reality. Actually, given everything we now know, it's rather astonishing that voters, following their instincts, didn't take longer.

The problem, as we have seen all along, was that the context was wrong. Voters needed Nixon and his henchmen to be lying to their faces as they lied to Woodward's. Voters needed to live the story. That's what I as a seventeen-year-old needed too. I didn't need facts. I had access to the same facts as my friends. But I fell into the trap of turning the story of Watergate into a referendum on my own beliefs and psychological needs (the need to justify my early decision to stick by Nixon after all of my friends had repudiated him) rather than a referendum on Nixon. It's not too far-fetched to think that my natural lie detector might have gone off even though Nixon was a practiced liar had I been able to see him up close as he was lying. And if I had been, my focus would have been on Nixon—where it belonged—and not on me.

The obvious lesson is that whenever possible we should try to put ourselves in a position where we can experience politics directly. If you have a chance to see a candidate up close and personal, grab it. If you can snag a ticket to a political convention—local, state, or national—make use of it. We are best at politics when we are engaged and can make full use of all of our physical senses—so long as we don't get so caught up in the moment that we surrender to our biases uncritically.

Most of us are not in a position to live a story the way journalists can. But this doesn't mean we have to be suckers for wily politicians. Science suggests there are ways we can navigate politics well even at a distance and even given the limitations of a brain that was designed for a Pleistocene world, not ours. In some cases, we can do this by making our instincts work for us rather than against us, and in others, by neutralizing them altogether. We aren't, as I said at the outset, fated to live out our lives as the victims of uncontrollable instincts. But first we have to learn to recognize when our reactions are being driven by instinct.

2.

While I was in the final stages of writing this book the news networks began carrying horrific stories of beheadings in the Middle East by the terrorist members of ISIS. The stories featured video clips showing innocent victims about to face the executioner's sword. One story was especially touching. It was about a handsome and idealistic former army ranger, Peter Kassig, who had been taken hostage by ISIS while he was on a mission to deliver medical supplies to people in need in Syria. He was twenty-six when he was killed.

Viewers reacted to these stories with anger. That was the right reaction. In this case, it's self-evident, we could trust our instincts. We didn't actually have to witness a beheading in person to feel the horror of it. The act of chopping off someone's head is so appalling we could almost feel it as if we were present. We could live the news even as we experienced it vicariously (especially since we could watch a video showing what happened, even if the networks cut away before the final fatal blow was struck). That was our Pleistocene brain working the way it should under modern circumstances.

But what should we do when it doesn't? One solution is to switch from System 1 to System 2. System 1, as you'll recall, is our automatic system. It's the system we use when our thinking is guided primarily by our emotions and instincts out of conscious awareness. System 2 is higher-order cognitive thinking, and it happens *in* conscious awareness. When we can't rely on System 1 we have to switch to System 2. In theory, this shouldn't be a problem. System 2 is designed for just such situations. When System 1 isn't giving us the results we need, System 2 is supposed to kick in automatically. The eminent psychologist Jeffrey Alan Gray proposed that the reason we as a species developed consciousness in the first place was to allow us to adapt when we encounter situations where our emotions and our instincts don't work. Consciousness, he explained, is an adaptive mechanism that allows humans to detect errors and make corrections. When System 1 isn't performing sufficiently well, our conscious system—System 2—is supposed to take over, giving us the ability to respond creatively to problems we encounter.

The trouble is that our signaling network often doesn't switch us over to System 2 when it should. Our brain's surveillance system should detect the fact that in politics the context is usually wrong and that we need to be switching to System 2 as a result. But it doesn't. This is why our Pleistocene brain, in the modern world, often seems to misfire.

In retrospect, when I was defending Nixon as a seventeen-year-old, I should have switched to System 2 thinking. As the evidence against him piled up I needed to question my assumptions and reevaluate my commitment. But my surveillance system didn't sound an alarm. So I stayed on autopilot, reacting to the news rather than thinking hard about it. If you had asked me, I would have told you I *was* thinking hard about Watergate. I was reading everything I could get my hands on about the scandal and was following the story's complicated twists and turns. But I didn't realize that System 1 instincts were guiding my reactions. That's because System 1 operates behind the scenes, in hiding places we seldom think to examine. I'd heard of cognitive dissonance. It was on the agenda of my Psych 101 class. But I didn't spot it in myself. It didn't occur to me to think that the more effort I put into my defense of Nixon the more I was likely to keep on defending him. I was using System 1 thinking but didn't realize it. I was confident I was thinking, not just reacting.

This suggests that one of our most urgent tasks is to study ourselves. This is hardly a revelation we needed science to tell us. Plato told us two thousand years ago to examine our lives. But it is not obvious that if we want to understand the modern world and make good political choices we have to start by understanding the 98 percent of our brain that is inaccessible to conscious awareness. Plato didn't mention that. What science teaches us is that as we look outward, we need to look inward simultaneously. We have to question our intuitions, which is counterintuitive.

In effect, we have to serve as our own watchdogs, ever on the lookout for System 1 thinking. We have to be our own "gotcha" cops. In the game of gotcha the media play, politicians are singled out when they commit a faux pas. Our job is to try to call ourselves out whenever we can when we catch ourselves operating on automatic pilot, particularly when serious issues are at stake. That's the only way we can be sure our Pleistocene brain is helping us react the way we should be. Sometimes, as we've seen in our reaction to the ISIS beheadings, our System 1 reaction is the right reaction. But the only way to know if we are reacting properly is to put our political reactions under a microscope. In effect, we have to keep ourselves under glass as if we were our own science experiment. Now it's not realistic to believe that we are going to be able to do this consistently. It would be too tiring to subject ourselves to this kind of self-scrutiny constantly. It's not even clear what reactions fall under the category of politics. Watching an ISIS beheading? That's clearly political. But how about walking past a homeless person lying on a sidewalk? We have a political reaction to that too, even when we step over the person and don't give them another thought; that seemingly non-reaction reaction is a reaction that reflects our unconscious assessment that homeless people don't count. Clearly, then, there are limits to what we can do. But that's no excuse for failing to try.

If I had scrutinized my own Watergate reactions I might have saved myself the agony of friction with my fellow students. I do not mean that friction is bad. Quite the contrary. But friction that is based on unexamined reactions is unhelpful. What would have been helpful? Engaging consciously in a debate about each of our mutual, natural reactions to the Watergate revelations. My friends might have conceded that they were ready to believe the worst of Nixon because their partisan brains inclined them to do so, a manifestation of our Pleistocene brain's Confirmation Bias. My friends never trusted Nixon and leaped at evidence he wasn't worthy of trust. And I might have suspected, if I were honest with myself, that my Pleistocene brain was leading me to defend Nixon because I was naturally inclined to double down on beliefs that I had invested so much of myself in. I might even have realized that the theory of cognitive dissonance I was reading about in my psychology class applied to me.

I probably would have continued to feel the *urge* to defend Nixon. But knowledge of System 1 thinking should have cured me of the assumption that I was reacting to the news purely rationally. It should, in short, have made me less sure I was right and that my friends were wrong. In a democracy, that's an invaluable lesson and one that happens to be backed up by science. The findings of science suggest we should be wary of ourselves. Not only are we not as smart as we think we are, as we've seen, we are often relying, when judging events, on instincts that don't work because the context is wrong.

How do we know when we should be on our guard? When our reactions are instant. That's when we know it's our System 1 intuitions that are in control and not our conscious System 2.

It's not just the instincts I've identified in the earlier parts of this book that we need to be cognizant of. Because our intuitions weren't designed to help us navigate the modern political world, we have to subject as many as possible to scrutiny. They can all misfire if the context is wrong, as it is likely to be in politics.

Take the powerful emotion of disgust. Experiments with fart spray show that our disgust emotion has such a strong effect that it can change our mood. But just because we feel disgusted doesn't mean we should. When Hitler paired images of Jews with rats in filmstrips, audience members recoiled when, in the next frame, they saw Jews alone. But they obviously shouldn't have. Jews weren't disgusting. The rats were. But the audience couldn't see the difference. Over time many came to think of Jews as rats. That dehumanized them, turning them into non-persons. And non-persons are easier to kill.

A modern example of the powerful effect of disgust can be seen on college campuses across the United States. In their ongoing campaign to turn Americans against abortion, pro-life activists have been erecting giant billboards depicting aborted fetuses. Their hope is that the pictures will turn students against abortion by associating it with something that triggers a reaction of disgust. But should our opinion of abortion be dictated by our emotional response to a picture that looks gruesome? Nature evolved a disgust reaction to save us from disease. That's why we turn away from feces. Disgust didn't evolve to make us recoil from abortion. As one professor who is upset by the antiabortion campaign has recently noted, there are lots of things that disgust her, including bugs in her hair and pictures of a human being's guts. But "these different things don't share the same moral status." As she aptly sums up, "our emotional reactions can mislead us."

So what should we do when a politician says something that really gets us going, whether it's a rhetorical flourish that plays on our patriotism or a slogan that makes the world's complicated events suddenly seem simple? We should hit the pause button before we let our emotional response dictate our decision to support a particular policy or favor a politician's bid for power.

We cannot stop ourselves from reacting the way we react. A picture of someone's guts will probably always draw a feeling of disgust. But knowing how we react to certain stimuli—like a picture of an aborted fetus—can change what we make of it. And that in turn can change how we think. Knowing how our brain works can change how it works. A person who's been taught to recognize biased thinking will think differently about things. Once we recognize the automatic reactions we have to certain stimuli—whether it's our reaction to a politician who seems sincere or our desire to go along with the feeling of the fellow members of a group—we can change how we make sense of our own judgments. We are unlikely to be able to change our instant reactions, but we can digest them differently. And every time we do that we change our brain. Thinking changes the neural networks. Every time you experience something and create a memory of it your brain changes. Brains are plastic.

That's one of the great discoveries of the last few decades. Our brain changes as we use it. One of the most famous examples of this was the finding a few years ago about London taxi cab drivers. To become a licensed driver in London you have to show a mastery of the city's complicated network of streets and detailed knowledge of its neighborhoods. You have to know how to get from point A to point B without consulting a map and also know the locations of hotels, theaters, and other destinations. This requires memorizing thousands of streets, forcing the drivers' hippocampi, which are critical to the functioning of memory, to work a lot harder. When researchers took fMRI snapshots of the drivers' brains they had a remarkable breakthrough. The hippocampi in the typical London cabbie were far larger than those in other people. We don't have the brain we were born with. It keeps changing. We can change it.

To be sure, the moral foundations of our beliefs are what they are, whether we like it or not. That's what the research of psychologist Jonathan Haidt proves. Some of us just lean conservative and some lean liberal. And many of our moral beliefs, like the belief that incest is a sin, are common to nearly all human beings and beyond rational debate. We are appalled by incest because we are appalled by incest. To demonstrate that this is the case, Haidt tells a story about Julie and Mark, who are sister and brother. One day they decide to have sex just for the fun of it. Both use protection and both are adults. Afterward, they say they enjoyed it but agree it was a onetime experiment. Anything wrong with what they did? People taking Haidt's moral foundations survey always say there is. But why? There's no danger of childbirth. The siblings insist it didn't damage their relationship. Both are consenting adults. So why we do we recoil from Julie and Mark copulating? Haidt's answer is that our moral foundations are deeply woven into our brain and are largely beyond the reach of our critical faculties. We believe because we believe. This suggests there are limits to our reasoning faculties. On some issues we simply hold firm opinions we can't really explain. But so what? So conservatives will think like conservatives and liberals will think like liberals. That doesn't preclude us from analyzing our biases and determining if our political opinions make sense in the context of modern politics.

3.

Knowing when we are likely being swept along by our instincts is just one challenge we face. Another is learning how to resist the pull of the wave. Fortunately, while our instincts are powerful, we aren't helpless before them. Science is teaching us why. It's because our instincts don't all pull in the same direction. They go every which way. Each of our evolved instincts evolved to confront a specific problem. Because no one designed us to be perfectly integrated beings, our instincts don't work seamlessly. Our head is filled with contested impulses. While we think of ourselves as integrated beings, we aren't. There's no homunculus—some little man in our head—at the controls.

Think of your reaction to 9/11. It's likely you didn't have just one reaction to that awful day's events. You had a series of reactions. The most-talked-about reactions were rage and revenge, two of the most common human emotions. But we also had another reaction that day. We wanted to understand why somebody would do such a thing. That impulse to understand the event gave us the opportunity to think and not just lash out. We really wanted to know. That became especially important when we saw videos of crowds in one Middle Eastern country after another cheering the terrorists' attack, as I discussed earlier. The crowds' reaction didn't square with our understanding of our role in the world or our self-identity. It was as if a dark, ominous cloud suddenly had appeared over our shining city on a hill.

To be sure, we wanted a quick explanation and a self-satisfying one, and President George W. Bush supplied it. Within days he began saying that the people who hated us didn't understand us. But a different political leader could have given us a different answer, and it could have been made to stick. We ourselves could have decided Bush's answer didn't quite sound right, as, indeed, professors nearly uniformly said it didn't: millions in those Middle Eastern countries where crowds had cheered had real grievances against the United States, and it wasn't because they didn't understand us. Appalling as their behavior may have been, they knew something about us that we didn't know about ourselves—that we are often careless with the lives of people who live in foreign places. Because of the pell-mell way our instincts evolved, we have the freedom to decide what weight to give them or if we should just ignore one and favor another. That's not true, to be sure, if a rock's coming at us and we have just a moment to react. But in most political situations we face that's not the case.

What in the end leads us to a decision in any particular situation is some combination of genes, personality, and circumstances. After 9/11 we may have been fated to seek revenge, but it doesn't follow that we had to subordinate all our other impulses to it. Science suggests we had the option of picking and choosing from our instincts, though some scientists have become convinced that genes play such an important role in behavior that our freedom of choice is limited.

The debate over immigration in the United States is an example of a controversy that triggers multiple instinctive reactions. One reaction, from white people who resent the flood of Mexican immigrants who illegally crossed the southern border in recent years, reflects a classic suspicion of outsiders. But this isn't the only instinct that comes into play in the immigration debate. We also happen to be a country of immigrants. Many of our stories celebrate immigrant success. As we've seen earlier, stories are particularly attractive when they are associated with national identity. There is no reason why we can't use the urge to celebrate immigrants with an evocative story to offset the urge to keep them at bay. We can make our instincts work for us. We can train ourselves to play one instinct off another when we ourselves want to neutralize an instinct our conscious brain tells us is unhelpful, as the suspicion of outsiders generally is in the modern world. We can reward politicians who appeal to our better instincts (instincts that suit the conditions of the twenty-first century) as President Obama did when he unveiled his plan in 2014 to allow millions of undocumented immigrants to obtain working permits. To convince Americans to support his plan, he related a story about a young woman named Astrid Silva. Here is what he told the television audience:

> Astrid was brought to America when she was four years old. Her only possessions were a cross, her doll, and the frilly dress she had on. When she started school, she didn't speak any English. She caught up to the other kids by reading newspapers and watching PBS, and became a good student. Her father worked in landscaping. Her mother cleaned other people's homes. They wouldn't let Astrid apply to a technology magnet school for fear the paperwork would out her as an undocumented immigrant—so she applied behind their back and got in. Still, she mostly lived in the shadows—until her grandmother, who visited every year from Mexico, passed away, and she couldn't travel to the funeral without risk of being found out and deported. It was around that time she decided to begin advocating for herself and others like her, and today, Astrid Silva is a college student working on her third degree. Are we a nation that kicks out a striving, hopeful immigrant like Astrid—or are we a nation that finds a way to welcome her in?

Notice what Obama didn't do. He didn't tell white Americans who want to keep immigrants out that they shouldn't feel what they're feeling. That was smart. We're going to feel what we're going to feel, as I have said repeatedly. In the early part of the speech he even conceded people had a right to feel resentful. "All of us," he said, "take offense to anyone who reaps the rewards of living in America without taking on the responsibilities of living in America." But then, in a calculated pivot, he laid out a vision of America that is welcoming to people in need. This was a bid to appeal to a different, more humane, instinct, one that better suits the circumstances in which we find ourselves.

Almost always in the modern world it's better when politicians trumpet appeals to our humane instincts. We aren't living in a Pleistocene dog-eat-dog world. Instincts geared to that world generally aren't appropriate in ours, not even when we go to war. Though in war we need to tap into animal spirits—to motivate an army you have to—it's possible even then for our leaders to remind us of the "angels of our nature." Abraham Lincoln repeatedly did that during the Civil War, especially in his second inaugural address, when he implored Americans to remember the humanity of their battlefield enemies:

> With malice toward none; with charity for all; with firmness in the right, as God gives us to see the right, let us strive on to finish the work we are in; to bind up the nation's wounds; to care for him who shall have borne the battle, and for his widow, and his orphan—to do all which may achieve and cherish a just, and a lasting peace, among ourselves, and with all nations.

And the Civil War was ghastly.

How we react to events depends in the end not on our instincts, per se, but on what our leaders and we ourselves choose to make of them. Think of what happened in the months after the first Ebola patient entered the United States in 2014. The initial reaction of many Americans was pure fear. They didn't want anybody with Ebola to come anywhere near the United States. That was their Pleistocene brain at work. Politicians like Chris Christie, the governor of New Jersey, exploited voters' fears, threatening to keep a nurse who had just returned from Africa locked up because he claimed to be worried that she was ill. (There was no evidence she was.) Healthcare officials uniformly tried to tamp down fears, reassuring the public that in this country people had little to worry about. They pointed out that people were far likelier to be struck by lightning or be hit by a car than be cut down by Ebola. It simply wasn't a serious threat to most Americans. After a short time fears subsided. Why? For one thing, Ebola cases slowed to a trickle. But what also helped immensely was that health care officials reacted calmly. This reassured people. By instinct we respect doctors and nurses. By nature we look to authority figures for guidance.

So to sum up what we've learned so far about when we should trust our instincts and when we shouldn't: we should trust them when they seem to fit the context of the modern world and seek to ignore them or neutralize them when they don't.

4.

At the outset of this book I said that science is giving us hope. You're probably thinking I haven't yet delivered on my promise to show you how to remain hopeful in the face of all of the evidence that we are driven by System 1 instincts that are likely to mislead us. Knowing that we have multiple instincts and that we can use these against one another isn't exactly a breaking-news story likely to prompt you to take to the streets to celebrate. But here's an example I think just might. It's what science has recently discovered we can do to stimulate people to vote, a discovery that we need to make use of—and fast. (In the 2014 midterms, barely 36 percent of eligible voters voted.)

As we know, millions of Americans don't get too excited about voting. The reason is that the process feels remote and irrelevant to their daily lives. Their instincts tell them to ignore the calls to civic responsibility. Why bother, they seem to tell themselves.

But now we know there's a way to make us feel differently about elections. Science proved it in 2010 in the course of a vast experiment during the midterm elections that year. Scientists at Facebook, working with political scientist James Fowler, sent messages to 61 million Facebook users. That's no misprint. They sent messages to *61 million* people—that's roughly the population of France. What they wanted to find out was whether they could use a simple message—like *Hey, people, voting's important, go vote*—to motivate them to vote. You will not be surprised by now to learn the answer. Simple messages did not work. Users who got a message to vote pretty much ignored it. A second finding was a little more encouraging. It showed the influence your Facebook friends can have on you even if they are not real friends, just virtual friends. If one of your virtual friends posted an "I Voted" icon on their page, it made you a little more likely to vote. But it was the third finding that was the important one. Close friends—real friends you see face-to-face on a regular basis—it turns out, can have an enormous influence on your behavior. Peer pressure works in close-knit networks. For every user who posted the "I Voted" sign bragging that they had voted, three of their close friends (real friends) followed suit and voted.

Usually, social scientists treat our instinct to follow others, which underlies contagious behavior, as a negative. But it can also have a positive effect. We can use an instinct that often undermines democracy—the general unwillingness to break ranks and question authority—to improve democracy.

Overcoming apathy is just one of the problems we now know how to solve as a result of large-scale projects like the Facebook study. What large-scale studies can show us is what will actually change human behavior. We no longer have to guess. We no longer have to rely on hunches or laboratory experiments or longitudinal studies (studies that monitor the behavior of individuals over a long period of time, often years and years). Those approaches all have their merits—even hunches do. After all, the invisible hand theory of eighteenth-century economist Adam Smith was based on a hunch, not hard data. But those other approaches do not offer the kind of proof that studies based on big data do. These big-data studies, which are part of an emerging field known as social physics, are transforming the way both business and government are motivating people.

One of the critical findings of the social scientists working with big data is particularly relevant to our concerns. It is the discovery that there is a single key that can unlock human creativity, and it is not sheer brainpower. It is the physical proximity of people to other people. The reason is remarkably straightforward. You want people to think creatively? You cannot just hire an Einstein and lock him in a room by himself and let him think big thoughts. However smart people are, they need to be in contact with other people to reach their full potential. This is because we are at our essence social creatures. If we cut ourselves off from contact with a broad swath of humanity, our thinking becomes narrower. Expose us to the ideas of lots of people by having us mingle with people from multiple walks of life, and we thrive. Mingling is the magic sauce in the recipe for creativity, whatever your dopamine level happens to be. It's why cities are idea factories. It's why civilization is so strongly associated with urban environments. It is in cities that people rub shoulders with other people who think differently.

This is fascinating—and unexpected. It suggests that what appears to be a Pleistocene advantage—individuals living in a small community where everybody knows everybody else—is not actually an unalloyed advantage. People living in such a community may not suffer from apathy. They may be able to read their leaders better than we can. But they are apt to be politically stunted. You wouldn't want to live in a Pleistocene community even if you had running water, paved streets, and a computer with access to the Internet. It's too small. We need a diverse group of people around us to stimulate our thinking.

MIT professor Alex Pentland, a leader in social physics, says that what he is finding is that big data prove there's a shortcut to social progress. You want to raise the educational level of people living in a large city? You want to lower crime? You can invest in expensive new schools or go on a hiring binge to pad the police rolls. You may or may not get good results. But focus instead on the improvement of neighborhoods by adding coffee shops, restaurants, and pretzel stands, so people can gather and talk, and amazing things happen. Density promotes creativity and keeps crime low. Combine living and working areas, and you can have a city where people thrive.

The opposite is true as well. Build a city where people live in one corner and work in another, and the place where they live will deteriorate. This is a powerful lesson of big data, and it has a strong bearing on politics. Remember the Nixonians who defended Nixon's conduct in Watergate? They couldn't change their way of thinking. They got stuck in 1974. What social physics suggests is that what happened to them is that their willingness to consider new viewpoints atrophied in the absence of direct and repeated contact with people who think differently than they do. The cure? If you find yourself in a tightly knit circle of like-minded people, get out and start talking to people with other ideas. What the Nixonians needed to do was mingle. But what was their instinct? It was to cut themselves off from people who think differently than they do. When the library director Timothy Naftali invited John Dean to speak, they moved to block Dean and punish Naftali. That was exactly the reverse of what they should have done.

A big study of the 2008 presidential election shows why. The purpose of the study was to find out how people form their political views. Are our views a function of individual reasoning or of the composition and influence of our social groups? To find out, social scientists tracked the interaction patterns of students living in a dormitory over the course of nine months. A digital monitor reported where they were, who they talked to, and how long they talked. This data was fed into a computer every five minutes. In the end the social scientists accumulated hundreds of gigabytes of data tracking the students' interactions over 500,000 hours. Nothing like this had ever been done before. The finding? The more we are exposed to people holding similar views, the more extreme our views become.

We cannot do much about our instincts. We love hanging out with people who think like we do. And if we hang out with a small group of people who think alike, our thinking is invariably going to be narrow and get narrower and narrower. That's because of how we're built. It's what happens to human beings who spend a lot of time with each other while cut off from others. But we have agency. We can choose to expand our social networks. We can deliberately put ourselves in contact with people who share different views. Do that and our thinking will naturally broaden.

We cannot change what we think when we are going on instinct. If, like my mother, we stare briefly into the eyes of a charismatic politician and are swept away, there is little we can do about our reaction. We'll feel what we're going to feel. But we can change our behavior and in doing so affect what we feel. We can do this by making conscious choices about whom we hang out with. That means, when we are on the Internet communicating with people through social media, we can make a conscious decision to interact with people who *don't* share our views. To promote social diversity, social media sites could reward users who reach out to people in other networks. As happens on some social media apps where people check in when they visit places like Starbucks, badges could go to people who actually meet in real places and not just virtually. The act of hanging out with people who think differently would naturally change how we think. We can make our instincts help us instead of hurt us.

The Nixonians' tight social circle is too tight. It is understandable why the members of the group cling to one another. They feel on the defensive. Their group identity rests on a shared set of grievances that Nixon was wronged. But their group identity comes at a cost. It has left them closed-minded. Is it worth it? Maybe the group is so important to them that they would say it is. Groups, after all, offer us a measure of security and can be a source of strength. But when we surrender our independence of thought to a group, the group can be a source of weakness. When we are willing to be taken hostage by a group, putting group loyalty above the truth, democracy suffers.

Mingling with others is no guarantee of open-mindedness, of course. That's the lesson of my own experience as a Nixon supporter at liberal Vassar. In my group of friends I was the lone Nixon supporter. The more my friends pushed me to defend Nixon the more stubbornly I stuck by him. But maybe I would have felt more open to change if I had had a few friends who believed as I did in Nixon's innocence. Having none—not one—I had no one with whom I could share my doubts. This led to a natural rigidity.

5.

Another reason to be hopeful is that science has now shown that we come equipped with an instinct that helps us recognize change, an instinct that works for us just as well as it did for our Pleistocene ancestors. It's anxiety. As we saw earlier, we get anxious when there's a mismatch between our expectations and reality. At a certain point, the social scientist George Marcus has instructed us, the burden of hanging on to a belief becomes greater than the cost of changing it, so we change it. This is extremely good news. This means we possess a natural proclivity to change.

We may not be well adapted for politics in the modern world. But anxiety in the end helps save us from ourselves. It gives us the incentive to change. And it works under most circumstances. Terrorists attack an American base in the Middle East? We grow anxious. Bankers on Wall Street rip off customers? We grow anxious. As long as the threat rises sufficiently high to draw our attention, our amygdala kicks into action, leading us to rethink our assumptions.

The only time we don't respond with anxiety to a big, bad news event is when it's really, really bad. That is, when we've got an immediate crisis on our hands. What do we do then? Neuroscientists tell us our brain skips the anxiety stage entirely. In a moment of crisis you don't want to be anxious. You don't want to have to think. Thinking takes time. In a crisis you want to be able to act. We cannot afford System 2 thinking in a crisis. We need System 1 thinking. After 9/11 we didn't want President George W. Bush sitting around the Oval Office for months on end trying to figure out a plan of action. We wanted instant action. He got us that and as a result we rallied behind him, as we saw earlier, giving him the highest sustained poll ratings of any president in history. In a real crisis our instincts tell us to follow the leader. Crises—true crises of the moment (think Pearl Harbor, not the Great Depression)—make us conservative. We look for allies we can trust and hunker down. It's not a time for asking questions. It's a moment for going with the old verities. It's one of those times when you really want to go with your gut. Bush's policy may have been misguided following 9/11, but our desire for national unity was the right instinct.

But at all other times of adversity, when we are facing challenges that don't put us in a crisis mentality, our instinct is to grow anxious. The worse things get in these circumstances, the more anxious we become. That feeling of anxiety forces us to reconsider our position. It even saves us from our biases, says Marcus. When we plan a large project we may, as a result of the Planning Fallacy, underestimate the cost and length of time it will take to complete it. In the immediate period after we discover our mistake the Perseverance Bias may keep us convinced that we have not made a mistake. But eventually, as the gap between our expectations and reality becomes fully apparent, triggering anxiety, we usually recognize the truth and accept it. When our heroes are unmasked as villains we stop treating them as heroes (though at a later time we may resurrect them, as the Russians have resurrected Stalin).

Because we are designed for survival, we are built to be realistic. Being realistic even helps us develop empathy. When we are in a situation where it is in our own self-interest not to acknowledge the harm we are inflicting on others, we can be downright obtuse. But if we hear a compelling story that helps us understand the suffering others are going through, the anxiety that story triggers can open our eyes. That did not happen during or after the Korean War, as we have seen, infuriating Freda Kirchwey. But that was probably because the media didn't devote much time to the story. All the voters had were facts. They needed compelling stories. But it did happen after Abu Ghraib, when Americans saw pictures showing our guards' torturing Iraqi war prisoners. Those pictures told a story that touched us. And, as we have learned, pictures and stories exert a powerful effect on us. In this case, they left us anxious. Anxiety over what US soldiers did led Americans to reevaluate the Iraq War and made us less complacent about our good intentions. All this is the astonishingly good news about the human brain that science has now begun to document.

And as Marcus and his colleagues showed in a recent test of the Theory of Affective Intelligence—the theory that our cognitive functions are deeply enmeshed with our emotions, and that anxiety is the key trigger for change—anxiety has roughly the same effect on us whether we are liberal or conservative. While scientists are finding more and more convincing evidence that liberals and conservatives really do think differently at the neural level—liberals in general are more open-minded and conservatives are inclined to stick with what they know and not question it, ways of thinking both liberals and conservatives come by genetically, in part—people across the ideological spectrum respond similarly to events that trigger anxiety. That's an amazingly hopeful discovery. It means that despite our differences, we can find ways to bridge the divide. We are not fated to drift apart. One study shows that an anxious response to events even draws us closer in line on issues that normally divide us, like tolerance, issues that raise deep moral questions. When we're anxious, whether we're liberal or conservative, we grow more tolerant.

Anxiety cannot turn ignorant voters into smart ones. It doesn't bring wisdom. When a voter eventually comes around to the viewpoint that a cherished leader has proved disappointing, that voter doesn't stop what they're doing and run to the library. Anxiety doesn't turn ordinary voters into philosopher kings. But it does tell them change is needed.

What results in consequence can look at first glance like irrationality, as happened in the 1930s. As one political science paper points out, the Great Depression prompted distinctly contradictory responses from voters in different parts of the world. Voters in the United States turned out of office stalwart Republicans who believed in laissez-faire, while voters in

Great Britain and Australia threw out Labour governments committed to public action. This suggests that people were not engaged in a thoughtful evaluation of the causes of the Great Depression or its likely remedies. They were just tossing out the incumbents willy-nilly, whatever those incumbents believed and however well or badly they were performing in office.

But is this really a sign of irrationality? Voters cannot be expected to know the correct course we should take when confronting hard problems. Usually, despite the bravado of politicians and pundits, no one really knows what to do. Even experts cannot predict the future. The social scientist Philip Tetlock tracked the predictions that hundreds of experts made over twenty years. In that period they made more than 28,000 predictions. How often were they right? Barely more than chance.

Human beings are bad at predicting the future because the future, by definition, is unknowable. All we have to go on is the past, and the past is often a poor guide, particularly in times of great flux. As historians are at pains to make clear, history seldom teaches neat little lessons. But as long as we are open to evidence, as long as we are willing to try new approaches, sooner or later we'll probably hit on a solution. That's the approach Franklin Roosevelt took during the Great Depression. "It is common sense to take a method and try it," FDR said in 1932, when he first ran for president. "If it fails, admit it frankly and try another. But above all, try something." That's not just a great quote. It also describes what human beings have done throughout history. It's the approach to life ratified by evolution. When things go wrong, try something new. Change. That's why our elections always come down to the question of change. If you like the way things are going, you vote for the incumbent party. If you don't, you vote for somebody new.

Now, because human beings are not all alike, not everybody reacts the same way at the same time. Where we live, who we hang out with, and what we've experienced all have an impact on how we react to events. Not even in national elections do we react to the same stimulus the same way. In 1916, a majority of American voters were mainly worried about war in Europe, but not everybody was. Those voters in New Jersey who dropped their support of Woodrow Wilson after suffering through a summer from hell weren't most concerned with war news. For them the important event of the moment was those shark attacks. It put them in a hopping-mad mood. They apparently weren't in the same emotional place as most other Americans. Those shark attacks changed their reality, triggering a deep reaction against the incumbent party. Unhappy, they voted for change. That might not have been rational. But given what we now know about evolution, it is entirely understandable and logical. It's what we do when bad stuff happens. It's anxiety doing its job. The fact that in this particular circumstance anxiety prompted an obviously irrational reaction does not mean that anxiety is not to be trusted. Nothing's better at keeping things real.

Anxiety, to be sure, is no magic potion. People in a state of high anxiety may go after minorities they fear are taking their jobs, lash out at politicians who are telling them hard truths they don't want to hear, and become susceptible to wild conspiracy theories. Wars have resulted when politicians have successfully played on the anxieties of voters about other countries' intentions, as happened in 2003 when National Security Advisor Condoleezza Rice warned that Saddam Hussein might be acquiring nuclear weapons ("We don't want the smoking gun to be in the form of a mushroom cloud"). And as we saw in the case of the followers of the Chicago housewife who predicted the end of the planet and in our encounter with the Nixonians, people living in an insular world as members of a close-knit group can persist in a state of illusion even when there are grounds to be anxious. Human beings will be human, after all. But as long as anxiety helps keep things real—and as long as the media are free to report the basic facts, it will in most cases—over time we'll adapt to change. And as science proves, that's the key to survival. Adapt or die. Thanks to anxiety, generally we adapt.

Do you see, though, the problem we face? We may adapt over time, but in the modern world, we often really need to adapt immediately to changing circumstances. Those Nixon voters who took eleven months to overcome their bias in favor of the president really needed to overcome it a lot sooner. The delay was costly. Divided and leaderless, the country drifted, Vietnam collapsed, inflation spiraled out of control, and the economy slipped into recession. Admittedly, not all of these problems resulted from the public's delay in coming to terms with Watergate. But Watergate distracted us from dealing with them.

And sometimes problems cannot wait. This is the situation we are facing with the debate over climate change. If the polar ice caps melt, we'll become anxious and act. But scientists tell us if we wait until then, it will be too late to reverse the long-term weather patterns that human activity will have set in motion. Once the caps melt, they're gone. To save ourselves, what we need is an immediate amygdala response. We cannot wait for the evidence of rising seas breaching the walls around our coastal cities. We need to be reacting to the signs of global warming *now*.

The trouble is that entrenched biases hinder us from taking climate change seriously. When the environmental activist George Marshall began writing a book to find out why so many people seem indifferent to the threat posed by climate change—and he discovered that even the people who lived through Katrina and Hurricane Sandy, which literally made the danger of climate change palpable, seemed uninterested in the subject—leading social scientists such as Daniel Kahneman and Paul Slovic warned him that most people are blind to threats like climate change.

Kahneman said he was "deeply pessimistic" about our acting before it is too late. "I really see no path to success on climate change." He gave four reasons: 1) Climate change lacks salience—this is the social scientist's way of saying climate change doesn't demand our attention. 2) "Paying costs now to mitigate costs in the future" is unappealing. 3) Information about climate change is contested, giving doubters grounds for indifference. 4) Doing something about climate change requires our taking losses, and, as a rule, human beings hate taking losses, as I noted earlier. Whatever gains we might make by preventing climate change, we'd feel our losses more.

Slovic offered more reasons. Climate change doesn't feel threatening. Bad weather is something we're used to. And the long-term effects of climate change are hard to imagine.

But what social scientist George Marcus has showed is that anxiety can break through our biases. This is one of the key lessons of the Theory of Affective Intelligence. An example of this is what we saw earlier is our reaction to a fire alarm. The Optimism Bias should stop us from responding to a fire alarm. When we hear it we should think it's just a false alarm and not worry. But that's not what we do. As Error Management Theory (EMT) predicts, when we hear an alarm go off we react, in the belief that it's safer to take a fire alarm seriously than risk the consequences of missing a threat that turns out to be real. That's anxiety doing its job.

What hurt us as a country in the 1950s when we overreacted to the possible threat of communist subversives can help us now. That's our natural concern that we might be destroyed by a missed red flag. This bias, which we see on display in all sorts of situations, is every bit as much a part of us as the biases Kahneman and Slovic worry will undermine our willingness to face climate change.

Anxiety, as it turns out, has already succeeded in convincing a solid majority of Americans—65 percent—that climate change is taking place or will in the coming decades, according to a Gallup Poll. And 70 percent, according to a *Washington Post*-ABC News Poll, favor limiting the "release of greenhouse gases from existing power plants in an effort to reduce global warming"—which suggests that they believe, on some level, that human activity is in part responsible. Only 20 percent are out-and-out deniers. What anxiety hasn't yet done is convince Americans that climate change is a real-enough problem for them to worry about it now. Most do not believe their lives will be substantially affected. That may explain why, when people are asked to rank the problems on their mind, climate change comes out near dead last.

This is troubling. Climate change is the crisis that doesn't feel like a crisis. And we're only built to feel crises that do. As George Marshall observes, because climate change "carries none of the clear markers that would normally lead our brains to overrule our short-term interests, we actively conspire with each other, and mobilize our own biases to keep it perpetually in the background." But we aren't stuck. There are things we can do to make it more likely that we will have the amygdala response we need to take action now. A good start would be to run thirty-second commercials on TV to make people anxious about climate change. If political spots can use anxiety to help turn voters against politicians, as the ads for President Lyndon Johnson did in the 1964 campaign against Barry Goldwater—"Vote for President Johnson on November 3rd. The stakes are too high for you to stay home"— there's no reason to think they can't be used to make voters feel anxious about climate change. TV spots work, especially negative spots, according to Kathleen Hall Jamieson, director of the Annenberg Public Policy Center, who has perhaps studied them more extensively than anybody else. What her work suggests is that we have the means to draw public attention to dangerous situations. This means we don't have to sit back and wait for the danger to arrive. We can use negative ads to make people anxious enough to reconsider their position.

We don't need to scare people. We just need to emphasize the importance of playing it safe. As George Marshall observes in his book, we play it safe all the time. It's why we spend billions of dollars on insurance. It's the reason governments spend trillions on defense. A campaign organized around this theme likely could trigger the amygdala response that's needed.

6.

The same science behind the Theory of Affective Intelligence, which is teaching us that we can trust the feeling of anxiety, is teaching us that we cannot trust our feelings of anger. Our brain may generate both emotions, but they have different effects on our politics. Anxiety, triggered by the amygdala, is associated with the positive effects described above, while anger, which is generated in the insula, has negative ones. What the research shows is that anxiety opens our minds and anger closes them.

In an experiment designed by George Marcus and colleagues to detect the difference between anxiety and anger, subjects were shown a news story about a fictitious college in Oregon that was using affirmative action to draw a more diverse student body. The story came in two versions. One put affirmative action in a positive light, the other in a negative light. What the study found was that people who were made anxious by the story they read finished it wanting to know more. They clicked on links to read more about affirmative action even if those articles contradicted their beliefs and made them feel even more anxious. But people who were made angry by what they read did not want to find out more. This was true of liberals who favored affirmative action and read a version of the story that put it in a bad light, and conservatives who opposed affirmative action and read the version that put it in a good light. These people, whichever camp they were in, liberal or conservative, did not want to read articles that conflicted with their own views. In short, they did not want to know more.

From an evolutionary perspective, anger was desirable when we were living as hunter-gatherers. In a crisis requiring quick action, anger gave us the focus we needed to succeed. Even in a fight with another human being it helped to be angry. An angry person is intimidating.

But in the modern world? In mainstream politics anger undermines democracy. People who are angry cannot see others' points of view. Angry people don't compromise.

And what is true now of our democracy? Americans by the millions are angry. It's no wonder politics in Washington, DC, suffers from gridlock. Anger is doing what it was designed to do: stiffen our will under grueling conditions. But it wasn't designed to help us survive in a multiparty cooperative system involving millions of citizens of the same country. Anger evolved to help us meet specific threats in settings where it was needed only for a short period. People in general did not remain in an angry state for months and years on end. But in our world they do stay angry in response to the taunts of grandstanding politicians and media demagogues. These days we don't get a chance to take a break from anger. It's all around us all the time. And we're surprised that the feeling of compromise is rare?

All anger is not alike, to be sure. Context counts, as I have repeatedly observed. Social scientists distinguish crisis events like 9/11 that leave us angry, from the ordinary day-to-day situations that leave us angry. In the wake of events like 9/11 we may be angry, but we also feel united. But the latter? They leave us divided. Think of how you feel when you listen to Rush Limbaugh. If you're a liberal, it's punishing, isn't it? The same goes for conservatives when they watch Rachel Maddow. She makes them mad. (Though contrary to stereotype, it appears that liberals are likelier to grow more angry hearing Limbaugh than conservatives are seeing Maddow.)

The lesson is obvious. If we are going to get along, we need to strongly discourage attempts to exploit people's anger at everyday events.

Anger is the fuel that drives social movements. It was anger at apathy that drove gay activists to form Act Up in the 1980s, and anger that drives the Tea Party today. Anger works. It draws people together and gives their efforts focus and purpose. To be human is to feel anger. It's the emotion we use when we want to force someone else to change his or her behavior. But we've overlearned the lesson of the past. Anger only works if a small minority uses it to advance an unpopular view. If the reaction to ordinary day-to-day politics by ordinary voters is anger by default, and if professional activists employ anger to recruit followers and draw donations, making anger routine, our democracy won't work the way it should. Under those circumstances, no one will get what they want. And that's the situation we're in now. So many people are angry, there's no room for compromise.

What science is teaching us is that we need to be on our guard whenever politics makes us feel angry. This is entirely doable. Our automatic System 1 mental processes may not be suited for democracy as it's practiced in the modern world, but science shows that we do not have to wait tens of thousands of years for the human brain to evolve. We possess the ability to recognize anger and switch to System 2 thinking when we feel ourselves surrendering to anger. We don't have to let ourselves get caught up in the fights triggered by seething media blowhards and politicians. We can resist.

The lesson of science? Minorities can use anger to trigger change. But majorities can't in circumstances that lead people to yell at one another as a matter of course. That just leads to gridlock.

7.

Over and over in this book we have seen that we can't change our instant reactions. But we can digest them differently if we so choose. This takes self-discipline, to be sure. But science shows that most humans can learn self-discipline, as Walter Mischel has shown. Mischel is the social-science pioneer credited with one of the most exciting and simple experiments ever devised, the justly celebrated Marshmallow Test. In the experiment, young children are told they can have a marshmallow right now if they want one, but if they wait a short time, they can have two. The difficulty is that the marshmallow is staring them in the face. Waiting becomes a mini-ordeal. As Mischel reports in his book about the Marshmallow Test, the kids dream up ingenious ways to keep themselves from giving in to temptation. They sing a song. They try staring at something else in the room. They bite their upper lip. And so on. Many fail after a short time and give in to desire.

But that wasn't what was most intriguing in Mischel's work. For years he tracked the children who took part in the experiment. What he found was that the kids who showed the most self-discipline ultimately did better in life. They did better in school. They got better jobs and earned more money. They even shared more matrimonial success, divorcing at a far lower rate than the kids who had given in to desire and eaten the marshmallow.

This suggested that self-discipline is another of those traits we appear to inherit and that some people are just lucky to have done so. In the genetic lottery of life, they got the self-discipline gene. But this wasn't actually the case, Mischel found. Discipline can be learned. This is one of the important lessons of the emerging science of cognitive therapy. How you are at four isn't how you are at forty. You can change.

Mischel reports that two strategies are particularly helpful. Say you are trying to decide how much money to set aside for retirement. If you think of making the decision right now you are probably not going to set aside enough, as surveys show is true of most Americans. The overwhelming reason is that your present needs seem a lot more pressing. We privilege the present over the future. We experience the present like a 3D movie in Technicolor, in contrast to the future, which seems distant, cold, and hard to imagine. The future is like watching television on an old RCA that only shows pictures in black and white. That's a problem because we always experience stronger feelings about things that are vivid rather than abstract. In an experiment at Stanford, subjects were divided into two groups and asked to make a decision about the amount of money they thought they would need for retirement. One group was primed to think in the present by showing them an avatar of their present self. Another group was primed to think of the future by showing them an avatar of what they'd look like when they are older. The participants who saw the avatars of themselves as older people decided they needed to save 30 percent more than the others.

What the Stanford experiment and others like it show is that if we want to make a good decision about an event in the future we have to make the future concrete. But it also showed something else. Flip the lesson on its head and it shows that if we want to insulate ourselves from undue emotionalism in the present we can do that by pretending to be making a decision about something far off in the future. If we want to enhance our ability to resist the marshmallow, we can do so by putting the marshmallow into a mental box we plan on eating later (years later). The distance turns Technicolor temptations into black-and-white movies with less appeal.

The Stanford study is part of a body of evidence that self-discipline isn't genetic. It can be taught and we are teachable. This suggests that if we want to resist the impulse to go with our political instincts, we should be able to. We don't have to let ourselves get carried away. We can follow events and listen to speeches without giving in to instinctive reactions. We can control our reactions by imagining how we might respond in the future. Using Mischel's terminology, we can turn off our hot system, what I have been calling System 1, and turn on our cool system, System 2.

A second approach Mischel endorses to improve our self-discipline is what's known as the if/then strategy. Here's how it works. Say you want to stop yourself from smoking cigarettes. An approach many have used with success is to figure out in advance how they are going to respond when they get their next itch to smoke. One remedy is to think of cancer patients lined up in a hospital ward waiting for a lung transplant.

It's not too far a stretch to think that this same technique could be applied to politics. If you know that you are a sucker for patriotic appeals even when you know they are being used by craven politicians to manipulate their way into your heart, you can prepare yourself by coming up in advance with a fixed reaction. Instead of letting yourself be carried away on a *Wizard of Oz* balloon festooned with red, white, and blue ribbons as "Stars and Stripes Forever" plays in the background, you can conjure up an image of Richard Nixon delivering his resignation speech. This is almost certain to disrupt the patriotic tune playing in your head.

If a politician appeals to your desire for a quick fix to a problem that you suspect is complicated but very much want to believe is susceptible to a quick fix, try to think immediately of all the times quick fixes have failed. To take one example, you can think of No Child Left Behind. This legislation, which passed Congress in 2001 with overwhelming bipartisan support (384 to 45 in the House of Representatives, 91 to 8 in the Senate), was supposed to fix American schools by failing schools whose students can't pass standardized performance tests. It didn't. Instead, teachers ended up doing what you might expect: they began teaching to the test and in some cases rigging the exams. Today, students seem little better off than they once were despite the expenditure of billions of dollars on the effort.

Or, to take another example, say a politician urges bombing another country to help protesters who claim they want to establish a free republic. What should you do? Think immediately of Libya. In the wake of the Arab Spring in 2011, as you'll recall, NATO came to the rescue of activists battling the government of dictator Muammar Gaddafi. Gaddafi was defeated and killed. The consequences were disastrous. Today Libya no longer exists as a country except in name only. Stockpiles of arms formerly under Gaddafi's control were confiscated by competing militias, turning large swaths of the country into armed camps. Thousands of weapons were smuggled out of Libya into the nearby country of Mali, where they wound up in the hands of rebels and terrorists affiliated with al Qaeda and helped destabilize the government there.

Why did we act in Libya? It was because the images of protesters being slaughtered registered so powerfully on our Pleistocene brain we felt the forceful urge to do something to stop it, the same urge we felt in the summer of 2014 to do something to stop ISIS. In both cases, the fact that we responded to human suffering was a sign that our brain was working as it should. We were showing empathy. But we can't let our empathy so affect our thinking that we succumb to the myth of the quick fix. Quick fixes, tempting as they are, as a rule don't last and need to be resisted.

Resisting temptation is always hard. It's why most people never manage to stick to their plans to lose weight and people with serious addictions often spend fruitless years trying to stop smoking or stop drinking. But people do succeed. What often helps? When they are at their wit's end they turn to self-help groups. This approach often works. The reason why is that when we are feeling weak it can help to have the support of others. In effect, what people in self-help groups do is use one instinct against another, in this case, peer pressure against the lure of a vice. Our hivishness, which worked against the Nixonians, can be made to work for us.

I don't expect self-help groups to suddenly start popping up to help us resist our political instincts. Not even the Scandinavians have tried that. But we already have in place institutions that can help. They're called schools. Schools teach children to play fair, resist bullies, and think critically. (At least, they're supposed to.) Perhaps we could ask educators to take on the additional role of teaching kids how to recognize System 1 responses to politics.

This undoubtedly would prove to be controversial. What conservative wants their child learning in school that conservatives are inclined to oppose the science of climate change because it makes them think immediately about government regulation? Not many. But the teacher could also point out that, when climate change is framed as a moral issue, conservatives have been shown in experiments to respond differently. Under those circumstances they accept climate change as a man-made assault on our moral purity. This is because, as Jonathan Haidt and other social scientists have discovered, conservatives respond strongly to moral appeals.

Too controversial? Perhaps. But it would be one helluva class, one that students likely would never forget.

8.

Science cannot help us overcome all of the instincts that conspire to mislead us in politics. There's no remedy for reading politicians wrong. We are going to keep reading them wrong because we aren't in a position to study them up close long enough to read them right. And while members of the media are generally in a position to render a detailed judgment based on careful examination, they are not likely to be well-enough informed to give us the well-rounded, warts-and-all perspective we need—particularly for presidential candidates.

A paradoxical effect hinders the effort of getting to know politicians better. The harder the press try to get to know politicians, the more the politicians hold back, which results in a vicious circle. In recent decades national campaigns have become so effective at keeping candidates in a self-protective bubble that not even the most persistent journalists have been able to pop it. Today, no reporter has access to presidents the way scores did in Franklin Roosevelt's day, when they crowded into his office at the White House for weekly off-the-record sessions. Because of Watergate, presidents have withdrawn access to the media; it's simply too risky to make themselves available given the culture of the modern media, which are now so hungry for a scoop that reporters are seemingly willing to do almost anything to get one—as political correspondent Matt Bai showed in his recent account of Gary Hart's career-ending 1988 presidential campaign. When journalists got word that Hart was cavorting with young women, they staked out his house and confronted him in his own driveway with questions about the identity of the woman he'd slept with the night before. In this case, we learned the truth that Hart cheated on his wife. But because Hart had declined to bring reporters into his inner circle the way FDR had, the public lacked a well-rounded perspective. We got the warts, but not much else.

But if it's likely we will keep making mistakes about the character of people in public life, particularly those who run for the White House (the people we need to know the most about), we are not entirely hamstrung. Careful scrutiny of the media can usually help us sift through the detritus to come to something of the truth about our politicians. There were plenty of clues that Richard Nixon wasn't trustworthy, Bill Clinton was a philanderer, and George W. Bush wasn't wise. In the end it's not our lack of knowledge about politicians that is likely to hamper our understanding, but a lack of knowledge about ourselves and the biases that cloud our perceptions.

What science is teaching us is that if we want to elect more honest politicians we first have to be honest with ourselves about our own limits.

Coda: The Widow's Advantage

And what we can learn from her

On June 6, 1927, Bessie and Nat Weiss had their fourth and last child. Her name was Phyllis. Jewish immigrants, Bessie and Nat had come to the United States as children in the late nineteenth century. They came from Austria. Like many immigrants, they found the adjustment to life in America difficult. One way Nat coped was by denying he *was* an immigrant. When anybody asked Nat where he was from, he always insisted he was born in America. His children didn't learn the truth until after he died.

The family lived on the Lower East Side of New York City, at Sixth Street and Second Avenue, in a second-floor walk-up. Nat, average in height, gave the appearance of somebody much taller. He had big arm muscles and, rare for a Jew, was often in fistfights. In the twenties, he earned a living as a bootlegger. In the thirties, after Prohibition ended, he opened a tavern where the local characters hung out. When the customers got rowdy, he'd cast a hard glance from his piercing brown eyes that could make the strongest man wince. Once, he literally threw a man out of the bar. The man he ejected—or so the family story went—was Bugsy Siegel, the infamous mobster, who supposedly was so astounded by this display of chutzpah that he just laughed it off.

Bessie's place, day and night, was home in the kitchen, a room with a window that opened on a dark brick shaft. From here she fed the world—her immediate family, her extended family, their friends, and the neighborhood's lost souls, which kept her tied to the kitchen from sunup until sundown and long after. Her only relief from the drudgery was to escape every now and then to Schrafft's—the restaurant "where ladies lunched"—and someone else, for a change, served her.

Bessie and Nat were determined to make life easier for Phyllis. When she went to sleep-away camp one summer and grew bored, they made the long trip to the mountains to bring her back home early. When she visited the tavern Nat would come running over, pick her up in the air, and exclaim, "My beautiful baby." When her teeth came in a little crooked she got braces, which was rare at the time. Bessie and Nat had suffered. Phyllis would not.

At age twenty, Phyllis met a young man named Sidney on a blind date arranged by friends. Nat and Bessie were delighted. But when Sidney, who ran a little hat store, came around to ask for their daughter's hand in marriage Nat had a question: "Are you going to support my little girl so she never has to work?" When he asked this, those strong brown eyes bore into Sidney with the same intensity as when Nat cast hard looks in the direction of unruly drunks at his bar. Bessie had her own concerns—which Phyllis only realized years later after she and Sidney had moved to the suburbs and one night gave a dinner party for a long table of friends, and Bessie and Nat drove in from the city to join them. Phyllis was in the kitchen preparing the food while the guests chatted in the dining room when she heard her mother come up behind her. Bessie was in a rage, her years of slaving away in front of a hot stove for the benefit of an unending stream of guests surfacing as she cried, "No child of mine is going to grow up to be a kitchen woman like me. No!"

Bessie need not have worried. Phyllis was no kitchen woman. *Leave It to Beaver*'s June Cleaver was more like it. She and Sidney had a deal. She would take care of the kids. He would take care of everything else. He paid the bills and got the car serviced. Phyllis didn't even have to worry about getting cash from a bank. Sidney, after a few years running his little hat store, had gone on to become a successful banker. When Phyllis was in need of cash, all she had to do was tell him and he would bring some home.

On March 12, 1990, Sidney suffered a massive stroke at home and promptly passed away. Phyllis, for the first time in her life, was on her own after forty-one years of marriage. She was sixty-two years old.

She had been raised to be a wife and a mother. She hadn't been taught how to be a widow. But now, after 15,225 days as a wife, she was one.

Phyllis didn't know anything about being a widow. She hadn't given much thought to the possibility of her being one. None of her close friends had lost their husbands. And hers, at age sixty-nine, hadn't seemed likely to face death anytime soon. Sidney's father had lived to seventy-five. His mother was *still* alive. And he hadn't retired. "Chrissakes," she would tell herself, he was still playing tennis almost every week.

But now he was gone, and she had to figure out how to be a widow. She had to learn how to dine alone. She had to deal with the anger she felt at losing her husband. And she had to make decisions, an endless series of decisions: Should she leave his clothes in the closet or give them away? Should she answer his mail? Should she join a support group? She also had to learn how to pay the bills, balance a checkbook, and retrieve cash from a bank.

That, in summary form, is Phyllis's story, which I know quite well because Phyllis, as you may have surmised, was my mother, the woman who fell in love with JFK. It's also the story, in broad outline, of millions of American women. Every year more than 800,000 become widows. And every year the new widows have to learn what the millions of widows before them learned: surviving widowhood doesn't just happen. It takes hard work. Like my mother, new widows figure out that they have to learn how to live alone. This is something that is particularly obvious to women in my mother's circumstances: women who never expected to be on their own who become widows without advance warning. But it's the epiphany all widows arrive at.

Voters, as it turns out, have the widow's problem. They, too, are on their own. In a way, no group is perhaps more on its own in our age than the ordinary citizen acting in their capacity as a voter. On who else's shoulders do we lay as many responsibilities with so little preparation, guidance, or support? When the average American turns eighteen and suddenly is eligible to vote, he isn't given an instruction manual on voting and isn't enrolled in a group to help him learn what voting involves. The government doesn't even tell him where to register to vote. What's more, he isn't given any help sorting out the issues voters are asked to decide or the criterion to be used in choosing one candidate over another. All he gets is a voters' pamphlet, which is usually less than enlightening.

More than four million people turn eighteen in the United States every year. That's more than four million new potential voters. And virtually none get the help they need. In all, there are more than 218 million eligible voters in the United States. And they don't get the help they need either. Unlike citizens in northern European countries, we generally don't convene study circles for people who want tutoring in complicated political subjects. Nor do we subsidize voters who want to take adult education classes to learn about issues. We can turn to the media for help. But they frequently overlook or underreport the stories people actually need to know about, preferring instead to focus on stories people will *want* to know about since those—fiery car wrecks, grisly murders, and police chases—are easy to digest, entertaining, and make no intellectual demands. You don't have to know anything to understand them.

Our being on our own is something new. In the past, voters got plenty of help—first and foremost, from church leaders. In the presidential election of 1840 the leading evangelical preacher in the country, Lyman Beecher (father of *Uncle Tom's Cabin* author Harriet Beecher Stowe), actually went on tour telling Protestant audiences whom they should vote for. It was for Tippecanoe, William Henry Harrison, he told them. They did. And that helped Harrison win what was a very close election in the popular vote.

Party bosses also offered voters direct help. Once the franchise became widespread the parties dominated politics (confounding the expectations of the Founding Fathers, who considered parties divisive), and the way they achieved their dominance was by recruiting voters *en masse*. The process often wasn't pretty. Frequently, the parties literally bought votes; in Indiana in the election of 1888 you could buy a vote for $2. New York City's Boss Tweed, who defended the practice of "honest graft," was nobody's model of civic virtue. But he and the other bosses who controlled politics through most of our history catered to voters in a way modern political parties don't. Today, government seems remote and party leaders far out of reach. Few voters today ever have personal contact with party leaders or their subalterns.

This is not how it was in the past. Nat Weiss, my mother's father, served as a Democratic Party precinct captain. In this position he had direct contact with party leaders. If someone on his block needed help with a task as basic as getting the garbage removed, all they had to do was see Nat, and he, in turn, would see to it that somebody in authority passed along the word to have the garbage picked up. Politics was personal. At election time Nat talked up the party's slate of candidates and got people excited about them. Say what you will about the system, it operated on a human scale. It wasn't bureaucratic as ours is now.

This accounts for one of the distinguishing phenomena of the party system in its heyday: the extraordinarily high turnout rates. In the 1790s, before the party system became entrenched, turnout was low, often no more than 25 percent. By the next decade it doubled. By the end of the nineteenth century turnout in national elections often exceeded 80 percent. (In the past four decades, in contrast, turnout rarely has reached 60 percent.) Voters turned out at elections because party leaders made sure they did. Party precinct captains like my grandfather cajoled voters and promised people jobs, which were handed out like bubble gum to people who often weren't qualified to hold them. Reformers in the late nineteenth century won enactment of a rule requiring federal civil service officeholders to pass written examinations to demonstrate their competence. An investigation of the New York Custom House found that many applicants failed the test even though it was simple. A sample question asked what the three branches of government are. A job candidate answered, the army and the navy. He got the job anyway, as did many others who failed, in violation of established procedures.

By the end of the nineteenth century voters began joining labor unions in large numbers, and the labor unions offered help too. No union member ever had to wonder which candidate was good for labor. His union told him (and often all but ordered him and his family members to vote the union-backed slate).

In the 1950s, this triumvirate—church, party, union—began to weaken and unravel. As the reputation of unions became tarnished by scandal and union bosses were sent to prison, a Republican Congress passed a law limiting the unions' power, and states passed so-called right-to-work laws. Union membership precipitously declined. This decline paralleled a decline in the old party system. As the labor bosses started going down one by one, so did the party bosses, ending the careers of machine politicians like Missouri's Tom Pendergast, who had been behind Harry Truman's rise to power.

A further factor in the decline of the old party system—probably the single biggest factor—was television. Once television became entrenched, candidates learned they could make an end run around the party bosses. They could win just by getting themselves on TV. The first politician to figure this out was Tennessee senator Estes Kefauver. In the early 1950s, he became a national celebrity when his hearings on organized crime drew blockbuster ratings at the dawn of the television age. Shortly after, over the opposition of the bosses, he became a candidate for the Democratic Party nomination for president and swept the primaries, winning ten of eleven of them. Though he failed to win the nomination—the bosses still had enough power to sabotage him at the convention—Kefauver paved the way for candidates like John Kennedy.

At the same time that unions and political parties were changing, the Internal Revenue Service issued a rule that hindered the ability of churches to play a direct role in politics. The rule was simple. No church could back a candidate. If it did, it could lose its tax-exempt status. For years, the IRS looked the other way when churches broke the rule. But in the 1990s the

IRS cracked down. When a conservative church took out a full-page ad in *USA Today* warning Protestants not to vote for Bill Clinton for president—"Christian Beware. Do not put the economy ahead of the Ten Commandments. . . . Bill Clinton is promoting policies that are in rebellion to God's laws"—the church was found to be in violation of the tax revenue code and lost its tax-exempt status.

Black and evangelical church leaders nonetheless persisted in helping voters sort out political issues, but by the end of the twentieth century most voters had no one they could turn to for authoritative help. Not party bosses, not labor bosses, not anybody who really understood politics and could be counted on to help them understand the issues and where their interests lay. Like Flag City USA's Jim P.—the Air Force veteran who didn't know if Barack Obama was a Muslim or a Christian ("It's like you're hearing about two different men with nothing in common")—voters felt at sea in finding the truth. They had the widow's problem: they were on their own. Unfortunately, they lacked the widow's advantage—a clear understanding of their situation.

When a widow finds herself on her own, what's the lesson she quickly learns? That you have to work at surviving. You can't ignore your responsibilities. If you do there are consequences. Neglect to pay the light bill and the lights go out. Forget to service your car and your car stops working. Fail to pay your taxes and the IRS pays you an unpleasant visit. Voters individually, in contrast, don't have to worry that they will pay a price for neglecting any of *their* responsibilities. Vote wrong and what happens to you? Nothing, absolutely nothing. Voting isn't like driving. You can vote recklessly over and over again and never lose your right to vote, even as the country goes to hell.

Because voters don't pay a price for citizen malpractice no lightbulb ever goes off in their head suggesting that they are performing badly. Indeed, all they hear from politicians and the media is how wonderful they are. This has consequences. Instead of working hard to understand the complicated business of politics, they just go with the flow, acting on instinct, and assume that instinct is sufficient. As we have seen, it isn't.

Jim P. should have gone to the library to do his own research on Barack Obama. Librarians could helpfully have told him which media sources he could trust. There was no reason for him to be as confused as he was. But, ultimately, he didn't make the effort because, baffled as he was by Obama, it didn't occur to Jim P. that he needed to.

It's not strange that people fail to realize the downside of being on their own. Being on our own is what we all strive for. Who wants party or union bosses telling us how to vote? But much was lost when the old system collapsed. Politics became more remote, and voters lost touch with people who could provide valuable cues. The result was that many of the errors to which we are prone by virtue of our Pleistocene brain grew worse. People on their own have a harder time summoning up the will to take part in politics, so more stay home on Election Day. Reading politicians becomes more difficult in the absence of personal contact with people in the politics business. Even our capacity for empathy may be impaired. To party bosses and labor bosses, peoples' problems were the problems of real human beings they encountered in the course of their everyday interactions with the public. The hard-luck stories they heard shaped their outlook and affected their politics, and this in turn shaped voters' outlook and *their* politics.

WHAT WE HAVE LEARNED IN THIS BOOK—what I learned doing my research for it and I hope you have learned by reading it—is that little in politics comes easy. Curiosity. Reading people. Realism. Empathy. These come naturally to us as human beings, but usually not as citizens.

If we want a democracy that works we can have one, even with our Pleistocene brain. But like the widow we have to work at it. While we busy ourselves with projects to reform the system, we need to work at reforming ourselves, too. Science, fortunately, shows us we can.

Acknowledgments

In a work of this kind, which is dependent on the research of scholars in a dozen or more disciplines, it behooves me to acknowledge, at the outset, my great debt, as I hope my endnotes show, to many people I have never met, but whose work proved informative and eye-opening.

As a historian and journalist operating in realms far outside my area of expertise, I repeatedly felt compelled to call on scholars for help in understanding the science and social science works I was reading. These scholars gave freely of their time. I feel my debt to them intensely: Christopher Achen, Larry Bartels, Peter Hatemi, Marco Iacoboni, Mary Lee Jensvold, Kurt and Gladys Lang, George Marcus, Michael Bang Petersen, Paul Slovic, and David Pizarro, whose brilliant 2010 Massey lecture at the University of Toronto helped crystalize my thinking about the key theme of the book—why we often seem so ill-prepared to deal with the political problems we face. David had the answer: a deeply ingrained emotional response that may have been an advantage in the Stone Age might not be advantageous now.

Among historians, I turned for help to Timothy Naftali and Luke Nichter. Both of them helped guide me through the often-complicated story of Watergate.

On a more personal note, I want to thank several friends with whom I batted around ideas: the late Dick Wesley, Rod Decker, and Bernard Weisberger. Now in his nineties, Bernie, as he is known, read early drafts, as he has done with all of my books stretching back to the late 1970s. No student ever had a better mentor.

John Wilson was gracious in helping me locate documents at the LBJ Library.

It was at the prompting of my agent, William Clark, in June 2011, at a wonderful lunch at Balthazar in New York City, that I began to think about writing this book. Unfortunately for him, this meant reading countless drafts of misguided proposals before I finally found my footing.

I have had the pleasure of working with three editors on the book. Lara Heimert, my charming and brilliant editor at Basic Books, who had the courage to take a risk on a historian doing a science book, offered sparkling insights and astute guidance. Roger Labrie line-edited the manuscript with great care and intelligence. John Wilcockson copyedited the final manuscript exquisitely, saving me from numerous inconsistencies.

Readers know the great debt I owe to my mother, from whom I got my love of politics. It was my dear hope that she would live to see the book's completion, but cancer, which she had beat twice, finally got her on the third round, before I finished.

I want to thank my sister, Randi Shenkman, too. At my side as I was writing my chapters on Watergate was Stanley Kutler's *Abuse of Power*, which she gave me years ago. On the flyleaf she wrote: "Happy birthday to one of Nixon's longest run loyalists." Having outed myself in this book as a onetime Nixon supporter, that is now no longer an inside family joke.

Speaking of outing myself, I have left my most important acknowledgment for last. It is for my husband, John Stucky, whom I have had the privilege of marrying four times: we first got married in Oregon, when gay marriage was suddenly made legal in 2004. Alas, gay marriage, just as suddenly, became illegal in Oregon, nullifying our consecrated document. In 2005, we got married again, this time in Vancouver, British Columbia. But it didn't sit right with us that we had had to leave the country to get married, so when it proved possible to get hitched in Connecticut, we leaped at the chance. Our fourth marriage happened without our having to do anything. In 2014, the State of Washington, where we live, automatically converted partnerships to marriages. And just like that our 2007 partnership became a marriage document. We have now been together fifteen years. These have been the best years of my life. If readers detect a joyousness in this book it is thanks to John, who is the best partner anyone could hope for. Each night as I returned home from the office after a day of research I made a full report on the discoveries I'd made that day. His keen questions about the material helped clarify my understanding of it. And when the task of writing the book seemed overwhelming, as it often did, he was there every step of the way to offer support.

I am glad the state now recognizes his role in my life. It has been one of the great surprises of my life that public opinion so swiftly changed about gay marriage that we were able to get married. As I show in the book, science has given us a reason to be optimistic about public opinion. So have the events of the last few years, as my little story about the evolution of our married life shows.

Notes

Introduction: The Mismatch

xi   **out of conscious awareness.** Radu J. Bogdan, *Interpreting Minds* (MIT Press, 2003), p. 115.

xii   **driven by instinct.** Nikolaas Tinbergen, *The Study of Instinct* (Oxford University Press, 1958).

xii   **cry or sneeze, after all.** William James, *The Principles of Psychology* (Henry Holt, 1890), p. 404.

xii   **feel good when we do.** Daniel Goleman, *Focus: The Hidden Driver of Excellence* (Harper, 2013), p. 66.

xiii   **other people's faces.** Carolyn C. Goren, Merrill Sarty, and Paul Y. K. Wu, "Visual Following and Pattern Discrimination of Face-like Stimuli by Newborn Infants," *Pediatrics* (October 1, 1975), Vol. 56, No. 4, pp. 544–549.

xiii   **one social scientist put it.** Timothy D. Wilson, *Strangers to Ourselves: Discovering the Adaptive Unconscious* (Harvard University Press, 2004). See also: Jason Weeden and Robert Kurzban, *The Hidden Agenda of the Political Mind: How Self-Interest Shapes Our Opinions and Why We Won't Admit It* (Princeton University Press, 2014), chapter 3.

xiii   **someone is lying to us.** Maria Hartwig and Charles F. Bond Jr., "Why Do Lie-catchers Fail?" *Psychological Bulletin* (July 2011), Vol. 137, No. 4, pp. 643–659.

·xiii   **by the age of four.** Simon Baron-Cohen, *Mindblindess* (MIT Press, 1997), p. 60.

xiii   **empathy for others.** Frans de Waal, *The Age of Empathy* (Broadway Books, 2010).

xiv   **emotions they are feeling.** Richard Restak, *The Naked Brain* (Three Rivers Press, 2006), p. 94.

xiv   **burden of childbirth.** Robert Trivers, "Parental Investment and Sexual Selection," in *Sexual Selection and the Descent of Man: 1871–1971*, ed. Bernard Campbell (Aldine Publishing Co., 1972), pp. 142–43. See also: Daniel Goleman, *Focus: The Hidden Driver of Excellence* (Harper, 2013), p. 66.

xv   **a thousand generations.** Christopher Boehm, *Hierarchy in the Forest: The Evolution of Egalitarian Behavior* (Harvard University Press, 1999), p. 198. E. O. Wilson, "A New Conception of Human Evolution," Seattle Townhall lecture (April 19, 2012). Scientists are agreed that human evolution has continued up to the present

253

day. But most evolutionary psychologists believe that the basic wiring of our brain was completed in the Pleistocene. Some scientists believe significant changes can take place over just hundreds of years. See, for example, Nicholas Wade's extended discussion in his controversial book, *A Troublesome Inheritance* (Penguin Press, 2014), p. 53ff, citing the research of Soviet-era scientist Dmitri Belyaev. Among those who insist that the brain has changed significantly in the last few hundred years is Marlene Zuk, *Paleofantasy: What Evolution Really Tells Us About Sex, Diet, and How We Live* (W. W. Norton, 2013).

xv   **"some problems than others."** Leda Cosmides and John Tooby, "Evolutionary Psychology: A Primer," website of the Center for Evolutionary Psychology (January 13, 1997). See also Cosmides and Tooby, "Evolution to Behavior: Evolutionary Psychology as the Missing Link," in *The Latest on the Best: Essays on Evolution and Optimality*, ed. John Dupré (MIT Press, 1987), and Peter Hatemi and Rose McDermott, eds., *Man Is by Nature a Political Animal: Evolution, Biology and Politics* (University of Chicago Press, 2011), esp. chapter 1. Two textbooks provide an excellent introduction to evolutionary psychology: *Evolutionary Psychology: The New Science of the Mind* (Pearson, 2012) by David Buss, and *Human Evolutionary Psychology* (Princeton University Press, 2002) by Louise Barrett, Robin Dunbar, and John Lycett. See also: *The Oxford Handbook of Evolutionary Psychology* (Oxford University Press, 2007), ed. Dunbar and Barrett, and *The Handbook of Evolutionary Psychology* (Wiley, 2005), ed. Buss.

xv   **good mood, you might not.** Gary Marcus, *The Birth of the Mind: How a Tiny Number of Genes Creates the Complexities of Human Thought* (Basic Books, 2004), p. 12ff. See also: Jonathan Haidt, *The Righteous Mind: Why Good People Are Divided by Politics and Religion* (Pantheon, 2012), pp. 130–131.

xv   **people when we're tired.** Walter Mischel, *The Marshmallow Test: Mastering Self-Control* (Little, Brown, 2014), pp. 169, 216, 235ff.

xv   **for months on end.** Steven Pinker, *The Better Angels of Our Nature: Why Violence Has Declined* (Penguin Books, 2012).

xvi   **they are maladaptive.** Even in our personal lives our instincts fall short. Why are so many Americans overweight? It is not because they lack self-control. As the Harvard scientist Daniel Lieberman notes, it is because we are not designed for a world in which sugary and fatty foods are abundant. We are designed for a world in which they are scarce. So we lack a regulator to prompt us to stop eating. Our systems tell us we should eat—and eat and eat and eat. Just as in politics, we have another mismatch. See *The Story of the Human Body: Evolution, Health, and Disease* (Pantheon, 2013).

xvi   **"hadn't been spelled out."** E-mail communication with the author, September 30, 2011.

xviii   **voters statewide in 1932.** Christopher Achen and Larry Bartels, "It Feels Like We're Thinking: The Rationalizing Voter and Electoral Democracy," paper delivered at the Annual Meeting of the American Political Science Association (August 28, 2006).

xx   **the Bush-Gore election of 2000.** Larry Bartels and Christopher Achen, "Blind Retrospection: Electoral Responses to Droughts, Flu, and Shark Attacks," paper delivered at the Annual Meeting of the American Political Science Association (September 2002).

xx   **and Atmospheric Administration (NOAA).** See "Historical Palmer Drought Indices—Temperature, Precipitation, and Drought—National Climatic Data Center (NCDC)" at the website of NOAA.

xxvi   **the incumbent government.** Andrew Healy, Neil Malhotra, and Cecilia Hyunjung Mo, "Irrelevant Events Affect Voters' Evaluations of Government Performance," *Proceedings of the National Academy of Sciences of the United States of America* (July 20, 2010), Vol. 107, No. 29, pp. 12804–12809.

xxvi   **droughts and floods have here.** Ryan E. Carlin et al., "Natural Disaster and Democratic Legitimacy: The Public Opinion Consequences of Chile's 2010 Earthquake and Tsunami," *Political Research Quarterly* (March 2014), Vol. 67, No. 1, pp. 3–15.

xxix   **he himself helped identify.** Daniel Kahneman, *Thinking Fast and Slow* (Farrar, Straus and Giroux, 2011), p. 417.

xxix   **less susceptibility to them.** Richard West, Russell Meserve, and Keith Stanovich, "Cognitive Sophistication Does Not Attenuate the Bias Blind Spot," *Journal of Personality and Social Psychology* (September 2012), Vol. 103, No. 3, pp. 506–519.

xxix   **others that are helpful.** I hasten to make the obvious point that instincts are complicated. And because they are we cannot write them all off. They work or don't work depending on our situation. In this book I will be harping on the situations in which they don't work. But I don't mean to imply that they never do. In some cases, even in the context of modern politics, they are absolutely essential. It is impossible to imagine, for example, that any human society on earth could survive for long if man lacked that most basic instinct of all, the instinct to get along well with others. That's our social instinct and it's vital.

Another instinct is our commitment to fairness. It's real and it's also vital. It has been confirmed by social scientists through experiments involving human beings throughout the world living under all kinds of social and political arrangements. In other words, it's universal, as demonstrated when people play the Ultimatum Game. In this game two players split a pot of money, say $100. How the money is split up is decided by only one player (the Decision Maker). Under the rules the other player can reject the offer if he deems it too low. When that happens neither get anything. It's game over. So what usually happens? The Decision Maker keeps $80 for himself, leaving $20 for the other player. If the Decision Maker leaves too small a sum for the other player he'll usually reject it even though anything he gets—$5 or 5¢—leaves him better off. Why do people reject low offers? It offends their sense of justice. See Robert Trivers, *The Folly of Fools* (Basic Books, 2011), p. 49.

Yale's Paul Bloom is of the opinion, which he characterizes as a strong hunch, that the main reason players share their proceeds is because of subtle social pressures. They want to look good in the eyes of their friends and others. We lack, he believes, a true Robin Hood instinct. But he concedes that we possess a powerful impulse to cooperate with others. See *Just Babies* (Crown, 2013), pp. 65–74.

xxix   **have the will to do so.** Haidt, *Righteous Mind*, chapters 9 and 10.

xxx   **northeast India are not.** Uri Gneezy et al., "Gender Differences in Competition: Evidence From a Matrilineal and a Patriarchal Society," working paper (January 2008). Evolutionary psychologists make the point that many differences in cultures are owing to different environments. The same evolved psychological mechanism may be operating in both cultures, but because the environments differ the same mechanism produces different results. Thus, in one culture people may share their food and in another not share it. Studies show that where a particular food is in short supply (for example, meat from hunting), sharing is common for that particular type of food. But where food is abundant, sharing is more rare. But the same evolved psychological mechanism, sharing, is present in both cultures.

Chapter 1: The Michael Jordan Lesson

4   **"Oh my God!"** Ira Berkow, "Looking Over Jordan," *New York Times* (January 31, 1999).

4   **for *Sports Illustrated* blared.** Roland Lazenby, *Michael Jordan: The Life* (Little, Brown, 2014), p. 495.

5   **renown in other sports.** "List of Multi-sport Athletes," Wikipedia (accessed October 2, 2013).

5   **medals in different sports.** "List of Athletes with Olympic Medals in Different Disciplines," Wikipedia (accessed October 2, 2013).

6   **surfing and rollerblading.** Freakonomics podcast, "What Do Medieval Nuns and Bo Jackson Have in Common?" (May 9, 2013).

6   **are not naturally suited.** Might Michael Jordan have become a great baseball player if he had worked at it as hard and as long as he worked at basketball? His biographer, Roland Lazenby, suggests that might have been the case. Lazenby notes that Jordan had difficulty as a ball player because he was competing with players who had hit hundreds of thousands of balls in their career (*Michael Jordan,* p. 500).

8   **"The Nervous Liberals."** Brett Gary, *The Nervous Liberals* (Columbia University Press, 1999).

10   **the polemic was me.** Rick Shenkman, *Legends, Lies and Cherished Myths of American History* (HarperCollins, 1988), *"I Love Paul Revere Whether He Rode or Not"* (HarperCollins, 1991), and *Legends, Lies and Cherished Myths of World History* (HarperCollins, 1993).

10   **have attracted attention.** These statistics are collected in Rick Shenkman, *Just How Stupid Are We* (Basic Books, 2008). See also: Michael X. Delli Carpini and Scott Keeter, *What Americans Know about Politics and Why It Matters* (Yale University Press, 1997).

11   **find the answer.** Eli Saslow, "In Flag City USA, False Obama Rumors Are Flying," *Washington Post* (June 30, 2008).

12   **of the twentieth century.** Eric R. Kandel, *In Search of Memory: The Emergence of a New Science of Mind* (W. W. Norton, 2006), chapter 11.

13   **our trump cards.** Curiosity, say researchers, is the reason behind our fascination with rumors. What's a rumor? Like a tip at a racetrack, it's a possible clue to the truth. We traffic in all kinds of rumors, both positive and negative. But the ones that gain the most traction are negative rumors. We want to know if the company we work at is folding, and seize on any rumors to that effect. See Nicholas DiFonzo, *The Watercooler Effect: A Psychologist Explores the Extraordinary Power of Rumors* (Avery, 2009).

Chapter 2: We're Political Animals

16   **a deliberative poll.** See the website of the Center for Deliberative Democracy, run by James Fishkin. See his two books: *The Voice of the People: Public Opinion and Democracy* (Yale University Press, 1997) and *When the People Speak: Deliberative Democracy and Public Consultation* (Oxford University Press, 2011).

16   **weekend of January 19–21.** Steven A. Holmes, "Broad Poll of the Public," *New York Times* (December 3, 1995).

17   **facts don't matter.** Fishkin, *Voice of the People,* chapter 5.

18   **to guide their thinking.** I should point out that ignorant voters are not uniformly ignorant. They tend to know a lot about subjects that affect them directly. And when the news concerns events like beheadings that all human beings

can readily relate to, overwhelming majorities evince a strong interest. NBC News reported in September 2014 that 59 percent of Americans were closely following the story of the beheadings by the Islamic State in Iraq and Syria (ISIS). No other story in the previous five years was followed as closely by as many people. Chuck Todd on NBC's *Nightly News* (September 9, 2014).

18 **unconstitutional, or defunded.** Robert Mutch, *Buying the Vote: A History of Campaign Finance Reform* (Oxford University Press, 2014).

19 **countries, surveys show.** Henry Milner, *Civic Literacy: How Informed Citizens Make Democracy Work* (Tufts, 2002), p. 18ff. See also Robert D. Putnam, *Bowling Alone* (Simon & Schuster, 2000).

20 **over a few years.** Rick Shenkman, "Sam Wineburg Dares to Ask If the Teaching American History Program Is a Boondoggle," History News Network (April 19, 2009).

Chapter 3: Your 150 Closest Friends

23 **to the larger community.** Christopher Boehm, *Hierarchy in the Forest: The Evolution of Egalitarian Behavior* (Harvard University Press, 2001).

25 **psychologist Steven Pinker.** Steven Pinker, *How the Mind Works* (W. W. Norton, 1997), p. 388.

25 **place the most emphasis.** Michael Bang Petersen, "Is the Political Animal Politically Ignorant? Applying Evolutionary Psychology to the Study of Political Attitudes," *Evolutionary Psychology* (2012), Vol. 10, No. 5, pp. 802–817.

25 **network is about 150.** Christmas cards are thought to be a particularly good indicator of a person's network. In Western societies this is the one time of year when people reach out to the people they care about. Robin Dunbar, *Grooming, Gossip, and the Evolution of Language* (Harvard University Press, 1996), p. 68ff.

26 **the magic number, 150.** Malcolm Gladwell, *The Tipping Point* (Little, Brown, 2002), p. 177ff.

26 **migrations in human history.** *Ibid.*, p. 73.

27 **some day find useful.** Nicholas Humphrey, "The Social Function of Intellect," in *Machiavellian Intelligence: Social Expertise and the Evolution of Intellect in Monkeys, Apes, and Humans* (Oxford University Press, 1988), ed. R. W. Byrne and Andrew Whiten.

28 **a startling discovery.** *Ibid.*

28 **As Albert Einstein is said.** Grenville Clark, letter to the editor, *New York Times* (April 22, 1955).

28 **people are complicated.** Dominance Theory suggests that one of the reasons for the emergence of higher cognition was the necessity to determine the status of primates competing for resources. As we'll see later, we come equipped with a psychological mechanism that allows us to determine by age three what our obligations are to one another. This capacity, known as deontic reasoning, allows us to determine who is of low and high status. This is vital in establishing a pecking order. See Denise Cummins, *The Evolution of Mind* (Oxford University Press, 1998), chapter 2.

28 **like any other man.** Clyde Kluckhohn and Henry Alexander Murray, *Personality in Nature, Society, and Culture* (Knopf, 1948), p. 35.

29 **in the Netherlands.** Frans de Waal, *Chimpanzee Politics: Power and Sex Among Apes* (Johns Hopkins University Press, 1998), esp. pp. xiii, 98, 103–104.

29 **Form bigger groups.** Which came first, which caused which? Did we have bigger groups and therefore get bigger brains? Or did our bigger brains allow us to form bigger groups? The change in our brain size apparently occurred about 1.8 million years ago as our ancestors emerged from the forests to live on the African

savannas. There, according to E. O. Wilson, we had ready access to meat, a high source of protein. Protein allowed our brains to grow larger. This is known as the savanna hypothesis. With a larger brain came larger groups. See Wilson, *The Social Conquest of Earth* (Liveright, 2012). An alternative hypothesis is that we evolved in response to unstable environmental conditions. As the environment shifted from hot to cold to wet climates, those who were able to adapt had higher fitness. The Smithsonian's Rick Potts has put forward this hypothesis. See Potts, *What Does It Mean to Be Human* (National Geographic, 2010).

30   **because they cannot talk.** Dunbar in *Grooming, Gossip, and the Evolution of Language*, and in his coauthored textbook, *Human Evolutionary Psychology* (Princeton University Press, 2002), p. 346.

32   **right size for us.** Jason Weeden and Robert Kurzban argue in *The Hidden Agenda of the Political Mind: How Self-Interest Shapes Our Opinions and Why We Won't Admit It* (Princeton University Press, 2014), that whites with little education are particularly susceptible to apathy (p. 190). The explanation, Weeden and Kurzban maintain, is that neither of the two main parties fights hard for the interests of such voters. That may be true. But this doesn't vitiate an EP explanation. In hunter-gatherer communities, people could see after their own interests because communities were small and largely egalitarian.

Chapter 4: Why We Are Surprised When Our Leaders Disappoint Us

37   **smart voters pick?** John Tierney, "Edwards Wins: A Theory Tested," *New York Times* (May 2, 2004).

39   **people in our midst.** Michael Bang Petersen, "Is the Political Animal Politically Ignorant? Applying Evolutionary Psychology to the Study of Political Attitudes," *Evolutionary Psychology* (2012), Vol. 10, No. 5, pp. 802–817.

40   **asked Edwards."** Charles Peters, "Tilting at Windmills," *Washington Monthly* (June 2003).

41   **one big lie.** Thomas Reeves, *A Question of Character* (Three Rivers Press, 1992), p. 186ff.

41   **swimming in the nude.** Mimi Alford, *Once Upon a Secret* (Hutchinson Radius, 2012).

42   **opponent George McGovern.** Keith Olson, *Watergate: The Presidential Scandal that Shook America* (University Press of Kansas, 2003), p. 110.

43   **to the concrete.** Christopher H. Achen and Larry M. Bartels, "Musical Chairs: Pocketbook Voting and the Limits of Democratic Accountability," Annual Meeting of the American Political Science Association (2004).

43   **liberal or conservative.** John Ehrman, *The Eighties: America in the Age of Reagan* (Yale University Press, 2005), pp. 47–48.

43   **simple answers appealing.** Biographers of both the left and the right 43 that millions found Reagan likable, even as the evidence piles up that he was always a polarizing figure, a central theme of Rick Perlstein's *The Invisible Bridge* (Simon & Schuster, 2014). Why did voters vote for Reagan, if not for his ideology? This is a complicated story. It's not only because Carter failed in many ways, prompting voters to vote for change. It's that Reagan told people what they wanted to hear. He reaffirmed their basic goodness by appealing to the classic American myth of exceptionalism and played down Watergate. Perlstein emphasizes that Reagan, alone among prominent politicians, said Watergate essentially didn't matter.

43   **that we know them.** See Nicholas Epley, *Mindwise*, esp. chapter 1.

44   **scientist Maria Elizabeth Grabe.** Maria Elizabeth Grabe, "News as Reality-Inducing, Survival-Relevant, Gender-Specific Stimuli," in *Applied Evolutionary Psychology*, ed. S. Craig Roberts (Oxford University Press, 2012), p. 362.

45   **vision is dominant.** David Eagleman, *Incognito: The Secret Lives of the Brain* (Pantheon, 2011), pp. 46–47.

45   **Ten million bps.** George Marcus, *Political Psychology: Neuroscience, Genetics, and Politics* (Oxford University Press, 2012), p. 107.

45   **vision was helpful.)** Eiluned Pearce, Chris Stringer, and Robin Dunbar, "New Insights into Differences in Brain Organization between Neanderthals and Anatomically Modern Humans," *Proceedings of the Royal Society B* (March 13, 2013).

46   **images they'd seen.** John Medina, *Brain Rules* (Pear Press, 2008), chapter 10.

46   **was dreading in 1984.** Leslie Stahl, *Reporting Live* (Simon & Schuster, 2000), p. 211.

47   **among the top three.** Kenneth Walsh, "Poll: 50 Years Later, JFK Lives On," *U.S. News & World Report* (October 15, 2013).

47   **of his assassination.** Steven M. Gillon, "Rethinking the JFK Legacy," History News Network (October 28, 2013).

47   **think about Kennedy.** "The Kennedy Half Century: National Polling Results," an online survey by Larry Sabato, author of *The Kennedy Half Century: The Presidency, Assassination, and Lasting Legacy of John F. Kennedy* (Bloomsbury USA, 2013).

48   **look like John Kennedy.** Wikipedia features a handy chart comparing a multitude of presidential ratings. See "Historical Rankings of Presidents of the United States."

49   **"read in his eyes."** Robert Caro, *The Years of Lyndon Johnson: The Passage of Power* (Knopf, 2012), p. 6.

49   **autistic people confront.** Simon Baron-Cohen, *Mindblindness* (MIT Press, 1997), chapter 7.

50   **in his direction too.** Tom Foulsham et al., "Gaze Allocation in a Dynamic Situation: Effects of Social Status and Speaking," *Cognition* (September 24, 2010).

50   **missing the message.** Peter R. Murphy et al., "Pupil-Linked Arousal Determines Variability in Perceptual Decision Making," *PLOS: Computational Biology* (September 2014), Vol. 10, No. 9.

50   **usually hard to see.** Richard Restak, *The Naked Brain* (Three Rivers Press, 2006), p. 139.

51   **the highest office.** Caro, *Passage of Power*, p. 33.

52   **face-to-face. We don't.** Bruce Hood, *Supersense* (HarperOne, 2009), chapter 9.

52   **a biographer tells us.** David Remnick, *The Bridge: The Life and Rise of Barack Obama* (Knopf, 2010), p. 371.

Chapter 5: 167 Milliseconds

53   **could kill you.** Gerd Gigerenzer, Peter M. Todd, and the ABC Research Group, *Simple Heuristics That Make Us Smart* (Oxford University Press, 1999), pp. 18–19.

53   **points out, is easy.** Daniel Kahneman, *Thinking Fast and Slow* (Farrar, Straus and Giroux, 2011).

54   **"of conscious awareness."** Michael Gazzaniga, *The Mind's Past* (University of California Press, 1998), p. 21.

54   **those involving consciousness.** George Marcus, *Political Psychology: Neuroscience, Genetics, and* Politics (Oxford University Press, 2012), p. 107. The distinction

between fast and slow thinking is now nearly universal among scientists who study the brain, but this by no means should imply a consensus about the distinction between them. A recent survey shows that scientists have developed twenty-eight different names for the dual-process system, each name corresponding to a different estimate of the nature of fast and slow thinking. The conceptual smorgasbord includes a difference of opinion about something as basic as whether fast or slow thinking is efficient. Some say fast thinking is efficient; some deny it adamantly. Both views are represented in the most recent comprehensive guide to dual-process research. See Jeffrey W. Sherman et al., eds., *Dual-Process Theories of the Social Mind* (Guilford Press, 2014); see Sloan, p. 77 (efficient) and Spunt and Lieberman, p. 280 (inefficient).

54 **refer to as heuristics.** Gerd Gigerenzer, *Gut Feelings: The Intelligence of the Unconscious* (Penguin, 2007).

54 **on us as happiness.** Gerd Bohner and Thomas Weinerth, "Negative Affect Can Increase or Decrease Message Scrutiny: The Affect Interpretation Hypothesis," *Personality and Social Psychology Bulletin* (November 2001), Vol. 27, No. 11, pp. 1417–1428.

54 **System 1 thinking.** Experiments by psychologist James Cutting show that we favor art with which we are familiar over art considered classics. See "The Mere Exposure Effect and Aesthetic Preference" in P. Locher, C. Martindale, and L. Dorfman, eds., *New Directions in Aesthetics, Creativity, and the Psychology of Art* (Baywood Publishing Co., 2006).

54 **his colleague, Amos Tversky.** Kahneman, *Thinking Fast*, p. 97ff.

56 **We just do.** *Ibid.*, p. 113ff.

56 **never met strangers.** Edward H. Hagen and Peter Hammerstein, "Game Theory and Human Evolution: A Critique of Some Recent Interpretations of Experimental Games," *Theoretical Population Biology* (2006), Vol. 69, pp. 341–342.

57 **shifts its gaze.** Bruce M. Hood, *Supersense* (HarperOne, 2009), pp. 112–113.

57 **looking at faces.** *The Oxford Handbook of Face Perception*, ed. Gillian Rhodes et al. (Oxford University Press, 2011), esp. p. 3.

57 **opposed to an object.** Elinor McKone and Rachel Robbins, "Are Faces Special?" in *Oxford Handbook of Face Perception*, chapter 9.

58 **seen upside down.** *Ibid.*, p. 151ff.

58 **Jesus in a coffee cup.** Kang Lee et al., "Seeing Jesus in Toast: Neural and Behavioral Correlates of Face Pareidolia," *Cortex* (April 2014), Vol. 53, pp. 60–77.

58 **go with their gut.).** Travis N. Ridout and Kathleen Searles, "It's My Campaign I'll Cry If I Want to: How and When Campaigns Use Emotional Appeals," *Political Psychology* (February 15, 2011).

59 **to quantify our ability.** Daniel J. Benjamin, and Jesse M. Shapiro, "Thin-slice Forecasts of Gubernatorial Elections," *Review of Economics and Statistics* (2009), Vol. 91, No. 3, pp. 523–536.

60 **couples, is 95 percent.** Malcolm Gladwell, *Blink: The Power of Thinking without Thinking* (Little, Brown, 2005), pp. 18–33.

60 **running a similar one.** Charles C. Ballew II and Alexander Todorov, "Predicting Political Elections from Rapid and Unreflective Face Judgments," *Proceedings of the National Academy of Sciences* (November 13, 2007), Vol. 104, No. 46.

61 **how good their marriage is.** It is possible that a photograph can indicate an individual's overall propensity for good health. For example, masculine features—a broad face and strong jaw—are produced in the womb when high levels of testosterone are present. Testosterone is correlated with compromised immune systems, which might lead you to believe that strong masculine features would be

a marker for bad health. Actually, just the opposite is the case. Only a healthy individual, it is surmised, can withstand the high testosterone levels associated with strong masculine features. Studies show that women worldwide overwhelmingly prefer male faces with masculine features, an indication that evolution has favored strongly masculine faces. A second facial feature strongly favored by women is symmetry. It too is associated with good health. See David Buss, *Evolutionary Psychology: The New Science of the Mind* (Pearson, 2012), pp. 122–123.

Earlobes may provide a clue to an individual's good mental health. In people who develop in the womb normally the earlobe extends below the point where the ear connects to the face. It droops. In people whose development in the womb is affected by a chemical imbalance, induced perhaps by the presence of alcohol or other drugs, the earlobe may not droop. Survey research shows that males born with an earlobe that doesn't droop are far more likely to be afflicted with hyperactivity disorder. This is a marker for later criminal activity. See Sarnoff A. Mednick, "Congenital Determinants of Violence," *Bulletin of the American Academy of Psychiatry and the Law* (1988), Vol. 16, No. 2, p. 107.

62   **"the House races."** The conventional wisdom is that voters favor politicians who are likable and trustworthy. Todorov's findings suggest that what voters prize most is competence.

62   **a person is strong.** Alexander Todorov et al., "Inferences of Competence from Faces Predict Election Outcomes," *Science* (2005), Vol. 308, No. 1623, pp. 1623–1626.

62   **warm and friendly).** Eugene Borgida et al., *The Political Psychology of Democratic Citizenship* (Oxford University Press, 2009), chapter 4.

63   **faces at 33 milliseconds.** Jonathan B. Freeman et al., "Amygdala Responsivity to High-Level Social Information from Unseen Faces" *Journal of Neuroscience* (August 6, 2014), p. 10574.

63   **after just 13 milliseconds.** Mary C. Potter et al., "Detecting Meaning in RSVP at 13 ms per Picture," *Attention, Perception, & Psychophysics* (February 2014), Vol. 76, No. 2, pp. 270–279.

63   **same kinds of calculations.** A good summary of the rich variety of factors that affect voting (such as genetics and personality) is provided by Avi Tuschman, *Our Political Nature: Evolutionary Origins of What Divides Us* (Pantheon, 2013).

63   **role in the decision.** Jeremy Bailenson et al., "Facial Similarity Between Voters and Candidates Causes Influence," *Public Opinion Quarterly* (2008), Vol. 72, No. 5, pp. 935–961.

63   **make various inferences.** Social scientists have discovered that human beings harbor unconscious biases against outsiders. This is commonly expressed in the form of racism, but the bias is not racial. We are biased generally against people who look different from the people who surrounded us in childhood. We also pick up biases from the general culture. The Implicit Association Test (IAT) administered by social scientists can detect expressions of bias of which we aren't even aware. Malcolm Gladwell, the product of a biracial couple, has revealed that the IAT indicated he harbored a bias against black people. Bias is not the same thing as racism. See Anthony Greenwald, *Blindspot: Hidden Biases of Good People* (Delacorte Press, 2013).

65   **than they knew theirs.** Another advantage the hunter-gatherers had was that in their world it made sense to find a correlation between the physical size of their leaders and high status. Physically larger men were more likely to be in a position to grab more resources than smaller men. So if you had to size someone up, you could do so quickly by sizing them up physically. The bigger the man, the more likely he was to be in a position of power. Unfortunately, we inherited a bias toward

larger and taller men. And in our world this is of little use in selecting a leader. What good is it whether a leader is tall or short? None. But whom do we select more often than not? The taller candidate. In the twentieth century, American voters selected the taller of the two main presidential candidates 83 percent of the time. It's not just voters who are influenced by height. So are the people who run corporations. Studies show that the taller you are the likelier you are to win a promotion and earn a higher salary. What we have here is another mismatch. J. S. Gillis, *Too Tall, Too Small* (Institute for Personality and Ability Testing, 1982).

65   **30 percent of the time.** Lee Ross and Richard E. Nisbett, *The Person and the Situation* (Pinter & Martin, 2011), pp. 2–3, 120–136.

66   **is usually circumscribed.** Lyn Ragsdale, *Vital Statistics on the Presidency* (CQ Press, 2014, 4th edition), pp. 3–5.

66   **the issue of spying.** Conor Friedersdorf, "Bush and Obama Spurred Edward Snowden to Spill U.S. Secrets," the *Atlantic* (August 22, 2014).

66   **Presidents matter.** Fred Greenstein, *The Presidential Difference: Leadership Style from FDR to Barack Obama* (Princeton University Press, 2009), pp. 1–3.

67   **"of political philosophy."** The Heston quote is in Gil Troy, *Morning in America* (Princeton University Press, 2005), p. 262. The Howard Phillips quote is from Shoon Kathleen Murray, *Anchors Against Change: American Opinion Leaders' Beliefs After the Cold War* (University of Michigan Press, 2002), p. 23. The William F. Buckley Jr. and George Will quotes are from *Tear Down this Wall: The Reagan Revolution—A National Review History* (Continuum, 2004), p. 166.

68   **he embraced them.** Beth Fischer, *The Reagan Reversal: Foreign Policy and the End of the Cold War* (University of Missouri Press, 1997).

68   **a death ray.** Frances Fitzgerald, *Way Out There in the Blue: Reagan, Star Wars and the End of the Cold War* (Simon & Schuster, 2000).

Chapter 6: Lying to Ourselves

71   **She was a chimpanzee.** Roger Fouts, *Next of Kin: My Conversations with Chimpanzees* (William Morrow, 1998).

72   **and humans in another.** *Ibid.*, p. 49ff.

73   **other animals seemed unclear.** Martin Schmelz et al., "Chimpanzees Know That Others Make Inferences," *Proceedings of the National Academy of Science* (February 15, 2011).

73   **later upped to 98.7 percent).** Kay Prüfer et al., "The Bonobo Genome Compared with the Chimpanzee and Human Genomes," *Nature* (June 13, 2012).

73   **shared a common matriarch.** Daniel C. Dennett, *Consciousness Explained* (Little, Brown, 1991), p. 189.

74   **recently people did not.** Euclid O. Smith, "Deception and Evolutionary Biology," *Cultural Anthropology* (1987), Vol. 2, pp. 50–64.

74   **lie to her face**. Interview with the author, December 14, 2012.

76   **two reasons, biologists say.** Peter Hatemi and Rose McDermott, eds., *Man Is by Nature a Political Animal* (University of Chicago Press, 2011), pp. 49–50.

76   **half a million years,** Ruggero D'Anastasio et al., "Micro-Biomechanics of the Kebara 2 Hyoid and Its Implications for Speech in Neanderthals," *PLOS ONE* (December 18, 2013).

76   **out of consciousness.** Jonathan Haidt, *The Righteous Mind: Why Good People Are Divided by Politics and Religion* (Pantheon, 2012), chapter 3.

76   **left postcentral gyrus.** Wu D et al., "Neural Correlates of Evaluations of Lying and Truth-Telling in Different Social Contexts," *Brain Research* (May 10, 2011).

77   **lies the others told.**

President	Example	Source
Jefferson	Falsely claimed he had nothing to do with the newspaper stories published by Philip Freneau against Alexander Hamilton.	James Thomas Flexner, *George Washington and the New Nation* (Little, Brown, 1970), pp. 375–376.
Monroe	Falsely claimed he would not reveal Hamilton's secret affair with Mrs. Reynolds.	Forrest McDonald, *The Presidency of George Washington* (University Press of Kansas, 1974), pp. 109–110.
Wm. H. Harrison	Falsely claimed to have been born in a log cabin.	Edward Pessen, *The Log Cabin Myth* (Yale University Press, 1984).
Polk	Falsely claimed that Mexican troops had killed Americans on American soil to justify the war with Mexico.	Charles G. Seller, *James K. Polk: Continentalist* (Princeton University Press, 1966), p. 409.
Pierce	Lied to his wife that he had not campaigned for his party's nomination.	Rick Shenkman, *Presidential Ambition* (HarperCollins, 1999), chapter 5.
Buchanan	Claimed not to know in advance of the Supreme Court's decision in the Dred Scot case, though he had personally intervened.	Philip Klein, *President James Buchanan* (Pennsylvania State University Press, 1962), pp. 269–272.
Grant	Claimed to be honest but repeatedly stood by friends who bilked the government.	Shenkman, *Presidential Ambition*, p. 173ff.
Hayes	Claimed to be honest but turned a blind eye to corruption in the Post Office and the New York Custom House.	Harry Barnard, *Rutherford B. Hayes* (Boobs-Merrill, 1954), *passim*.
Garfield	Failed to disclose the whole truth about a bribe he was paid in the Crédit Mobilier scandal.	Allan Peskin, *Garfield* (Kent State University Press, 1978), p. 362.
Arthur	As president lied about his health, concealing a fatal illness, Bright's Disease.	Shenkman, *Presidential Ambition*, chapter 10.
Cleveland	As president lied about his health, concealing cancer.	Shenkman, *Presidential Ambition*, pp. 235–241.
B. Harrison	Lied about the circumstances that led to the American takeover of Hawaii.	Shenkman, *Presidential Ambition*, pp. 247–248.

(continues)

President	Example	Source
Teddy Roosevelt	Falsely claimed that the US government was not behind the Panamanian revolution.	Henry F. Pringle, *Theodore Roosevelt* (Harcourt Brace, 1931), p. 221ff.
Wilson	Misled the country about his health.	Thomas Fleming, *The Illusion of Victory* (Basic Books, 2003), p. 418ff.
Harding	Cheated repeatedly on his wife, failed to reveal corruption in his administration, misled the country about his health.	Francis Russell, *The Shadow of Blooming Grove* (McGraw-Hill, 1968), *passim.*
F. D. Roosevelt	Cheated on his wife, lied about the Nazi attack on the USS *Greer*.	Shenkman, *Presidential Ambition*, p. 310.
Eisenhower	Concealed serious health problems prior to running for president and lied about the U-2 spy flights.	Robert Gilbert, *The Mortal Presidency* (Fordham University Press, 1992), chapter 4; James Pfiffner, *The Character Factor* (Texas A&M University Press, 2004), p. 41.
Kennedy	Lied about his health and the missile gap and failed to acknowledge he agreed to withdraw Jupiter missiles from Cuba in exchange for Soviet withdrawal of missiles from Cuba.	Thomas Reeves, *A Question of Character* (Three Rivers Press, 1992), passim; John Mearsheimer, *Why Leaders Lie* (Oxford University Press, 2011), p. 66.
L. B. Johnson	Lied about the Tonkin Gulf attack.	Pfiffner, *Character Factor*, p. 55ff.
Nixon	Lied about Watergate.	Pfiffner, *Character Factor*, p. 120ff.
Reagan	Lied about Iran-Contra.	Pfiffner, *Character Factor*, p. 56ff.
G. H. W. Bush	Lied about Iran-Contra.	Pfiffner, *Character Factor*, p. 45ff.
Clinton	Lied about affair with Monica Lewinski.	Starr Report.
G. W. Bush	Lied about the Iraq War.	Mearsheimer, *Why Leaders Lie*, pp. 49–55.
Obama	Made multiple statements that were not true about health care coverage.	PolitiFact.

77   **who came after him.** Garry Wills, *Cincinnatus: George Washington and the Enlightenment* (Doubleday, 1984).

78   **today. It is.** This is the story I tell in *Presidential Ambition*.

78   **published during his lifetime.** Hugh Gallagher, *FDR's Splendid Deception: The Moving Story of Roosevelt's Massive Disability—And the Intense Efforts to Conceal it from the Public* (Vandamere, 1999), p. 94.

78   **into his first term.** Ron Reagan Jr., *My Father at 100* (Viking, 2011).

78   **out of the White House.** Leslie Stahl, *Reporting Live* (Simon & Schuster, 2000), p. 211.

79   **wouldn't be affected.** Shenkman, *Presidential Ambition*, p. 236ff.

80   **questions about their beliefs.** Michael Shermer, *The Believing Brain: From Ghosts and Gods to Politics and Conspiracies—How We Construct Beliefs and Reinforce Them as Truths* (St. Martin's Griffin, 2012), pp. 133–135.

80   **"acquired than belief."** Daniel Gilbert, "How Mental Systems Believe," *American Psychologist* (February 1991), Vol. 46, No. 2, p. 110. See also: Gilbert, "You Can't Not Believe Everything You Read," *Journal of Personality and Social Psychology* (August 1993), pp. 221–231. Denise Cummins points out that when we are engaged in what's known as indicative reasoning—"where reasoners are asked to test the truth of a rule"—we instinctively look for evidence that confirms the rule. We don't try to disprove the rule. If we are told that all swans are white, we look for evidence that backs up the claim. We don't immediately look for a black swan. See Cummins, "Evidence of Deontic Reasoning in 3- and 4-Year-Old Children," *Memory and Cognition* (1996), Vol. 24, No. 6, p. 824.

80   **expresses open skepticism).** Jeremy Dean, "Why You Can't Help Believing Everything You Read," PsyBlog (September 17, 2009).

81   **We aren't built that way.** Gilbert, "How Mental Systems Believe."

81   **because they are ours.** There are two elements to our desire to believe in our leaders. One is simply that we are inclined to belief, not doubt, as Daniel Gilbert reports in "How Mental Systems Believe." More specifically, we are inclined to believe in our leaders, according to Justification Theory, because we prefer to think that everything that is, is ordained. Rich people are rich because they deserve it. Poor people are poor because they are lazy. See Melvin Lerner, *The Belief in a Just World: A Fundamental Delusion* (Springer, 1980). Recent research suggests that some people, notably conservatives, are more susceptible to this way of thinking than liberals. See John T. Jost et al., "A Decade of System Justification Theory: Accumulated Evidence of Conscious and Unconscious Bolstering of the Status Quo," *Political Psychology* (December 2004), Vol. 25, No. 6, p. 881ff. Other theories that affect human's willingness to believe in their leaders rest on a belief in multilevel selection. This is the minority view among biologists that evolution took place both within groups (favoring selfishness) and between groups (favoring hivishness). All other things being equal, says Haidt, *Righteous Mind*, chapter 9, selfish individuals will be favored over altruists within groups, but groups made up of altruists will be favored over those made up of the selfish. Multilevel selection suggests that altruists will put the needs of the group above their own. This is likely to favor a belief in the existing hierarchy.

82   **inauguration in 1861.** Nikita Stewart and Michael E. Ruane, "Like Lincoln, Obama Will Ride the Rails to D.C.," *Washington Post* (December 16, 2008).

82   **Obama as a little weird.** David Brody, "The Obama Memorial?" Christian Broadcasting Network website (December 16, 2008).

82   **children by age three.** Robert Trivers, *The Folly of Fools* (Basic Books, 2011), p. 19.

82   **"God in embryo."** Amy Chua And Jed Rubenfeld, "What Drives Success," *New York Times* (January 25, 2014).

82   **in its own virtue.** Ross Hammond and Robert Axelrod, "The Evolution of Ethnocentrism," *Journal of Conflict Resolution* (December 2006), Vol. 50, No. 6.

82   **of evolutionary psychology.** Richard Dawkins, *The Selfish Gene* (Oxford University Press, 2009), p. 184ff; Gerd Gigerenzer and Klaus Hug, "Domain-Specific Reasoning: Social Contracts, Cheating, and Perspective Change," *Cognition* (1992), Vol. 43, p. 127ff; and William J. Ray, *Evolutionary Psychology: Neuroscience Perspectives Concerning Human Behavior and Experience* (SAGE, 2012), p. 326–327. In recent years some scientists have embraced multilevel selection, building on work by Darwin. See E. O. Wilson, *The Meaning of Human Existence* (Liveright, 2014), chapter 6.

82   **It's all against all.** This suggests that some form of group selection may have affected our development as a social species. Theories abound. One is that communities of well-meaning social cooperators may have been favored over communities of cheaters. This naturally would lead over time, it is thought, to the predominance of genes for altruism. But most scientists still are leery of theories of group selection, though Darwin believed in it. See Christopher Boehm, "Emergency Decisions, Cultural-Selection Mechanics, and Group Selection," *Current Anthropology* (December 1996), Vol. 37, No. 5, pp. 763–793; Edward O. Wilson, *The Social Conquest of Earth* (Liveright, 2012), p. 91.

83   **"carrying a log together."** Haidt, *Righteous Mind*, p. 204–207.

83   **in their courtship.** Jared Diamond, *The Third Chimpanzee* (Harper, 2006), p. 172ff.

84   **"have been sharpened."** Trivers, *Folly of Fools*, p. 5.

85   **was actually a positive.** *Ibid.*

85   **those of non-cheaters.** Raoul Bell and Axel Buchner, "Enhanced Source Memory for Names of Cheaters," *Evolutionary Psychology* (2009), Vol. 7, No. 2, pp. 317–330. When we are engaged in deontic tasks—those involving our duties as members of a community—we look for violators, as Cummins points out in "Evidence of Deontic Reasoning in 3- and 4-Year-Old Children," p. 824. We do this automatically, suggesting it's a task involving the emotions. This jibes with the findings of Joshua Greene, who discovered that fMRI scans show that subjects in the process of making moral judgments use emotional modules in the brain. In other words, when we confront a moral choice, we get emotional. Deontic judgments are emotional. See Greene, "The Secret Joke of Kant's Soul," in volume 3 of *Moral Psychology: The Neuroscience of Morality: Emotion, Disease, and Development* (MIT Press, 2007), ed. W. Sinnott-Armstrong. Jonathan Haidt argues that moral perceptions are driven by emotion. In his celebrated metaphor, emotion is the elephant and reason the rider on the elephant. Who's in charge? The elephant. When it shifts this way and that, the rider responds. The rider isn't in charge. This is why we often cannot explain our moral reasoning. We just believe it because we believe it. See *The Righteous Mind*, p. 65ff.

86   **"visited in Barbados."** Ralph Andrist, ed., *George Washington: A Biography in His Own Words* (*Newsweek*/Harper & Row, 1972), pp. 29, 50.

86   **ambitiousness at an early age.** See Shenkman, *Presidential Ambition*, chapter 1.

87   **matters of coincidence.** *Ibid.*, pp. 95–120.

87   **That is impossible to know.** Buchanan never married. In recent years some have speculated that he may have been gay. For years he roomed with Senator William King, another bachelor, who at the least seems to have had a crush on Buchanan. King was cruelly referred to by others as Miss Nancy and confided in

letters after he was named ambassador to France that he sorely missed Buchanan. Buchanan's being gay would go a long way toward explaining the mysterious distance he kept from Ann. As I explain in *Presidential Ambition*, p. 102, "he may have been at war with himself, one very powerful force pushing him toward Ann, another pushing him away, leaving him, pathetically, in a desperate state of ambivalence." But whether he was straight or gay, to use modern terminology, doesn't absolve him of the charge that he likely went after Ann for her money. If he was gay his courtship could only have been for the sake of the social advantages it offered. If he was straight we are back to the problem of the mysterious distance he maintained after the engagement was announced, which suggests that he wanted her more as a prize than as a partner.

88   **simply find desirable.** E. O. Wilson, *On Human Nature* (Harvard University Press, 2004), p. 126.

89   **dooming his plans.** Justin A. Nelson, "Drafting Lyndon Johnson: The President's Secret Role in the 1968 Democratic Convention," *Presidential Studies Quarterly* (February 16, 2004), p. 688–713.

89   **"until he has tried it."** David Donald, *Lincoln* (Simon & Schuster, 1995), p. 491.

90   **presidents run again and again.** Coren L. Apicella et al., "Testosterone and Financial Risk Preferences," *Evolution and Human Behavior* (November 2008), Vol. 29, No. 6, pp. 384–390. Michael Shermer points out that recent research indicates dopamine may not provide a reward as such. Rather, it may act as a motivator by keeping at bay the feeling of anxiety, as if your brain is telling you, *Hey, win the game and I'll make sure you don't feel anxious.* See *The Believing Brain*, p. 118.

90   **end in their death.** Hatemi and McDermott, *Man Is by Nature a Political Animal*, p. 269.

90   **position of superiority.** David Buss, *Evolutionary Psychology: The New Science of the Mind* (Pearson, 2012), p. 363.

90   **more intensely than gains.** Daniel Kahneman, *Thinking Fast and Slow* (Farrar, Straus and Giroux, 2011), chapter 26.

91   **and that's what matters.** *Ibid.*, pp. 118–119.

91   **natural oxytocin levels).** Paul Zak, *The Moral Molecule: The Source of Love and Prosperity* (Dutton, 2012), p. 79.

92   **"and I'm tired of it."** *New York Times* (March 28, 1992), p. 9.

92   **"time he had to do to win.** Herbert S. Parmet, *George Bush: The Life of a Lone Star Yankee* (Scribner, 1997), p. 114.

93   **five different ways.** William von Hippel and Robert Trivers, "The Evolution and Psychology of Self-Deception," *Behavioral and Brain Sciences* (2011), Vol. 34, pp. 1–56.

93   **person doing the lying.** In an exciting study published in 2014 scientists found that when experts are allowed to engage in active questioning of subjects in an experiment they had an accuracy rate for detecting liars of 97.8 percent. When students were asked to watch the experts at work their accuracy rate was 93.6 percent. The researchers concluded: "The data suggest that experts can accurately distinguish truths from lies when they are allowed to actively question a potential liar, and nonexperts can obtain high accuracy when viewing expertly questioned [people]." See Timothy R. Levine et al., "Expertise in Deception Detection Involves Actively Prompting Diagnostic Information Rather Than Passive Behavioral Observation," *Human Communication Research* (July 2014), Vol. 40, pp. 442–462.

94   **even if it wasn't.** Robert Caro, *The Years of Lyndon Johnson: The Passage of Power* (Knopf, 2012), pp. 82–83.

95   **knows the difference.** Dingcheng Wu et al., "Neural Correlates of Evaluations of Lying and Truth-Telling in Different Social Contexts," *Brain Research* (2011).
Some researchers report that when we consciously tell a lie our health suffers. See:
"Lying Less Linked to Better Health, New Research Finds," news release issued by
the American Psychological Association (August 4, 2012).

95   **the more we do it.** Anil Ananthaswamy, "The More You Lie, the Easier
It Gets," *New Scientist* (February 8, 2011).

96   **"power of self-deception."** Joseph T. Hallinan, *Kidding Ourselves: The Hidden Power of Self-Deception* (Crown, 2014).

96   **perhaps life-threatening circumstances.** Trivers, *Folly of Fools,* pp. 2–4.
Confirmation of Trivers's work came in 2014 when researchers found that society rewards the overconfident. The researchers concluded: "These findings suggest that people don't always reward the most accomplished individual but rather
the most self-deceived. We think this supports an evolutionary theory of self-
deception." See Shakti Lamba and Vivek Nityananda, "Self-Deceived Individuals
Are Better at Deceiving Others," *PLOS ONE* (August 2014).

Chapter 7: Do We Really Want the Truth?

100   **"time for him to go.** Gladys and Kurt Lang, *The Battle for Public Opinion:
The President, the Press, and the Polls During Watergate* (Columbia University Press,
1983), p. 27ff.

100   **to Watergate as events unfolded?** A good general survey is provided by
James M. Perry, "Watergate Case Study," in Tom Rosenstiel and Amy S. Mitchell,
Thinking Clearly: Cases in Journalistic Decision-Making (Columbia University Press,
2003).

100   **"in the Watergate investigation."** Carl Bernstein and Bob Woodward,
"Mitchell Controlled Secret GOP Fund," *Washington Post* (September 29, 1972).

100   **edge he had in August.** Harris Poll (September 14, 1972).

101   **"Democratic campaign workers."** Carl Bernstein and Bob Woodward,
"FBI Finds Nixon Aides Sabotaged Democrats," *Washington Post* (October 19, 1972).

101   **"Incident at Watergate."** *Los Angeles Times* (October 5, 1972).

101   **attention to Watergate.** Keith Olson, *Watergate: The Presidential Scandal
That Shook America* (University Press of Kansas, 2003), p. 65ff. This is the source
for polls cited in the next few paragraphs.

102   **"votes in the 1972 election."** *Ibid.*

103   **voting in American history.** Paul Lazarsfeld, Bernard Berelson, and Hazel
Gaudet, *The People's Choice: How the Voter Makes Up His Mind in a Presidential Campaign*
(Columbia University Press, 1944).

104   **"get their feet wet."** The Columbia study convinced many that the media's
role in elections is vastly overstated. But research by Kurt and Gladys Lang in the
1950s demonstrated that the media can have a profound effect on voters. In one
study they proved that people viewing the national political conventions in 1952 on
television took away a different impression of what was transpiring depending on
the network they were watching. CBS, which had the strongest journalistic bench
of any of the three networks, provided viewers with enough information to be able
to follow events closely, leaving viewers feeling that the convention was well organized. NBC, which focused on personalities, left viewers feeling disdain for Sam
Rayburn, who ran the convention, after he silenced delegates who wanted to speak.
CBS explained his tactics. NBC did not, leaving viewers to infer that Rayburn was
a bully. ABC's coverage was sporadic and unfocused, leaving its viewers in a state
of confusion. See Gladys and Kurt Lang, *Television and Politics* (2002).

106   **traceable to our genes.** James H. Fowler, Laura A. Baker, and Christopher T. Dawes, "Genetic Variation in Political Participation," *American Political Science Review* (May 2008), Vol. 102, No. 2, pp. 233–248.

106   **who share our views.** Rose McDermott et al., "Assortative Mating on Ideology Could Operate Through Olfactory Cues," *American Journal of Political Science* (September 2014, pp. 997–1005).

106   **novelty is largely genetic.** Jonathan Haidt, *The Righteous Mind: Why Good People Are Divided by Politics and Religion* (Pantheon, 2012), pp. 312–313.

106   **of conscious reasoning.** Jonathan Haidt in *The Righteous Mind* argues that our political opinions are shaped by our natural affinity for different values ranging from our concern for loyalty (mostly a conservative value) to a concern for caring (mostly a liberal value). John Jost, in *Social and Psychological Bases of Ideology and System Justification* (Oxford University Press, 2009), argues that ideology is a function of psychology. It is our psychology that divides us, with some of us, for example, being more prone to stereotyping than others. As I note later in this chapter Jason Weeden and Robert Kurzban, in *The Hidden Agenda of the Political Mind: How Self-Interest Shapes Our Opinions and Why We Won't Admit It* (Princeton University Press, 2014), argue that what drives our political ideas are our interests, broadly construed.

106   **become more moralistic.** David A. Pizarro et al., "Disgust Sensitivity Predicts Intuitive Disapproval of Gays," *Emotion* (2009), Vol. 9, No. 3. Interview with David Pizarro by the author, January 10, 2013, pp. 435–439.

107   **the truth to prevail.** Steven Pinker, *How the Mind Works* (W. W. Norton, 1997), p. 305. See also: Charles Taber and Milton Lodge, "Motivated Skepticism in the Evaluation of Political Beliefs," *American Journal of Political Science* (July 2006), Vol. 50, No. 3, pp. 755–769.

107   **should not surprise us.** Hugo Mercier and Daniel Sperber, "Why Do Humans Reason? Arguments for an Argumentative Theory," *Behavioral and Brain Sciences* (2011), Vol. 34, pp. 57–111.

107   **undermine our opinions.** Partisans display both Confirmation Bias and Disconfirmation Bias. In a study published in 2014 researchers found that when things go wrong (as when people found they couldn't access the Obamacare website) partisans blame the other party even when experts weigh in with a contrary opinion. Partisanship trumps knowledge, in short. See Jeffrey Lyons and William P. Jaeger, "Who Do Voters Blame for Policy Failure? Information and the Partisan Assignment of Blame," *State Politics and Policy Quarterly* (September 2014), Vol. 14, No. 3, pp. 321–341.

107   **pigheadedness, research shows.** Cordelia Fine, "Biased but Brilliant," *New York Times* (July 30, 2011).

107   **are discussing government regulation.** Dan M. Kahan, Hank Jenkins-Smith, and Donald Braman, "Cultural Cognition of Scientific Consensus," *Journal of Risk Research* (2011), Vol. 14, pp. 147–174. An additional reason why a businessperson might be a climate change denier is their conservative outlook. Fundamental to conservatives is a belief in the status quo. This turns conservatives into "system justifiers," as social scientists put it. As a system justifier a businessperson is likely to engage in biased thinking. See John T. Jost and David Amodio, "Political Ideology as Motivated Social Cognition: Behavioral and Neuroscientific Evidence," *Motivation and Emotion* (March 2012), Vol. 36, No. 1, pp. 55–64.

108   **the supply of virgins.** Weeden and Kurzban, *The Hidden Agenda of the Political Mind*.

108   **rather overreact than underreact.** David Buss, ed., *Handbook of Evolutionary Psychology* (Wiley, 2005), p. 240ff.

109   **"our evolutionary past."** Dominic D. P. Johnson et al., "The Evolution of Error: Error Management, Cognitive Constraints, and Adaptive Decision-Making Biases," *Trends in Ecology and Evolution* (August 2013), Vol. 28, No. 8, pp. 474–481.

109   **identified by social scientists.** See Andrew Newberg and Mark Waldman, *Why We Believe What We Believe* (Free Press, 2006); Daniel Kahneman, *Thinking Fast and Slow* (Farrar, Straus and Giroux, 2011).

110   **instinct—their first choice.).** Scott O. Lilienfeld et al., *50 Great Myths of Popular Psychology: Shattering Widespread Misconceptions about Human Behavior* (Wiley-Blackwell, 2010), chapter 16.

110   **Bias met their needs.** Gerd Gigerenzer, *Gut Feelings: The Intelligence of the Unconscious* (Penguin, 2007).

111   **avoid contact with it.** Timothy D. Wilson and Nancy Brekke, "Mental Contamination and Mental Correction: Unwanted Influences on Judgments and Evaluations," *Psychological Bulletin* (1994), Vol. 116, No. 1, p. 117ff.

112   **often get things right.** Jonathon D. Brown, *The Self* (Psychology Press, 2014).

113   **with Self-Serving Bias.** Tali Sharot, *The Optimism Bias: A Tour of the Irrationally Positive Brain* (Pantheon, 2011), p. 15.

113   **succeed in a chosen task.** Peter Hatemi and Rose McDermott, eds., *Man Is by Nature a Political Animal: Evolution, Biology and Politics* (University of Chicago Press, 2011), p. 247.

114   **attacking the Soviet Union.** *See* Tali Sharot, *The Optimism Bias,* p. 186ff chapter 11.

115   **but not ourselves.** Margarete Vollrath et al., "Personality, Risky Health Behaviour, and Perceived Susceptibility to Health Risks," *European Journal of Personality* (1999), Vol. 13, pp. 39–50.

115   **chance of dying.** Kahneman, *Thinking Fast and Slow,* p. 170ff.

115   **tells them the truth.** Walter Mondale, *The Good Fight* (Scribner, 2010), p. 294.

116   **earlier in the book.** Gigerenzer, *Gut Feelings.*

116   **not entirely different.** Douglas T. Kenrick and Vladas Griskevicius, *The Rational Animal* (Basic Books, 2013); Martie G. Haselton and David M. Buss, "Biases in Social Judgment: Design Flaws or Design Features?" in *Social Judgments: Implicit and Explicit Processes,* ed. Joseph P. Forgas et al. (Cambridge University Press, 2003).

117   **We become less analytical.** Norbert Schwarz, Herbert Bless, and Gerd Bohner, "Mood and Persuasion: Affective States Influence the Processing of Persuasive Communications," in *The Message Within: The Role of Subjective Experience in Social Cognition and Behavior,* ed. Herbert Bless and Joseph Forgas (Psychology Press, 2000), p. 252.

117   **looked in a certain direction.** Hatemi and McDermott, *Man Is by Nature a Political Animal,* p. 16.

118   **they cast their ballot.** Peter Gray, *Psychology,* 5th ed. (Worth Publishers, 2007), p. 494.

118   **as a result of Watergate.** Christopher Achen and Larry Bartels, "It Feels Like We're Thinking: The Rationalizing Voter and Electoral Democracy," paper delivered at the Annual Meeting of the American Political Science Association (August 28, 2006).

119   **They saved us all.** Leon Festinger, Henry Riecken, and Stanley Schachter, *When Prophecy Fails: A Social and Psychological Study of a Modern Group That Predicted the Destruction of the World* (Harper Torchbooks, 1964).

120 **to confirm our assumptions.** Bruce M. Hood, *Supersense* (HarperOne, 2009), p. 10ff.

121 **emphasizes in his work.** George Marcus, *Political Psychology: Neuroscience, Genetics, and Politics* (Oxford University Press, 2012), pp. 70–73.

121 **only Swedes drank more.** William Rorabaugh, *The Alcoholic Republic: An American Tradition* (Oxford University Press, 1979), pp. ix, 6, 10, 20–21, 26, 48, 55, 64, 84, 125, 151, 163, 169–170. Mark Edward Lender and James Kirby Martin, *Drinking in America: A History* (Free Press, 1982), pp. 2, 3, 7, 11, 30, 32–34.

121 **historian David Hackett Fischer.** David Hackett Fischer, *Growing Old in America* (Oxford University Press, 1978).

122 **Now, being younger was.** Our very use of the word *revolution* to describe the Revolution is revealing. We use the term to refer to a radical break with the past. But by definition something that revolves is not a radical break with the past at all. It's a return to something we previously experienced. It's a stop in the cycle of life, a turn of the wheel. Our use of the word reflects our older understanding of history as a series of familiar occurrences. Spring following winter, death following birth. It was our attempt to make even the Revolution seem predictable. See Marcus, *Political Psychology*, pp. 70–73.

122 **decades after its publication.** Walter Laqueur, "Putin and the Art of Political Fantasy," *Standpoint Magazine* (January/February 2015).

122 **and he smites you.** Marc Ambinder, "Falwell Suggests Gays to Blame for Attacks," ABC News website (September 14, 2001). Social scientist Nicholas Epley points out that we like to anthropomorphize nature. He notes that when Katrina struck, New Orleans mayor Ray Nagin remarked, "Surely God is mad at America. Surely he's not approving of us being in Iraq under false pretense. But surely he's upset at black America, too. We're not taking care of ourselves." See Epley, *Mindwise: How We Understand What Others Think, Believe, Feel, and Want* (Knopf, 2014), p. 61.

122 **abhor disorder and uncertainty.** A study in 2005 found that ill patients perceived themselves more sick when given diagnoses that indicated higher uncertainty. The greater the uncertainty, the more they believed their health was in jeopardy. See Y. Kang, "Effects of Uncertainty on Perceived Health Status in Patients with Atrial Fibrillation," *Nursing in Critical Care* (July–August 2005), Vol. 4, pp. 184–91.

122 **president in our history.** Lyn Ragsdale, *Vital Statistics on the Presidency* (3d ed., Congressional Quarterly Press, 2009), p. 248.

123 **man and the moment met.** Americans generally rally behind presidents in a moment of crisis. In 1979, after the Iranians took over the US embassy and held the staff hostage, Americans even rallied behind the unpopular Jimmy Carter. His approval rating increased from the low thirties to the midfifties. The crisis atmosphere continued for more than a year until the Iranians finally released the hostages. But voters did not stick with Carter through the crisis. Just three months after the ordeal began his approval ratings headed south and kept going in that direction. The reason was that he no longer offered certainty. To many he seemed bewildered and inadequate.

123 **are "ridiculously specific."** John Medina, *Brain Rules* (Pear Press, 2008), p. 224.

123 **different odor molecules.** Robin Reineke, "It's Right Under Our Noses: The Importance of Smell to Science and our Lives," 2000 Third Web Report.

124 **more than three choices.** Barry Schwartz, *The Paradox of Choice: Why More Is Less* (Ecco, 2012).

124   **four say they prefer it.** Samuel McClure et al., "Neural Correlates of Behavioral Preference for Culturally Familiar Drinks," *Neuron* (October 14, 2004), Vol. 44, No. 2, pp. 379–387.

126   **psychological immune system.** Daniel Gilbert et al., "Immune Neglect: A Source of Durability Bias in Affective Forecasting," *Journal of Personality and Social Psychology* (September 1998), Vol. 75, No. 3, pp. 617–638.

126   **had left them embarrassed.** Elliot Aronson and Judson Mills, "The Effect of Severity of Initiation on Liking for a Group," *Journal of Abnormal and Social Psychology*, (September 1959), Vol. 59, No. 2 , pp. 177–181.

127   **"that isn't worth it."** Interview with Carol Tavris, Brain Science Podcast (2011), episode 43. See also: Carol Tavris and Elliot Aronson, *Mistakes Were Made (But Not by Me)* (Houghton Mifflin Harcourt, 2007).

127   **they had in his survival.** For a long time, social scientists believed that what voters need are the facts. Information would cure ignorance. This is increasingly regarded as naïve. Numerous studies have demonstrated that voters who are supplied with correct information will insist on holding wrongheaded beliefs when the facts conflict with their ideological assumptions. Indeed, several well-designed studies show that voters who are supplied with correct information will come to hold their views "more fervently than those who did not receive a correction." The authors of one of these studies calls this perverse. Who can blame them? You provide a correction and people still insist they are right to hold their belief? That is truly depressing. See Brendan Nyhan and Jason Reifler, "When Corrections Fail: The Persistence of Political Misperceptions," *Political Behavior* (2010), Vol. 32, pp. 303–330.

128   **children in Birmingham, Alabama.** Shelby Steele, *A Bound Man: Why We Are Excited About Obama and Why He Can't Win* (Free Press, 2007). Ironically, having accurately analyzed Obama's appeal to white voters, Steele wrongly predicted that Obama would lose the election of 2008. His mistake, he later admitted, was in thinking that Obama could not maintain the mask he donned as a nonthreatening black man. Steele also said he hadn't put a lot of thought into his prediction.

128   **anything else he ever did.** This section is based on a Skype interview with George E. Marcus by the author (March 20, 2013).

130   **because of Ann and Sue.** Emotion was becoming a key subject in multiple social science fields, and in particular psychology. Freud had taught that we should be concerned with the mind, but you couldn't test any of his insights empirically. They weren't testable. How could you test the impact of the id on someone? In a revolt in the 1920s against Freudianism, psychologists embraced behaviorism. Behaviorism seemed scientific because it was concerned with things you could measure, such as the response time of a rat to positive and negative reinforcements. But by the 1950s psychologists began to rethink their commitment to behaviorism. Behaviorists believed that we are blank slates, and anybody can be taught anything through a system of rewards and punishments. But it turned out not to be true. Human beings, as we have seen, are not blank slates. Much of our behavior is the result of biology. We cry when we are sad. We laugh when we are happy. We don't have to be taught to react in these ways. We just do. See Haidt's *The Righteous Mind* (Pantheon, 2012).

131   **emotion and reason work together.** See Joseph LeDoux, *The Emotional Brain* (Simon & Schuster, 1996), Ronald de Sousa, *The Rationality of Emotion* (MIT Press, 1990), and Antonio Damasio, *Descartes' Error: Emotion, Reason, and the Human Brain* (Penguin, 2005).

132   **this happens is anxiety.** The literature I relied on in writing this section includes: Marcus, *Political Psychology*; George Marcus, W. Russell Neuman, and

Michael MacKuen, *Affective Intelligence and Political Judgment* (University of Chicago Press, 2000); W. Russell Neuman, George Marcus, Michael MacKuen, and Ann N. Crigler, eds., *The Affect Effect: Dynamics of Emotion in Political Thinking and Behavior* (University of Chicago Press, 2007); and George Marcus, *The Sentimental Citizen: Emotion in Democratic Politics* (Pennsylvania State University Press, 2002).

132   **rusting metal of our preconceptions.** George Marcus, W. Russell Neuman, and Michael MacKuen, "Ideology, Affect, Context, and Political Judgment: When Conservatives and Liberals Share Feelings and When They Don't," paper presented at the Annual Meeting of the American Political Science Association (August 2014).

Chapter 8: Everything Happens for a Reason

134   **laid to rest in Bloomer, Wisconsin.** "The Pledge of Private Treptow," *New York Times* (January 21, 1981); Edmund Morris, *Dutch* (Random House, 1999), pp. 412–413.

134   **a story that wasn't true.** Alan Barrie Spitzer, *Historical Truth and Lies about the Past: Reflections on Dewey, Dreyfus, de Man, and Reagan* (University of North Carolina Press, 1996), p. 108ff.

135   **It is stories.** Peggy Noonan, *What I Saw at the Revolution: A Political Life in the Reagan Era* (Random House, 2003), pp. 143ff, 184. Why Reagan was so beholden to his stories has been the subject of speculation. Rick Perlstein says in *The Invisible Bridge* (2014) that it was because of Reagan's chaotic childhood. Stories in which he played the hero were a refuge from the instability of his family life. His father was an alcoholic. The family moved more than a dozen times during his childhood. Once Reagan found his father splayed out in the snow in a drunken stupor. Given his history it is little wonder Reagan found simple stories with heroes and villains in which the heroes always won preferable to reality. As a youngster they helped keep him sane. As I indicated earlier in the endnotes, Perlstein observes that Reagan, alone among leading American presidential prospects in the 1970s, downplayed Watergate and defended Nixon to the hilt. Insiders were baffled. But Reagan couldn't help himself, explains Perlstein. He felt strongly compelled to concoct a fake world in which the president ruled with wisdom and justice. Many Americans found this vision far more appealing than what the Democrats offered: doom and gloom during Watergate.

135   **leaders have in common.** Howard Gardner, *Leading Minds: An Anatomy of Leadership* (Basic Books, 1996), pp. 41ff.

136   **ourselves a new story.** Yuval Noah Harari, *Sapiens: A Brief History of Humankind* (Harper, 2015), p. 34.

136   **decided to find out.** Fritz Heider and Marianne Simmel, "An Experimental Study of Apparent Behavior," *American Journal of Psychology* (1944), Vol. 57, pp. 243–259.

138   **relief from his seizures.** Marlon S. Matthews et al., "William P. van Wagenen and the First Corpus Callosotomies for Epilepsy," *Journal of Neurosurgery* (2008), Vol. 108, pp. 608–613.

138   **another curious anomaly.** Michael S. Gazzaniga, "Principles of Human Brain Organization Derived from Split-Brain Studies," *Neuron* (February 1995), Vol. 14, pp. 217–228; David Wolman, "The Split Brain: A Tale of Two Halves," *Nature* (March 14, 2012).

139   **describes what happened.** Michael S. Gazzaniga, *Who's in Charge: Free Will and the Science of the Brain* (Ecco, 2011), p. 81ff.

140   **answer that sounded reasonable.** Michael S. Gazzaniga, "The Split Brain in Man," *Scientific American* (1967), Vol. 217, No. 2, p. 29. See also: Jason

Weeden and Robert Kurzban, *The Hidden Agenda of the Political Mind: How Self-Interest Shapes Our Opinions and Why We Won't Admit It* (Princeton University Press, 2014), p. 51.

140   **ventromedial prefrontal cortex.** Maria-Dorothea Heidler, "Is Your Brain Lying to You? How the Brain Leads Us to Believe False Truths," *Scientific American* (March 2014), Vol. 25, No. 2, pp. 40–44.

140   **"was expected at court."** Armin Schnider, "Orbitofrontal Reality Filtering," *Frontiers in Behavioral Neuroscience* (June 10, 2013), Vol. 7, p. 67.

141   **The two got mixed up.** Armin Schnider, "Spontaneous Confabulation and the Adaptation of Thought to Ongoing Reality," *Nature Reviews Neuroscience* (August 2003), Vol. 4, pp. 662–671.

141   **It's another feature.** Further evidence that we are prewired to think in stories is the recent discovery that young children remember much more of what happened to them as three-year-olds if their mothers had told them stories about their activities. See Patricia Bauer, "The Onset of Childhood Amnesia in Childhood: A Prospective Investigation of the Course and Determinants of Forgetting of Early-life Events," *Memory* (November 18, 2013), pp.907–924.

141   **mistake but animals won't.** Michael S. Gazzaniga, *The Cognitive Neurosciences III* (MIT Press, 2004), p. 1194.

142   **"the pattern-recognition engine."** Michael Shermer, *The Believing Brain: From Ghosts and Gods to Politics and Conspiracies—How We Construct Beliefs and Reinforce Them as Truths* (St. Martin's Griffin, 2012), pp. 59–60. It is Steven Pinker who coined the phrase "baloney generator." See Pinker, *The Blank Slate: The Modern Denial of Human Nature* (Penguin Books, 2003), p. 43.

142   **brain activity goes up.** Jeremy Dean, "The Psychology of Storytelling and Empathy, Animated," PsyBlog (January 31, 2014).

142   **It privileges stories.** Paul Zak, *The Moral Molecule: The Source of Love and Prosperity* (Dutton, 2012), p. 72.

143   **writings of Richard Nixon.** Rick Perlstein, ed., *Richard Nixon: Speeches, Writings, Documents* (Princeton University Press, 2008), p. 3.

144   **was contemplating using.** Sigma 1, Part 1, National Security File, Agency File, box 30, LBJ Library.

145   **as one historian notes.** H. R. McMaster, *Dereliction of Duty* (Harper, 1997), p. 89ff. My account relies on the war game study cited above, McMaster's account, and this: Dominic D. P. Johnson et al., "Overconfidence in Wargames: Experimental Evidence on Expectations, Aggression, Gender and Testosterone," *Proceedings of the Royal Society* (June 20, 2006), Vol. 273, pp. 2513–2520.

147   **admits to it in his memoirs.** Robert McNamara, *In Retrospect* (Crown, 1996), p. 208.

147   **"others felt the same way."** William Bundy, unpublished memoir appendix, LBJ Library.

149   **in history? Joseph Stalin.** Maria Lipman et al., "The Stalin Puzzle" (Carnegie Endowment for International Peace, 2013).

149   **Myths bring us closer.** Jonathan Haidt, *The Happiness Hypothesis: Finding Modern Truth in Ancient Wisdom* (Basic Books, 2006), p. 73ff.

151   **"the reporters felt that way."** Alicia Shepard, *Woodward and Bernstein: Life in the Shadow of Watergate* (Wiley, 2007), p. 57.

Chapter 9: It's Like It Was Still 1974

153   **Nixon resigned from office.** This section is based on a Skype interview with Timothy Naftali by the author, April 15, 2013.

154 **Democratic National Committee headquarters.** The original Watergate exhibit can be found online at the Nixon Library website: www.nixonlibrary.gov /themuseum/exhibits/oldwatergatetour.php.

155 **president says on the tapes.** Ken Hughes, "Nixon's Biggest Crime Was Far, Far Worse than Watergate," History News Network (June 5, 2012).

156 **blatantly hypocritical statements.** Drew Westen, *The Political Brain* (PublicAffairs, 2007), pp. xi–xv.

157 **my solutions to the problem.** Kate Zernike. "Unlikely Activist Who Got to the Tea Party Early," *New York Times* (February 27, 2010).

157 **as a consequence were "losers."** Wikipedia entry, "Rick Santelli," accessed September 24, 2013.

157 **back the House of Representatives.** The more Santelli talked the more it seemed he was irrational. In the face of overwhelming evidence that the risk of inflation was low, he continually predicted it was heading out of control. See Paul Krugman, "Rick Santelli and Affinity Fraud," *New York Times* (July 14, 2014).

158 **behavior and strange ideas.** Alex Pentland, *Social Physics* (Penguin, 2014), chapter 8.

158 **their own leads the way.** Nicholas A. Christakis and James H. Fowler, *Connected: The Surprising Power of Our Social Networks and How They Shape Our Lives* (Little, Brown, 2009), p. 295.

159 **oversees all presidential libraries.** Christopher Goffard, "At Nixon Library, The Old Game of Hardball Against a New View of Watergate," *Los Angeles Times* (December 14, 2011).

160 **"no skin in the game."** Adam Nagourney, "Watergate Becomes Sore Point at Nixon Library," *New York Times* (August 6, 2010).

161 **"reflect favorably" on presidents.** Memo from Ronald Walker to the National Archives, "Memorandum for Sharon Fawcett, Assistant Archivist, Office of Presidential Libraries, National Archives and Records Administration" (August 2010).

161 *Start with Watergate.* Victor Lasky, *It Didn't Start with Watergate* (Dell Publishing, 1977).

163 *by Politics and Religion.* Jonathan Haidt, *The Righteous Mind: Why Good People Are Divided by Politics and Religion* (Pantheon, 2012), chapter 4.

163 **Our morality is social.** David Sloan Wilson, *Darwin's Cathedral: Evolution, Religion, and the Nature of Society* (University of Chicago Press, 2002).

163 **what Haidt calls universalism.** Haidt, *Righteous Mind*, pp. 138–141. The six conservative traits are: a high regard for people who make sacrifices, giving people rewards in proportion to their contribution to an effort, loyalty, a high regard for hierarchy, reverence for the sacred, and enthusiasm for liberty.

165 **to know what happened,** See, for example, Ethan Rarick, *Desperate Passage: The Donner Party's Perilous Journey West* (Oxford University Press, 2008).

165 **cold steel, mathematical approach.** Louise Barrett, Robin Dunbar, and John Lycett, *Human Evolutionary Psychology* (Princeton University Press, 2002), pp. 64–65.

166 **found the same pattern.** Nicholas Wade, *Before the Dawn: Recovering the Lost History of our Ancestors* (Penguin, 2006), p. 159ff.

166 **toward one another.** Barrett, Dunbar, and Lycett, *Human Evolutionary Psychology*, p. 25ff.

167 **into future generations.** Richard Dawkins, *The Selfish Gene* (Oxford University Press, 2009), *passim*. My discussion is based primarily on Dawkins and Barrett, Dunbar, and Lycett, cited above.

167   **are prewired for attachment.** Patricia Churchland, "Self as Brain," Seattle Townhall lecture (September 24, 2013).

167   **the lesson of the Donner Party.** In a study published in 2014 researchers report that clear patterns of altruism show up in primates only when children are cared for by large familial networks: mothers, fathers, aunts, uncles, and grandparents. Of fifteen species of primates, only humans and callitrichid monkeys, a family of New World monkeys that live in small highly cooperative groups, show these patterns of altruism. See J. M. Burkart et al., "The Evolutionary Origin of Human Hyper-Cooperation," *Nature Communications* (August 2014), Vol. 5, No. 4747, pp. 1–9.

168   **with their biological parents.** David Buss, ed., *Handbook of Evolutionary Psychology* (Wiley, 2005), p. 631.

169   **It's your spouse.** *Ibid.*

169   **began to test it.** William J. Ray, *Evolutionary Psychology: Neuroscience Perspectives Concerning Human Behavior and Experience* (SAGE, 2012), pp. 162–167, 175, 286–287, 292, 313–316.

169   **when approached by strangers.** *Ibid.*, p. 167.

170   **relationship to one another.** Barrett, Dunbar, and Lycett, *Human Evolutionary Psychology*, pp. 61–62.

170   **between families and groups.** As I mentioned earlier in the endnotes of chapter 6, in recent years some scientists, including Harvard's E. O. Wilson, have questioned Hamilton's Rule in a broad attack on the theory of individual selection. (See E. O. Wilson's *The Meaning of Human Existence* [Liveright, 2014], chapter 6 and the appendix.) These dissenters believe in multilevel selection. That is, they believe we are subject as animals to both individual selection and group selection. Individual selection favors selfishness while group selection favors altruism. Darwin himself was a believer in multilevel selection. It was the only way he had of accounting for altruism.

When social scientists began studying altruism in the twentieth century they discovered several mechanisms by which it could be favored by evolution, mechanisms of which Darwin was unaware. One method is known as tit for tat. People get ahead in the classic prisoner's game by adopting a simple strategy of cooperation on the first round, but not on the second, unless the other person playing the game responds in kind. Hence, the name, tit for tat. Players who adopt this strategy usually prevail over players who adopt more selfish strategies. See Ray, *Evolutionary Psychology*, p. 322. Tit for tat helps explain how cooperative people might be able to survive in a population of ruthlessly selfish individuals, solving the familiar free rider problem. (Free riders take advantage of cooperative individuals at every turn.)

Recently, Paul Zak, an economist-turned-neuroscientist, found that the single molecule oxytocin triggers altruistic responses in all animals, including humans. See Zak's *The Moral Molecule: The Source of Love and Prosperity* (Dutton, 2012). Zak argues that altruism was required from the beginning of the evolution of mammals. As he points out, only animals that trust one another will lower their guard long enough to copulate. When we trust others, they trust us, in a virtuous circle. What Zak's research suggests is that all humans possess the ability to demonstrate trust even as they compete as individuals for scarce resources. What determines if we show trust? The situation, though clearly some people are inclined to be less trustworthy than others, probably a result of some combination of genes and the environment.

What Zak's work shows is that Hamilton's Rule alone cannot account for altruism. We're altruistic by nature. But his rule still helps us understand why the members of families so often seem to show a higher degree of altruism toward one another than non-family members do toward other non-family members, including friends. But it is likely research will show that patterns of altruism arise from more complicated relationships than we currently understand.

170   **one white, one black.** My account relies mainly on the special report published by the *Boston Globe,* "102 Hours in Pursuit of Marathon Suspects" (April 28, 2013).

171   **when they heard the news?** "Bomb Suspects' Mother Defends Sons," *Daily Beast* (April 19, 2013), and "Bombing Suspect's Father Speaks," *Daily Beast* (April 19, 2013).

172   **evolution teaches us is survival.** Evolution does seem to select for people who can control their antisocial impulses. Joiners and good citizens are rewarded. Robbers and bullies are punished; in primitive societies they were often put to death. Evolutionary success goes to those who get along. The effect of this is to make society more moral. But evolution doesn't care whether we are moral, per se. Evolution doesn't have a purpose. Some forms of behavior are rewarded with higher fitness. But we aren't actually designed for anything. When we say we are designed for this or for that, the word "designed" should not be taken literally. See Christopher Boehm, *Hierarchy in the Forest: The Evolution of Egalitarian Behavior* (Harvard University Press, 1999), p. 28ff.

173   **illnesses (such as depression).** Tegan Cruwys et al., "Feeling Connected Again: Interventions That Increase Social Identification Reduce Depression Symptoms in Community and Clinical Settings," *Journal of Affective Disorders* (February 2014), Vol. 159, pp. 139–146.

175   **"operation that needs to win."** "After Election Setbacks. Diehards Battle Pragmatists for Control of GOP," McClatchy Newspapers (December 6, 2012).

176   **says Jonathan Haidt.).** Haidt, *The Righteous Mind,* chapter 11.

176   **visit the library again.** Interview with Naftali, April 15, 2013, by the author: "He told me he'd never step foot in the library as long as I was there because I brought John Dean."

179   **"teach the Devil tricks."** Edward J. MacKenzie Jr., "Breaking Legs for Whitey," *Boston Magazine* (May 2003).

179   **columnist was William Safire.** William Safire, "His Brother's Keeper," *New York Times* (December 5, 2002).

180   **the phenomenon of groupthink.** Irving L. Janis, *Groupthink* (Houghton Mifflin, 1982).

180   **power of group conformity.** Richard Thaler and Cass Sunstein, *Nudge: Improving Decisions About Health, Wealth, and Happiness* (Penguin Books, 2009), p. 56.

180   **a pleasurable dopamine rush.** Zak, *Moral Molecule,* p. 98.

Chapter 10: When It Happens to You

183   **"during World War II."** "Air Battle of South Korea," Wikipedia (accessed March 25, 2014).

183   **which are mind-boggling.** Except where otherwise noted, the facts in this section are based on Marilyn Young, "Bombing Civilians from the Twentieth to the Twenty-First Centuries," in *Bombing Civilians,* ed. Yuki Tanaka and Marilyn Young (New Press, 2009).

185   **seemed indifferent to it.** Freda Kirchwey, "Liberation by Death," *Nation* (March 10, 1951).

185   **force, not less force.** Roger Dingman, "Atomic Diplomacy during the Korean War," *International Security* (Winter, 1988–1989), Vol. 13, No. 3, p. 81.

185 **of all weapons, nukes.** The claim, as it happens, is not true. Eisenhower never threatened to use nuclear weapons, as Roger Dingman demonstrates in the article cited in the preceding note.

186 **"he's accomplished anything."** Young, "Bombing Civilians," p. 158.

187 **"effect on the flow."** *Ibid.*, p. 164.

188 **bombardment in history."** Mark Clodfelter, *The Limits of Air Power: The American Bombing of North Vietnam* (Bison Books, 2006), p. 56ff.

189 **than when they cannot.** Jonah Lehrer, *How We Decide* (Mariner Books, 2009), p. 187.

190 **ordinary meat and flour.** Quote from Comedy Central's *The Daily Show*, March 4, 2014.

190 **"the son we love."** Rob Portman, "Gay Couples Also Deserve Chance to Get Married," *Columbus Dispatch* (March 15, 2013).

190 **now favored gay marriage.** "Rob Portman Reverses Gay Marriage Stance After Son Comes Out," Huffington Post (March 15, 2013).

191 **a classic virtuous circle.** Paul Zak, *The Moral Molecule: The Source of Love and Prosperity* (Dutton, 2012), p. 165ff.

191 **better father and husband.** *Ibid.*, p. 135ff.

192 **the chimps, 36.** Nicholas Epley, *Mindwise: How We Understand What Others Think, Believe, Feel, and Want* (Knopf, 2014), preface.

193 **We'd show less.** *Ibid.*, p. 41ff.

193 **but not by much.** *Ibid.*, p. 93ff.

193 **wouldn't bother them.** *Ibid.*, p. 173.

194 **doesn't last very long.** Zak, *Moral Molecule*, p. 158ff.

194 **hostility to strangers.** Paul Bloom, *Just Babies: The Origins of Good and Evil* (Crown, 2013), p. 174.

195 **group of anonymous victims.** Deborah Small, George Lowenstein, and Paul Slovic, "Sympathy and Callousness: The Impact of Deliberative Thought on Donations to Identifiable and Statistical Victims," *Organizational Behavior and Human Decision Processes* (March 2006), Vol. 102, pp. 143–53.

195 **married couples produced.** Nicholas Epley, "Understanding the Minds of Others," Seattle Townhall lecture (February 27, 2014).

Chapter 11: The Accountant's Syndrome

197 **stuck with me ever after.** Anthony Lewis, "The Real Mr. Ford," *New York Times* (October 25, 1976).

198 **than high-status people.** Denise Cummins, ed., The *Evolution of Mind* (Oxford University Press, 1998), p. 40ff. See also Michael Inzlicht and Sukhvinder Obhi, "Powerful and Coldhearted," *New York Times* (July 27, 2014).

198 **human being to another.** Yoel Inbar, David A. Pizarro, Joshua Knobe, and Paul Bloom, "Disgust Sensitivity Predicts Intuitive Disapproval of Gays," *Emotion* (2009), Vol. 9, No. 3, pp. 435–439.

198 **of high-status people.** Nicholas Epley, *Mindwise: How We Understand What Others Think, Believe, Feel, and Want* (Knopf, 2014), p. 43ff.

199 **Monopoly we're talking about.** Kathleen D. Vohs et al., "Merely Activating the Concept of Money Changes Personal and Interpersonal Behavior," *Current Directions in Psychological Science* (2008), Vol. 17, No. 3, p. 209. See also: Nicholas Kristof, "The Compassion Gap," *New York Times* (March 1, 2014), and Robert Burton, "A Judge without Empathy Is Inhuman," *Salon* (May 12, 2009).

199 **alpha males were favored.** Alpha males who wanted to take a leadership role in a community may have not needed to be particularly empathetic, but they did

need to avoid offending a community's sense of right and wrong. Anthropologists who have studied hunter-gatherer communities report that leaders who behave brutishly are eventually driven off. See Christopher Boehm, *Hierarchy in the Forest: The Evolution of Egalitarian Behavior* (Harvard University Press, 1999).

199   **at a high speed.** Susan T. Fiske, "Envy Up, Scorn Down: How Comparison Divides Us," *American Psychologist* (November 2010), pp. 698–706.

199   **majority grew even larger.** There is one well-known exception to the general rule that the privileged are less likely to extend a helping hand than the underprivileged. In the immediate aftermath of a victory of some sort, even including something as banal as a sports victory, winners are more likely to show compassion than losers. The winners can afford to focus on others. But the losers? They are so consumed with their loss they cannot focus on anyone else's pain. See Nancy Eisenberg, "Emotion, Regulation and Moral Development," *Annual Review of Psychology* (2000), Vol. 51, pp. 665–697.

199   **easier time understanding you.** Paul Zak, *The Moral Molecule: The Source of Love and Prosperity* (Dutton, 2012), chapter 4.

200   **MPFC doesn't activate.** Both David Hume and Adam Smith argued that it is vital for human beings to sympathize with others. Hume contended this was a simple matter of absorbing their feelings. Emotions, he said, "readily pass from one person to another." Smith took a less optimistic line. He held that it takes "moral imagination" to understand what another person is feeling. Hume, who is right about so many things (particularly the way our mind works; Hume held that reason is a "slave to the passions"), is clearly wrong in thinking that what we call empathy is automatic. Adam Smith was right. It takes moral imagination to get inside the head of someone else. Gerald Ford's problem was that he lacked moral imagination. See "Adam Smith's Moral and Political Philosophy" in the online Stanford Encyclopedia of Philosophy (February 15, 2013).

201   **difficulty relating to people.** Anthony I. Jack et al., "fMRI Reveals Reciprocal Inhibition between Social and Physical Cognitive Domains," *NeuroImage* (February 2013), Vol. 66, No. 1, pp. 385–401.

201   **supposed to be consumed."** Samuel L. Popkin, *The Reasoning Voter* (University of Chicago Press, 1994), pp. 1–5.

202   **heartwarming hormone, oxytocin.** Zak, *Moral Molecule*, pp. 71–75.

202   **emphatic with every bite.** Epley, *Mindwise*, p. 45.

202   **from Möbius syndrome.** Marco Iacoboni, *Mirroring People: The New Science of How We Connect with Others* (Farrar, Straus and Giroux, 2008), p. 115.

203   **an ice cream cone.** Sandra Blakeslee, "Cells That Read Minds," *New York Times* (January 10, 2006). This story in the *Times* was probably responsible for the wide circulation of the ice cream story. It remains on the newspaper's website, though it's never been confirmed by the people involved. It was the *Times* that contributed the colorful detail that the monitor went "Brrrrrip." See Iacoboni, *Mirroring People*, p. 11.

203   **what others are feeling.** Patricia Churchland, "Self as Brain," Seattle Townhall lecture (September 24, 2013), says she is a doubter. Her main objection is that mirror neurons don't seem to endow the monkeys that possess it with empathy, suggesting something else is responsible for empathy. See also Gregory Hickok, "Three Myths About the Brain," *New York Times* (August 1, 2014).

204   **"like shooting at him."** Epley, *Mindwise*, p. 45.

205   **time was $83 billion.** *Historical Statistics of the United States* (United States Census Bureau, 1975), Vol. 1, pp. 356, 966; Vol. 2, p. 1104.

205   **welfare rolls were exploding.** Lou Cannon, *Reagan* (Simon & Schuster, 1982), pp. 175–184.

205   **of the country to the other.** R. Richard Ritti and Drew W. Hyman, "The Administration of Poverty: Lessons from the 'Welfare Explosion' 1967–1973," *Social Problems* (December 1977), Vol. 25, No. 2, pp. 157–175.

205   **the public as Linda Taylor.** Paul Krugman, "Republicans and Race," *New York Times* (November 19, 2007).

206   **and possibly murder.** Josh Levin, "The Welfare Queen," *Slate* (December 19, 2013).

206   **and the elderly.** Arloc Sherman, Robert Greenstein, and Kathy Ruffing, "Contrary to 'Entitlement Society' Rhetoric, Over Nine-Tenths of Entitlement Benefits Go to Elderly, Disabled, or Working Households," Center on Budget and Policy Priorities (February 10, 2012).

206   **meet the state's requirements.** Ritti and Hyman, "The Administration of Poverty," p. 163.

206   **the welfare-rights movement.** Felicia Kornbluh, *The Battle for Welfare Rights* (University of Pennsylvania Press, 2007).

206   **an exhaustive study concludes.** Ritti and Hyman, "The Administration of Poverty."

207   **explicitly to appeal to racists?** Kornbluh, *Welfare Rights,* p. 91.

207   **that welfare recipients are lazy.** Dan T. Carter, *The Politics of Rage: George Wallace, the Origins of the New Conservatism, and the Transformation of American Politics* (Louisiana State University Press, 2000), p. 374.

207   **on welfare are lazy.** Michael Bang Petersen, "Social Welfare as Small-Scale Help: Evolutionary Psychology and the Deservingness Heuristic," *American Journal of Political Science* (January 2012), Vol. 56, No. 1, pp. 1–16.

207   **the World Values Survey.** Michael Bang Petersen et al., "Who Deserves Help? Evolutionary Psychology, Social Emotions, and Public Opinion about Welfare," *Political Psychology* (June 2012), Vol. 33, No. 3, pp. 395–418.

208   **shapes many whites' attitudes.** I don't mean to minimize the role that racism played in the debate over welfare. It's telling that welfare benefits tend to be most generous around the world in countries that are homogenous, and least generous in countries that are heterogeneous. See Alberto Alesina and Edward Glaeser, *Fighting Poverty in the U.S. and Europe: A World of Difference* (Oxford University Press, 2004).

209   **because of some personal flaw.** Lee Ross and Richard E. Nisbett, *The Person and the Situation* (Pinter & Martin, 2011).

210   **demoralizing as it was shocking.** Chana Joffe-Walt, "Unfit for Work: The Startling Rise of Disability in America," NPR's *All Things Considered* (April 2013).

210   **government reported that.** "Aid to Disabled Children Now Outstrips Welfare: As SSI Expands, Debate Intensifies," *Boston Globe* (August 28. 2014).

210   **to those on welfare.** R. Kent Weaver, *Ending Welfare As We Know It* (Brookings Institution Press, 2000), p. 173.

Conclusion: A Way Forward

213   **the boy was Bob Woodward.** Alicia Shepard, *Woodward and Bernstein: Life in the Shadow of Watergate* (Wiley, 2007).

214   **looking at other things.** Paul Bloom, "Psych 110: Introduction to Psychology," Open Yale Courses, lecture 4, available online.

214   **"called [Henry] Kissinger, 'Henry.'"** Shepard, *Woodward and Bernstein,* p. 54.

215   **"had done anything wrong."** Bob Woodward and Carl Bernstein, *All the President's Men* (1974), pp. 95–101.

217　**to problems we encounter.** Jeffrey Alan Gray, *Consciousness: Creeping up on the Hard Problem* (Oxford University Press, 2007), pp. 75ff. I thank George Marcus for pointing me to Gray's work.

220　**recoil from abortion.** Rachel Herz, *That's Disgusting: Unraveling the Mysteries of Repulsion* (W. W. Norton, 2012).

220　**reactions can mislead us."** Carol Hay, "Gross Violations," *Aeon* (November 19, 2014).

221　**those in other people.** Katherine Woollett and Eleanor Maguire, "Acquiring 'the Knowledge' of London's Layout Drives Structural Brain Changes," *Current Biology* (December 20, 2011), Vol. 21, No. 24–2, pp. 2109–2114.

221　**because we believe.** Jonathan Haidt, *The Righteous Mind: Why Good People Are Divided by Politics and Religion* (Pantheon, 2012), p. 45ff.

222　**at the controls.** David Eagleman, *Incognito: The Secret Lives of the Brain* (Pantheon, 2011), chapter 5.

222　**freedom of choice is limited.** Michael S. Gazzaniga, *Who's in Charge: Free Will and the Science of the Brain* (Ecco, 2012), and Bruce M. Hood, *SuperSense: Why We Believe in the Unbelievable* (HarperOne, 2009). David Eagleman, *ibid.*, is one of the scientists who doubts free will.

225　**of eligible voters voted.** "2014 November General Election Turnout Rates," Election.Project.org (November 20, 2014).

225　**61 million Facebook users.** Alex Pentland, *Social Physics* (Penguin, 2014), p. 64ff.

226　**longer have to guess.** *Ibid.*, p. 199ff.

226　**hunch, not hard data.** Alex Pentland, "'Social Physics:' Engaging with the Big Data Around Us," Seattle Townhall lecture (February 6, 2014).

226　**think big thoughts.** Pentland, *Social Physics*, p. 35.

226　**shortcut to social progress.** *Ibid.*, p. 167ff.

227　**presidential election shows why.** *Ibid.*, p. 49ff.

230　**we are liberal or conservative.** See: George Marcus, W. Russell Neuman, and Michael MacKuen, "Ideology, Affect, Context, and Political Judgment: When Conservatives and Liberals Share Feelings and When They Don't," paper presented at the Annual Meeting of the American Political Science Association (August 2014).

230　**really do think differently.** See Haidt, *Righteous Mind*, and James H. Fowler, Laura A. Baker, and Christopher T. Dawes, "Genetic Variation in Political Participation," *American Political Science Review* (May 2008), Vol. 102, No. 2, pp. 233–248. See also: John R. Hibbing, Kevin B. Smith, and John R. Alford, *Predisposed: Liberals, Conservatives, and the Biology of Political Differences* (Routledge, 2014).

230　**we grow more tolerant.** Leonie Huddy, Stanley Feldman, and Erin Cassese, "On the Distinct Political Effects of Anxiety and Anger," in *The Affect Effect: Dynamics of Emotion in Political Thinking and Behavior,* ed. by W. Russell Neuman, George Marcus, Michael MacKuen, and Ann N. Crigler (University of Chicago Press, 2007), pp. 202–230.

230　**parts of the world.** Jonathan McDonald Ladd and Gabriel S. Lenz, "Does Anxiety Improve Voters' Decision Making?" *Political Psychology* (2011), Vol. 32, No. 2, pp. 347–361.

231　**made over twenty years.** Philip E. Tetlock, *Expert Political Judgment: How Good Is It? How Can We Know?* (Princeton University Press, 2005).

232　**wild conspiracy theories.** Michael Shermer, *The Believing Brain: From Ghosts and Gods to Politics and Conspiracies—How We Construct Beliefs and Reinforce Them as Truths* (St. Martins Griffin, 2012), p. 79.

232   **other countries' intentions.** Guido den Dekker et al., "From Human Insecurity to International Armed Conflict," 50th Pugwash Conference on Science and World Affairs (August 2000), and Richard Restak, *Poe's Heart and the Mountain Climber: Exploring the Effect of Anxiety on Our Brains and Our Culture* (Three Rivers Press, 2004).

232   **generally we adapt.** Anxiety is idiosyncratic, it is important to note. People with a large amygdala feel more anxious than people with a smaller one. Caren Chesler, "The Coward," *Aeon* (October 30, 2014).

233   **are hard to imagine.** George Marshall, *Don't Even Think About It: Why Our Brains Are Wired to Ignore Climate Change* (Bloomsbury, 2014), p. 57ff.

233   **according to a Gallup Poll.** Gallup Poll, "In U.S., Most Do Not See Global Warming as Serious Threat" (March 13, 2014).

233   **is in part responsible.** *Washington Post*-ABC poll, "EPA Rules on Greenhouse Gases" (June 2, 2014).

234   **comes out near dead last.** A good summary of poll findings is provided by Ira Chernus, "Don't Blame Climate Change Deniers," History News Network (September 24, 2014).

234   **"perpetually in the background."** George Marshall, *Climate Change*, p. 228.

234   **to reconsider their position.** Kathleen Hall Jamieson, *Everything You Think You Know About Politics . . . and Why You're Wrong* (2000), p. 105ff and Jamieson, *Packaging the Presidency: A History and Criticism of Presidential Campaign Advertising* (Oxford University Press, 1996), p. 220.

234   **spend trillions on defense.** Marshall, *Climate Change*, p. 67.

234   **George Marcus and colleagues.** Michael MacKuen, Jennifer Wolak, Luke Keele, and George Marcus, "Civic Engagements: Resolute Partisanship or Reflective Deliberation," *American Journal of Political Science* (April 2010), Vol. 54, No. 2, pp. 440–458.

235   **conservatives are seeing Maddow.** Marcus, Neuman, and MacKuen, "Ideology, Affect, Context, and Political Judgment."

236   **efforts focus and purpose.** It is, therefore, no surprise that one recent study found that angry comments on the Chinese social media website Weibo spread far more quickly than others. See Rui Fan, Jichang Zhao, Yan Chen, and Ke Xu, "Anger Is More Influential Than Joy: Sentiment Correlation in Weibo," arXiv (September 2013), 1309.2402 [cs.SI].

236   **no room for compromise.** One reason why politicians and activists constantly appeal to our angry side is not only because it works, but also because anger is one of the most fleeting emotions. Generally, we don't remain in an angry state very long. Compared with other emotions, the duration of a normal period of anger is short. According to one recent study we remain sad far longer than we remain angry. But hatred lasts nearly as long as sadness. And in politics the point of anger is nearly always to inspire hatred. See: Philippe Verduyn and Saskia Lavrijsen, "Which Emotions Last Longest and Why: The Role of Event Importance and Rumination," *Motivation and Emotion* (October 31, 2014).

236   **celebrated Marshmallow Test.** Walter Mischel, *The Marshmallow Test* (Little, Brown, 2014), pp. 127–128.

237   **true of most Americans.** Don Taylor, "Two-thirds of Americans Don't Save Enough," Bankrate.com (October 7, 2014).

238   **for a lung transplant.** Mischel, *Marshmallow Test*, p. 66ff.

238   **billions of dollars on the effort.** Andrea Orr, "What Went Wrong with No Child Left Behind?" Economic Policy Institute (March 18, 2010). www.epi.org

/publication/what went wrong with no child left behind/.

239   **destabilize the government there.** "Libya Weapons Aid Tuareg Rebellion in Mali," *Los Angeles Times* (June 12, 2012).

239   **strongly to moral appeals.** Matthew Feinberg and Robb Willer, "The Moral Roots of Environmental Attitudes," *Psychological Science* (December 10, 2012), Vol. 24, pp. 56–62.

240   **with the night before.** Matt Bai, *All the Truth Is Out: The Week Politics Went Tabloid* (Knopf, 2014).

Coda: The Widow's Advantage

243   **fell in love with JFK.** Like all family stories ours is based on reminiscences related long after the events they describe took place. I have had only one document to rely on: my grandfather's birth certificate—and even that may not be accurate. It indicates he was born in Austria, though family lore was that his people came from Romania. At one time Romania was part of the Austro-Hungarian empire, but there's enough ambiguity here to justify doubts of all kinds about the stories that were passed down, including where exactly he was born.

244   **often exceeded 80 percent.** Sean Wilentz, *The Rise of American Democracy: Jefferson to Lincoln* (W. W. Norton, 2005), pp. 138–139, 505.

245   **violation of established procedures.** Rick Shenkman, *Presidential Ambition* (HarperCollins, 1999), pp. 198–199.

245   **candidates like John Kennedy.** Rick Shenkman, "Television, Democracy, and Presidential Politics," *The Columbia History of Post-World War II America*, ed. Mark C. Carnes (Columbia University Press, 2007), pp. 255–284.

245   **its tax-exempt status.** *Branch Ministries, Inc. versus Charles O. Rossotti*, Civil Action No. 95–0724 (PLF), www.irs.gov/pub/irs-utl/branch_ministries.pdf. See also: Barry W. Lynn, *Piety & Politics: The Right-Wing Assault on Religious Freedom* (Harmony, 2006), p. 150ff.

Index

RICK SHENKMAN is an award-winning investigative reporter, a *New York Times* best-selling author, and the publisher and editor of the History News Network, the website that puts the news into historical perspective. An elected fellow of the Society of American Historians, he appears regularly on Fox News, CNN, and MSNBC. He lives in Seattle, Washington.